CLASSICAL ARMINIANISM

A Theology of Salvation

F. LEROY FORLINES

EDITED WITH AN INTRODUCTION BY
J. MATTHEW PINSON

randall house

114 Bush Rd | Nashville, TN 37217 | randallhouse.com

Classical Arminianism

© 2011 by F. Leroy Forlines

Published by Randall House Publications
114 Bush Road
Nashville, TN 37217
Visit www.randallhouse.com

Text compiled and edited from a previous work by Leroy Forlines, *The Quest for Truth*, published by Randall House in 2001.

13-ISBN   9780892656073

Printed in the United States of America

Table of Contents

Introduction by J. Matthew Pinson iv

CHAPTER 1
Human Nature, Total Depravity, and the Image of God 1

CHAPTER 2
The Theology of Election 35

CHAPTER 3
Proof Texts for Unconditional Election: Romans 9 97

CHAPTER 4
Proof Texts for Unconditional Election: Other Texts 147

CHAPTER 5
Scriptural Support for Conditional Election 169

CHAPTER 6
The Nature of Atonement and Justification 199

CHAPTER 7
The Condition of Salvation 251

CHAPTER 8
Sanctification 273

CHAPTER 9
The Perseverance of the Saints 303

CHAPTER 10
Apostasy and Assurance: Doctrinal and
Practical Considerations 337

Introduction
by J. Matthew Pinson

Leroy Forlines has been at the forefront of a growing movement that many are calling "Reformed Arminianism."[1] During his college days at Free Will Baptist Bible College in the late 1940s and early 1950s, Professor Forlines began to develop his views on Classical Arminianism. Key to his early theological development was a course entitled "Arminian Theology" taught by President L. C. Johnson.[2] During that course, Forlines began to read the works of Jacobus Arminius. He was particularly struck by Arminius's disputation on the threefold office of Christ. In that disputation, Arminius, in a discussion of Christ's priesthood, advocated a penal satisfaction view of atonement. He painstakingly argued that Christ's penal sacrifice on the cross satisfied the just demands of a holy God against sinful human beings.

How different Arminius was, Forlines concluded, from "Arminian" authors such as Charles Finney or John Miley or Orton Wiley.[3] They had taught a governmental view of atonement similar to that of Hugo Grotius. That theory held that God could freely pardon sinners without any satisfaction for the violation of divine law, because such a pardon was within God's discretion as governor or sovereign. Thus the sacrifice of Christ is accepted by God as governor or ruler rather than as judge. The death of Christ, in this view, is a symbol of the punishment sin may induce. God uses this symbol as a deterrent. The penalty for sin is therefore set aside rather than paid. So, upon faith, the believer is pardoned as a governor would pardon a guilty criminal, and all past sins are forgotten.

However, in Arminius's disputations on the priesthood of Christ, he plainly articulated a more Reformed understanding of atonement that accorded with the Belgic Confession of Faith and the Heidelberg Catechism, to which he eagerly subscribed.[4] For Arminius, Christ, in His execution of the role of priesthood, becomes the human victim that is offered up to God to appease His justice. Indeed, as the priest-sacrifice, Christ offers Himself up as an oblation to God. This oblation, this offering, consists of the sacrifice of His body—His shedding of blood and subsequent death. Arminius describes this oblation as a payment that Christ renders to God as the price of redemption for human sin. In Christ's oblation, Arminius argues, Christ as priest and sacrifice suffers the divine punishment that is due for human sin. This suffering constitutes the satisfaction or payment to the divine justice for redemption of humans from sin, guilt, and divine wrath. Thus Arminius presents an understanding of atonement, in the context of his view of the priestly office of Jesus Christ, that is consistent with the penal-substitution motifs regnant in sixteenth- and early seventeenth-century Reformed theology.[5]

Professor Forlines had heard this approach to atonement preached, in less articulate form, while growing up as a Free Will Baptist in rural eastern North Carolina.[6] In Arminius, he now found a theological expression of it from a non-Calvinist vantage point. And on this view of atonement hinged an entire system of theology that was at once Arminian but also Reformed in important ways. That system was Arminian in the sense of how one *comes to be* in a state of grace (predestination, free will, grace). But it was Reformed on the *meaning* of sin and redemption. Put another way, Reformed Arminians agree with Augustinian-Reformed theology on the sinfulness of humanity and the way God has accomplished redemption through Christ and applied it in justification and sanctification. Yet they see the issue of *just how* redemption is applied in a different way than Calvinists do.[7]

At the same time that Forlines began teaching this kind of Arminian theology in the 1950s, Carl Bangs (whom Forlines never knew personally) was working out a historiography of it.[8] Bangs argued that Arminius, far from being a former supralapsarian Calvinist as many earlier historians had mistakenly held, simply reflected and systematized a non-Calvinist undercurrent that had been present in the Reformed churches since before Calvin's time. Bangs presented "Arminius as a Reformed Theologian," positing a milieu within the continental Reformed churches in the late sixteenth century that was broader than Calvinist predestinarianism.[9]

From this Reformed/Arminian posture on atonement, Forlines extrapolated a Reformed doctrine of justification through faith alone by the imputed righteousness of Christ alone, similar to that articulated by Arminius. This account of atonement and justification affected many doctrines that had traditionally separated Arminians from Calvinists. For example, Forlines's doctrine of atonement presupposes the seriousness of sin and the complete depravity and inability of people to desire God without a radical intervention of divine enabling grace.

Forlines's Reformed understanding of justification as the imputation of the active and passive obedience of Christ shifts the focus from the believer's good works to the merit of Christ. His merit alone clothes believers and gives them their righteous position before God the Judge. Reformed Arminians do not resort to a doctrine of entire sanctification to deal with the problem of sin in the believer's life. They see a lack of assurance in much Arminian thought and piety that necessitates a doctrine of entire sanctification or Christian perfection. They also see an attenuated doctrine of justification—more in terms of simple forgiveness or pardon rather than imputation—as being at the heart of predominant Arminian views on perseverance, which focus on the believer's good works as necessary for maintaining God's forgiveness.

By contrast, Professor Forlines presents believers as secure in Christ, because they have been imputed with the active and passive obedience of Christ. Forlines's view of perseverance, similar to that of Arminius, holds that believers maintain the freedom to cease to be believers and thus to decline from salvation.[10] Like Arminius as well as Calvin, Forlines believes that justification results in sanctification, that true faith will produce "works befitting repentance" (Acts 26:20). Yet believers are "kept by the power of

God through faith" (1 Pet 1:5), not through works. This approach militates against the lack of assurance characteristic of much Arminianism, in which believers can lose their salvation again and again by committing sins and must regain it through repentance to maintain their justification before God.[11]

Thus, there is in Forlines's theology a logical outgrowth from the Reformed doctrines of atonement and justification. In short, an Arminian acceptance of a Reformed account of atonement and justification affects one's doctrine of perseverance. Believers persevere solely in union with Christ, imputed with His righteousness; thus continuance is not grounded in forgiveness of post-conversion sins. Apostasy is a once-for-all, irremediable event, a complete shipwreck of saving faith. This *sola fide* approach to perseverance and apostasy bases assurance on the believer's position in union with Christ rather than on one's efforts. If an Arminian does not accept this perspective, entire sanctification is more compelling as a way to achieve full assurance of salvation.

Another unique feature of Forlines's Classical Arminianism that arises from a more Reformed understanding of theology is his focus on the election of individuals rather than on corporate election. Unlike many Arminians, Forlines "camps out" in Romans 9 for fifty pages. He does not shrink from the concept that Paul in that chapter is describing the personal election of individuals, not the election of the church or people of God as a corporate entity. Long before E. P. Sanders's concept of covenantal nomism became commonplace, Professor Forlines was teaching his students in his courses on Romans that Paul in Romans 9 was dealing with the tension in Jewish thought between salvation by works of the law on the one hand and salvation by corporate election of the people of God on the other. In a careful way, Forlines articulates nuanced crosscurrents with aspects of Sanders's thought. Yet at the same time, Forlines explicates a thoroughgoing penal substitutionary view of atonement together with a doctrine of justification that posits the imputation of Christ's righteousness to the believer.

In this work, Professor Forlines presents the traditional Arminian view of God's simple, exhaustive foreknowledge of all future events. Thus he eschews the novel attempts of open theists—so-called "free will theists"—who grant the Calvinists/determinists their argument that God can foreknow only those events that He foreordains. Against both determinism and open theism, Forlines posits God's exhaustive foreknowledge of all events alongside the significant freedom of personal beings created in His image. However, he also avoids the idiosyncratic views of the Jesuit theologian Luis de Molina known as "middle knowledge." Forlines believes this construct to be unhelpful and overly speculative as an account of the divine foreknowledge.

Forlines engages in a helpful and extensive discussion of the value of an "influence-and-response" model of divine-human relations as opposed to the "cause-and-effect" model of determinist metaphysics, with which he classes Calvinistic views of divine sovereignty. He has a thorough knowledge of Calvinistic approaches to sovereignty and different types of determinism, including Calvinistic attempts at defending a compatibilist or "soft" determinist account of free will. His discussion of these issues will illuminate them for readers on both sides of the libertarian-determinist debate. Calvinists will be pleased with the way Forlines strives to be eminently fair in representing and interacting with their views despite his respectful disagreement with them.

In 2000, Randall House published F. Leroy Forlines's systematic theology, *The Quest for Truth*. Evangelical scholars such as I. Howard Marshall, Jonathan Wilson, Fisher Humphreys, and L. Igou Hodges praised the book as a model of Arminian scholarship. Forlines's combination of theological clarity with a winsome, conversational style has gained the book many devotees. The volume's growing importance for the Arminian-Calvinist dialogue has been noted many times in various reviews and online discussions. Since its publication, *The Quest for Truth* has been used as a text in Arminian schools and even in moderate Calvinist ones.[12]

One reason that more and more people outside Free Will Baptist circles are reading *The Quest for Truth* and *Grace, Faith, Free Will*, by Forlines's long-time colleague Robert E. Picirilli, is that classical Calvinism is on the rise.[13] Traditional Calvinism is so aggressive in its growth that it has become the leading view at many Southern Baptist seminaries. The "New Calvinism" even made it into a *Time* magazine cover story entitled "10 Ideas Changing the World Right Now" (even *Time* thinks traditional theology can still change the world—it was number three on the list!). In this environment, Arminians across denominations desire theologically solid resource material from an Arminian vantage point, and Calvinists need works that will acquaint them with perspicacious Arminian scholarship. *The Quest for Truth* is, as I. Howard Marshall said, probably the best of such resources.

However, a number of non-Free Will Baptist scholars and teachers— both Arminian and moderate Calvinist—have wished that the material on salvation from *The Quest for Truth* could be extracted from it and put under a different cover for a shorter book just on the topic of Arminianism. Many readers, who are not interested in reading a larger systematic theology, will purchase and read a smaller monograph on a specialized topic.

Thus, this new volume is a revised and completely reformatted version of the soteriological material in *The Quest for Truth*, arranged in an order that is more conducive to the contours of the Arminian-Calvinist conversation. The result is a smaller, more topic-specific book that will find an entirely new audience among Arminians and Calvinists alike. It is published in the hopes that readers from diverse confessional backgrounds will realize F. Leroy Forlines's maxim, which has characterized him personally and professionally: that biblical truth is for the whole of life.

---

[1]See Stephen M. Ashby, "Reformed Arminianism," in J. Matthew Pinson, ed., *Four Views on Eternal Security* (Grand Rapids: Zondervan, 2002). The term seems to have been coined by Robert E. Picirilli, who used it in his 1987 preface to Professor Forlines's theological commentary on the epistle to the Romans. See

F. Leroy Forlines, *Romans* in the *Randall House Bible Commentary*, ed. Robert E. Picirilli (Nashville: Randall House, 1987). Picirilli later began to use the term "Reformation Arminianism." Forlines uses the term "Classical Arminianism," which he sees as the Arminianism closest to Arminius.

[2]F. Leroy Forlines, *The Quest for Truth* (Nashville: Randall House, 2000), 507, n.5.

[3]Professor Forlines found more affinity with the moderate Calvinist evangelical theologian Henry Clarence Thiessen (*Lectures in Systematic Theology* [Grand Rapids: William B. Eerdmans Publishing Company], 1949). Forlines disagreed with Thiessen's soteriology only on the question of the eternal security of the believer. It is interesting that Thiessen's book was later revised, after his death, to teach four-point Calvinism.

[4]Jacobus Arminius, *The Works of James Arminius*, trans. James Nichols and William Nichols (Nashville: Randall House, 2007), Public Disputation 14, "On the Offices of Our Lord Jesus Christ," 2.211-25. See 2.690 for Arminius's agreement with the Belgic Confession and Heidelberg Catechism.

[5]See J. Matthew Pinson, "The Nature of Atonement in the Theology of Jacobus Arminius," *Journal of the Evangelical Theological Society* (forthcoming).

[6]This pre-Wesleyan approach to Arminianism had been taught by the forefathers of American Free Will Baptists, the seventeenth-century English General Baptists. Their most outstanding theologian, Thomas Grantham, summed up their theory of atonement in the title of Section V in book two, chapter three of his book *Christianismus Primitivus*, which reads, "According to the Will of God, and his Eternal Wisdom, Christ did, in the place and stead of Mankind, fulfil that Law, by which the whole World stood guilty before God." In this section, Grantham explains "how deeply Mankind stood indebted to the Righteous God of Heaven and Earth, and how unable he was to pay that score; and how consequently he must inevitably undergo the eternal displeasure of God, with the malediction of his Righteous Law." He later says: "That God imputes Righteousness to Men without Works, is so plain, that it can never be denied. What is thus imputed, is not acted by us, but expressly reckoned as a matter of free Gift, or Grace; and this can be the Righteousness of none but Christ . . . because no other way can the Righteousness of God be made ours . . . there is none righteous, no not one. Except therefore the Righteousness

of Christ be laid hold on, there is no Righteousness to be imputed to Sinners."
Grantham's theory of active and passive obedience as essential aspects of the
atonement is brought directly to bear on his doctrine of justification: "Now
whether the Passive Righteousness of Christ only, or his Active Righteousness
also, be that which is imputed to Sinners, is doubtful to some; but for my part
I take it to be both. . . . The whole Righteousness of Christ, Active and Passive,
is reckoned as ours through believing" (Thomas Grantham, *Christianismus
Primitivus*, or *The Ancient Christian Religion* [London, 1678], book II, 62, 67,
68). See also Grantham's *St. Paul's Catechism* (London, 1687), 28. A more in-
depth discussion of Grantham's soteriology and how it contrasts with that of
the Arminian Puritan John Goodwin can be found in J. Matthew Pinson, "The
Diversity of Arminian Soteriology: Thomas Grantham, John Goodwin, and
Jacobus Arminius," presented at the national meeting of the American Society of
Church History, Florida State University, Tallahassee, Florida, March 1998.

[7]I give a much fuller description of the ways in which Arminius defies both
modern Calvinistic and Arminian interpretations in J. Matthew Pinson, "Will
the Real Arminius Please Stand Up? A Study of the Theology of Jacobus
Arminius in Light of His Interpreters," *Integrity: A Journal of Christian Thought*
(Summer 2003): 121-39.

[8]Carl Bangs, "Arminius and Reformed Theology," doctoral dissertation,
University of Chicago, 1958; Carl Bangs, *Arminius: A Study in the Dutch
Reformation* (Nashville: Abingdon Press, 1971); Carl Bangs, "Arminius as a
Reformed Theologian," in *The Heritage of John Calvin*, ed. John H. Bratt (Grand
Rapids, Michigan: William B. Eerdmans Publishing Company, 1973)

[9]See J. Matthew Pinson, "Introduction," in *Four Views on Eternal Security*, 14.

[10]Cf. Arminius, *Works*, 1.742.

[11]See, e.g., Wesleyan theologian Steve Harper's comments that, for Wesley,
Christ's atonement "totally accomplishes our deliverance, but the efficacy of
that deliverance must include our ongoing appropriation of it." Harper later
states approvingly that, for Wesley, "voluntary sins—deliberate violations of
the known laws of God—do, however, become mortal if we do not repent of
them. The subject of eternal security rests (in both categories of sin [involuntary
and voluntary]) on the matter of ongoing repentance." ("A Wesleyan Arminian
View," in *Four Views on Eternal Security*, 226, 240. For more on traditional

Wesleyan soteriology, see J. Matthew Pinson, "Atonement, Justification, and Apostasy in the Thought of John Wesley," *Integrity: A Journal of Christian Thought* (Summer 2008), 73-92.

[12]When I say "moderate Calvinist," I am referring to the *via media* of many Baptists and other evangelicals who have emerged from a Calvinistic theological heritage but have moderated their Calvinistic soteriology to include many elements of Arminian thought. For an excellent example of this, see the first edition of Henry C. Thiessen's *Lectures in Systematic Theology* (Grand Rapids: Eerdmans, 1949). For a more recent example of this from a Southern Baptist perspective, see David Allen and Steve Lemke, eds., *Whosoever Will: A Biblical-Theological Critique of Five-Point Calvinism* (Nashville: B&H Academic, 2010).

[13]Robert E. Picirilli, *Grace, Faith, Free Will: Contrasting Views of Salvation—Calvinism and Arminianism* (Nashville: Randall House, 2002).

CHAPTER 1

Human Nature, Total Depravity, and the Image of God

The psalmist asks one of the most important questions ever to be raised by a human being in Psalm 8:4: "What is man, that You art mindful of him?" The answer to this question is not simply an exercise in mental curiosity by those seated at the intellectual round table. Our whole being cries out for an answer.

Proper identification is important. Even a machine requires proper identification. A motor requires proper identification in order that the right fuel may be used, the proper function may be understood, the right adjustments may be made, the right parts may be ordered for replacement, etc. Improper identification can have serious results. The same can be said of plants. What may be fatal to one plant may not be harmful at all to another. The same can be said of animals. Improper identification can be dangerous and even fatal because it can result in an improper prescription.

It seems absurd, in a way, even to talk about improper identification of human beings since we are all human. We observe others and are observed by them. The problem rests in the danger of an improper description of man. Two conflicting views of human beings demand our attention. One view describes man as a being related to the animal world. He has an animal history. He has the needs of an animal of his type. The other view describes man as created by God in God's image. He is accountable to God.

It is obvious that the prescriptions written for man's needs will differ greatly according to which of these views a person embraces. If the wrong prescription can cause malfunction and even disastrous results for a machine, it should be more obvious that the wrong prescription for a human being can have *the most serious consequences*. We need a proper prescription for our lives. Proper prescriptions can come only after we have proper identification. It is only when we have a prescription based on our design that we can know true happiness.

Special divine revelation takes the guesswork out of identification. Identification comes to us as a "given" from the Creator. The real nature of man's personality and what it takes to meet human needs will never be discovered by observation and experience. It must come to us as a "given."

I am not suggesting that the whole picture of man comes so fully amplified that there is no room for study. I am saying, however, that revelation does give us the basics and that all amplification of details must involve reflection upon the data of revelation. Also, we must be constantly subjecting whatever may be known through research and observation to the authority of revelation.

One of the important things to observe about a system is that nothing in a system can be fully identified without reference to its other parts. Every part of a system is tied into the system by relationships to other parts. These relationships must be touched on in identifying a part. The matter of relationship in identification is clearly revealed in the statement: "Man is created in the image of God." To identify man without identifying God, and then to elaborate the meaning of "the image of God," is disastrous.

THE MEANING OF BEING CREATED IN THE IMAGE OF GOD

It is a mistake to begin our identification of human beings by saying, "Man is a sinner." That is true, but there is something more fundamental in explaining what a human being is. Human beings are created in the image of God.

If the man at a body shop is going to work to restore a wrecked automobile, he will need to know what it was like before it was wrecked. So it is with human beings. While it is necessary for us to recognize that "all have sinned," we need to know what human beings were like before they sinned. Saying that a human being is a sinner tells us about a serious problem he has, but it does not tell us what a human being is. It is important in identifying man to say that God created him, but that still does not tell you what a human being is. God also created plants and animals. We have not told what a human being is until we say that he or she is created in the image of God.

Once we know what it means to be created by God in His image, then we can begin to address the fact that man is a sinner, the problems that presents, and the hope and meaning of redemption. What human personality is and how human personality functions are understood by knowing the meaning of being created in the image of God. The basic needs of human beings are determined by knowing the design of human beings as they came from the hand of the Creator.

That man is created in the image of God is declared in Genesis 1:26–27. The meaning is that man is patterned after God. In what sense is man patterned after God? That it was not a physical likeness is too obvious to require proof.[1]

A Rational Likeness

We get clues from Colossians 3:10 and Ephesians 4:24 regarding what is involved in being created in God's image. In Colossians 3:10 we read: "And have put on the new man who is renewed in knowledge according to the image of Him who created him." The image of the Creator in man is linked to rationality. Therefore, we conclude that being created in the image of God involves human rationality. We do not make people rational by educating them. We can educate people because by the design of creation they are rational.

Human beings are created as rational beings, and this makes it possible for us to think, reason, and learn. It is astounding what human minds have been able to accomplish. All of this has been possible because God created human beings with intelligence. As created, rational beings, not only are we able to think and reason, but we also have rational needs. We *need* knowledge and understanding. People need answers to the *inescapable questions of life*: Is there a God? If so, what is He like? How can I know Him? How do we account for the origin of the universe and man? What is a human being? How do I know what is right and what is wrong? Is there life after death? If there is, how do I get ready for it? Human beings are in desperate need of answers to these questions. Human beings need a worldview. When a person starts answering these questions, he or she is developing a worldview.

A Moral Likeness

In Ephesians 4:24 Paul wrote: "And that you put on the new man, which was created according to God, in true righteousness and holiness." We conclude from this text that the image of God in man makes man a moral creature. In thinking of morals at this point, we should think in the broadest sense of the word to include the whole scope of what is involved in holiness, love, wisdom, and ideals. We do not make people moral by teaching them morals. We can teach them morals because by the design of creation they are moral. Paul tells us that every human being has the law of God written on his or her heart (Rom. 2:14-15).

The need to live according to God's moral standard and to appreciate beauty and excellence is designed in every human being. We cannot decide whether we need to live according to God's moral standard. *God decided that* when He created us. We can decide whether we want to live according to God's moral teachings, but we cannot decide whether we need to. God has already decided that. A human being cannot go contrary to God's moral law without suffering consequences.

Since we all have to deal with our own sinfulness, it helps us when we can see moral issues addressed in the Bible. Yet general revelation does a good job of informing us on basic morality. At the judgment, no person will honestly be able to say to God, "I didn't know it was wrong to lie. I didn't know it was wrong to steal. I didn't know it was wrong to murder. I didn't know it was wrong to have sex outside marriage." The suppression of the Truth will no longer work.[2]

Until Jesus Christ returns, we will always have to contend with sin. No sin will be exterminated from the human race prior to His return. But there is a decided difference between the presence of sinful behavior and the idealizing of such behavior. It was this problem that Paul addressed in Romans 1:32, "They not only do the same, but also give hearty approval to those who practice them" (NASB). The word that is translated "give hearty approval to" is *suneudokeō*. The literal meaning is "to think well with." When wrong behavior is approved and idealized, we have reached a new low.

Likeness Summed Up in the Word *Person*

The word *person* sums up the idea of rationality and morality. God is personal. Man is personal. The basic thrust of the idea of being created in the image of God is that man is a personal being. A person is one who thinks, feels, and acts.

The Meaning of *Mind*

We think with our minds. The mind is referred to in Matthew 22:37; Romans 14:5; and Hebrews 8:10. The words *think, reason,* and *understanding* are used too often in Scripture to require a list of proof texts. We think with our minds. We grasp ideas. We reason. We make judgments. We draw conclusions. We size up situations.

The Meaning of *Heart*

The heart is referred to in Matthew 22:37; Romans 10:1, 9; Hebrews 8:10; and many other passages. We feel with our hearts. The heart is the seat of the emotions. With the heart we feel the reality of the truth that we know with our mind. The heart registers the value we place on things. It is with the heart that we feel sorrow and sadness. Sorrow and sadness reflect feelings of negative value or disvalue. Feelings of positive value are joy, happiness, satisfaction, peace, and contentment. Heart involvement represents the involvement of our deepest inner self. The human heart cries out for more than a mere objective grasp of knowledge.

THE MEANING OF *WILL*

The New Testament does not use the noun form of will to refer to the faculty of choice in man. However, the verb form (*thelō*) is used (Mt. 16:24; 21:29; 23:37; Mk. 8:34; Jn. 7:17; Rev. 22:17; and others). By will, we mean power of choice. Every command, every prohibition, every exhortation, and every entreaty in the Bible made to people presupposes they are capable of making choices.

Whether we want to think of the act of willing as the function of a faculty of the person or simply the person making a choice, the fact remains that the ability to choose is part of being a person. That ability of choice is what we call *will*. In his totality, man is a thinking, feeling, acting being. He thinks with his mind, feels with his heart, and acts with his will.

THE CONSTITUTIONAL AND FUNCTIONAL LIKENESS OF GOD IN MAN

What has been said about man as a personal, rational, moral creature is frequently referred to as the formal likeness of God in man.[3] I prefer to speak of it as the constitutional likeness of God in man. The image of God in man at creation included more than constitutional likeness; it also included functional likeness (also referred to as material content[4]). The functional likeness means that man as created thought, felt, and acted in a way that was pleasing to God.

The distinction between constitutional and functional likeness is made clearer if we divide the scope of person into *personhood* and *personality*.

Personhood would embrace the constitutional likeness of God—that is, all the elements that go together to constitute a person. Personality refers to the way in which a person thinks, feels, and acts. At times *person* and *personality* are used synonymously, but there is usually a difference. In this study, personality will be used as defined above. Man as created was in the likeness of God with respect to both his personhood and his personality.

THE TWO LEVELS OF PERSONALITY

The functioning of personality occurs on two levels: the conscious level and the subconscious level. Man as created and as he developed after creation, up to the time of the fall, functioned both on the conscious and subconscious level in the likeness of God.

The subconscious mind is programmed with ideas, attitudes, and responses. *Mind,* as it is referred to here, is used in the broad sense to include mind, heart, and will. It is this use of the word *mind* that we employ when we say, "I have made up my mind to do so and so." *Mind* in this instance involves more than the reasoning, thinking mind. It involves our total personality: our mind, heart, and will.

Through study, thought, observation, and meditation, we store knowledge or ideas into our subconscious mind. Only a very limited part of our knowledge is at any given moment in our conscious mind. It is stored for recall in our subconscious mind. The storage of ideas is much like the programming of a computer. Our mind is programmed with a vast store of ideas that can be brought to the surface with differing degrees of speed.

In the process of meditation, ideas to which we are committed take on the appropriate attitudes in the heart. We are programmed to think and feel a certain way under certain circumstances. The programming of the subconscious mind of Adam and Eve was constituted with ideas and attitudes that were in the likeness of God before the fall. In their innermost being they were like God. I agree with Berkhof when he says, "The image of

God in which man was created certainly includes what is generally called 'original righteousness,' or more specifically, true knowledge, righteousness, and holiness. . . . Man's creation in this moral image implies that the original condition of man was one of positive holiness, and not a state of innocence or moral neutrality."[5]

In theological writings, references are frequently made to "original righteousness" and "original sin." I have been unable to find anyone who comments on the meaning of the word *original* when discussing the meaning of original righteousness and original sin. Most commonly, we think of original as meaning "first" as distinguished from some other place in the order of numerical sequence. Sometimes, we take the meaning to be the original as distinguished from a copy. Neither of these meanings properly modifies righteousness or sin in the terms "original righteousness" or "original sin."

According to the *Oxford English Dictionary*, one of the meanings of original is "innate." That seems to fit the meaning of original righteousness and original sin. When we speak of man, as created, as possessing original righteousness, we mean he was innately righteous. Righteous thoughts, feelings, and actions flowed from the very design of his nature. By original sin, we mean that since the fall of Adam and Eve human beings are born with an innately depraved nature. There is an innate proneness to sin.

DESIGNED FOR RELATIONSHIPS

Inherent in the constitutional likeness of God in man and demonstrated in the functional likeness is the fact that man is designed for relationships. A human being cannot be adequately described apart from these relationships. In fact, people will die, suffer malfunction, or be less than human according to what relationship or relationships are involved and depending upon the extent to which they are deprived, or deprive themselves, of these relationships. These relationships are (1) man's relationship to God; (2) his relationship to other people; (3) his relationship to the created order; and (4) his relationship to himself.

DESIGNED FOR A RELATIONSHIP WITH GOD

Human beings are designed for a relationship with God. Man's relationship to God is seen in his fellowship with and his responsibility to God. After we are told of the creation of man by God, we read, "Then God blessed them, and God said to them, 'Be fruitful and multiply; fill the earth and subdue it; have dominion over the fish of the sea, over the birds of the air, and over every living thing that moves on the earth'" (Gen. 1:28). We read also of man's moral responsibility when God said, "But of the tree of the knowledge of good and evil you shall not eat, for in the day that you eat of it you shall surely die" (Gen. 2:17). From the reference to God walking in the garden immediately after the fall, we would infer that He had done so before and that Adam and Eve had enjoyed fellowship with God. Before the fall Adam and Eve functioned properly and in a way that was becoming to God in their relationship with Him. We do not make people religious by teaching them about God. We can teach them about God because they are religious by the design of creation. Human beings are in desperate need of a meaningful relationship with God. As Augustine said, "Thou madest us for thyself, and our heart is restless, until it repose in Thee."[6]

DESIGNED FOR INTERPERSONAL RELATIONSHIPS

Human beings are designed for social relationships. In Genesis 2:18, God said, "It is not good that the man should be alone; I will make him a helper comparable to him." The direct reference here is to making a wife for Adam. However, considering that a human being is a member of a race, it is obvious that social relationships are a part of the design of God. A person's need for reciprocal social relationships is no less real than his need for air, water, and food. God created this need for social relationships in our basic design, and it cannot be ignored without serious consequences. We can infer from Genesis 2:18 that it is not good for man to be a loner.

DESIGNED FOR A RELATIONSHIP WITH THE CREATED ORDER

Human beings are designed for a relationship to the created order (Gen. 1:26, 28-30; Ps. 8:6-8). God designed man for the responsibility of exercising dominion over the earth, plants, and animals. This meant that man had a management responsibility over the created order. That responsibility was to be used to meet his needs and to serve his purposes. It is often referred to as the "Cultural Mandate."

Our relationship with the material universe is more than a means of survival. God designed it for our pleasure and enjoyment. It presents us with a challenge. It is an opportunity for us to put our creative minds to work. The Cultural Mandate sanctifies and elevates to the level of divine service the work of farmers, housekeepers, skilled workers, helpers, scientists, engineers, artists, etc. The list could go on. When done for the glory of God, all that we do is a divine service. The challenge is great. Work was a part of the original plan of God for man. It did not involve the undesirable aspects that it does now, but work has always been a part of the divine plan.

This managerial responsibility must also involve a concern for ecology. We must be concerned about the condition of things as we pass them on to future generations.

In the Cultural Mandate, God is saying to every human being: I have made you in My image. I have given you a mind. Your mind is capable of taking what I have given you in the physical universe and achieving much that will be for your enjoyment, comfort, deep satisfaction, and My glory. The possibilities of creative achievement are limitless. I have given you a moral nature. My laws are written in your heart. As you carry out this Mandate, your mind is to do its work under the supervision of your moral nature. See what you can do with the challenge that is before you. One day, I will have you report to Me to see how good a steward you have been of the opportunities you have had.

The fall of man complicated matters in the fulfillment of this Mandate. But the Mandate still remains in force. Stephen M. Ashby reminds us that "it is our responsibility as stewards of this divine command to educate people to think Christianly with an integrated and unified field of knowledge in regards to their faith with their learning."[7]

DESIGNED FOR AN INTRAPERSONAL RELATIONSHIP

Man was designed for a relationship with himself. Anytime there is responsibility and challenge, there is also a place for self-examination. How did I do? How can I face the challenge that is before me? Genesis 2 presents two clear illustrations of responsibility: the responsibility (1) to refrain from eating of the tree of the knowledge of good and evil (Gen. 2:17) and (2) to exercise dominion over the earth and its inhabitants.

To eat of the forbidden fruit was to reap the consequences of death. It would also make man guilty. Guilt when recognized by a person becomes self-judgment on the negative side. To refrain from eating would have produced self-acceptance on the positive side. The responsibility to exercise dominion over the earth has the same basic results so far as self-judgment and self-acceptance are concerned. The moral tone may not be as strong, but the same basic principles are involved.

In connection with the responsibility placed upon man and the challenge given to him, we see that man is goal-oriented. Achievement with its rewards, as well as failure with its losses, are inescapable parts of human beings that were designed in them by their Creator.

THE IMPORTANCE OF THE FACT THAT MAN WAS CREATED IN THE IMAGE OF GOD CONTRIBUTES TO A PROPER SENSE OF WORTH

The image of God in man gives dignity and places a sense of worth on him. Psalm 8:5-8 reads:

For You have made him a little lower than the angels,
And You have crowned him with glory and honor.
You have made him to have dominion over the works of Your hands;
You have put all things under his feet, All sheep and oxen—
Even the beasts of the field,

The birds of the air,
And the fish of the sea
That pass through the paths of the seas.

As a result of the fall, there is a dark side to human nature, but even in fallen man there are still signs of nobility. Jesus was talking about fallen man when He said, "Look at the birds of the air, for they neither sow nor reap nor gather into barns; yet your heavenly Father feeds them. Are you not of more value than they?" (Mt. 6:26). Jesus appealed to the greater worth of man than animals when He defended His healing of the man with a withered hand on the Sabbath day: "Then He said to them, 'What man is there among you who has one sheep, and if it falls into a pit on the Sabbath, will not lay hold of it and lift it out? Of how much more value then is a man than a sheep? Therefore it is lawful to do good on the Sabbath.'" (Mt. 12:11-12).

INFLUENCE AND RESPONSE, NOT CAUSE AND EFFECT

In some sense, an individual's actions are both his own and under his control. If this were not the case, he or she would be less than a person. Yet the fact that human beings are relational creatures means that their actions cannot be explained as independent in the absolute sense. *Influence* is brought to bear on their actions. *Influence* in personal decisions can never be equated with *cause* as in mechanical cause and effect relationships. *Influence* and *response* are more appropriate terms, where persons make decisions, than the terms *cause* and *effect*.

In many of our decisions, we are both active and acted upon. To have to make a choice between active and passive is to equate personal relationships with mechanical cause and effect relationships. These principles relate to our relationships to both God and other human beings. It is only when we distinguish between influence and response and cause and effect that we can begin to understand how God works with us as human beings.

The Factor of Human Design

When we see the full meaning of the fact that (1) we are designed to be personal, rational, moral beings and (2) we are designed for the four basic relationships, then we can determine our needs according to our design. The design of human beings represents not only possibilities, but also needs. It is possible for us not only to be rational and moral and to have functioning relationships, but we also need to function rationally and morally and properly in the framework of the four basic relationships. Failure in any of these areas means loss. All rational, moral, and spiritual functions are functions of the personality. A Christian psychology, sociology, and system of ethics must have as a part of its foundation an acquaintance with what it means to be made in the image of God. It is utterly impossible for human beings through observation and experience alone (empiricism) ever to arrive at an adequate understanding of human needs and human behavior. Only when we let special divine revelation inform us about human design and its implications can we develop an adequate understanding of human need and how to minister effectively to those needs. Then and only then can we help our fellow human beings be what they are designed to be and become what they can by redemption.

We pay very close attention to design and how it determines need in machines. We are very careful when we buy fuel for our automobiles. We get diesel fuel if that is what our car was designed for. We get gasoline if our car was designed for gasoline. Shall we be less careful in finding out what we are designed for? Will we ignore the question of human design and recommend that people create their own meaning and purpose or simply go along with what society is saying? We know better than to pour water in the fuel tank of our car. It is even more important that we live according to the design that the Designer designed into our being when He made us in His own image.

The Origin of the Immaterial Part of Man

By origin of the immaterial part of man, I am not referring to the original creation by God, but to the origin of the immaterial part as it relates to those who have descended from Adam and Eve. In one sense, this discussion may not belong under the discussion of man as created, but in another sense it does. The design of providing the immaterial part of man is not related to the fall, but was already a part of the divine plan before the fall. The same plan would have been followed if there had been no fall of man into sin.

There are three approaches: (1) The pre-existence theory teaches that the immaterial part of man existed prior to the creation of the body. Since orthodox Christians have never accepted this view, I do not deem it necessary to deal with it. There are no reasons for anyone even to be confused about whether the Bible supports such a view. (2) The creationist theory teaches that God creates the immaterial part of each person and places it in the body sometime between conception and birth. (3) The traducian theory teaches that the immaterial part of man is transmitted through propagation just as the body is.

The Creationist View

One of the main reasons people have advocated the creationist view is that it is felt this was the only way for Christ to be born without depravity. It is felt that traducianism would result in a depraved nature for Christ. I would suggest that the same divine act of conception that could provide Jesus with a body that did not bear the marks of depravity could also sanctify the immaterial part of man.

The most serious objection to the creationists' view is how the immaterial part becomes corrupt. One thought, which is sometimes associated with the federal headship view of Adam's sin and the race, suggests that God created the immaterial part of man corrupt because Adam violated the covenant God made with him when he sinned. I cannot conceive of

God creating anything corrupt. Another view states that God creates the immaterial part sinless, but that it becomes corrupt upon contact with the body. There is a close relationship between the spirit and the body, but to blame the total process of perpetuating the depravity of the race on the body is more than can be justified. The depravity of the spirit is far more basic in our depravity than that of the body.

The Traducian View

The traducian theory most easily accounts for the perpetuation of depravity in the human race and its effect on the total person. Some are of the opinion that the Bible does not give a clear-cut case for either creationism or traducianism. I do not think this is the case. In Genesis 5:3 we read, "And Adam . . . begot a son in his own likeness, after his image, and called his name Seth." If the creation of man in God's image included the personhood and personality of Adam, certainly the begetting of Seth in Adam's image included Seth's personhood and personality. Personhood and personality cannot be based on body alone but must embrace the spirit also. Traducianism offers the only adequate explanation of Adam's begetting Seth in his own image.

The Effect of the Fall on the Image of God in Man

Concerning the effect of the fall on the image of God, Carl F. H. Henry explains: "The fall of man is not destructive of the formal image (man's personality) although it involves the distortion (though not demolition) of the material content of the image."[8] Louis Berkhof comments: "As created in the image of God man has a rational and a moral nature, which he did not lose by sin and which he could not lose without ceasing to be man. This part of the image of God has indeed been vitiated by sin, but still remains in man even after his fall into sin."[9] Gordon H. Clark says, "Sin has interfered with but does not prohibit thought. It does not eradicate the image but causes it to malfunction."[10]

As was stated previously when discussing the meaning of being made in the image of God, I prefer "constitutional likeness" to "formal image" and "functional likeness" to "material content," but the meaning is the same whichever way it may be stated. I made a further distinction between personhood and personality. This distinction will be particularly helpful in explaining the effect of the fall on the image of God in man.

The Effect on the Constitutional Likeness

The fall did not change the fact of the constitutional likeness. The personhood of man remains intact. He is still a thinking, feeling, acting being. He is still morally constituted. All of the constituent parts of personhood remain intact after the fall. The parts have suffered damage, but they all remain. The damage reflects itself in the personality.

The Effect on the Functional Likeness

The effect of the fall is seen in the functional likeness. A basic and drastic change occurred in man's personality. Before the fall, man thought, felt, and acted both on the conscious and subconscious levels in absolute conformity to the likeness of God. After the fall, this was no longer true. Man no longer thinks, feels, and acts in a way that is pleasing to God. This is true both on the conscious and subconscious levels. However, it is not as simple as saying that man is the precise opposite of what he was before the fall. We must avoid oversimplified explanations of how the fall affected the image of God.

The Problem of Giving a Simple Description of Fallen Man

It is clear that man fell from a state of holiness into a state of sin (Is. 53:6; Rom. 3:23). It is clear that sin has placed man under condemnation before God (Rom. 6:23; Rev. 21:8). It is clear that fallen man cannot please God and has no fellowship with God (Eph. 2:1-3; Rom. 8:7-8). It is clear that man cannot come to God without the drawing power of the Holy Spirit (Jn. 6:44). It is clear that a work so drastic as to be called a new birth is required for man's salvation (Jn. 3:3-7). But we also find areas where the state and condition of man are not so clearly understood.

Henry is grappling with the difficulty of giving a clear statement on the effect of the fall on the functional likeness in man, as indicated in the quotation given earlier. He states that while there is a "distortion," there is not a "demolition" of the material content (functional likeness). Berkhof and Clark also indicate the difficulty of making a clear statement. What we are dealing with here is: How depraved is man? What do we mean when we say there is not a demolition of the functional likeness? I am not raising the question of whether man is totally depraved but rather what is meant by total depravity. Charles C. Ryrie correctly argues that total depravity does not imply that depraved people cannot do good things before God or man, but simply that those things cannot bring salvation. Total depravity also does not means that human beings have no conscience that enables them to distinguish between good and evil. Still, "that conscience has been affected by the fall so that it cannot be a safe and reliable guide." Finally, total depravity does not imply "that people indulge in every form of sin or in any sin to the greatest extent possible."[11] In commenting on these three points, Ashby explains:

(1) There is such a thing as "relative good." But depraved people do not do the right thing, with the right motive, to satisfy the righteous expectations of a holy God.

(2) I agree that fallen man has a conscience—but it is skewed and judges trivial things as important and monumental things as trivial.

(3) Total depravity is not absolute depravity. Every person is not a Hitler or a Charles Manson. But every aspect of one's being is conditioned by sinful inclinations.[12]

In summary, *total* means that the corruption has extended to all aspects of man's nature, to his entire being; and *depravity* means that, because of that corruption, there is nothing man can do to merit saving favor with God.

The Effect of the Presence of the Image of God in Fallen Man on Human Behavior

Why is it that every sinner does not exhibit his depravity as thoroughly as he could? Why is it that every sinner does not commit every sin? Why is it that a degree of moral concern can be found among sinners? Why is it that sinners perform some good deeds? The answer goes back to the understanding that sinners still retain personhood. They are still personal, rational, moral beings by constitution and design.

Man did not become non-moral in the fall anymore than he became non-rational. A being must be moral (that is, morally constituted) to be immoral. He must be rational (that is, rationally constituted) to be irrational. It is the moral constitution of man that Paul is discussing in Romans 2:15 when he speaks about the Gentiles, "Who show the work of the law written in their hearts."

The sinner, still bearing the image of God, is so constituted that he has the categories of right and wrong. Right is considered a plus factor, and wrong is considered a minus factor. No human being does what he knows to be wrong without considering it, to some extent, to be a minus factor. This fact cannot be obliterated.

I do not say this as a person who has been out of touch with the problem side of human nature. I have had considerable experience dealing one on one with troubled people. I have learned to listen when people give clues concerning what is happening in their deep inner selves.

I remember one day listening to a talk show when a prostitute called in. She said, "I am a prostitute. I don't like what I am doing. But I don't know anything else to do." Recently, I saw a program on television that was dealing with prostitution in Russia. As one of the women was interviewed, she said, "I don't want my daughter to know what I am doing. I am humiliated. I feel dirty. I receive dirty money."

Some time ago, I watched a program detailing one method of dealing with deeply troubled teenagers. A member of the group would sit before the others for a period of very hard questioning which attempted to get to the bottom of what was bothering the person. This was not a religious treatment center. One girl broke down and cried, "I had an abortion. I killed the baby that was within me."

Sin has introduced a foreign element into man's being. Man was made for righteousness. He was not made for sin. A human being can never live in sin and have self-acceptance and full harmony of being. Sin has placed man in conflict, contradiction, and confusion. Sin puts a person at cross purposes with the image of God within from which there is no escape. To whatever extent a person has forfeited the morality of the Ten Commandments, to that extent, he or she is in trouble—not only with God, but also with himself or herself. No person who lives in gross violation of the morality of the Ten Commandments is happy. If you doubt this statement, start listening, and you will gather your own evidence.

Since people cannot totally erase moral concern, they try to enter into label changing. They try to place the label "right" on what they want to do. The effort never totally succeeds. Regardless of what may go on in the conscious mind, people can never accept in their deep inner beings the violation of the basic morality of the Ten Commandments. Ten thousand arguments will never make these violations acceptable. Notice the lack of self-respect among those who try this route. Notice the need of alcohol and of drugs. Notice the presence of misery, despair, and depression. All of these tell us that the deep inner self is not going along with the attempt to set aside basic human morality. The image of God within cries out for Truth, a right use of reason, moral uprightness, forgiveness for guilt, and an experience of beauty, excellence, and order. The image of God longs to experience what it means to be in the likeness of God. The image of God within can be neglected, but not without a high cost.

Man is in drastic need of approval both from himself and from others. This fact gives rise to worthy deeds among sinners. Every person feels good when he by conscious choice does what he believes to be right. Every person feels good when he by conscious choice accommodates another person.

The categories of right and wrong, with right being a plus factor and wrong being a minus factor, indelibly written in the constitution of man, produce some good in the sinner. This good will never provide acceptance before God, neither will it meet the needs of the person himself. It is the presence of this moral constitution in man that provides a point of contact for the gospel. If fallen man were a moral blank, or had the categories of right and wrong reversed, there would be no point of contact for the gospel. There would be no grounds for conviction of sin.

ASSESSING THE TRUE NATURE OF DEPRAVITY

In assessing the seriousness of the power and influence of depravity, we must keep in mind that the truest picture of sin does not always manifest itself in overt acts. Everyone has imagined committing sins that he has not committed. The same capacity that can imagine evil can commit evil. Everyone has kept in check some desire for evil that he has had. With the same capacity with which we desire evil, we can also commit evil. Sometimes people enjoy seeing sin committed by others. The same capacity that enjoys evil can commit evil.

THE IMPOSSIBILITY OF FALLEN MAN'S ATTAINING A RIGHT STANDING BEFORE GOD BY HIS OWN EFFORTS

It is possible and sometimes happens that unbelievers reach a measure of decency and uprightness in society. They may perform humanitarian deeds, but all of these fall far short of meeting divine approval (Rom. 3:23). The presence of sin in their lives still renders them unrighteous before a holy God. The power of sin in their lives makes them stand in need of the new birth.

THE QUESTION OF THE FREEDOM OF THE WILL

Probably the most enduring controversy over depravity centers on the will. Does fallen man have a free will? If descendants of Adam do not in some sense have freedom of will, they have lost their personhood. One of the factors involved in being a person is to have power of choice or the ability to will. The will can choose and act only to the extent that it is free. To deprive the will of freedom is to deprive it of being a will. I think the debate between Calvinism and Arminianism should be framed over whether fallen man is a functioning, personal being. Does he have a functioning mind, heart, and will?

THE MEANING OF FREEDOM OF THE WILL

Before proceeding to discuss the effect of depravity on the will, let us make a few things clear about what is and is not meant by freedom of will. The freedom of the will does not mean that forces or influences cannot be brought to bear on the will. In fact, the very nature of freedom of the will means that forces or influences will be brought to bear on the will. It does not mean that these forces cannot be a contributing factor in the exercise of the will. It does mean that these influences or forces *cannot guarantee or determine* the action of the will. We are dealing with influence and response, not cause and effect.

THE FRAMEWORK OF POSSIBILITIES AND THE MEANING OF FREEDOM OF THE WILL

Freedom of will is a freedom within a *framework of possibilities*. It is not absolute freedom. Man cannot be God. He cannot be an angel. The freedom of a human being is in the framework of the possibilities provided by human nature. Also, the influences brought to bear on the will have a bearing on the framework of possibilities.

Before Adam and Eve sinned, it was in the framework of possibilities within which they operated to remain in the practice of complete righteousness, or to commit sin. After they sinned, it no longer remained within the framework of possibilities for them to practice uninterrupted righteousness. The same is true for fallen man now (Rom. 8:7-8). If anyone understands *freedom of will* to mean that an unconverted person could practice righteousness *and not sin*, he misunderstands the meaning of freedom of will for fallen human beings. Romans 8:7-8 makes it clear that Scripture does not teach this.

Jesus makes it clear that it does not fall within the framework of possibilities for a sinner to respond to the gospel unless he is drawn by the Holy Spirit (Jn. 6:44). The influence of the Holy Spirit working in the heart of the person who hears the gospel brings about a framework of possibilities in which a person can say yes or no to the gospel. If he says yes, it is his choice. If he says no, it is his choice. To say less than that is to raise serious questions about the existence of real personhood after the fall. If a human being is not in some sense a *self-directed* being, he or she is not a person. The self-direction may have a high degree of dependence at times, but it is still self-direction. As has already been made clear, I am not suggesting that fallen man can choose Christ without the aid of the Holy Spirit. In fact, I strongly reject such an idea. I am saying, however, that no matter how much or how strong the aid of the Holy Spirit may be, the "yes" decision is still a decision that can rightly be called the person's decision. After all, one can say no.

The view that I hold is the same as that Jacobus Arminius advocated. Very few individuals throughout history have had so many viewpoints wrongly attributed to them as Arminius. J. Matthew Pinson has done considerable research in order to clarify what Arminius taught and did not teach. Pinson explains that Arminius believed that human beings are not able to seek God "unless they are radically affected by his grace." Most interpreters have assumed that Arminius was a semi-Pelagian, thus espousing a view of freedom of the will that "makes individuals totally able to choose God or spurn him." Yet, Pinson argues, Arminius holds that human beings have no freedom to do anything good in God's sight. Rather, "for Arminius, the basic freedom which characterizes the human will is freedom from necessity. . . . [Yet] he states unequivocally that the will is not free from sin and its dominion." Pinson quotes from Arminius as follows: ". . . the free will of man towards the true good is not only wounded, maimed, infirm, bent, and (*nuatum*) weakened; but it is also (*captivatum*) imprisoned, destroyed, and lost: And its powers are not only debilitated and useless unless they are assisted by grace, but it has no powers whatever except such are excited by grace."[13] Thus, as Pinson explains, "fallen humanity has no ability or power to reach out to the grace of God on its own."[14]

THE DIFFERENCE BETWEEN MY VIEW AND CALVINISM

Faith can be called a gift in the sense that it would not have been possible without divine aid. It is not a gift in the sense that it exists outside the person and is given to him, nor is it a gift in the sense that God believes for the person. The person himself does the believing by divine aid. I think Calvinism errs in its understanding of "dead in trespasses." Cornelius Van Til, in his explanation of the Calvinistic interpretation, argues that sinful man is dead in trespasses and "unable of himself even to stretch forth his hand to receive salvation." However, "Scripture continues to deal with him as a responsible being. He is called to faith and repentance. Yet faith is a gift of God. Lazarus lay in the tomb. He was dead. Yet Jesus told him to come forth. And he did come forth."[15]

The above interpretation interprets "dead" in "dead in trespasses" (Eph. 2:1) as meaning lifeless. The dead body of Lazarus had no life in it. It was capable of no action until it was made alive by Jesus. If "dead in trespasses" means dead in the same way, the logic of Calvinism follows. Sinners would be both deaf and speechless. They would know nothing about God, sin, and salvation until God made them alive through the new birth. Then and only then would they be able to hear and to speak.

I think "dead in trespasses and sins," or spiritual death, means that man is separated from God, dead in relationship to God. There is no communion and no fellowship with God. The principle is similar to that spoken of by Paul when he said, "By whom the world is crucified to me, and I to the world" (Gal. 6:14). Both Paul and the world were alive in the sense that they were not lifeless. They were not alive so far as a functioning relationship between them was concerned.

Spiritual death, if this is the correct interpretation, refers to the fact that the sinner is cut off from communion and fellowship with God. This is true both because a holy God demands that it be so until sin is taken care of, and also because the bias of the sinner's heart is against God. The fact that sinners are not in communion with God does not mean that they are totally deaf to God's communication. If that were the case, sinners could not even distort the message of God. You cannot distort that to which you are totally deaf. That a person is a sinner does mean he does not hear well. He tends to resist and oppose the Truth and to distort the Truth. The gospel has to go forth against great opposition. The Holy Spirit must work before there can be a successful communication of the gospel to the sinner and before there will be conviction and response from the sinner. This approach recognizes the seriousness of sin, the necessity of the enlightening and drawing power of the Holy Spirit, and the personhood of the sinner.

I believe that saving faith is a gift of God in the sense that the Holy Spirit gives divine enablement without which faith in Christ would be impossible (Jn. 6:44). The difference between the Calvinistic concept of faith and my concept of faith *cannot* be that theirs is *monergistic* and mine is *synergistic*. In *both* cases it is synergistic. Active participation in faith by the believer means that it must be synergistic. Human response cannot be ruled out of faith. Justification and regeneration are monergistic. Each is an act of God, not man. Faith is a human act by divine enablement and therefore cannot be monergistic.

The Consequences of Adam's Sin for the Race

The questions to be answered regarding the consequences of Adam's sin for the human race are as follows: First, is Adam's sin imputed to the race? Second, if it is imputed, how and why? Third, how is depravity transmitted?

Romans 5:12-19

The key passage in deciding the consequences upon the race of Adam's sin is Romans 5:12-19. How do we interpret the phrase "death passed upon all men, for that all have sinned" in verse 12 (KJV)? "Death passed upon all men" is the effect. "All have sinned" is the cause. Concerning the Greek word translated "have sinned" in the KJV, there are two possibilities insofar as Greek grammar is concerned. "Have sinned" is a translation of *hēmarton*, which is the aorist. If we understand the aorist as a simple aorist, we would translate "all sinned." It would mean that all sinned at some time in the past. This would mean that death passed upon the race because the race sinned at some time in the past.

If we understand the aorist as being a gnomic aorist, we would translate it "all sin." If we understand it to be a culminative aorist, we would translate it "all have sinned." Whether we understood the Greek to be a gnomic aorist or a culminative aorist, the interpretation would be the same. It would mean that death passes upon all men because all people sin.

If we understand that death passed upon all men because all men sinned at some time in the past, death would pass upon all because all sinned in Adam. If we understand that death passes upon all men because all sin, death would pass upon each person because of his own sins, not the sin of Adam. The context must decide which of these interpretations is correct.

The chart below will help us see how the context decides the question.

CAUSE	EFFECT
5:12 "All have sinned" or "All sinned"?	"Death passed upon all men"
5:15 "The offence of one"	"Many be dead"
5:16 "By one [person]"	"Condemnation"
5:17 "One man's offence"	"Death reigned"
5:18 "The offence of one" (The Greek means "one offence.")	"Judgment came upon all men to condemnation"

On the "effect" side of the chart, it is obvious that the effect in 5:15-18 is the same as the effect in 5:12. If it is clear what the cause of the effect is in 5:15-18, that should help clarify what the cause is in 5:12. The cause in 5:15-18 is "one person," "one man's offence," and "one offence." Putting that together, it is clear that the cause is the one offense committed by Adam when he ate the forbidden fruit.

If 5:12, 15-18 all give the same effect, it is to be expected that 5:12, 15-18 will all give the same cause. The cause is clear in 5:15-19. This interprets the cause in 5:12. While Greek grammar may allow the statement in 5:12 to refer to each individual's sin, the context decides against it and in favor of the other grammatical possibility. It is clear in the total context that 5:12 is to be interpreted, "all sinned in Adam."

Romans 5:12-19 definitely settles the fact that the sin of Adam is imputed or placed on the account of the whole race. The question to be decided now is how and why was this done?

THE APPROACHES USED TO EXPLAIN THE IMPUTATION OF ADAM'S SIN TO THE RACE

One view would say that the answer is found in Adam's natural headship of the race. The other would declare that while Adam is the natural head of the race, the natural headship did not furnish the grounds for imputing the sin of Adam to the race. Adam was appointed federal head of the race and the grounds of imputation are found in the federal headship of Adam.

According to the view that grounds imputation in the natural headship of Adam, sin is imputed to the race because the race, by being in Adam, was a part of Adam when he sinned, thus identified with him in his sin and the guilt of that sin. This view accepts the traducian view of the origin of the human spirit. The process of propagation transmits depravity.

According to the federal headship view, Adam became the representative of the race by divine appointment. The reason for Adam's being chosen was his natural headship, but natural headship did not of itself involve the race in Adam's sin. God entered into a covenant with Adam promising to bestow eternal life on him and his posterity should he obey God. Corruption and death would pass on to his posterity should he disobey God. It is the covenant relationship of the race with Adam, by virtue of his being appointed as the representative of the race, that involves the race in the consequences of his sin. Instead of saying that the race sinned in Adam, this view would say, "All are accounted as sinners."

COMPARISON OF NATURAL AND FEDERAL HEADSHIP THEORIES

NATURAL HEADSHIP VIEW	FEDERAL HEADSHIP VIEW
1. Traducianist	1. Creationists as a rule, but could be traducianist
2. Adam representative of the race because the race was in him	2. Adam representative of the race because of divine appointment
3. Sin imputed because of identification by being in Adam	3. Sin imputed to the race because Adam, as appointed representative of the race, violated the covenant
4. All sinned	4. All are accounted as sinners
5. Immaterial part transmitted with a depraved nature	5. Immaterial part created by God with corrupt and depraved nature, or created without corruption and corrupted by contact with a corrupt body. (A few would go along with the traducian view, but this is not the usual view.)

THE FEDERAL HEADSHIP VIEW

While a person may be a traducianist and hold to the federal headship view, a creationist must hold to the federal headship view if he believes in the imputation of the sin of Adam to the race. Being in Adam from only a physical viewpoint would not furnish an adequate basis for imputing the sin of Adam to the race as it relates to the total personality.

The federal headship view works on the assumption that the federal headship principle of imputation explains the imputation of the death and righteousness of Christ to the redeemed. It then seeks to build a parallel view of the imputation of Adam's sin to the race.

While there may be some people who accept the federal headship view of Adam who do not accept unconditional election, the federal headship principle fits logically in the Calvinistic system. The covenant made with Adam, because of Adam's disobedience, brought condemnation to all who were in the covenant. In this case, it was the whole race. The covenant made with Christ, because of His obedience in death and righteousness, brought eternal life to all who were in the covenant. In this case, according to Calvinism, only those who were unconditionally elected to be parties of the covenant were in the covenant.

By an act of His own will and based on His own reasons, God chose to include the whole race as the recipient of the guilt and consequences of Adam's sin. He could have chosen to do it otherwise. There was nothing in the nature of things that made it necessary for it to be that way. By an act of His own will and based on His own reasons, God did not choose to elect the whole human race and make them participants in the benefits of Christ's obedience. There was nothing in the nature of the case that required Him to limit the number of the elect. I mention these observations here because in systematic thinking we must see the possible bearing on other parts in a system of the way we interpret principles and their application in a particular place.

ROMANS 5:12 – SUPPORT FOR FEDERAL HEADSHIP VIEW OR NATURAL HEADSHIP VIEW?

Does the Scripture aid in our choice between the natural headship view and the federal headship view? I think it does. The evidence presented above supports the conclusion that Romans 5:12 is to be interpreted as "All sinned in Adam."

The language of Romans 5:12 is more appropriate for the natural headship view because the language of Romans 5:12 and of the natural headship view are identical. The "all sinned" of Romans 5:12 must be twisted to mean "all are accounted as sinners" for the federal headship view. "All sinned" is in the active voice. "All are accounted as sinners" would require the passive voice.

The Natural Headship View

We have some difficulty accepting with our total being the conclusion that the whole race was condemned for Adam's sin. This is made far more acceptable when we see that the nature of things made it necessary that the race be charged with Adam's sin than to think that God made the decision in no relationship to necessity. There are those who say in rebuttal that God can do anything. God cannot be limited by necessity. This is to misunderstand the case. God must act in accord with His nature. As an expression of His own nature, God has built certain principles and guidelines into the nature of reality. He is obligated to abide by these principles and guidelines in order that He may maintain a rational consistency with His creation. The objectionable features of the creationist view of the origin of the spirit and how it becomes corrupt have already been discussed earlier in the chapter and need not be repeated here.

Let us now return to a further discussion of the natural headship view. We have already seen that it best accords with Scripture. Now let us look at the logical defense. The race was in Adam and has descended, body and spirit, from him. This means that we were in Adam and were identified with him in his sin. It necessitates our being partakers with him in his guilt and condemnation. To say otherwise would say that not all of Adam was condemned, because that which was in Adam's loins, which was the race potentially, was as much a part of Adam as any other part. No matter how many subdivisions there may be, the parts never lose their real identification as being a part of the original whole. We have never lost our identification with Adam in his sin.

I would not accept some of the ideas that have usually been associated with this view. In explaining this perspective, A. H. Strong says, "The powers which now exist in separate men were then unified and localized in Adam; Adam's will was yet the will of the species. In Adam's free act, the will of the race revolted from God and the nature of the race corrupted itself."[16] It sounds as if Strong may be saying that the will of every human being acted in Adam's will. I do not think that this is the case. The wills did not exist. Only the potential for those wills existed. Our wills came into being only when we came into being as individual persons. To say that all sinned in Adam must not be understood to say that their wills were active in Adam. We could say that his will was the will of the race since the race was in him and descended from him, but we cannot speak of the wills of the race being combined in his will.

The Parallel Between the Imputation of Adam's Sin and the Imputation of Christ's Death and Righteousness

The principle involved in imputation of something from one to another is *identification by being in or in union with the person*. This is true whether it is sin or whether it is righteousness. The Scripture knows of no other way that the action of one person can be imputed to another. This is the principle involved in the imputation of the death and righteousness of Christ to the believer.

The Bible knows of no imputation from one to another except in a manner that makes it so that the action can in some sense be said to be *the action of the person himself*. Paul said in Galatians 2:20, "I am [or I have been] crucified with Christ." By being in union with Christ, Paul became so identified with Christ that it could be said he was crucified with Christ. Paul was not actually crucified with Christ in the sense of experiencing the sufferings of Christ. By identification with Christ, the death of Christ became his so that he could get credit for its benefits. (For a more thorough explanation of this, see the discussion on union with Christ in connection with the doctrine of justification.)

In a similar sense that the death of Christ is ours, the sin of Adam is ours. We did not perform the sin by an act of our own will, but we were in Adam when he committed the sin. We were identified with him. We were in Adam at the time of his sin. Our connection with him is maintained by an unbroken continuity between Adam and us. We were not in Christ at the time of His crucifixion, but were placed in Him when we exercised faith. We are now in Him.

I think the federal headship principle misinterprets both the imputation of Adam's sin and the imputation of the death and righteousness of Christ. The Scripture knows of only one principle of imputation of the actions of one person to another, and that is identification by union. The *natural headship view*, not the federal headship view, *maintains the parallel between Christ and Adam* in connection with the principle involved in imputation. (If the reader has problems at this point, I would suggest that he skip over and read what is said about union with Christ as it relates to justification. The whole case is better elaborated there.)

THE QUESTION OF THOSE DYING IN INFANCY

A question that always arises in this connection is: What about those dying in infancy? I will reserve the discussion of this until later. Let me just say at this point that I believe in infant salvation. The discussion belongs more properly to the doctrines of atonement and salvation.

OTHER VIEWS ON THE IMPUTATION OF ADAM'S SIN TO THE RACE

There are two more views that should be mentioned. The theory of mediate imputation denies that the guilt of Adam is imputed to the race. We receive depravity from him, and depravity forms the basis of guilt and condemnation. The sin of Adam is the indirect cause, not the direct cause, of the race being charged with guilt. This imputation of guilt precedes personal acts of sin. This view does not accord with Scripture, as we have seen from our discussion above.

Another view that is frequently referred to as the Arminian view does not teach that the race is charged with the guilt of Adam's sin. Depravity is inherited from Adam and causes people to sin. They are not condemned before God until they commit individual sin upon becoming responsible persons. The discussion above shows the inadequacy of this view.

While it is true that some Arminians have advocated this view, it is by no means universally accepted and should not be called the Arminian view.

This is especially true since it was not the view held by Arminius himself. It is somewhat puzzling why people with good scholarly credentials would say that Arminius denied the imputation of Adam's sin to the race. This is the position set forth by A. H. Strong under the heading, "The Arminian Theory, or Theory of Voluntarily Appropriated Depravity."[17] In his book, *With Wilful Intent*, David Smith attributes this view to Arminius and uses Strong as his authority for it.[18]

Pinson sets the record straight. He explains that Arminius's approach to original sin is Augustinian. He quotes Arminius as saying that "the whole of this sin . . . is not peculiar to our first parents, but is common to the entire race and all their posterity, who, at the time when his sin was committed, were in their loins, and who have since descended from them by natural propagation."[19] Pinson goes on to explain that Arminius held that all people "sinned in Adam, and are guilty in Adam, apart from their actual sins." He cites Arminius's *Private Disputations*, in which Arminius states that "all men who were to be propagated from [Adam and Eve] in a natural way, became obnoxious to death temporal and death eternal, and [*vacui*] devoid of this gift of the Holy Spirit or original righteousness."[20]

One of the chief concerns of Arminians has been to deny that infants go to hell. Some have sought support for this denial by denying guilt before individual guilt enters the picture. Many others have believed that the guilt of Adam was imputed to the race but removed for all in atonement. Arminius himself believed in the salvation of all who died in infancy. He did not work on the basis of a non-involvement in Adam's sin as a basis for believing that those who die in infancy go to heaven when they die.[21]

---

[1] See *The Quest for Truth*, 65-66, for a discussion of the spiritual nature of God.

[2] See *The Quest for Truth*, 32-36, for a discussion of general revelation.

[3] Carl F. H. Henry, "Image of God" in *Evangelical Dictionary of Theology*, Walter A. Elwell, ed. (Grand Rapids: Baker Book House, 1984), 547.

[4] Ibid., 341.

[5]Louis Berkhof, *Systematic Theology*, 3rd ed. (Grand Rapids: William B. Eerdmans Publishing Company, 1941), 204.

[6]Augustine, *The Confessions of Saint Augustine*, 1 (See *The Quest for Truth*, Chapter 3, note 22).

[7]From a private communication with Stephen Ashby (See *The Quest for Truth*, Chapter 2, note 2).

[8]Henry, "Image of God" in *Evangelical Dictionary of Theology*, 547.

[9]Berkhof, *Systematic Theology*, 204.

[10]Gordon H. Clark, "Image of God" in *Baker's Dictionary of Christian Ethics*, Carl F. H. Henry, ed. (Grand Rapids: Baker Book House, 1973), 313.

[11]Charles Ryrie, "Depravity Total" *Evangelical Dictionary of Theology*, 312.

[12]From a private communication with Stephen Ashby (See *The Quest for Truth*, Chapter 2, Note 2).

[13]James Arminius, *The Works of James Arminius*, trans. James Nichols and William Nichols (Nashville: Randall House, 2007), 2:193.

[14]J. Matthew Pinson, "Will the Real Arminius Please Stand Up? A Study of the Theology of Jacobus Arminius in Light of His Interpreters," *Integrity: A Journal of Christian Thought* 2 (2003), 134.

[15]Van Til, Cornelius, "Calvinism," in *Baker's Dictionary of Theology*, Everett F. Harrison, ed. (Grand Rapids: Baker Book House, 1960), 340-341.

[16]A. H. Strong, *Systematic Theology*, (Philadelphia: Griffith and Rowland, 1907), 619.

[17]Ibid., 601-603.

[18]David L. Smith, *With Wilful Intent: A Theology of Sin* (Wheaton: Victor Books, 1994), 363.

[19]Arminius, 2:156.

[20]Pinson, "Will the Real Arminius Please Stand Up?" 15-16 The bracketed "Adam and Eve" is Pinson's bracketed addition. The bracketed *vacui* is the translators.

[21]Arminius, *Works*, 2:10-14.

CHAPTER 2

The Theology of Election

While Arminians and Calvinists share much common ground, there are major points of difference. Nothing calls attention to that difference like a study of decrees and election. My plan in this chapter is first to survey Calvinistic and Arminian thought on decrees and election. I will deal with the main concepts that are involved in treating these subjects. I will show what I consider to be problems in Calvinistic thought, and then I will build a case for the Arminian position on these subjects.[1] In Chapters 3 and 4, I will show what I believe to be the proper interpretation of the passages that Calvinists use to support unconditional election. In Chapter 5, I will give the biblical support for conditional election.

THE CALVINISTIC VIEW OF UNCONDITIONAL ELECTION

Unconditional election says that God, in eternity past, chose or elected certain ones from the fallen race of men for salvation. This election was in no way related to God's foreknowledge of faith on the part of the individual. Those who were thus elected will in due time be saved. God has provided the death and righteousness of Christ for their justification. In the course of time, those who have been chosen will be called. This call is an irresistible call (or an effectual call). It cannot fail to result in saving faith. This salvation is an absolute gift. Man did not in any way do anything to merit it or receive it. The elect are in no way responsible for having faith. That faith is theirs as an absolute gift of God.

The Order of Decrees in Calvinism

Millard Erickson explains the wording for the decrees regarding salvation as follows:[2]

SUPRALAPSARIANISM
1. The decree to save (elect) some and reprobate others.
2. The decree to create both the elect and the reprobate.
3. The decree to permit the fall of both the elect and the reprobate.
4. The decree to provide salvation only for the elect.

INFRALAPSARIANISM
1. The decree to create human beings.
2. The decree to permit the fall.
3. The decree to elect some and reprobate others.
4. The decree to provide salvation only for the elect.

SUBLAPSARIANISM
1. The decree to create human beings.
2. The decree to permit the fall.
3. The decree to provide salvation sufficient for all.
4. The decree to save some and reprobate others.

Most Classical Calvinists are Infralapsarian. Supralapsarianism, in making the decree to elect some and to reprobate others precede the decree to create, is sometimes referred to as Hyper-Calvinism. While in a minority, Supralapsarians have been accepted among Classical Calvinists. Many theologians do not list Sublapsarianism as a separate category. The particular significance of Sublapsarianism is that, in making the decree to provide atonement to precede the decree to elect, it takes the position of unlimited atonement—thus, four-point Calvinism. All of the above approaches to decrees are in agreement on unconditional election.

CALVINISM, DETERMINISM, AND FREE WILL

I must confess that it is not simple to answer the question, Do Calvinists believe in free will? Some seem to reject the concept of free will. Others claim to believe in free will. Then there is the problem of how they define free will. In order to get a clearer picture of how Calvinists deal with the concept of free will, we must first examine their approach to determinism.

THE QUESTION OF DETERMINISM IN CALVINISM

There are various forms of determinism. Our concern is with theistic determinism. Norman Geisler explains that, according to theistic determinism, every event, including human conduct, is determined or caused by God. Jonathan Edwards exemplified this view, contending that "free will or self-determinism contradicted the sovereignty of God. If God is truly in control of all things, no one could act contrary to his will, which is what self-determinism must hold. Hence, for God to be sovereign he must cause every event, be it human or otherwise."[3] J. A. Crabtree defines divine determinists as those who believe that "every aspect of everything that occurs in the whole of reality is ultimately caused and determined by God."[4] John S. Feinberg points out that "the fundamental tenet of determinism (and the various forms of Calvinism are forms of determinism) is that for everything that happens, in the light of prevailing conditions, the agent could not have done other than he did. For determinists, there are always sufficient conditions that decisively incline the agent's will to choose one option or another."[5]

These definitions of determinism bring up the question: "What about the scope of determinism?" Let us look now at how Calvinists deal with this problem.

The Scope of Determinism
The Whole of Created Reality (Unlimited Determinism)

It is obvious that Jonathan Edwards would take his stand with those who make the scope of determinism coextensive with the whole of reality. Gordon H. Clark makes divine determination cover everything, including the sinful acts of men. In commenting on Proverbs 21:1 and Ezra 7:6, he argues that God determines all policies and decisions of governments: "God controls all governmental policies and decisions. Not only did God cause Pharaoh to hate the Israelites, he caused Cyrus to send the captives back to build Jerusalem. He also caused Hitler to march into Russia and he caused Johnson to escalate a war in Vietnam. God turns the mind of a ruler in whatever direction he wants to."[6] In commenting on the action of Joseph's brothers when they sold him into slavery, Clark remarks that, if Joseph's brothers had murdered him as they had contemplated, "then God would have been mistaken. The sale had to take place. Does this mean that God foreordained sinful acts? Well, it certainly means that these acts were certain and determined from all eternity. It means that the brothers could not have done otherwise."[7]

Most Calvinists who make determinism coextensive with the whole of reality are not looking for opportunities to make statements like those that Clark makes. If they had to comment, they would try to soften their remarks. Yet they cannot deny what Clark said.

Soteriology (Limited Determinism)

Richard A. Muller gives a different perspective on determinism than Clark gives. He argues that, contrary to Arminian allegations, Calvin's and other Reformed theologians' use of biblical examples of divine determination in their arguments for predestination does not indicate determinism of all actions. This, he argues, confuses philosophy with soteriology—the latter being the true debate between Arminians and Calvinists. Muller contends that the biblical examples Reformed theologians used historically pointed more toward the bondage of the human will to sin, the resultant inability to choose salvation, and the necessity of grace in salvation. This is far from asserting that God determines all events—especially individual sins. The view that God predetermined moral acts, Muller explains, is as far from the Reformed view as saying that God determined the fall of Adam without regard to Adam's will to sin.

> The divine ordination of all things is not only consistent with human freedom; it makes human freedom possible. As J. S. K. Reid has argued of Calvin's theology, the divine determination so belongs to the ultimate order of being that it cannot be understood as a philosophical determinism in and for the temporal order of being: human responsibility is assumed and God is not the author of sin. This overarching providential determination (which includes the divine ordination of and concurrence in freedom and contingency) is, moreover, distinct from predestination: predestination is the specific ordination of some to salvation, granting the inability of human beings to save themselves. Again; this is not a matter of philosophical determinism, but of soteriology.[8]

Muller also argues that, according to Reformed theology, some events are contingent, "having a 'cause that by its nature could have acted differently.'" Other events result from "divine persuasion," and others result from "human free agency or deliberation." According to Muller, traditional Reformed thinkers said simply that "the beginning of the redeemed life is solely the work of God."

Thus, they posited a distinction between "the general decree of providence that establishes all things, whether necessary, contingent, or free, and the special decree of predestination that establishes salvation by grace alone." Thus, he contends, the traditional Reformed position avoids "a rigid metaphysical determinism of all human actions, a form of necessitarianism (which was never Reformed doctrine in any case). Predestination regards only salvation, not "a determinism of all human actions."[9]

Muller further cites the sixteenth-century strict Calvinist, William Perkins: "Human beings move about with a natural freedom, can eat and drink; they can also exercise their humanity freely in the arts, trades, and other occupations; they can practice 'civill vertue, justice, temperance, liberalitie, chastitie'; and they may freely exercise the ecclesiastical duties of outward worship."[10]

Muller should not think it strange when Arminians interpret Calvin and other Reformed theologians to mean that "predestination indicates 'a divine determination of all human actions.'" Well known Calvinists interpret divine determination to be coextensive with the whole of reality. Calvinists as well as Arminians need to be aware that there is not unanimous agreement among Calvinists on this point.

The Question of Free Will in Calvinism

It is not a simple matter to find out where Calvinists stand on the subject of free will. It is denied, affirmed, defined, and ignored.

The Denial of Free Will

In a chapter entitled "Free Will," Clark launches an attack on the concept of free will for human beings. One clear statement is found in connection with a comment on Ephesians 1:11. He comments, "This verse states in particular that God works our own willing. It is clear therefore that man's will is not free, but is directed by the working of God."[11]

R. K. McGregor Wright leaves no doubt where he stands on the question of free will. He comments, "The Arminian form of the freewill theory is behind every important issue in evangelical apologetics today. However unpopular and threatening this type of probing may be, evangelical freewillism cannot be allowed to remain unquestioned. Too much is at stake."[12]

The Acceptance of Free Will

J. Oliver Buswell, Jr., remarks that to deny free will constitutes "purely arbitrary philosophical dogmatism, entirely contrary to reasonable evidence and to the biblical view." He argues that there are no biblical, philosophical, or psychological reasons for believing "that a personal being may be free to choose between certain motives, and having chosen, is personally responsible for his choice. If God is angry with sin, then it follows that the sinner is blameworthy, cosmically, ultimately, absolutely."[13] In support of his position, Buswell points out that "the answer to question thirteen of the Westminster Shorter Catechism tells us, 'Our first parents, being left to the freedom of their own will, fell from the estate wherein they were created by sinning against God.'" The Westminster Standards, he states, "repeatedly and emphatically answer the question of the possibility of free will in the affirmative."[14]

The Acceptance of Freedom, but Unclear About Free Will

It is hard to see where Boettner stands on the issue of free will. He comments: "Human nature since the fall retains its constitutional faculties of reason, conscience and free agency, and hence man continues to be a responsible moral agent."[15] Later in his book where he deals with "Objections Commonly Urged Against the Reformed Doctrine of Predestination" he explains what he means by free agency and foreordination. He points out, "By a free agent we mean an intelligent person who acts with rational self-determination; and by Foreordination we mean that from eternity God has made certain the actual course of events which takes place in the life of every person and in the realm of nature."[16]

He gives further confirmation of his belief in free agency when he says, "Predestination and free agency are the twin pillars of a great temple, and they meet above the clouds where human gaze cannot penetrate."[17]

Boettner seems willing to use the term *free agent*, but he shies away from using the term *free will* with affirmation. He says that if free will means that "absolute determination" is placed in human hands, then "we might as well spell it with a capital F and a capital W; for then man becomes like God,—a first cause, an original spring of action,—and we have as many semi-Gods as we have free wills." In other words, the only way to admit this sort of human free will is to surrender divine sovereignty. "It is very noticeable—and in a sense it is reassuring to observe the fact—that the materialistic and metaphysical philosophers deny as completely as do Calvinists this thing that is called **free will** [emphasis added]."[18]

Boettner leaves us wondering what the difference is between *free agency* and *free will*. What he says about free will is not supported from any source. It is a caricature of free will. The way it is described, no one would claim it. I must confess that I find Boettner's use of "self-determination" surprising when he gives his definition of "free agency" in the quotation given above. I am surprised that he would affirm *any* use of the term "self-determination" in referring to human beings.

Feinberg speaks of a freedom that he thinks is compatible with determinism. He explains that, like other determinsts, he believes "there is room for a genuine sense of free human action," despite his belief that the action is "causally determined." Such freedom, he argues, is not "indeterministic." Rather, determinists who believe in free will argue that there are two sorts of causes that "influence and determine actions": constraining causes and nonconstraining causes. Constraining causes force people to act against their wills. While nonconstraining causes are able to cause an action, they do not "force a person to act against his will, desires, or wishes." Thus, Feinberg says that a free act can be causally determined and still be free, "so long as the causes are nonconstraining. This view is often referred to as *soft determinism* or *compatibilism*, for genuine free human action is seen as *compatible* with nonconstraining sufficient conditions which incline the will decisively in one way or another."[19]

Later, in commenting on human responsibility, Feinberg argues that what makes people "morally responsible for their actions" is the fact that those actions are free. "I agree that no one can be held morally accountable for actions that are not free." However, he argues, compatibilism lets people act freely while at the same time their actions are causally determined. "The key is not whether someone's acts are causally determined or not, but rather how they are determined. If the acts are constrained, they are not free and the agent is not morally responsible for them."[20]

Let us take a look at what Feinberg is saying. He says, "Like many other determinists, I claim that there is room for a genuine sense of free human action, even though such action is *causally determined*." Later he comments, "The key is not whether someone's acts are causally determined or not, but rather *how* they are determined. If the acts are constrained, they are not free and the agent is not morally responsible for them."[21]

Feinberg's determinism is coextensive with the whole of reality. The determinism of Muller that is referred to above is restricted to soteriology. Feinberg and Muller would be in essential agreement when it comes to election. However, they differ sharply when it comes to other matters.

It is important to observe that for Feinberg and those who make determinism coextensive with the whole of reality, *God causes all human acts*. When he talks about the agent being responsible, he is particularly talking about sin. This is true since there would be no question about action that is acceptable to God. The *only cause* that he has in mind in his determinism is God. This is true because the determinism under consideration is *divine determinism*. That means that God is the cause not only of faith on the part of those who believe but also for the sins of dishonesty, murder, rape, and so forth. The reason the person is responsible for such action, though it is "causally determined," is that he did what God caused him to do freely, not by constraint. In *unlimited determinism*, God causes people to lie, steal, murder, and to commit rape, but they are not constrained to do so.

Since Muller limits his determinism to soteriology, all acts that are not related to soteriology *are not causally determined*. This would mean that in these areas there would be no essential reason that his view would have to differ from Arminianism.

I will wait until I present my own thinking before I make any critical observations.

Foreknowledge and Free Will in Calvinism

Foreordination, for most Calvinists, takes the mystery out of foreknowledge. As Boettner explains, Arminian objections to divine foreordination equally apply to divine foreknowledge. Actions that God foreknows "must, in the very nature of the case, be as fixed and certain as what is ordained." Thus he argues that, if foreordination is inconsistent with human freedom, then so is foreknowledge. "Foreordination renders the events as certain, while foreknowledge presupposes they are certain." Furthermore, he explains, Arminianism's rejection of divine foreordination constitutes a rejection of "the theistic basis for foreknowledge. Common sense tells us that no event can be foreknown unless by some means, either physical or mental, it has been predetermined."[22]

Feinberg, in arguing for his position of soft determinism, says, "If indeterminism is correct, I do not see how God can be said to foreknow the future. If God actually knows what will (not just might) occur in the future, the future must be set and some sense of determinism applies."[23] Crabtree also sees a problem of divine foreknowledge of free human events. He explains, "No one, not even God, can know the outcome of an autonomous decision that has not been made, can he? To assert the possibility of such knowledge is problematic."[24]

Buswell does not see a problem with God's having knowledge of free acts of human beings. He remarks that he does not know how God can know a future free act. Yet neither does he know how he "can have knowledge by analysis, by inference from reason or from causes, or from statistical data reported by intuition, or (if it is insisted upon) by innate ideas."[25] Thus, Buswell argues, knowledge is a mystery, and divine foreknowledge of future free events is a revealed mystery that we can accept based on what Scripture teaches.

The Strength of Calvinism in Theological Scholarship

The strength of Calvinism in the world of scholarship is evident. For example about 80 percent of the commentaries on Romans I have surveyed will support the concept of unconditional election. For those who are interested in treatments on unconditional election, I recommend the comments on Romans 8:29–30 and Romans 9 in the following commentaries: Haldane, Harrison, Hendriksen, Hodge, Murray, Olshausen, Plumer, and Shedd. For treatments that support the position of conditional election see the following commentaries on Romans 8:29-30 and Romans 9: Clarke, Godet, Greathouse, Lenski, Meyer, Picirilli, and Sanday and Headlam. It should be pointed out that though Lenski and Meyer in their comments support the concept of conditional election, as Lutherans, they would not use the term "conditional election."

One may wonder why Calvinists have produced so many more scholarly writings than Arminians. A significant factor is that the emphasis on scholarship among Presbyterians has resulted in the production of scholarly works greater in proportion than their numerical strength.

The tendency among Arminians is to be more inclined to activity than to scholarly pursuits. Also, Arminians are inclined to think that common sense would direct people to take the Arminian approach. The list is short when you look for good works on conditional election. On the popular level, a host of people believe in "once saved, always saved" but believe in conditional election. These people have not come forth with outstanding works on conditional election. For many years a widely used book by the respected theologian Henry C. Thiessen taught conditional election.[26] When Vernon D. Doerksen revised this book, it was changed so that the book now teaches unconditional election.[27] In this move, a book that had been widely used to voice the position of conditional election became a voice for unconditional election.

A Debt of Gratitude to Calvinism

Calvinists work on the assumption that unconditional election is necessary in order to maintain the doctrines of the sovereignty of God, the total depravity of fallen man, and that salvation is absolutely free. The theological world owes a debt of gratitude to Calvinism for its insistence that salvation is the free gift of God. I am sure that Arminians have needed this reminder. However, I am in sharp disagreement with those Calvinists when they make the claim that unconditional election is necessary if salvation is to be free. Calvinists have not hesitated in criticizing Arminians. I am sure they will be understanding if some criticism is returned. My advice to fellow Arminians is that, if we expect to be treated with seriousness, then we must give time and effort to producing some well-thought-out treatments of our doctrine.

An Introduction to Classical Arminian Thought on Decrees and Election
Three Basic Assumptions or Convictions of Calvinism

I will be giving my answer to Calvinism as I explain and build my case for Classical Arminianism. The unconditional election taught in Calvinism seems to rest on three basic assumptions: first, that the sovereignty of God requires unconditional election and thus precludes conditional election; second, that total depravity precludes the response of faith from a sinner unless he is first regenerated by the Holy Spirit; and third, that the fact that salvation is free precludes conditional election. If these three assumptions are true, Calvinism has made its case. If these three assumptions are not true, Calvinism is in trouble.

An Answer to the First Assumption of Calvinism

The first and probably the most foundational of these assumptions of Calvinism is that the sovereignty of God requires unconditional election and thus precludes conditional election. Calvinistic thought rests on two great pillars in the history of theological thought: Augustine of Hippo and John Calvin. It appears to me that Augustine's doctrine grew out of his thought that depravity was so strong that it could be dealt with only by unconditional election. It appears that Calvin's view grows more out of the idea that unconditional election is the only view of election that is consistent with the sovereignty of God.

In Calvinism, the central truth to be reckoned with is that *everything else must harmonize with the sovereignty of God*. The Calvinistic concept of the sovereignty of God, as I see it, is developed along the lines of *cause* and *effect*. This is why Calvinists have a special difficulty dealing with the origin of sin. It is hard to find good discussions on the origin of sin in Calvinistic writings. Also, this is why some Calvinists are unlimited determinists. This stress on a *cause* and *effect* approach to interpreting the sovereignty of God is also the reason that those who want to restrict determinism to matters relating to salvation when discussing theology on its broader points sound like they are unlimited determinists. In fact, it is hard to find out where many Calvinists stand on whether determinism is unlimited or limited.

The answer to Calvinism's assumption that the sovereignty of God requires unconditional election and thus precludes conditional election will be lengthy. It must deal with the following concerns: (1) *Influence* and *response* versus *cause* and *effect*, (2) the meaning of freedom of will, (3) the need of a theology of personality, (4) the question of divine determinism, and (5) the question of the foreknowledge of God in relation to the free acts of human beings.

Cause and *Effect* or *Influence* and *Response?* An Arminian Answer

Calvinism has oversimplified the way that God carries out His sovereignty. In so doing it has oversimplified the relationship of God to man in the application of redemption. It is very important to distinguish between *cause* and *effect* relationships and *influence* and *response* relationships. In the relationship of the physical to the physical, or the relationship of the parts of a machine to one another, we are dealing with *cause* and *effect* relationships. The concepts of active and passive apply in their simple meaning. When a hammer hits a nail, the hammer is active and the nail is passive. The hammer *causes* the nail to be driven into the wood. The nail had no choice. A force outside the nail caused the nail to be driven into the wood.

Interpersonal relationships do not submit to such a simple analysis. *Influence* and *response* are more appropriate terms. A person is one who thinks with his mind, feels with his heart, and acts with his will. In the simple sense of the terms *cause* and *effect*, one person cannot *cause* another person to do anything. This does not depend on the lack of ability that one person has to influence another. Rather, the inability of one person to *cause* another person to do something grows out of the nature of what it means to be a *person*. When an appeal is made to a person, it is inherent within the nature of a person to consider the appeal and then make a decision. There is no such thing as a person's doing or not doing something *without having made a decision*. This is true regardless of how strong the influence may be upon him or her.

Calvinism's approach to irresistible grace (or effectual call) sounds more like cause and effect than influence and response. When the appropriate time comes with regard to the elect, God regenerates him or her. As a regenerated person, he or she is caused by God to have faith in Jesus Christ as Lord and Savior. In such a view, faith is considered a gift. It is problematic for faith to be considered an individual's choice, act, or response. The possibility of a negative response does not exist. It was a guaranteed response. The fact that it was guaranteed makes the terms *cause* and *effect* appropriate. Calvinism considers all of this necessary if salvation is to be a gift.

In explaining the gift of faith in that way, the Calvinist is thinking along the lines of cause and effect. The only problem is that, if being a person means anything beyond being a smoothly operated puppet with conscious awareness, it is impossible to describe the experience of a person in such a manner. We must keep in mind that human beings are personal beings because God has made them that way. This is necessary to the very notion of being made in the image of God. Can anyone really deny that faith is a personal response to the working of God with that individual? At least in some sense, the response of faith is a decision in which the person who believes actively participates. Even Calvinism must admit this.[28]

In my opinion, it has been a mistake over the centuries to focus the conflict between Calvinists and Arminians on whether fallen or redeemed man has a *free will*. The real question is: Is fallen man a personal being, or is he sub-personal? (The same question can also be asked concerning redeemed man.) Does God deal with fallen man as a person? If He does, He deals with him as one who thinks, feels, and acts. To do otherwise undercuts the personhood of man. God will not do this—not because something is being imposed on God to which He must submit, but because God designed the relationship to be a relationship between *personal beings*. Human beings are personal beings by God's design and were made for a *personal relationship* with a personal God. God will not violate His own plan. The nature of the case does not demand that God work in a cause and effect relationship with human beings.

We dare not take the position that God is unable to work with human beings within the framework of influence and response. Are we going to settle for the thinking that the inability of *fallen man* results in the *inability of God*, that is, the inability of God to work with fallen man and redeemed man in an influence and response relationship? I hope not! Are we going to say that the very *nature* of God's *sovereignty* requires Him to work in a cause and effect relationship and prohibits Him from working in an influence and response relationship? I hope not!

I am sure that Calvinists would want to say that they do not believe in "mechanical" cause and effect as it relates to the way God deals with human beings. While they would object to the word *"mechanical,"* if they opt for any form of *determinism*, they cannot successfully reject the words *cause* and *effect*. My reading of Calvinistic writings suggests that Classical Calvinists would not object to these terms. If anyone doubts this observation, I would suggest that he reread the quotations above that are taken from Calvinistic writings. I think the description of God's relationship to man that Calvinists would give would be much like my description of influence and response. However, the result is thought to be *guaranteed*. When the result is guaranteed, they would simply have a softened form of cause and effect. Any time the result is guaranteed, we are dealing with cause and effect. When the *guarantee* is gone, Calvinism is gone.

From a Calvinistic viewpoint, it will not do to say that cause and effect describes God's relationship to us, but influence and response describes our relationship to one another. The entirety of that which falls within the scope of determinism falls within the scope of cause and effect. There is no influence and response. Yet, I get the impression when I read Calvinistic writings that they are trying to persuade me. Persuasion is a form of *influence*. I get the impression that they think I could and should agree. I do not think they have any different idea about persuasion than I do. I have a statement that I make sometimes, "Calvinists are Arminian except when they are making Calvinistic statements."

I need to point out that in common speech we frequently tend to use the terms *influence* and *response* and *cause* and *effect* somewhat interchangeably. We may say, "He caused me to do it." To be technical, we should say, "He influenced me to do it, and I chose to do it." Though the terms may be interchangeable (to a certain extent) in common speech, I do not believe any confusion will develop from my using them the way I do in a theological work.

The Meaning of Freedom of the Will

The discussion of cause and effect and influence and response sets the stage for a discussion of the meaning of the freedom of the will. I am going to restate briefly some of what I said about the meaning of free will in Chapter 1.

The New Testament does not use the noun form of *will* to refer to the faculty or organ of choice in man. Instead, the verb form (*thelō*) is used (Mt. 16:24; 21:29; 23:37; Mk. 8:34; Jn. 7:17; Rev. 22:17; and others). By *will* we mean power of choice. Every command, every prohibition, every exhortation, and every entreaty made in the Bible to human beings presupposes that they are capable of making choices.

Whether we want to think of the act of willing as the function of a faculty of the person or simply the person making a choice, the fact remains that the ability of choice is part of being a person. That ability of choice we call will. In his totality, man is a thinking, feeling, acting being. He thinks with his mind, feels with his heart, and acts with his will.

Let us make a few things clear about what is and is not meant by freedom of will. The freedom of the will does not mean that forces or influences cannot be brought to bear upon the will. In fact, the very nature of freedom of the will means that forces or influences will be brought to bear upon the will. It does not mean that these forces cannot be a *contributing factor* in the exercise of the will. It does mean that these influences or forces cannot *guarantee* or *determine* the action of the will. We are dealing with influence and response, not cause and effect.

The Framework of Possibilities and the Meaning of Freedom of the Will

Freedom of will is a freedom within a framework of possibilities. It is not absolute freedom. We cannot be God. We cannot be angels. The freedom of a human being is in the framework of the possibilities provided by human nature. Also, the influences brought to bear on the will have a bearing on the framework of possibilities.

Before Adam and Eve sinned, it was in the framework of possibilities within which they operated to remain in the practice of complete righteousness, or to commit sin. After they sinned, it no longer remained within the framework of possibilities for them to practice uninterrupted righteousness. The same is true for fallen man now (Rom. 8:7–8). If anyone reads the meaning of freedom of will to mean that an unconverted person could practice righteousness and not sin, he misunderstands the meaning of freedom of will for fallen human beings. Romans 8:7-8 makes it clear that Scripture does not teach this.

Jesus makes it clear that it does not fall within the framework of possibilities for a sinner to respond to the gospel unless he or she is drawn by the Holy Spirit (Jn. 6:44). The influence of the Holy Spirit working in the heart of the person who hears the gospel makes possible a framework of possibilities in which a person can say yes or no to the gospel. If he says, "yes," it is his choice. If he says, "no," it is his choice. To say less than that is to raise serious questions about the existence of real personhood after the fall. If a human being is not in some sense a *self-directed being*, he or she is not a person. The self-direction may have a high degree of dependence at times, but it is still self-direction. As has already been made clear, I am not suggesting that fallen man can choose Christ without the aid of the Holy Spirit. In fact, I strongly reject such an idea. I am saying, however, that no matter how much or how strong the aid of the Holy Spirit may be, the "yes" decision is still a decision that can rightly be called the person's decision. Also, he could have said no.

When I say that human beings have a free will, I mean that they can rationally consider a matter and make a choice. In bringing a person to the point of saving faith, the Holy Spirit makes it possible for a person to give the response of faith. At the same time, this work of the Holy Spirit can be resisted. The person can say no. What puts Arminians at odds with Calvinists is that, in Calvinism, when God works with a person to bring him or her to faith, he or she *cannot say no.* Yes is the only answer he or she can give. Calvinists believe that, apart from irresistible grace, nobody could be saved. Irresistible grace is not simply the way God chooses to work in saving people. It is the only option open to God to save lost people. Total depravity, according to Calvinism, makes it impossible for a human being to respond apart from irresistible grace. The sovereignty of God, as viewed by Calvinism, is incompatible with a "no" answer. Thus, resistible grace, according to Calvinism, is ruled out.

TERMS USED IN DEFINING FREE WILL

I have run across the terms *spontaneity, indifference, libertarian,* and *self-determination.* No Calvinist would deny that human beings have a will. However, as we have seen, some Calvinists deny outright that human beings have a free will. Others want to use the term *free will* but define it in a way that is consistent with their version of Calvinism. A few others want to maintain real freedom of the will.

Liberty of Spontaneity and Liberty of Indifference

It would appear from what I have read that thoroughgoing Calvinists who affirm a belief in the freedom of the will would concur that there is *liberty of spontaneity*, but not the *liberty of indifference*. Crabtree gives the following explanation of these terms: "One exercises the liberty of spontaneity when what he does is done in accordance with his own will and desires. One exercises the liberty of indifference when what he does is such that he could have done otherwise."[29]

Ronald H. Nash explains that the liberty of indifference is the capability to do something or not—in other words to do something or refrain from doing it. The liberty of spontaneity, however, is the capability to do whatever one wants to do. "On this second view, the question of the person's ability to do otherwise is irrelevant. The key question is whether he is able to do what he most wants to do."[30]

The *Oxford English Dictionary* (*OED*) is helpful in this regard. It defines spontaneity as follows:

Spontaneous, or voluntary and unconstrained, action on the part of persons; the fact of possessing this character or quality. 1651 C. CARTWRIGHT *Cert. Relig.* 1.181 Thus we see how Bernard doth agree with Calvin in making the freedome of mans will to consist in a spontaneity and freedom from coaction [constraint, coercion]. 1702 *Le Clerc's Prim. Fathers* 348. Freedom in his opinion, is only a meer Spontaneity, and doth not imply a Power of not doing what one would. [*sic*][31]

The help in the *OED* on the liberty of indifference was found under "indifferency." One of the meanings for indifferency is "Indetermination of the will; freedom of choice; an equal power to take either of two courses, *Liberty of Indifferency*, freedom from necessity, freedom of will. Obs."

These references given in the *OED* make it clear that at one time the liberty of spontaneity was used to mean that the will was free in that it was not coerced. It was not speaking of a freedom to make a different decision. Liberty of indifference was freedom to choose a different course of action.

Crabtree's and Nash's definitions of these terms are consistent with what we learn from the *OED*.

Determinism rules out the liberty of indifference. I would accept the liberty of indifference in the way Crabtree, Nash, and the *OED* define it. However, I am not happy with adding the words "an equal power to take either of two courses," as seen in the *OED* definition. I think that oversimplifies the matter. Also, there may be more than two options.

If we could maintain this distinction between "spontaneity" and "indifference," I think they would be very useful in helping us distinguish between an Arminian view of free will and a Calvinistic view of free will. Most Calvinists would accept the liberty of spontaneity and reject the liberty of indifference. Arminians would accept both the liberty of spontaneity and the liberty of indifference as these terms are defined above.

However, there is a problem in using the term *liberty of indifference*. It is loaded with other possible connotations. It could also mean unconcerned or disinterested. Unconcerned or disinterested is not what I mean by freedom of the will. Even Berkhof, usually a careful scholar, fails to grasp the historic meaning of *liberty of indifference*. In raising the question of whether "the predetermination of things was consistent with the free will of man," his response was that it was not, if free will is seen as "indifferentia (arbitrariness), but this is an unwarranted conception of the freedom of man. The will of man is not something altogether indeterminate, something hanging in the air that can swing arbitrarily in either direction.[32] I do not know of anyone who would define free will that way. These kinds of comments complicate discussion between Calvinists and Arminians.

Freedom of the will does not mean that a person is free from being influenced or even being pressured. People are pressured frequently in their daily experiences. The whole point of what it means to be a person is that a person is presented with options. Influences are brought to bear upon the person, seeking to influence him or her to choose one of these options. The person rationally considers the options and makes a choice. The problem is that, if he is reasoning from faulty premises, then the conclusions will be invalid. Bias and prejudice can blind a person to the truth. This blindness especially works on the level of premises.

If we will use the terms *liberty of spontaneity* and *liberty of indifference* with their original intended meaning, I think they will be very helpful in establishing meaningful communication between Arminians and Calvinists.

LIBERTARIAN

Libertarian is a term used to describe a person who believes in free will. The dictionary meaning of libertarian is, "An advocate of the doctrine of free will." But it also means, "A person who upholds the principles of absolute and unrestricted liberty esp. of thought and action."[33] I would qualify as a libertarian by the first definition. But the term libertarian conjures up too many objectionable ideas in people's minds for me to want to be identified by the term.

SELF-DETERMINED

Self-determined is sometimes used in discussions of determinism and free will. Norman Geisler advocates the use of this term and the view of free will associated with it. He points out that both Thomas Aquinas and C. S. Lewis hold to this view. Geisler explains that advocates of moral self-determinism sometimes use free will as if it were the "efficient cause of moral actions." This, he says, provokes the question of what is the cause of free will.

> But a more precise description of the process of the free act would avoid this problem. Technically, free will is not the efficient cause of a free act; free will is simply the power through which the agent performs the free act. The efficient cause of the free act is the free *agent*, not the free will. Free will is simply the power by which the free agent acts. We do not say that humans are free will but only that they *have* free will .... So it is not the power of free choice which causes a free act, but the *person* who has the power.[34]

Later in his treatment, Geisler comments that God causes the "fact" of freedom, while human beings cause the "acts" of freedom. "God gives people power (of free choice), but they exercise it without coercion. Thus God is responsible for bestowing freedom, but human beings are responsible for behaving with it.[35]

John Miley, the Methodist theologian whose *Systematic Theology* appeared near the end of the nineteenth century, would be in agreement with Geisler's statement: "The efficient cause of the free act is the free *agent*, not the free will. Free will is simply the power by which the free agent acts." Miley explains that "we find the higher meaning of the term [agent] only in personality. There we reach the power of rational self-energizing with respect to ends. There is no such power in the will itself. It is simply a faculty of the personal agent." Thus, he argues, freedom of the will "cannot be the true question of freedom. The fact means nothing against the reality of freedom, but points to its true location in our own personal agency, and in the result will make it clearer and surer."[36]

To place the real freedom in the personal agent is to place it in the person or personality. I think this has much to commend itself. But the term *free will* is so firmly fixed in theology as a theological term to express freedom that we cannot escape using and defining the term.

I think Geisler's view has much to commend itself. There is a technical turn in what he is saying that most people will not want to work through, but I think he is on the right track. The term *self-determinism* by itself could be subject to gross distortion. It could picture a person as a loose canon out of control. No one who reads what Geisler says will get such an idea. But apart from a context it could suffer such distortion.

Properly understood, my view would be self-determinism, though I prefer to speak of human beings as *self-directed*. Self-determination of human beings must be understood in the context of their relationship with a sovereign God who is bringing influences to bear on them, granting them freedom (permission) of choice, and carrying out His purposes. Anything less will fail to measure up to biblical Christianity.

My problem with Geisler is how he combines his view of self-determinism with "soft determinism."[37] The problem with determinism whether it is called "hard determinism" or "soft determinism" is that it is still determinism. When Geisler speaks of soft determinism, it is divine determinism.

Geisler explains his approach to the relationship between foreknowledge and determinism by arguing that, given the fact that God does not "pass through temporal successions," He has forever thought what He thinks. God does not really foreknow; He simply knows in His eternal now what we freely do. Thus, "there is no problem of how an act can be truly free if God has determined in advance what will take place . . . . God is not foreordaining from his vantage point, but simply ordaining what humans are doing freely. God sees what we are freely doing. And what he sees, he knows. And what he knows he determines. So God determinately knows and knowingly determines what we are doing freely."[38]

The key words in understanding Geisler's view, as I see it, are: "And what he sees, he knows. And what he knows he determines." Geisler's divine determinism is based on *what God knows*. In genuine determinism, knowledge is based on *what is determined*. Bringing up the concept of Eternal Now does not change that. I will deal with this problem later in this chapter under the heading, "The Question of How God Could Have Foreknowledge of Free Human Choices." It seems to me that Geisler does a better job in building his case for self-determinism (free will) than he does linking self-determinism with divine determinism.

THE CONSISTENCY OF THE INFLUENCE AND RESPONSE MODEL WITH THE TEACHINGS OF SCRIPTURE

I think that anyone who does not come with philosophical presuppositions that would prevent agreement would agree that influence and response is the way human beings deal with one another. Those who have not already made up their minds to the contrary would also most likely accept the idea that God would work with us, as human beings, within the framework of an influence and response relationship. The question for the Christian is, will it stand the test of Scripture?

Philippians 2:12-13

Gordon Clark remarks that this passage so clearly denies free will that he cannot "see how anyone could possibly misunderstand it. In Philippians 2:12-13 the Apostle Paul tells us to 'work out your own salvation with fear and trembling; for it is God who works in you both to will and to do for *His* good pleasure.'"[39] As we have already noted, not all determinists reject free will as Clark does. But any consistent unlimited determinist would interpret these verses within a cause and effect framework. I can see why they would do this. However, these verses present no problem when interpreted in keeping with the influence and response model.

In Romans 5:3 Paul says, "Tribulation produces perseverance." What Paul is saying is that it is the design of tribulation to produces perseverance. The design does not come to fruition in every case. Some people become very impatient in times of tribulation. There is no reason whatever that the work of God to get us to will and to do of His good pleasure could not be interpreted in terms of *design* and *purpose* in a manner in keeping with influence and response. The meaning would be that God works in us to influence and to enable us to will and to do for His good pleasure.

We are not to think of human beings as operating outside the realm of divine influence. At the same time, we know that they do not always respond properly to this divine influence. This is true of both the saved and the unsaved. We do, of course, insist that there is a compliance that makes a difference between the saved and the unsaved. To say that human beings *always* respond properly to divine influence would say something about God, as the One who does the influencing; that I do not think we want to say. We cannot attribute all that is happening in the world to the influence of God. Nor can we make Him the cause or the determiner of all that is happening. This is the kind of thinking that inclines many to atheism. It is unthinkable that a sovereign, holy, just, fair, and loving God would be the determining cause of everything that is happening in our world. There is something within us that rebels against such a thought.

The influence and response model has room for disobedience. It does not require divine determinism as the basis of all that happens. While there is room for obedience or disobedience, we are not to limit human freedom to mere obedience or disobedience. We are not to think of God as giving a list of minute details requiring yes or no answers for every move we make. Human freedom leaves room for creativity in obedience to the divine commandment—to human beings exercising dominion over the earth and its inhabitants (Gen. 1:26). Christians are given freedom and are encouraged to exercise stewardship over their gifts and callings (1 Pet. 4:10 and Tit. 1:7), the mysteries of God (1 Cor. 4:1-2), and the gospel (1 Cor. 9:17 and Eph. 3:2). Stewardship involves a creative thinking and planning responsibility. It is not possible to harmonize *divine determinism* and *stewardship responsibility* to God.

THE NEED FOR A THEOLOGY OF PERSONALITY

Human freedom is a freedom to function as persons. It is the freedom to think, plan, and act. I would invite you to examine several books on systematic theology. Turn to the index in each set and find the word *personality*. Over and over again you will find references to divine personality, but no reference to human personality. It will be a very rare find when you discover one that makes any reference to "human personality." One of the rare finds where a theologian develops the meaning of human personality is found in Arminian theologian John Miley's *Systematic Theology*.[40]

Why is it so hard to find a theology book that defines and expands the treatment of human personality? I think it is because there is not much place for it in deterministic thinking. Calvinists do not have much place for a development of thought on the function of human personality. Calvinists are afraid that if they say very much about the function of human personality they will take something away from God. Calvinists have produced most of the outstanding works on theology. Arminians have tended to follow the Calvinist model; however, they merely give an Arminian interpretation. Since Calvinists do not usually deal with the meaning of human personality in their writings, most Arminians do not either. I think I can safely say that a person will find more references to human personality in this book than in all of the others systematic theology and doctrine books combined. Treatments are given to mind, heart, and will. But it will be rare to find where the term *personality* is used in connection with these treatments. Christian ministry is in great need of an understanding of human personality in reaching lost people and in ministering to the needs of Christians. The foundational thinking of human personality, how it functions, and how personality change is made should be done by *theologians*. While library research is essential, our understanding of human personality needs to be hammered out in the arena of life.[41]

God's Foreknowledge and Human Freedom

Classical Calvinism has problems with the idea that God can have foreknowledge of the actions of those who have free will in the Arminian sense of free will. In unlimited determinism, the fact that God has determined everything that will happen is considered to be the foundation for God's foreknowledge. There is no need of foreknowledge of free acts in unlimited determinism because free acts do not exist. Calvinists who have a place in their thought for free will in the sense of liberty of indifference would have to acknowledge that God has foreknowledge of free acts of human beings. The reader may want to review the material given above under, "The Question of Foreknowledge and Free Will in Calvinistic Thought."

Arminianism on Foreknowledge and Human Freedom

In Classical Calvinism, there is agreement that God has absolute knowledge of the future down to the smallest detail. There is not agreement on how to deal with the question of human freedom or whether human freedom exists. In Arminianism, there is agreement that human beings have freedom of choice. This includes the freedom to place faith in Christ upon hearing the gospel or to refuse to place faith in Christ.

Contemporary Arminians do not agree on the question of foreknowledge as it relates to free acts of human beings. Classical Arminianism agreed with Calvinism that God has absolute knowledge of the future down to the smallest detail. This, of course, would require that God has foreknowledge concerning the free acts of human beings. In recent years, some Arminians have rejected the view that God has foreknowledge of the free acts of human beings.

A Denial of Divine Foreknowledge of Human Free Choice

Clark Pinnock is the best known of those who do not believe that God has foreknowledge of the acts of free agents. In an autobiographical account entitled, "From Augustine to Arminius: A Pilgrimage in Theology," Pinnock describes how he changed from a Calvinist rooted in Augustinian thought to an Arminian. He explains that he had to ask himself if Scripture made it possible to hold God's complete foreknowledge "of everything that can be known" and at the same time hold that the free choices of human beings are not known by God "because they are not yet settled reality." He argues that human choices that are not made yet cannot be known by God because they do not exist. "They are potential—yet to be realized but not yet actual. God can predict a great deal of what we will choose to do, but not all of it, because some of it remains hidden in the mystery of human freedom."[42] Thus, Pinnock relates, "It has become increasingly clear to me that we need a 'free will' theism, a doctrine of God that treads the middle path between classical theism, which exaggerates God's transcendence of the world, and process theism, which presses for immanence."[43]

At the heart of what concerns Pinnock is how God's sovereignty is administered in the light of man's free will. He explains that, while God as Creator is basically sovereign, He has elected to give human beings significant freedom. He goes on to say:

> In keeping with this decision, God rules over the world in a way that sustains and does not negate its structures. Since freedom has been created, reality is open, not closed. God's relationship to the world is dynamic, not static. Although this will require us to rethink aspects of conventional or classical theism, it will help us relate sovereignty and freedom more coherently in theory and more satisfactorily in practice.[44]

Another advocate of "free-will" theism is Richard Rice. He comments that the interaction of God with a world in which human beings have genuine freedom does not require a denial of God's foreknowledge, but only a careful redefinition of its scope. Rice argues that God knows much about the future. For example, He knows everything that will ever happen as the direct result of factors that already exist. He knows infallibly the content of his own future actions, to the extent that they are not related to human choices. Since God knows all possibilities, he knows everything that could happen and what he can do in response to each eventuality. And he knows the ultimate outcome to which he is guiding the course of history.

The only thing that God does not know is "the content of future free decisions, and this is because decisions are not there to know until they occur."[45] In further elaborating on his view, Rice points out "that God is dynamically involved in the creaturely world."[46] In commenting on God as a loving parent, Rice explains that God is "genuinely personable and lovable." Furthermore, Rice argues, God "is vulnerable"; He can "take risks and make sacrifices," and is "momentarily delighted and disappointed, depending on our response to his love."[47]

The driving concern of Pinnock and Rice seems to be: (1) that we have a view of God and His foreknowledge that allows for genuinely free acts on the part of human beings, and (2) that our view of God be such that it contributes to a warm personal relationship with God while we experience the real encounters of life.

AFFIRMATION OF ABSOLUTE DIVINE FOREKNOWLEDGE

Arminius makes it unquestionably clear where he stands on the question of God's foreknowledge. He comments, "I am most fully persuaded that the knowledge of God is eternal, immutable and infinite, and that it extends to all things, both necessary and contingent, to all things which He does of Himself, either mediately or immediately, and which He permits to be done by others."[48]

On the contemporary scene, Jack Cottrell speaks out for absolute divine foreknowledge. Acknowledging that non-Calvinists disagree with regard to divine foreknowledge, Cottrell affirms that God has "true knowledge of future free-will choices without himself being the agent that causes them or renders them certain." God's foreknowledge "is grounded in— and is thus conditioned by—the choices themselves as foreknown. This is how God maintains sovereign control over the whole of his creation, despite the freedom he has given his creatures."[49] In another place Cottrell comments: "To say that God has foreknowledge means that he has real knowledge or cognition of something before it actually happens or exists in history. This is the irreducible core of the concept, which must be neither eliminated nor attenuated. Nothing else is consistent with the nature of God."[50] To make it emphatically clear, he remarks, "Surely God foreknows everything about the life of every individual. He cannot help but foreknow, just because he is God."[51]

Robert E. Picirilli makes it very clear where he stands on God's foreknowledge when he says, "All things that occur are *certainly* foreknown by God. Every happening is certain and known as such from all eternity."[52]

In summing up an excellent chapter, "God's Knowledge of the Present, Past, and Future," William Lane Craig argues that the Old and New testaments portray God as knowing all past, present, and future events. "This foreknowledge would seem to extend to future free acts . . . which could not possibly be inferred from present causes and which in any case are not so represented by the biblical authors." Craig argues that there are countless biblical examples of divine foreknowledge of future free events, "including even the thoughts which individuals shall have. It does not, therefore, seem possible to deny that the biblical conception of God's omniscience includes foreknowledge of future free acts."[53]

A Critical Evaluation of Calvinistic Approaches to the Basis for God's Foreknowledge

Hard Unlimited Determinism

Calvinists who are hard, unlimited determinists solve the problem by eliminating free acts. God determines everything down to the minutest detail. God knows the future because He determines what the future will be. God is the cause of all that happens. The logic of this view is easy to follow. Unconditional election and unconditional reprobation fit logically into unlimited determinism. The problem arises when one tries to harmonize it with the biblical view of God and man.

If God has determined everything that will be, He is the cause of everything. This cannot be harmonized with the biblical view of the holiness of God. A holy God did not and will not determine and cause all of the lying, stealing, hatred, bitterness, depression, mental anguish, pain, suffering, alcoholism, drug addiction, divorce, child sex abuse, rape, abortion, murder, and so on. The law of noncontradiction means nothing if the sin that we are experiencing and seeing can be harmonized with the causal determination of a holy and loving God. No retreat to the inscrutable wisdom of God is acceptable to justify such obvious contradiction.

If God is the cause of everything, why would He cause James Arminius, John Wesley, Adam Clarke, Richard Watson, John Miley, H. Orton Wiley, the Arminians that I have mentioned in this chapter, and a host of others to be Arminian? Why did He also cause Augustine, John Calvin, Augustus Toplady, John Gill, Charles Spurgeon, Jonathan Edwards, Charles Hodge, Benjamin Warfield, those referred to in this chapter, and a host of others to be Calvinists? Would a rational God cause devout believers to arrive at conclusions that are diametrically opposed to one another? He did if unlimited determinism is true.

When it comes to sin, guilt, judgment, and punishment for sin, in deterministic thinking, the problem is not solved by saying that the person did what he wanted to do, that he or she was not coerced. The point is that in determinism the "want to" is determined by God. Yet, if unlimited determinism is true, we see God punishing people for doing what He causally determined that they would do.

Soft Unlimited Determinism

Soft determinists are compatibilists. They believe in both determinism and free will. Their concept of free will would be the liberty of spontaneity as distinguished from the liberty of indifference.

The key to understanding the *liberty of spontaneity* is the kind of influences that can be brought to bear upon a person to influence him or her to make a choice. As mentioned earlier, Feinberg says that, as a compatibilist or soft determinist, he can affirm that an act can be caused without violating human freedom as long as the cause is a nonconstraining cause. He argues that nonconstraining causes "are sufficient to bring about an action, but they do not force a person to act against his will, desires, or wishes."[54]

Feinberg speaks of "constraining causes which force an agent to act against his will." From his standpoint, causes that would force an agent to act against his will can exist only in theory. In the real world there could be no such thing, because God has determined all causes. The causes that are determined by God, according to Feinberg would never force a person to act against his or her will. Since God determines all causes in unlimited determinism, there would be no room for real causes or influences in our world that would coerce a person.

Let me repeat another statement from Feinberg. He points out that the basic affirmation of determinism and Calvinism "is that for everything that happens, in the light of prevailing conditions, the agent could not have done other than he did. For determinists, there are always sufficient conditions that decisively incline the agent's will to choose one option or another."[55]

What makes Feinberg's view determinism is, as can be seen from the last quotation, that no decision that is ever made could be different from what it was. God determines every action. Feinberg makes this clear in other places. He remarks, "God decides what will happen in our world and then sees that his decisions are carried out."[56] Later on he refers to Calvin's thought with approbation, "For Calvin, then, God's sovereignty means he governs all things according to his will. This means God not only overrules in the affairs of men, but also determines what will happen in their lives. This providential determination extends to every area of our lives."[57]

Soft determinism clearly denies freedom of choice in the sense that a person could have done differently. I agree with Picirilli when he says, "A choice that actually can go but one way is not a choice, and without this 'freedom' there is not personality."[58]

Soft determinism seeks to come across as being milder than hard determinism. Yet as long as it remains "unlimited determinism," it cannot escape the criticism that I made above against hard determinism. The basis for the criticism that I made was the fact that it is *unlimited* determinism, not that it is *hard* determinism. Changing from "hard" to "soft" determinism brings no relief at all from the criticism that is directed toward determinism *qua* determinism. For example, if a person believes that capital punishment is wrong, changing the method of execution from electrocution or hanging to lethal injection does not make capital punishment acceptable. It may be that if capital punishment will take place in spite of his best efforts to stop it, that the person who opposes it would prefer lethal injection rather than some other form of execution. But it would not make capital punishment acceptable to the person. It may well be that a person who is opposed to unlimited determinism would prefer that a person promote soft determinism rather than hard determinism. However, he would still have all the objections he had against unlimited determinism *qua* unlimited determinism.

Limited Determinism

As we have seen earlier in this chapter, Richard Muller believes in limited determinism. He limits determinism to soteriology, arguing that "the Reformed exegesis of biblical passages related to predestination, far from indicating a determinism of all human actions, indicates the ultimate determination of God in matters pertaining to salvation."[59] It appears that Muller restricts determinism to "the beginning of the redeemed life." He not only states that determinism is limited to soteriology in his own thinking, he insists that it is the Reformed or Calvinistic position. It is obvious that many Calvinists would not agree with him on this limitation of determinism.

Before I evaluate Muller's position, I will refer again to a statement from him that gets to the heart of his objection to Arminianism. He comments: "The Arminian God is locked into the inconsistency of genuinely willing to save all people while at the same time binding himself to a plan of salvation that he foreknows with certainty cannot effectuate his will." Yet he says that Calvinism "respects the ultimate mystery of the infinite will of God, affirms the sovereignty and efficacy of God, and teaches the soteriological consistency of the divine intention and will with its effects."[60]

It would appear that, outside of the beginning of salvation, Muller would believe in the liberty of indifference. What he says certainly points to such a conclusion. If that is the case, he would apparently believe that God has perfect foreknowledge of the free acts of human beings that He has not determined.

Muller's major criticism of Arminianism is of the Arminian view that God has a genuine desire for the salvation of all human beings while at the same time His foreknowledge tells Him that His desire for the salvation of all will not be fulfilled. That would be a failure. Sovereigns do not fail to accomplish their goals or purposes. In Calvinism, God's desire to save extends only toward those He has elected. God's desires will be effectuated.

It appears that, as it relates to the rest of mankind and the decisions of believers other than those related to the beginning of salvation, Muller's concept of free will would not be essentially different from the view I hold. The questions that I would like to have an answer to are: Does God have any kind of desires regarding the mass of unbelievers who are left out of God's elective plan? Are all of these desires met? Or, should we say that God has no desires at all for those who are unbelievers? Are they totally beyond God's concern so that no matter what they do it does not matter to God?

I ask these questions because, if those who hold Muller's view can admit that there is any incompatibility whatever between what a Sovereign God desires and what actually happens, then the question still remains: "Would that mean that God has forfeited His sovereignty?" If the answer is no, it should help us (and them) to understand that, if God desires the salvation of all and it does not take place, then neither does it mean that God has forfeited His sovereignty. If Muller's view of free will for the non-elect and many of the decisions of the elect is what it appears to be, then those who take such a position could make some meaningful contributions to our understanding of the relationship between God's sovereignty and the free will of man.

Another point to be made is that the person who limits determinism to unconditional election must accept the position that God can have foreknowledge of free acts of human beings. That is the only way God can know that those individuals that He would choose to elect would exist. It is impossible for a particular individual to exist apart from having a certain set of parents, grandparents, great-grandparents, and so forth, all the way back to Adam and Eve. In that chain of events, there would be numerous free acts that God must have knowledge of before He could know that a particular individual would exist. Once it is admitted that God can have knowledge of free human acts, there is no reason, as far as the exercise of foreknowledge is concerned, that God could not have used the approach of conditional election.

I think it would be very helpful if Calvinist theologians would declare themselves on whether they believe in unlimited determinism or limited determinism. It would help if we knew whether they believe only in the liberty of spontaneity or whether they believe that the liberty of indifference applies to some areas of human experience. If the liberty of indifference applies to some areas, what are these areas? If the liberty of indifference applies to any areas at all, in these areas it would be helpful if Calvinists and Arminians could engage in discussion on: (1) The question of God's foreknowledge of free acts of human beings, (2) How the failure of free agents to obey God does not mean that God has forfeited His sovereignty, and (3) The problem of limiting God's sovereign control to the area of soteriology.

The Question of How God Could Have Foreknowledge of Free Human Choices

As we have observed above, many Calvinists work on the assumption that it is impossible for God to have foreknowledge of the free choices and free acts of human beings. These Calvinists also believe that God has foreknowledge of all that will ever take place. Thus, they believe that the only basis that God can have for His foreknowledge is for Him to be causally related, by divine determinism, to all that will ever happen in the future. God knows the future because He determines the future. Since God determines everything that has happened, is happening, or ever will happen, these Calvinists deny free will in the sense of the liberty of indifference. Some Arminians, as we have seen, also deny that God can have foreknowledge of the free choices and free acts of human beings. They thus limit the omniscience of God. Most Arminians, however, believe that the foreknowledge of God includes the free choices of human beings.

We will now turn our attention to some of the attempts theologians have made to explain how God has foreknowledge of free human choices and acts.

God's Foreknowledge of Free Acts Based on God's Being Timeless

The most common way theologians describe God's eternity is to refer to it as timelessness. It is said that God has no past and no future. Everything with God is one "eternal now." Time is said to be a creation of God and will be terminated by Him. Time is characterized by past, present, and future and has succession of events. Eternity has only the present, thus no succession of events.[61]

This approach to God's timelessness has been used by some to explain how God could know what the free acts of human beings will be before they occur. Again, Geisler, as one who holds to this view, argues that God does not really foreknow things but knows them as present in His "eternal now." Thus, "God is not foreordaining from his vantage point, but simply ordaining what humans are freely doing. And what he sees, he knows. And what he knows, he determines. So God *determinately* and *knowingly* *determines* what we are freely deciding."[62] Those who hold this view explain that, from a technical viewpoint, God does not have foreknowledge of free acts since all knowledge to God is Now. However, it would be viewed as foreknowledge by us.

This view has problems. It gives God a *direct perception* of all that is happening. This direct perception of what is happening is God's way of knowing human events whether they are past, present, or future to us. But what about contingencies that never happen? In explaining the inadequacy of this view to explain how God knows the free acts of human beings, Arminius astutely observes:

> That reasoning, however, does not exhaust all the difficulties which may arise in the consideration of these matters. For God knows, also, those things which may happen, but never do happen, and consequently do not co-exist with God in the Now of eternity, which would be events unless they should be hindered, as is evident from 1 Sam. xxiii, 12, in reference to the citizens of Keilah, who would have delivered David into the hands of Saul, which event, nevertheless, did not happen.[63]

There is another problem in trying to use the Eternal Now view of God as a basis for His foreknowledge of free human acts. The question is: Is this a valid view of God's relationship to time? There is one big problem. How can events be eternally now to God when in fact they have not always existed? I do not have any trouble seeing that God can see the past, the present, and the future with equal vividness. But He sees the past as past. It does not have present objective reality to God. He sees the future with equal vividness to the present, but He sees it as future. The future does not have objective reality to God. If these observations are correct, the Eternal Now view is without merit.[64]

God's Foreknowledge of Free Acts Based on God's Middle Knowledge

One of the chief proponents of this view, on the current scene, is William Lane Craig. In his promotion of middle knowledge, Craig has a twofold purpose: (1) He desires to show how God does, in fact, have foreknowledge of free acts of human beings, and (2) He wishes to present a view that will be acceptable to both Calvinists and Arminians. In doing so he hopes to bring Calvinists and Arminians closer together.

The founder of this view was the Spanish Jesuit Luis de Molina (1535-1600). Craig says concerning Molina, "By means of this doctrine he proposed to avoid the Protestant error of denying genuine human freedom, yet without thereby sacrificing the sovereignty of God."[65] Craig calls attention to Molina's error in soteriology. Yet he thinks that we are shortsighted if we allow Molina's soteriological errors to keep us from appreciating his approach to divine sovereignty and human free will. Craig argues that Molina affirmed both doctrines, claiming that the doctrine of middle knowledge enabled him to do so. Molina "boldly asserted that had the doctrine of middle knowledge been known to the early church, then neither Pelagianism nor Lutheranism would have arisen. The resolution of the tension between God's sovereignty and man's freedom is an admirable objective that ought to interest any Christian."[66] In following

Molina, Craig asserts that there are three types of divine knowledge. He gives the following table in explaining his view:

The Three Logical Moments in God Knowledge
[logical as distinguished from chronological]

1. Natural Knowledge: God's knowledge of all possible worlds. The content of this knowledge is essential to God.
2. Middle Knowledge: God's knowledge of what every possible free creature would do under any possible circumstances and, hence knowledge of those possible worlds which God can make actual. The content of this knowledge is not essential to God.

God's Free Decision to Create a World

3. Free Knowledge: God's knowledge of the actual world. The content of the knowledge is not essential to God.[67]

God's natural knowledge is innate. God must have natural knowledge or He would not be God. According to Craig, natural knowledge includes the laws of logic. In getting to the point of how this line of thinking helps us to understand how God has foreknowledge of free events, he explains that God's "natural knowledge" entails the knowledge of "all possibilities." Thus, God knows "all possible individuals that he could create, all the possible circumstances he could place them in, all their possible actions and reactions, and all the possible worlds or orders which he could create. God could not lack this knowledge and still be God; the content of natural knowledge is essential to him."[68]

Natural knowledge gives God the knowledge of every person who would make up all possible worlds. Middle knowledge gives God the knowledge of how each person would respond to each hypothetical encounter. As Craig points out, "Middle knowledge is the aspect of divine omniscience that comprises God's knowledge, prior to any determination of the divine will, of which contingent events would occur under any hypothetical set of circumstances."[69]

Both natural knowledge and middle knowledge are logically prior to God's decision to create one of these possible worlds. Craig tells us, "Indeed, God's decision to create a world is based on his middle knowledge and consists in his selecting to become actual one of the possible worlds known to him in the second moment."[70] After (logically after, not temporally after) God's decision to create, God possessed foreknowledge of the world that he would actually create.

In all of the possible worlds that God could create, the individuals were free. This would mean that the individuals in the one that God did choose to create were free. Those who hold this view assert that they have an explanation for believing in human free will and God's foreknowledge of the free acts of human beings. Since God chose to create this world rather than one of the other worlds that He could have created, they conclude that this world and *the individuals and their free acts were predestinated (or predetermined)*—thus preserving the concerns of both Calvinism and Arminianism.

AN EVALUATION OF THE MIDDLE KNOWLEDGE APPROACH

As I see it, there is a fatal flaw in this approach. The problem is found in the explanation of natural knowledge. In a quotation given above, Craig explains that God's natural knowledge "includes knowledge of all possibilities. He knows all possible individuals that he could create, all the possible circumstances he could place them in, all their possible actions and reactions, and all the possible worlds or orders which he could create."[71]

A careful look at this explanation of God's natural knowledge will reveal that it already presupposes God's foreknowledge of free human choices and acts. Let us limit our discussion to the statement "He knows all possible individuals that he could create." The only individuals in the human race that God could have foreknown without having foreknowledge of free human choices and acts, if human beings were to have true free will, would have been Adam and Eve. From that point on free choices were involved in every conception and every birth. For God to know that I would exist would require knowledge of all the free acts from Adam and Eve to me that were involved in every marriage, every conception, and every birth of my endless number of grandparents, and my parents. If He knew that, He already had knowledge of free human choices and acts.

If my observations are correct, this view would not be the grounds of an explanation of how God has foreknowledge of free acts of human beings because it already assumes such foreknowledge in the definition of God's natural knowledge. Also, I contend that the only individuals that have free will are real persons. Fictitious individuals (only theoretically possible individuals) do not have free will. They are moved about, not by a will of their own, but the will of the one who imagines their existence.

God's Foreknowledge of Free Acts a Mystery

The majority of those who have believed in God's foreknowledge of free human choices have not attempted to give an explanation of how God was able to have this kind of foreknowledge.

Arminius makes the concession, "I do not understand the mode in which He knows future contingencies, and especially those which belong to the free-will of creatures, and which He has decreed to permit, but do not of Himself."[72]

Let me repeat a part of a quotation given earlier in this chapter, where Buswell, a Calvinist, said that he saw no problem in foreknowledge of free acts of human beings. He explains:

> To the question then how God can know a free act in the future, I reply I do not know, but neither do I know how I can have knowledge by analysis, by inference from reason or from causes, or from statistical data reported by intuition, or (if it is insisted upon) by innate ideas. Knowledge is a mystery in any event, and God's knowledge of free events in the future is only one more mystery, revealed in Scripture. We have good and sufficient grounds to accept, and no valid ground to reject, what Scripture says on this subject.[73]

I cast my lot with those who do not understand the way God is able to foresee future free acts. The Bible makes it quite clear that God does possess foreknowledge of all future events, including free acts. Berkhof reminded us in a quotation used above, "It is perfectly evident that Scripture teaches divine foreknowledge of contingent events, 1 Sam. 23:10-13; 2 Kings 13:19; Ps. 81:14, 15; Isa. 42:9; 48:18; Jer. 2:2, 3; 38:17-20; Ezek. 3:6; and Matt. 11:21."[74]

As we can see, the Bible makes it clear that God has foreknowledge of free human choices and acts. I believe God's foreknowledge of free acts is also necessarily implied from God's foreknowledge of His own actions. It would have been impossible for God to have had foreknowledge of sending Jesus Christ into the world apart from knowledge of the free acts of human beings, that is, unless a person takes the position of unlimited determinism. For God to have foreknowledge of the exact identity of the human nature of Jesus Christ required that He have foreknowledge of His exact ancestry. For God to have this knowledge required that He have a foreknowledge of free acts of human beings.

I cannot explain how God created the universe *ex nihilo* (from nothing), but I believe it. I do not know how Jesus worked His miracles, but I believe He did. Why should I be concerned if I do not know how He has foreknowledge of free human choices and acts? As Buswell reminds us, there is much about our own ability to gain knowledge that we do not understand. I have sometimes made the statement that our knowledge of God is more adequate for our needs than our understanding of human personality. We cannot reach a consensus about whether human beings have a free will, what free will means, whether human beings are trichotomous or dichotomous or unitary beings, what human personality is, and how human personality is changed.

There are many things about God that we do not understand. I cannot comprehend that God had no beginning. Yet I believe it. I cannot think of God in any other way. Though I cannot understand how God has foreknowledge of free events, I still believe it. I cannot think of God in any other way. I can identify with Jack Cottrell when he says, "Surely God foreknows everything about the life of every individual. He cannot help but foreknow, just because he is God."[75] We must all agree that some things about God are inscrutable!

Divine Foreknowledge Not to Be Equated With Divine Causality

It is important for us to realize that causality cannot be ascribed to foreknowledge. Nor can divine cause be required for foreknowledge. These conclusions are necessary if there is to be the possibility of real contingencies in human experience. Picirilli, who acknowledges a debt to James Arminius and Richard Watson, has an excellent treatment on this subject. He explains: "The Arminian insists that there are things that actually can go either of two ways, and yet God knows which way they will go. He knows all future events perfectly. This means that they are all certain, else He would not know what will be."[76]

Picirilli goes on to say:

> The Arminian insists that there is no conflict between "certainty" and true "contingency," although explanation of this requires a careful and technical discussion of three important terms: certainty, contingency, and necessity. The distinction between these plays an important role in the issues related to predestination. I would venture that, in this matter alone, there is more room for misunderstanding and more to be gained from clarity than almost any other point in dispute.[77]

In explaining the terms "contingency" and "necessity," Picirilli posits the contingency of "the free acts of morally responsible persons." A contingency, he explains, is "anything that really can take place in more than one way. The freedom to choose does not contradict certainty. Certainty relates to the 'factness' of an event, to *whether* it will be or not; contingency relates to its *nature* as free or necessary. The same event can be both certain and contingent at the same time."[78] Necessary events must "inevitably be the way they are." For necessary events, "there were causes leading to the event that allowed no freedom of choice, causes that necessarily produced the event. Whenever God, for example, 'makes' something happen the way it does without allowing for any other eventuality, that event is a necessity."[79]

Picirilli goes on to argue that "God foreknows everything future as certain." However, necessity is not what makes future events certain. Rather, their "simple factness" is what makes them certain. "They will be the way they will be, and God knows what they will be because He has perfect awareness, in advance, of all facts. But that knowledge *per se*, even though it is foreknowledge, has no more causal effect on facts than our knowledge of certain past facts has on them."[80]

Further on he says:

> The Calvinist errs, on this subject, in suggesting that God knows the future certainly only because He first unconditionally foreordained (predestinated) it. But that is to confuse knowledge with active cause and so in effect take away contingency. God's foreknowledge, in the sense of prescience, is part of His omniscience and includes all things as certain, both good and evil, contingent, and necessary. It is not in itself causal.[81]

Picirilli makes a solid case for God's foreknowledge of future free human choices. God's foreknowledge of events means that it is certain that they will occur, but it does not make the events necessary. I have already referred to God's knowledge of hypothetical contingencies. If divine cause had to be the basis for knowledge of that which is neither past nor present, that would rule out knowledge of hypothetical contingencies. That would mean that any reference to hypothetical cases in Scripture by God would be only educated guesses. Such a view of God is unthinkable.

DIVINE FOREKNOWLEDGE OF FREE HUMAN CHOICES AND ACTS NOT BASED ON A SPECTATOR ROLE

It is important to keep in mind that in eternity past God did not observe the future as a mere spectator any more than He occupies the position of a mere spectator now. At the present time, God is deeply involved in what is taking place. As a holy, loving, caring, personal, omnipotent, omniscient, wise, and sovereign God, He is deeply concerned about and deeply involved in what is happening in the human race. There is a consistency between all of God's attributes and of His actions as a divine Sovereign.

God is not an impassible being who cannot be moved by the concerns of human beings. He cares deeply about people. He cares deeply about people because it is His nature to care. He cares deeply about people because He created them for His glory in His image. He wants us to care deeply about people. He feels the pain and suffering of people. He wants us to feel the pain and suffering of people as well.

It is the kind of God that I have just attempted to describe who foresaw the future from all eternity. As He foresaw the future, He saw it as it would progressively unfold from: (1) The result of His creative activity and His divine influence. (2) The result of the devastating influence of sin. (3) The result of the response that human beings would give as a result of the redemptive work of Jesus Christ, the ministry of the Holy Spirit, the ministry of the Word of God, and the ministry of the redeemed. (4) The result of all of the influences that would come from all sources outside Himself. (5) The result of all the influence that He would bring on people through His power and His infinite wisdom. He saw then, everything that He sees and is doing now. He is the same God now that He was then. Everything that He is doing now is just as real as it would be if He had not known it in advance.

THE CONSISTENCY BETWEEN THE SOVEREIGNTY OF GOD AND THE *INFLUENCE AND RESPONSE* MODEL

Up to this point in this chapter, I think I have been able to raise some serious objections to the *cause* and *effect* model of how God plans and carries out His plan for the human race. The question before us now is: Is the *influence* and *response* model consistent with the sovereignty of God? I believe it is. I may not be able to answer all of the questions that I may be confronted with about this model, but I think it will have considerably fewer problems than the cause and effect model.

A Point of Clarification

Are the following two questions the same? (1) Is free will in the sense of the liberty of indifference consistent with the sovereignty of God? (2) Is free will in the sense of the liberty of indifference consistent with divine determinism? If the only way that a sovereign God can maintain His sovereignty in dealing with human beings is through a cause and effect approach, then these questions are essentially the same, and the answer to both questions is no. However, if a sovereign God can maintain His sovereignty through an influence and response approach, the questions are not the same. The answer to the first question is yes, and the answer to the second question is no.

THE QUESTION OF LIMITING THE SOVEREIGNTY OF GOD

It is usually assumed that, if God is going to grant free will to human beings in the sense of the liberty of indifference that it would impose a limitation on the sovereignty of God. Arminians frequently make this concession. My first question to the suggestion of a limitation is: What kind of limitation? Does the use of the word *limitation* mean to make God weaker? If so, my response is that a God who can grant true freedom of will and still retain His sovereign control is a much greater God than a God who must limit His approach to sovereign control to determinism. I am in agreement with Cottrell when he says that it is wrong to think "that God's control varies according to the degree that he causes things or the degree of freedom bestowed on his creatures." God's sovereignty entails that he have total control. However, "the issue is whether such total control requires a predetermination or causation of all things. I contend that it does not; God's sovereignty is greater than that!"[82]

My next question with regard to whether free will imposes a limitation on God is: A limitation in comparison to what? Why is it a limitation on

God if He should choose to govern human beings through an *influence* and *response model* rather than a cause and effect model?

The two models do have some significant differences. If God had chosen to make man a machine with conscious awareness, he could have carried out His sovereign control with absolute precision. There would have been an absolute correlation between divine cause and effect as human beings would have experienced it. Certainly no one would claim that all we see happening in today's world is in exact conformity to the desire of a holy and loving God! This is the fatal flaw of unlimited determinism, whether hard or soft.

According to the *influence* and *response model*, it would have been possible for Adam and Eve and the human race to have lived a life of absolute obedience. This would comport with a *liberty of indifference*. But, as we know, it did not actually work out that way. This did not spell the end of God's sovereignty. It did mean that He had to follow through on the warning that He gave to Adam and Eve when He said, "But of the tree of the knowledge of good and evil you shall not eat, for in the day that you eat of it you shall surely die" (Gen. 2:17).

In the *influence* and *response model*, once sin entered the picture, there would not be an exact correspondence between divine desire and human response. Divine sovereignty took on a new direction. God placed human beings under the sentence of death and cursed the earth. In Genesis 3:15, He made a promise to Adam and Eve that we know in the light of further revelation involved the promise of redemption through Jesus Christ. He is carrying out that plan with the human race. It is being done through the influence and response model.

The Influence and Response Model and the Fulfillment of God's Sovereign Purposes

One of the most important questions for theologians to answer is: Is the *cause* and *effect model* the only way that a sovereign God can carry out His purposes? Or, can God work effectively in carrying out His purposes through the *influence* and *response model*?

There is absolutely no reason that a sovereign God cannot carry out His sovereign purposes while using an *influence* and *response model*. Once sin entered the picture, there would not be a precise, exact correlation between God's desires and human action. To say what I am saying is not the same as saying that God will not accomplish what He plans to do. *God's plan will not be thwarted!*

If God is going to be sovereign—and I cannot imagine God not being sovereign—then He must be able to make plans and carry them out. It cannot be otherwise. However, if God works with human beings through an *influence* and *response model* in accordance with both the liberty of spontaneity and the liberty of indifference, we would necessarily use different criteria for judging His effectiveness as sovereign than we would if He operated through cause and effect.

The *cause* and *effect model* would expect an exact correlation between God's desire and what follows. Determinism is required for the *cause* and *effect model*. The smallest failure between God's desire and what follows would mean the collapse of God's sovereignty.

In influence and response, there is an exact correlation between what God sets out to do and what follows. If God says something will happen, it will happen. But that is not the same as saying that there is an exact correlation between what God desires and what follows. I think we can safely say that God does not desire for lying, hatred, murder, rape, and thievery to occur. At the same time, this does not mean that God will not accomplish the purposes He sets before Himself.

The purposes that God set before Himself, as they relate to human beings, are best explained by the influence and response model. God purposed to create human beings with a free will. He purposed that they would be free to obey Him or disobey Him, to please Him or displease Him. It turned out that Adam and Eve disobeyed God. God obviously did not desire that they disobey Him. Such an attitude would be prohibited by His holiness. Their disobedience did not mean that God had ceased to be sovereign.

God was not caught off guard. He knew what would happen. He set in motion the processes that would bring about the plan of redemption through Jesus Christ. This plan was to be based on the fact that Jesus Christ would pay in full the penalty for the sins of human beings. He would provide absolute righteousness to meet the demand for absolute righteousness. He would offer this free salvation to all who would believe in Jesus Christ. He would have this message preached. He would have the Holy Spirit work to draw people to Christ as the gospel is preached. All of this would be done in keeping with the influence and response model. The end result of all of this would be "that in the dispensation of the fulness of the times He might gather together in one all things in Christ, both which are in heaven and which are on earth—in Him" (Eph. 1:10). All of this is being done "according to the purpose of Him who works all things according to the counsel of His will" (Eph. 1:11).

Many seem to think that God would be helpless when it comes to carrying out His sovereign purpose if He did not work through cause and effect. That this is not a necessary conclusion is seen by the way human beings work. The way human beings work with one another is through influence and response. Many things are accomplished this way. Contractors sign contracts and build buildings. For them to accomplish this goal, they have to influence people to work for them.

They have to influence them to do what they ask them to do. They may not always get the ones to work that they ask. But they get others. They succeed with the project.

Human contractors can deal with those who are free in the sense of the liberty of indifference through the influence and response model. If they can, cannot a sovereign and wise God accomplish His purposes with those who are free in the sense of the liberty of indifference through the influence and response model?

In the last several pages, I have made my case for the position that a sovereign and wise God is not required to use the cause and effect model in order to maintain His sovereignty and accomplish His purposes. I believe that God can and does work through the influence and response model. That being true, there is no reason that a sovereign God could not use the approach of conditional election.

We will now turn our attention to the second assumption of Calvinism.

An Answer to the Second Assumption of Calvinism

The second assumption of Calvinism is that total depravity precludes the response of faith from the sinner unless the Holy Spirit first regenerates him. As I pointed out earlier, the view that the nature of depravity requires that the sinner be regenerated before he or she can respond with faith had its origin with Augustine.

To place regeneration before faith poses some serious problems for Calvinism. This will be dealt with in Chapter 7. For a more thorough treatment please refer to "An Inconsistency in Calvinism."

Calvinism is faced with two important assumed impossibilities: First, it is impossible for a person to believe unless he or she is first regenerated. Second, it is impossible for sanctification to take place prior to justification. A Classical Calvinist will not argue against either of these statements. In Chapter 7, I give support for these two assertions from Robert Haldane and Louis Berkhof. The Calvinistic credentials of these men are not in question. In Classical Calvinism, the order is regeneration, faith, justification, and sanctification. *In placing regeneration before justification Calvinism has a problem.* By anybody's definition, regeneration is a life-changing experience. Berkhof tells us that "regeneration is the beginning of sanctification."[83] If regeneration is the beginning of sanctification, this means that Classical Calvinism has the process of sanctification beginning before justification occurs. This cannot be!

Calvinists have, by and large, adhered to the satisfaction view of atonement and justification. If a person is consistent in developing the implications of the satisfaction view of atonement, it is clear that God cannot perform the act of regeneration (an act of sanctification) in a person before he or she is justified. God can move in with His sanctifying grace only after the guilt problem is satisfied by justification. To think otherwise is to violate the law of non-contradiction. I realize that when we talk about the *ordo salutis* (order of salvation) we are talking about logical order instead of chronological order. But that logical order is inviolable!

Regeneration is not an act of God that prepares the way for redemption. It is a redemptive act. I commend Calvinists for upholding the satisfaction view of atonement and the imputation of the death and righteousness of Christ as the ground of justification. Yet I believe they need to reexamine the question of whether *the redemptive act of regeneration* can be performed on a person before the death and righteousness of Christ is actually imputed to his or her account.

THE NECESSITY OF THE DRAWING POWER OF THE HOLY SPIRIT

It is evident that it is no simple matter for a person who is under the bondage of sin to be brought to an exercise of saving faith. Jesus drove that point home when He said, "No man can come to me, except the Father which hath sent me draw him" (Jn. 6:44).

We dare not take the depravity of human beings lightly. Apart from the drawing power of the Holy Spirit, none would come to Christ. If a person cannot exercise faith in Christ unless the Holy Spirit *first* regenerates him or her, those who believe in the satisfaction view of atonement and justification are in trouble as we have seen above. For a person to be regenerated *before* he or she is justified contradicts the logical priority of justification to sanctification. To avoid this contradiction, a way must be found that will place justification before regeneration. I believe that in the influence and response model we can maintain a strong view of depravity and at the same time maintain the *ordo salutis* to be faith, justification, regeneration, and sanctification.

We know that Adam and Eve were created with original righteousness. They had a righteous and sinless nature. By a satanic attack through the serpent, Eve responded in a way that *contradicted* her righteous nature.

She disobeyed God and obeyed the serpent. Then Adam, following the example of Eve, responded in a way that contradicted his righteous nature. All of this happened through an influence and response relationship. Satan influenced Adam and Eve and they responded.

It is a matter of historical fact that Adam and Eve by the influence of Satan acted contrary to their nature. Satan did not perform some transforming act on them to give them a depraved nature, making it possible for them to sin. We grant that Adam and Eve, through Satanic influence, an influence which did not first change their nature, were brought to sin. Will we say that God cannot, without first regenerating sinners, influence sinners through the Word of God and the Holy Spirit, so that some of them will contradict their sinful nature and be brought to Christ? How can a person acknowledge the factualness of what happened to Adam and Eve and deny the possibility that a person could exercise saving faith by the aid of the Holy Spirit without first being regenerated?

God made human beings in His image. He made them personal beings. He made them to live in an influence and response relationship with Himself. While depravity puts human beings in a state of being that requires divine aid before they can respond to the gospel, there is no reason to believe that God cannot continue to work with human beings in keeping with the influence and response model. That is the only way consistent with the personhood of human beings.

The image of God still remains in fallen creatures and can be appealed to by the moral teachings of the Bible, the message of sin and guilt, God's provision of atonement through Jesus Christ, and the offer of salvation through Christ alone through faith alone. When sinners are confronted with this message, the Holy Spirit can and will work to draw sinners to Christ. They can be brought to that point in which they are enabled to say either yes or no.

To make it clear that I have a very serious view of sin and depravity, let me state again what I said in Chapter 1 under the heading, "The Problem of Giving a Simple Description of Fallen Man": It is clear that man fell from a state of holiness into a state of sin (Is. 53:6; Rom. 3:23). It is clear that sin has placed man under condemnation before God (Rom. 6:23; Rev. 21:8). It is clear that fallen man cannot please God and has no fellowship with God (Eph. 2:1-3; Rom. 8:7-8). It is clear that man cannot come to God without the drawing power of the Holy Spirit (Jn. 6:44). It is clear that a work so drastic as to be called a new birth is required for man's salvation (Jn. 3:3-7). But we also find areas where the state and condition of man are not so clearly understood.

I think I have shown that Calvinists are in deep trouble when they place regeneration, which clearly includes sanctification, ahead of justification in the *ordo salutis*. That problem alone should spell a deathblow to the Classical Calvinist insistence that regeneration must precede faith and justification. I think I have shown that there is no reason to believe that God cannot use the influence and response model in working with sinners to lead them to Christ.

AN ANSWER TO THE THIRD ASSUMPTION OF CALVINISM

The third assumption of Calvinism is that the only way salvation could be free is by unconditional election. My treatment of atonement and justification in Chapter 6 will make it unquestionably clear that I believe justification is a gift. It is by grace. Not one thing that I have ever done or ever will do is placed on my account with God as part of the price of my redemption. The only way God, as Supreme Judge of the universe, can justify a member of the fallen human race is to have Christ's righteousness and Christ's death placed on his account. That and that alone is the ground for justification. That is it and nothing else. Justification is by *Christ alone* by (conditioned on) *faith alone*. That is pure and uncorrupted grace!

Is anyone really going to insist that for God to require faith in Christ *as a condition for receiving* the death and righteousness of Christ would mean justification by works? Does not Paul insist in Romans 4 that to be justified by faith (faith as a condition, not ground) is in contradiction to justification by works? Even a Calvinist believes that faith is a condition of salvation.

Earlier in this chapter, I pointed out that the unconditional election taught in Calvinism seems to rest on three assumptions. These assumptions are: First, the sovereignty of God requires unconditional election and thus precludes conditional election. Second, total depravity precludes the response of faith from a sinner unless the Holy Spirit first regenerates him. Third, that salvation is free precludes conditional election. I pointed out that if these three assumptions are true, Calvinism has won its case. I also pointed out that if these three assumptions are not true, Calvinism is in trouble. I believe that I have shown that these assumptions do not rest on solid ground.

Now I want to turn our attention to the question of decrees in Arminian thought.

Types of Decrees Consistent With Arminian Theology

The decrees of God are His eternal purpose or purposes. Decrees could be called God's eternal will or His eternal plan. I will consider three basic types of decrees: efficacious decrees, decrees to influence, and decrees to permit.

Efficacious Decrees

Efficacious decrees are decrees in which God decrees that certain things will come to pass. In these decrees, God Himself will be responsible for their fulfillment. There are two types of efficacious decrees: unconditional efficacious decrees and conditional efficacious decrees.

Unconditional Efficacious Decrees

Unconditional efficacious decrees are not dependent upon any conditions for their fulfillment. The work of creation would be an example of this kind of decree. The provision of hell for the wicked and the provision of atonement through Jesus Christ would also be examples of this kind of decree. Because of God's foreknowledge of sin, by the necessity of His holy nature, He decreed to prepare hell for the wicked. On the occasion of God's foreknowledge of sin, God was moved by His love to decree the provision of atonement.

It is important to note that it can be seen by the use of foreknowledge in these two unconditional efficacious decrees how foreknowledge was used in the "determinate counsel" of God in Acts 2:23. It is not necessary to consider foreknowledge in this case to be causal. It is possible to consider foreknowledge to be instrumental in the decree to predestinate the crucifixion of Christ. In this case, foreknowledge would furnish God with the information necessary for Him to make the plans for the provision of atonement through the death of Christ. By the help of His foreknowledge, God could decree the death of Christ in a way that would not violate the freedom of choice of the persons who would be involved.

Conditional Efficacious Decrees

In conditional efficacious decrees, God efficaciously decreed that certain things would take place when certain conditions were met. These decrees were made because God, on the basis of His foreknowledge, knew that these conditions would be met. An example of this kind of decree would be the justification and regeneration of a person when he believes. It is for this reason that I can say that a believer's justification and regeneration were efficaciously decreed. Justification and regeneration are monergistic. They are solely the work of God.

Decrees to Influence

Decrees to influence refer to the action of God through which He would work with His responsible creatures to bring about desired responses. While there is a desired response on the part of God, that response is not guaranteed by the influence of God. The drawing power of the Holy Spirit upon the unsaved when they read or hear the gospel would be an example of this kind of decree. I have not seen this terminology (or any synonym) used elsewhere. I do not believe that we can successfully understand the workings of God with man apart from this decree or one by another name that says the same thing. It is the lack of tolerance for an idea of this kind that puts Calvinism into an awkward position in trying to explain the origin of sin without making God responsible for sin.

Decrees to Permit

These decrees have reference to the action of God in permitting certain things but not efficaciously bringing them about. All events that God foreknows (which embraces all that ever will happen) are either efficaciously decreed or permitted. All acts of human beings (or free agents) come under this permission *whether evil or good*.

While the *permission* and the *events* that follow, whether evil or good, are decreed, both are not decreed in exactly the same sense. The permission itself is a divine act. The events that follow, which are our present concern, are human acts—some in obedience and some in disobedience. As it relates to those acts that are good, God has the relationship of both influence and permission. As it relates to those acts that are evil, God's relationship to their occurrence is permission only. As William G. T. Shedd says, "The permissive decree relates only to moral evil. Sin is the sole and solitary object of this species of decrees."[84]

It is a mistake to limit permission to disobedience. The decrees to influence and the decrees to permit are God's way of dealing with persons made in His own image. They are permitted to either obey or disobey. They are permitted to be good stewards or bad stewards. In this arrangement, some things happen that please God and some things happen that displease God. It pleased God to make man in His own image and give man a choice in matters. The plan pleased God. But He is not pleased with the sinful deeds of human beings.

AN ORDER OF DECREES CONSISTENT WITH ARMINIANISM

In the first edition of his *Systematic Theology*, Henry C. Thiessen adopted a modified form of Sublapsarianism. He argues that "the decrees are in this order: 1. the decree to create, 2. the decree to permit the fall, 3. the decree to provide salvation for all, and 4. the decree to apply that salvation to some, to those who believe."[85] Thiessen modified the fourth point of Sublapsarianism to conform to his doctrine of conditional election. This modification of Sublapsarianism would be compatible with Arminianism.

Conclusion

I believe that I have shown in this chapter that there are no *a priori* reasons that would prohibit God from working through the approach of conditional election. The remaining question is: What is the biblical teaching on election? That will be the subject of the next three chapters.

---

[1]Some of the material in this chapter is adapted from F. Leroy Forlines, "Observations About Election," *The Randall House Bible Commentary: Romans*, Rober E. Picirilli, ed. (Nashville: Randall House Publications, 1987), 232-238.

[2]Millard J. Erickson, *Christian Theology* (Grand Rapids: Baker Book House, 1985), 918.

[3]Norman L. Geisler, "Freedom, Free Will, and Determinism," *Evangelical Dictionary of Theology*, Walter A. Elwell, ed. (Grand Rapids: Baker, 1984), 429.

[4]J. A. Crabtree, "Does Middle Knowledge Solve the Problem of Divine Sovereignty?" *The Grace of God, the Bondage of the Will*, Thomas R. Schreiner and Bruce A. Ware, eds. (Grand Rapids: Baker Books, 1995), 2:429.

[5]John S. Feinberg, "God, Freedom, and Evil in Calvinistic Thinking," *The Grace of God, the Bondage of the Will*, 2:463-464.

[6]Gordon H. Clark, *Biblical Predestination* (Philadelphia: Presbyterian and Reformed Publishing Company, 1969), 60.

[7]Ibid., 45.

[8]Richard A. Muller, "Grace, Election, and Contingent Choice: Arminians Gambit and the Reformed Choice," *The Grace of God, the Bondage of the Will*, 2:269-270.

[9]Ibid., 271.

[10]Ibid., 276. Quoted material from William Perkins, *A Treatise of God's Free*

Grace and Man's Free Will, in *Workes*, I:704, IA, 709.2C-710.IC.

[11]Clark, *Biblical Predestination*, 121.

[12]R. K. McGregor Wright, *No Place for Sovereignty: What's Wrong with Freewill Theism* (Downers Grove: Inter Varsity Press, 1996), 41.

[13]James Oliver Buswell, Jr., *A Systematic Theology of the Religion*, vol. 1, (Grand Rapids: Zondervan Publishing House, 1960) 267.

[14]Ibid.

[15]Loraine Boettner, *The Reformed Doctrine of Predestination* (Philadelphia: The Presbyterian and Reformed Publishing Company, 1969), 78.

[16]Ibid., 208.

[17]Ibid., 222.

[18]Ibid.

[19]Feinberg, "God Ordains All Things," *Predestination and Free Will: Four Views of Divine Sovereignty and Human Freedom*, eds. David Basinger and Randall Basinger (Downers Grove: InterVarsity, 1986), 24-25.

[20]Ibid., 37.

[21]Ibid., 24-25, 37. Emphasis mine.

[22]Boettner, *The Reformed Doctrine of Predestination*, 42.

[23]Feinberg, "God Ordains All Things," 32.

[24]Crabtree, "Does Middle Knowledge Solve the Problem of Divine Sovereignty?" *The Grace of God, the Bondage of the Will*, vol. 2, 436.

[25]Buswell, *A Systematic Theology*, vol. 1, 60.

[26]Henry Clarence Thiessen, *Introductory Lectures in Systematic Theology* (Grand Rapids: William B. Eerdmans Publishing Company, 1949), 344-349.

[27]Henry C. Thiessen, *Introductory Lectures in Systematic Theology*, rev. ed., rev. by Vernon D. Doerksen (Grand Rapids: Wm. B. Eerdmans Publishing Company, 1979), 257-262. The only hint of a change from Thiessen's view of conditional election in the first edition to the view of unconditional election in the revised edition is found in the "Preface to the Revised Edition." Doerksen explains, "Several of the portions, such as those on inspiration, election,

foreknowledge, creation, demons, imputation of sin, and pretribulationism, have been rather extensively revised" (p. ix). [I hardly think anyone unfamiliar the first edition's teaching of conditional election would have imagined it after reading the revised edition's treatment supporting unconditional election.]

[28]See "The Question of Synergism," Chapter 7.

[29]J. A. Crabtree, "Does Middle Knowledge Solve the Problem of Divine Sovereignty?" *The Grace of God, the Bondage of the Will*, 2:449, footnote 18. (Crabtree calls attention to the fact that William Lane Craig alludes to these terms. Then he gives an explanation.)

[30]Ronald H. Nash, *The Concept of God: An Exploration of Contemporary Difficulties with the Attributes of God* (Grand Rapids: Zondervan Publishing House, 1983), 54.

[31]*Oxford English Dictionary.*

[32]Berkhof, *Systematic Theology*, 68.

[33]*Merriam Webster's Collegiate Dictionary*, Tenth Edition.

[34]Norman L. Geisler, "God Knows All Things," *Predestination and Free Will: Four Views of Divine Sovereignty and Human Freedom,* eds. Davis Basinger and Randall Basinger (Downers Grove: InterVarsity, 1986), 76.

[35]Ibid., 79.

[36]John Miley, *Systematic Theology*, vol. 2 (New York: The Methodist Book Concern, 1894), 2:273.

[37]Geisler, "God Knows All Things," *Predestination and Free Will: Four Views of Divine Sovereignty and Human Freedom*, 73.

[38]Ibid.

[39]Gordon H. Clark, *Biblical Predestination*, 120.

[40]Miley, *Systematic Theology*, 1:166-169.

[41]Soon I want to get back to work on a manuscript that is well over half finished, for which I am using the working title, "Understanding Yourself and Others."

[42]Clark Pinnock, "From Augustine to Arminius: A Pilgrimage in Theology," *The Grace of God, the Will of Man: A Case for Arminianism*, Clark Pinnock, ed.

(Grand Rapids: Zondervan Publishing House, 1989), 25.

⁴³Ibid., 26.

⁴⁴Clark Pinnock, "God Limits His Knowledge," *Predestination and Free Will: Four Views of Divine Sovereignty and Human Freedom*, eds. David Basinger and Randall Basinger (Downers Grove: InterVarsity, 1986), 144.

⁴⁵Richard Rice, "Divine Foreknowledge and Free-Will Theism," *The Grace of God, the Will of Man: A Case for Arminianism*, Clark Pinnock, ed. (Grand Rapids: Zondervan Publishing House, 1989), 134.

⁴⁶Ibid., 135.

⁴⁷Ibid., 136.

⁴⁸James Arminius, *The Writings of James Arminius*, trans. James Nichols (Grand Rapids: Baker Book House, 1956), 3:66.

⁴⁹Jack Cottrell, "The Nature of the Divine Sovereignty," *The Grace of God, the Will of Man: A Case for Arminianism*, Clark Pinnock, ed., 111.

⁵⁰Jack Cottrell, "Conditional Election," *Grace Unlimited*, Clark H. Pinnock, ed. (Minneapolis: Bethany House, 1975), 59.

⁵¹Ibid., 60.

⁵²Robert E. Picirilli, *Grace, Faith, Free Will* (Picirilli is a professor emeritus and former Academic Dean at Free Will Baptist Bible College. For years he was academic dean. He has taught Pauline Writings, Greek, Philosophy, and Calvinism and Arminianism.) The material quoted here can be found in "Chapter 3: The Classical Arminian Doctrine of Predestination," under "Areas of Disagreement," under the sub-point, "The relationship between, certainty, contingency, and necessity."

⁵³William Lane Craig, *The Only Wise God: The Compatibility of Divine Foreknowledge and Human Freedom* (Grand Rapids: Baker Book House, 1987), 37.

⁵⁴Feinberg, "God Ordains All Things," 24-25.

⁵⁵Feinberg, "God, Freedom, and Evil in Calvinistic Thinking," *The Grace of God, The Bondage of the Will*, vol. 2, 463-464.

⁵⁶Ibid., 460.

[57]Ibid., 451.

[58]Picirilli, *Grace, Faith, Free Will* "Chapter 3: The Classical Arminian Doctrine of Predestination," under the heading, "Areas of Disagreement," under sub-point, "An emphasis on the nature of man as personal."

[59]Muller, "Grace, Election, and Contingent Choice: *Arminius's Gambit and the Reformed Response, The Grace of God, the Bondage of the Will*, 2:271.

[60]Ibid., 277-278.

[61]F. Leroy Forlines, *The Quest for Truth: Theology for Postmodern Times* (Nashville: Randal House Publications, 2001), 67-70.

[62]Geisler, "God Knows All Things," *Predestination and Free Will: Four Views of Divine Sovereignty and Human Freedom*, 73.

[63]Arminius, *The Writings of James Arminius*, 3:66.

[64]See my more thorough treatment in Chapter 5 of *The Quest for Truth*.

[65]William Lane Craig, "Middle Knowledge: A Calvinistic-Arminian Rapprochement," *A Case for Arminianism: The Grace of God, the Will of Man*, Clark Pinnock, ed. (Grand Rapids: Zondervan Publishing House, 1989), 141.

[66]Ibid., 141-142.

[67]Craig, *The Only Wise God: The Compatibility of Divine Foreknowledge and Human Freedom*, 131.

[68]Ibid., 129.

[69]Craig, "Middle Knowledge: A Calvinistic-Arminian Rapprochement," 147.

[70]Ibid., 130-131.

[71]Craig, *The Only Wise God*, 129.

[72]Arminius, *The Writings of James Arminius*, 3:66.

[73]Buswell, *A Systematic Theology*, 1:60.

[74]Berkhof, *Systematic Theology*, 67.

[75]Jack Cottrell, "Conditional Election," 60.

[76]Picirilli, Grace, *Faith, Free Will*, 36.

[77]Ibid.

⁷⁸Ibid., The "b" sub-point under "1. The relationship between certainty, contingency, and necessity."

⁷⁹Ibid., The "c" sub-point.

⁸⁰Ibid.

⁸¹Ibid.

⁸²Cottrell, 111.

⁸³Berkhof, *Systematic Theology*, 536.

⁸⁴William G. T. Shedd, *Dogmatic Theology*, (1888; reprint, Nashville: Thomas Nelson Publishers, 1980), 1:406.

⁸⁵Thiessen, *Introductory Lectures* (1949), 344.

CHAPTER 3

Proof Texts for Unconditional Election: Romans 9

In the last chapter, I dealt with the theological problems that must be considered in a study of election. The views on unconditional election and conditional election were set forth. Attention was given to decrees, determinism, the sovereignty of God, the meaning of free will, and so on. I set forth two differing models for the way God carries out His sovereign purposes with human beings: the *cause* and *effect* model and the *influence* and *response* model. The cause and effect model best serves unconditional election. The influence and response model best serves conditional election. I believe that the influence and response model best maintains theological consistency.

The most important question before us is: What does the Bible teach? The ultimate test of a theological viewpoint is: Will it stand the test of biblical exegesis? If unconditional election is true, there must be at least one passage of Scripture that irrefutably teaches unconditional election. Calvinists would agree that they consider Romans 9 to be the passage that unquestionably and irrefutably teaches unconditional election. Romans 9 is considered the bedrock of Calvinism. The question for us to decide is: Does Romans 9 teach unconditional election? Once that question is decided, we will examine other passages.

When I wrote my commentary on Romans,[1] which was published in 1987, I examined about 40 commentaries on Romans 9. As a result of that study, about 80 percent of the commentaries I surveyed set forth the view of unconditional election. If conditional election is going to stand, those who believe it must be able to deal with Romans 9 adequately and with integrity.

Calvinism on Romans 9:14

The case for unconditional election in Romans 9 stands or falls on the meaning of the question that Paul raises in verse 14. In Romans 9:14, Paul asks: "What shall we say then? There is no injustice with God is there? May it never be!" (9:14, NASB). If we miss the meaning of Paul's question in verse 14, we will likely come away from Romans 9 with a wrong view of what Paul means to convey. It is absolutely necessary for us to understand why Paul asks the question in verse 14, if we are going to be able to understand the contribution that Romans 9 gives to our understanding of election.

It is assumed by those who believe in unconditional election that Paul is raising the question of whether God was unrighteous or unjust in unconditionally choosing Jacob while rejecting Esau. Robert Haldane explains, "The Apostle anticipated the objection of the carnal mind in this doctrine. Does not loving Jacob and hating Esau before they had done any good or evil, imply that there is injustice with God?"[2] Everett F. Harrison observes, "God's dealings with Jacob and Esau might be challenged as arbitrary, on the ground that Esau was the object of injustice."[3] William S. Plumer says, "The meaning is this: Does God's treatment of Isaac and Jacob display injustice to Ishmael and Esau?"[4] William G. T. Shedd explains: "The objection is raised that in such discrimination as that between Jacob and Esau, God acts unjustly."[5] John Piper comments, "When Paul said that God chose to bless Jacob over Esau apart from any basis in their actions but simply on the basis of his choice (*ek tou kalountos*, Rom. 9:12), his opponent objected that this would call God's righteousness into question (9:14).[6]

It is obvious that these commentators are of the opinion that, in setting forth the choice of Jacob and the rejection of Esau (verses 10-13), Paul has established the doctrine of unconditional election. They take the question that Paul raises in verse 14 to be dealing with an objection to the doctrine of unconditional election.

THE CONTEXT OF THE QUESTION IN ROMANS 9:14

The question before us is: Is Calvinism's interpretation a proper assessment? If Paul is, in fact, raising the question of whether God is unrighteous in unconditionally electing Jacob for salvation while not extending the same privilege to Esau, Calvinism has won the debate. This is true because unconditional election would already be implied in the question in Romans 9:14. I do not concede to Calvinism. I believe that Calvinism has *wrongly interpreted* the question in verse 14. Calvinists have wrongly interpreted the question in verse 14 because they have wrongly interpreted verses 6-13, particularly verses 11 and 12. A proper understanding of verses 6-13 should help us understand why Paul posed the question of whether there is injustice in God in verse 14.

Three Views of Verses 6-13 as Related to Election

There have been basically three views given of this passage (verses 6-13) as it relates to election. Interpreters have given major attention to how this passage climaxes in verses 10 and 11.

First, most who believe in conditional election have taken the position that this passage has nothing to do with election or rejection with regard to individual salvation. Rather, it is understood to refer to the election of Jacob as the third of the patriarchal ancestors (the other two being Abraham and Isaac) of the nation of Israel. Thus, the Covenant Seed of Abraham were chosen through Jacob rather than Esau. Jacob was elected as the third patriarch. Esau was rejected with the result being that his descendants were not a part of the Covenant Seed of Abraham. (See Clarke,[7] Godet,[8] and Sanday and Headlam.[9])

Second, some who believe in unconditional election agree that the passage deals with the election of Jacob as the third patriarchal head of the Covenant Seed of Abraham and the rejection of Esau for the position. However, this approach goes on to view Jacob and Esau as types. Shedd explains that Jacob and Esau, "like Isaac and Ishmael, are *types* of two classes that have been spoken of: viz: the "children of the promise," and the "children of the flesh" (v. 8). The theocratic election of Isaac and Jacob illustrates the spiritual election of individuals; and the theocratic reprobation of Ishmael and Esau illustrates the spiritual reprobation of individuals."[10] Hodge also takes this position.[11]

Third, the more common view among those who support unconditional election would be to understand the passage as being directly concerned with unconditional election rather than to support it by analogy. This view is held by Hendricksen,[12] Murray,[13] and Piper.[14] Let us take a serious look at verses 6-13 and see what the context is for the question in verse 14.

THE JEWISH PROBLEM

A Belief that God Unconditionally Promised All Jews Eternal Life in the Abrahamic Covenant

It must be noted that recent translations usually translate *sperma* as "descendant" or "offspring." These are valid and helpful translations. However, since the terminology "Abraham's Seed" has so fixed itself in eschatological literature, I will use the term "Abraham's Seed" in this treatment except when I quote other sources.

To find out why Paul raised this question in verse 14, we need to review the context. In verses 1-3, Paul expressed his deep concern over the many Jews who were not saved. This created a serious problem for the Jews. The unbelieving Jews were not prepared for such an observation. That large numbers of Jews, who were the Covenant People of God, would be lost and under God's wrath was for them unthinkable.

Observations on the Jewish Understanding of Salvation

The New Testament confronts us with two seemingly contradictory concepts concerning the viewpoint of the Jews on their own salvation.

The first is the concept of unconditional salvation of all Jews as the seed of Abraham. It was this viewpoint that caused John the Baptist to say, "Therefore bring forth fruit in keeping with your repentance; and do not suppose that you can say to yourselves, we have Abraham for our father; for I say to you, that God is able from these stones to raise up children to Abraham" (Mt. 3:9; see also Jn. 8:33-40).

The other viewpoint is that the Jews were depending on their own works. Paul set forth this viewpoint when he said. "But Israel, pursuing a law of righteousness, did not arrive at *that* law. Why? Because *they did* not *pursue* it by faith, but as though it *were* by works" (Rom. 9:31-32).

It appears that even their thinking about salvation by works was not referring to the salvation of an individual Jew by works. Rather, the reference seems to be to a corporate righteousness. That a strong sense of corporate righteousness was prevalent among the Jews can be seen from the apocryphal book 2 Esdras, in which the writer expresses his bewilderment over what appeared to be the preferred treatment given to Gentiles. He was desperately concerned about why God had delivered Israel over to Babylon. In his prayer he expressed his bewilderment over the matter. In 3:27-36, he complains:

> [27]So thou didst deliver the city [Jerusalem] into the hands of thy enemies. [28]Then I said in my heart, Are the deeds of those who inhabit Babylon any better? Is that why she has gained dominion over Zion? [29]For when I came here I saw ungodly deeds without number, and my soul has seen many sinners during these thirty years. And my heart failed me, [30]for I have seen how thou dost endure those who sin, and hast spared those who act wickedly, and hast destroyed thy people, and hast preserved thy enemies, [31]and hast not shown to anyone how thy way may be comprehended. Are the deeds of Babylon better than those of Zion? [32]Or has another nation known thee besides Israel? Or what tribes have so believed thy covenants as the tribes of Jacob [33]Yet their reward has not appeared and their labor has borne no fruit. For I have traveled widely among the nations and have seen that they abound in wealth, though they are unmindful of thy commandments. [34]Now therefore weigh in a balance our iniquities and

those of the inhabitants of the world; and so it will be found which way the turn of the scale will incline. [35]When have the inhabitants of the earth not sinned in thy sight? Or what nation has kept thy commandments so well? [36]Thou mayest indeed find individual men who have kept thy commandments, but nations thou wilt not find.[15]

It appears that these two observations about salvation among the Jews are mutually exclusive. However, from all I can gather, Jews were not as concerned with harmonization as some of us are. They were more content to let some loose ends dangle in their thought.[16] As E. P. Sanders astutely observes, "The Rabbis were not concerned with the internal systematic relationship of their statements."[17] Their concept of unconditional corporate election of all Jews was by far the more basic of the two thoughts. All the rest of their thoughts must be weighed in the light of that foundational thought.

The following lengthy passage from Charles Hodge's comments on Romans 3:3 clarifies this concept:

It is plain that the whole first part of this chapter is an answer to the objections of the Jews to the apostle's doctrine that they were exposed to condemnation. This is clear as to the first verse, and the fifth and those that follow it . . . . Their great objection to Paul's applying his general principles of justice to their case was that their situation was peculiar: "God has chosen us as his people in Abraham. If we retain our relation to him by circumcision and the observance of the law, we shall never be treated or condemned as the Gentiles." Traces of this opinion abound in the New Testament, and the Jewish writers openly avow it. "Think not," says the Baptist, "to say within yourselves, We have Abraham to our father," Matt. iii.9. "We be Abraham's seed," John 8:33. Comp. Rom. 2:17; 9:6; and other passages, in which Paul argues to prove that being the natural descendants of Abraham is not enough to secure the favour of God. That such was the doctrine of the Jews is shown by numerous passages from their writings. "If a Jew commit all manner of sins," says Abarbanel, "he is indeed of the number of sinning Israelites, and will be punished according to his sins; but he has, notwithstanding, a portion in eternal life." The same sentiment is expressed in the book Torath Adam, fol. 100, in nearly the same words, and the reasons assigned for it, "That all Israel has a portion in eternal life . . . ." Justin Martyr, as quoted by Grotiuson chap. ii.13, attributes this doctrine to the Jews of his day: "They suppose that to them universally, who are of the seed of Abraham, no matter how sinful and disobedient to God they may be, the eternal kingdom shall be given."[18]

Douglas J. Moo raises the question of whom the Israel is that God promises salvation. According to Moo, "the standard view among Paul's Jewish contemporaries was that this Israel was made up of all those physically descended from Jacob, the heir of Abraham and Isaac, who was himself named 'Israel.' Only those who had refused their inheritance by outright apostasy would be excluded from Israel to whom the promises belonged."[19]

This Jewish thinking was based on the promise of the eternal possession of the land to Abraham and his seed (Gen. 13:14-15 and 17:8). The eternal possession of the land meant, to them, the promise of eternal life in the next life. Since the Jews are the Covenant Seed (descendants, or offspring) of Abraham, they took this to mean that in the Abrahamic Covenant an unconditional promise of eternal life was given to them. Paul's suggestion that some of them were not saved ran counter to their understanding of the Abrahamic Covenant.

The Jews believed in the unconditional corporate election of all Jews based on the promises of the Abrahamic Covenant. In this case, corporate election means more than the election of a group of people who came to be known as Jews. It embraced each individual who descended from Abraham through Jacob. Hodge sees their interpretation of the Abrahamic Covenant as the foundation of their thinking in terms of the corporate salvation of all Jews. He explains:

It should be remembered that the principal ground on which the Jews expected acceptance with God, was the covenant which he had made with their father Abraham, in which he promised to be a God to him and to his seed after him. They understood this promise to secure salvation for all who retained their connection with Abraham, by the observance of the law and the rite of circumcision. They expected, therefore, to be regarded and treated not so much as individuals, each being dealt with according to his personal character, but as a community to whom salvation was secured by the promise made to Abraham.[20]

Having in mind the Jewish viewpoint of the unconditional corporate election of all Jews as the seed of Abraham, we can see why Paul's suggestion that many Jews were not saved (verses 1-3) would not be received by the Jews. The claim that only those Jews believing in Christ would be saved was totally unacceptable in their thinking. To them, it was an attack on the promise that God had made to Abraham. It was an attack on the veracity, righteousness, or justice of God.

Additional Information on Jewish Thought About Salvation

As we have seen, the prevailing thought among Jews in New Testament times appears to have been that all Jews were unconditionally saved. However, it does seem that there was some modification of opinion and some variety of views. I will call brief attention to this problem. The article "Resurrection" in *The Jewish Encyclopedia* gives us insight into Jewish thought:

It became a matter of dispute between the older school of the Shammites, represented by R. Eliezer, and the Hillelites, represented by R. Joshua, whether or not the righteous among the heathen have a share in the future world, the former interpreting the verse, "The wicked shall return to Sheol, even all the Gentiles that forget God" (Ps. ix. 18 [R. V. 17]), as condemning as wicked among the Jews and the Gentiles such as have forgotten God; the latter interpreting the verse as consigning to Sheol only such as have actually forgotten God (Tos Sanh. xiii. 2). The doctrine "All Israelites have a share in the world to come" (Sanh. xi. i), based upon Isa. ix. 21 (Hebr). "The people all of them righteous shall inherit the land," is therefore identical with the Pharisaic teachings as stated by Josephus (Ant. xviii. 1. § 3; "B. J." ii. 8 § 14), that the righteous will rise to share in the eternal bliss. It is as deniers of the fundamentals of religion that heathen, Samaritans, and heretics are excluded from future salvation (Tos. Sanh. xiii.; Pirke R. El. xxxviii.; Midr. The. xi. 5). Regarding plurality of opinions in favor of the salvation of righteous non-Jews, and the opinions those who adhere to the national view, see Zunz, "Z. G." pp. 371-389. Related to the older, exclusive view also is the idea that the Abrahamic covenant releases the Israelites from the fire of Gehenna (Gen. R. xlviii; Midr. The. vii. I; 'Er. 19a).[21]

Another factor to keep in mind while trying to understand Jewish thought is that it also appears that they held to a remote possibility of loss of salvation. While the quotation that I will give came from the eighteenth century, it probably represents the thinking of some in biblical days. "Rabbi Israel Baal Shem Tov, founder of Hasidism, is reported to have said: 'Every Jew is an organ of the Shekhinah. As long as the organ is joined to the body, however tenuously, there is hope; once it is cut off, all hope is lost.'"[22]

It appears that some thinking might have already existed before the time of Christ that might have been in conflict with the view that all Jews were saved. In 2 Esdras 7:47-48 the writer says:

> And now I see that the world to come will bring delight to few, but torments to many. For an evil heart has grown up in us, which has alienated us from God, and has brought us into corruption and the ways of death, and has shown us the paths of perdition and removed us far from life—and that not just a few of us but almost all who have been created. (See also 7:59-61 and 8:1-3.)

The Development of My Thinking on the Jewish Understanding of Salvation

I think it is incumbent upon me to address this problem, at least, briefly. My thinking on the way Jews looked at the basis for their salvation has gone through some changes over the years. For a while, I went along with the popular view that Jews believed in salvation by works. By the time I wrote my commentary on Romans, published in 1987, I had given considerable attention to the Abrahamic Covenant. In the light of Genesis 13:14-15 and 17:8, I could see why the Jews, as implied in Matthew 3:9

and John 8:33-39, believed that the Abrahamic Covenant promised them that they would have eternal life and the land of Canaan would be their eternal inheritance. In the study that I did for writing the commentary, the greatest help that I received came from Charles Hodge's comments in his *Commentary on the Epistle to the Romans*.

In 1970, I wrote a Th.M. thesis entitled "Jesus and the Pharisees" for Chicago Graduate School of Theology. That experience helped me to have a better understanding of Jewish thinking at the time of Jesus. The emphasis in that thesis was on Oral Tradition. In writing it, I became convinced that there was a considerable amount of misunderstanding about the Pharisees. The knowledge that I gained about the Pharisees has been useful to me as I have tried to understand their view of election or salvation, but I did not address that issue in the thesis. The conflict that Jesus had with the Pharisees dealt with the issue of *ethical legalism* rather than *soteriological legalism*.

The Pharisees correctly worked on the assumption that the whole of life should be lived out in submission to God. Their problem came from the conviction that this responsibility to God could be spelled out in minute detail in terms of laws. These laws were to be spelled out by the properly recognized Jewish authorities. This was passed along to the people in the form of Oral Tradition or Oral Law. It is referred to in the KJV as the Tradition of the Elders. The individual did not have the freedom to use on-the-spot judgment to go contrary to these laws. There was no room to use common sense and to be extemporaneous in showing mercy if it went contrary to the prescription of the Oral Tradition. (See Mt. 15:1–20 and Mk. 7:1–23.)

It is possible for a person to be an *ethical legalist* (relying heavily on laws to express moral and ethical responsibility), and not be a *soteriological legalist* (depending on obedience to laws as a way to be saved). A failure to make this distinction has contributed and continues to contribute to a lot of confusion. Just because a person has strict convictions and seeks to get other people to live by them does not necessarily mean that he or she believes in salvation by works (soteriological legalism).

I think that, beyond doubt, the prevailing opinion among the Jews of Paul's day was that in connection with the call and the covenant that God made with Abraham, He unconditionally promised salvation to all Jews. That does not mean that the rest of Jewish thought worked itself out logically in the same pattern that we might expect of a systematic theology today. It is our responsibility to recognize that the Jews did believe in the unconditional salvation of all Jews and then see, to the best of our ability, how the rest of the pieces of the puzzle fit together. These other pieces of the puzzle include statements made in the New Testament that seem to connect Jews to salvation by works and statements from Jewish writings that seem to imply that salvation is by works.

If, in our attempt to understand the Jewish view of salvation, we do not begin with the Jewish concept of a covenant relationship between God and Israel and how the Jews perceived that covenant relationship, we will be hopelessly confused. That covenant relationship was instituted by God when He established the covenant with Abraham and His seed. The Jews understood that they were the Covenant Seed of Abraham. Through the Abrahamic Covenant, God elected or chose Israel to be His people. This relationship was to be an eternal relationship. All Jews were considered saved. They believed in corporate salvation or corporate election. This election included each individual Jew, but Jews did not believe they were not chosen individually. Election applied to them as individuals because they were members of the group.

While the Jews believed in the unconditional election or salvation of all Jews, in the arena of life this presented them with real problems. What place does merit have in a person's relationship with God? What about the descendant of Abraham who becomes an apostate and turns against God and the Law of Moses? They did not want to ignore these problems. But they did not want to reject the conviction that all Jews are saved. If we start with what they say about works and merit, we will conclude that at least in some measure they thought that salvation is by works. If we take this approach, we will never understand the place that their concept of a covenant relationship with God had in their thinking. It seems that is where most people have started. With such an approach, it will be impossible to understand Romans 9.

It seems to me that if we get to the bottom of Jewish thinking it would be summed up like this: God unconditionally elected all Jews as a group. It is to be expected that individual Jews will manifest an interest in serving God. If they do not, it puzzles Jews in a way similar to the way it bothers us as Christians when other Christians do not take their relationship to God as seriously as we think they should. But the Jews assume that such people are in the covenant. Though they assume that these people are safely in the covenant, what they say may not always sound consistent with that conclusion. It may sound like that for an individual Jew to keep his place in the covenant he must maintain obedience. But at the same time, it seems that his place in the covenant is unconditionally secure. It seems that the more fundamental aspect of their thinking is that the covenant is unconditional.

It seems to me that the only way Jewish thinkers are, in any way, willing to alter the "all" in "all Jews are saved" is the elimination of those who are guilty of apostasy. Such cases would be rare. I have quoted from sources above that will support the fact that such thinking has existed in Jewish thought. It is not that Jews believed they must do something to be saved or remain saved. They believed that Jews are saved and will remain saved unless they commit apostasy. That there is such a thing as apostasy for Jews seemed to be a rather reluctant conclusion, but one that they could not dismiss.

Though it seems that apostasy would be the only way, in Jewish thinking, that a person would be eliminated from the blessings of the covenant, some things that Jewish thinkers said sound as if obedience to the covenant is required to remain in the covenant. That type of inconsistency prevailed in Jewish thought. I do not think that this means that they had no concern about the law of non-contradiction.

They lived knowing that, with the information available to them, they could not remove the apparent contradiction. I would say that a systematic harmony of the doctrines of a sovereign, holy, and loving God, and sin, guilt, grace, and forgiveness can be developed only in the light of the incarnation, atonement, and the resurrection of Christ. At best, Jewish theology without Jesus Christ would, of necessity, fall short of a harmonious, consistent systematic theology. This would be true of their theology before Jesus came. It would also continue to be true of their theology after the coming of Jesus if they leave Him out of their thinking.

If the position that I have described is the true understanding of the Jewish approach to salvation, what about the passages in the New Testament that would suggest that Jews had a problem with salvation by works? Before I respond, let me say again that the Jews were not as concerned as we are about bringing a systematic harmony to their thinking.

In trying to answer the question of why we get the impression in some places that the Jews believed in salvation by works, I would make the following observations. My first observation is that pastors and teachers face many problems in their personal encounters with people that are not found in scholarly treatments. For example, among those who believe that loss of salvation is possible, there are some who take the position that if a Christian commits one sin he is lost until he confesses that sin. Though a person may encounter that as he works with people, I doubt that there has ever been a scholarly treatment that set forth that view. Yet, it must be dealt with because there are people who think that way.

Paul was not just dealing with the members of the Sanhedrin. He was not just dealing with famous Rabbis. He was dealing with the Jews who attended the synagogue and wherever else he might meet them. I do not think it would have been uncommon for Jews to have referred to the corporate superiority of the Jews to the Gentiles. It would not be hard at all to see how the question of works could get into the picture. When Paul drew the discussion away from corporate salvation to individual salvation, it is not hard to see how particular individuals would defend themselves on the grounds of moral superiority—particularly as compared with Gentiles.

E. P. Sanders's View of the Jewish Understanding of Salvation

My introduction to Sanders came after most of my thinking had been developed. Sanders has made a significant contribution to our understanding of the thinking of the Jews of Paul's time. His conclusions have been shocking to many, and have given rise to a lot of controversy. Sanders argues that the pattern of the Jewish approach to salvation starts with God's election of Israel and Israel's acceptance of that election. After that election, God commanded Israel to obey His laws, promising to reward obedience and punish disobedience. If man fails to obey God's commands, he can repent and have his sins atoned for. "As long as he maintains his desire to stay in the covenant, he has a share in God's covenantal promises, including life in the world to come. The intention and effort to be obedient constitute the condition for remaining in the covenant, but they do not earn it."[23]

Sanders chooses to call his view "covenantal nomism." He defines this phrase as "the view that one's place in God's plan is established on the basis of the covenant and that requires as the proper response of man his obedience to its commandments, while providing a means of atonement for transgression.[24] In another place, he says:

> The all-pervasive view is this: all Israelites have a share in the world to come unless they renounce it by renouncing God and his covenant. All sins, no matter of what gravity, which are committed within the covenant, may be forgiven as long as a man indicates his basic intention to keep the covenant by atoning, especially by repenting of transgression.[25]

Sanders is sharply critical of the fact that so many Christians have understood the Jews of New Testament times to be obsessed with a rigid, legalistic approach to salvation.[26]

An Assessment of Sanders's View

It seems to me, as I have emphasized up to this point, that the Jews of Jesus and Paul's day worked on the assumption that all Jews were saved. They started in life as being one of God's chosen, covenant people. The only thing that could change that would be an act of outright apostasy. If they worked on that assumption, they had to believe in unconditional salvation. If that is true, they did not believe in salvation by works. Sanders has a right to be perturbed about this.

I agree with Sanders that in making a study of Jewish thought we must start with their concept of their covenant relationship with God. It is hopeless to understand Jewish thought any other way. Whatever they say about works and merit must always be understood in that light. At least, we should attempt to understand it in that light. We cannot force an absolute harmony on Jewish thought. We may say that some of their statements sound like works salvation. But when understood in the context of an unconditional covenant, we must back off of the charge.

When Sanders says, "The intention and effort to be obedient constitute the *condition for remaining in the covenant*, but they do not *earn it*," he is struggling with trying to be fair and as near as possible accurate in describing Jewish thought. Even that must be understood in the context of the conviction that all Israel will be saved. The idea that intention and effort constitute a condition for remaining in the covenant, but do not earn remaining in the covenant, may sound contradictory to us. But the Jews chose to live with such seeming conflict of ideas.

It seems to me that the bottom line is that the Jews did not exactly look at obedience as a condition for remaining in the covenant. They viewed that as an unconditional blessing of God. They did not have to do anything to stay in the covenant. But if they renounced God and Judaism, they would lose their place in the covenant. At the same time they would say things that made it look as if they did believe that obedience was a condition of remaining in the covenant.

The problem with the Jews in the New Testament was not that they thought works saved them. It was that they did not need to be saved, each on an individual basis, but that they were saved collectively and corporately. Paul's aim is to get them to see that this was a mistaken idea. They needed to be saved as individuals, and that was on the condition of faith in Jesus as the Messiah.

A Challenge

Extensive research and writing needs to be done on the Jewish concept of the unconditional salvation for all Jews, the possibility of apostasy, the question of salvation by works, the question of whether few or many will be saved, and the Jewish thinking about the salvation of Gentiles, and how all of this affects our interpretation of the Gospels and the rest of the New Testament.

Paul's Burden in the Book of Romans

While Paul was the Apostle to the Gentiles, he had a heavy burden for the Jews who were unsaved. I am convinced that the *burden of Paul in the Book of Romans was his deep concern that so many of his own kinsmen, the Jews, were not saved.* While the most intense statement of the burden is found in 9:3, Paul's burden for the Jews comes across before we get to chapter 9.

Paul's Appeal to the Jews to Get Them to See That They Were Under the Wrath of God

The evidence of Paul's burden for the Jews comes early in the book. In showing that the Gentiles who had only general revelation were lost in 1:19-32, Paul took only 14 verses to make his case. In trying to show the Jews that they were lost in 2:1–3:8, he took 37 verses.

That should get our attention. We consider it much harder to show people that the heathen who have only general revelation are lost than we do to show that those who have been confronted with special revelation are lost apart from Jesus Christ. It was harder for Paul to show the Jews, who had received special revelation, that they were lost than it was for him to show the Gentiles, who had only general revelation.

Paul was intensely interested in getting the Jews to see that the only way to be saved was by Jesus Christ on the condition of faith alone. This was true of both Jews and Gentiles. Paul's concern for the Jews could not be dealt with in isolation from the fact that a host of Gentiles were being saved while many Jews, according to Christian thought, were lost. If he was going to make any headway with his desire to reach Jews, he had to give the Jews an explanation of why so many Gentiles were being saved, while so many Jews were lost.

Paul's Appeal to the Abrahamic Covenant

The appeal to Abraham and the Abrahamic Covenant in Romans 4 had a threefold purpose: (1) To show that in the covenant that God made with Abraham, faith and faith alone was the condition of justification. (2) To show that Gentiles who have faith in Christ are also justified by faith alone. (3) To show that it was God's plan in the Abrahamic Covenant for Gentiles who believe to become Abraham's seed and thus heirs with him and the Jewish believers.

Paul's Answer to the Jewish Concern About the Law

The major concern of Romans 7:7-25 was to deal with Jewish concerns. In verse 7, Paul asks the question, "Is the law sin?" Why would Paul raise the question, "Is the law sin?" Because the emphasis up to this point is on what the law cannot do. The law cannot justify (3:20). The law works wrath (4:15). The law tended to make sin abound (5:20). To be out from under the law was supposed to be a plus factor so far as righteous living was concerned (6:14 and 7:6). The law stirred the passions of sins in us into activity (7:5).

We need to keep reminding ourselves how important the law was to the Jewish people of that day, especially in Phariseeism. Law to them was supreme. Even a converted Jew would have difficulty understanding the removal of law from the center of the picture. It is not hard at all to see why a Jew would raise the question, and why he would need an answer.[27]

The Depth of Paul's Burden for the Jews

In chapter 8, Paul speaks of the glorious blessings of the one who has placed his faith in Jesus Christ. Chapter 8 ended on a triumphant note. While in this emotion-filled state, Paul suddenly thought of his kinsmen—the Jews. When he did, the deep compassion and concern which he had for his kinsmen was activated within him. It is out of this deep concern that he speaks. In anguish of heart he said, "For I could wish that I myself were accursed, *separated* from Christ for the sake of my brethren, my kinsmen according to the flesh" (Rom. 9:3, NASB).[28]

In this state of deep concern, Paul reviews the unique position of Israel in the history of redemption. They were uniquely blessed. All of the redemptive covenants were made with Abraham and the Covenant Seed. The redemptive promises were made to them. It was to Israel that the Messianic prophecies were given. The Gentile believers were indebted to the Jews. It was through Israel that God gave the world, as it comes to us from Hebrew, the "Messiah," and as it comes to us from Greek, the "Christ" (9:4-5).

Paul's Appeal to the Jews to Convince Them of the Fallacy of Their Reasoning

Against the background of thought that God had unconditionally promised eternal life to all Jews, Paul said, "But *it is* not as though the Word of God has failed" (9:6, NASB). If God had unconditionally promised eternal life to all Jews through the Abrahamic Covenant, His promise would have failed if large numbers of Jews, as Paul taught, were unsaved. On the other hand, as John Piper explains, "If Paul can show that God's ultimate 'purpose according to election' never included the salvation of every individual Israelite, then the situation described in Rom. 9:1-5 would not so easily jeopardize God's reliability."[29]

Jewish thought assumed that if masses of Jews were unsaved, that would mean that God's promise had failed. That would mean that God would be unrighteous or unjust because He would be failing to live up to His promise of eternal life to all Jews, as it was given in the Abrahamic Covenant. With great concern, Paul attempted to show the Jews that God's promise had not failed. He revealed that God had never promised to save all Jews.

Romans 9:6

Paul's first step in trying to convince the Jews that God had not promised salvation to all Jews was to say, "For they are not all Israel who are descended from Israel" (9:6, NASB). In this verse, Paul is saying that the name "Israel" has a broad and a narrow use. In the broad use, it refers to all of those who have descended from Abraham through Jacob. These are the Covenant Seed of Abraham. It is true that the promises of the Abrahamic Covenant were made to all of those who descended from Abraham through Jacob. But the question is: *Does this mean that all are saved?*

Paul is saying we are not to understand that all who have descended from Abraham through Jacob are saved. This suggests that there is a second use of the name "Israel." This use of the name "Israel" refers to those who descended from Abraham through Jacob who will actually be the beneficiaries of the promises of the Abrahamic Covenant. According to Paul, these are the ones who believe in Jesus Christ for salvation. These are "True Israel."

We could illustrate Paul's point this way. We could say that all who descended from Abraham through Jacob are "A." Those who descended from Abraham through Jacob and are also the ones who will actually be the beneficiaries of the promises of the Abrahamic Covenant are "B." The diagram will illustrate this for us:

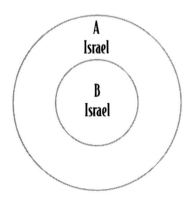

"A" represents all of the Covenant Seed who descended from Abraham through Jacob. "B" represents those who are the part of the Covenant Seed who will actually receive the eschatological promises made in the Abrahamic Covenant. All "B" are "A," but not all "A" are "B." In Jewish thought all "A" would be "B." In their thinking "A" and "B" would be coextensive. Paul's aim in Romans 9 is to show the Jews that such thinking is wrong. If he can get them to see that, it will greatly increase the possibility that they will place their faith in Jesus as the true Messiah and Lord and Savior.

Romans 9:7-13

It takes more than a mere statement on Paul's part to convince the Jew. So what follows is designed to get the Jew to come to an understanding of the truth that God did not unconditionally promise eternal life to all who descended from Abraham through Jacob.

The basis for the Jewish misunderstanding was that in Genesis 13:14-15 and 17:8, the everlasting promise of the land, which implies resurrection and eternal life, was offered to the seed of Abraham. No mention is made of the fact that not all of the seed (offspring or descendants) of Abraham would be saved. However, Paul is going to show that even the Jews do not believe in the unconditional promise of eternal life to *all of the descendants of Abraham.*

In verse 7, Paul observes, "Nor are they all children because they are descendants, but: 'THROUGH ISAAC YOUR DESCENDANTS WILL BE NAMED'" (NASB). The Jews understood well that though Ishmael and the descendants of Abraham through his children by Keturah were *Abraham's descendants,* they were not considered a part of *the Covenant Seed of Abraham.* They were also well aware that not even all of *the descendants of Isaac* were a part of this Covenant Seed. They understood that the descendants of Isaac through Jacob *were* the Covenant Seed of Abraham, while the descendants of Isaac through Esau *were not* the Covenant Seed of Abraham.

The Jews recognized that though the descendants of Ishmael and Esau were the seed (descendants) of Abraham, they were not the Covenant Seed of Abraham. This meant that the Jews were already admitting that the blessings promised in Genesis 13:14-15 and 17:8 did not apply to all of the descendants of Abraham. This being true, there was nothing inherent in the promise made to Abraham that required that all who made up the Covenant Seed of Abraham would be saved. This was the point that Paul was calling to their attention in verses 7-12.

The language of Genesis 13:14-15 and 17:8 did not spell out the limitation of whom among the descendants of Abraham would make up the Covenant Seed of Abraham. That clarification came later in the Book of Genesis (21:12 and 25:23). These verses did not spell out who would be or who would not be the ones who would actually inherit the eschatological promise of eternal life. That was the clarification that Paul was desperately trying to make.

If there is no contradiction between the promise made in Genesis 13:14-15 and 17:8 and the limitation of the Covenant Seed of Abraham to those who descended from Isaac through Jacob, then there is no contradiction between Genesis 13:14-15 and 17:8 and a further limitation of Israel to a true Israel that is made up of believers only.

Romans 9:10-13

Since these verses have been a mainstay of Calvinism, I will give special attention to them. It is important to observe that these verses are in a context that has as its purpose to show that there is no reason to believe that all of the Covenant Seed of Abraham (those who descended from Abraham through Jacob) are saved. This means that Paul uses verses 10-12 to show that not all of the natural descendants of Abraham were saved. If this consideration of the context is not taken into account, the meaning of these verses will be missed.

Verses 10-13 are of particular importance because they point out that even though God had said, "THROUGH ISAAC YOUR DESCENDANTS WILL BE NAMED" (verse 7, NASB), not even all of Isaac's descendants made up the Covenant Seed of Abraham. In view of their importance, I will quote these verses 10-13:

> And not only this, but there was Rebekah also, when she had conceived twins by one man, our father Isaac; for though the twins were not yet born, and had not done anything good or bad, so that God's purpose according to His choice [election] would stand, not because of works but because of Him who calls, it was said to her, "THE OLDER WILL SERVE THE YOUNGER." Just as it is written, "JACOB I LOVED, BUT ESAU I HATED" (NASB).

117

The words "And not only this" in verse 10 tell us that Paul is developing the same line of thought that he had been in verses 7-9. He had shown them that in selecting the Covenant Seed of Abraham, God had chosen Isaac rather than Ishmael. He had one more step to make. He showed that God chose Jacob rather than Esau. Abraham was the first patriarch, Isaac was the second patriarch, and Jacob was chosen as the third patriarch. The Covenant Seed would be called through Jacob, the third patriarch. This final limitation of who would make up the Covenant Seed of Abraham was made. All of the descendants of Jacob are the Covenant Seed of Abraham. But this does not mean that all of the descendants of Jacob are saved. If God could determine that the descendants of Ishmael and Esau would not make up the Covenant Seed of Abraham, He could also determine that not all of the Covenant Seed of Abraham through Jacob would be saved. That is Paul's case with the Jews. Paul was not debating this part just to win a debate. He was trying to win people—his kinsmen according to the flesh.

Before saying more about my thinking regarding verses 10-13, I will examine John Piper's view of verses 6-13.

John Piper's Approach to Romans 9:6-13

I am choosing Piper's treatment to deal with because I think he has given the most thorough and most able treatment of this passage from the side of unconditional election. To get Piper's thinking before us, I will quote his own summary of his understanding of what Paul was trying to accomplish in Romans 9:1-13. He explains:

> The basic problem described in 9:1-5 is that many Israelites, to whom, as a nation, saving promises had been made, are now accursed and cut off from Christ (9:1-3). The condemnation of so many Israelites to eternal destruction raises the question whether God's word has fallen. Paul denies it (9:6a) and defends his denial in 9:6b-13. In defense of God's faithfulness to his word, in spite of many Israelites being accursed, Paul argues that God's "purpose" from the beginning of Israel's history was a

purpose "according to election" (9:11), that is, a purpose not to save every individual Israelite, as though descent from Abraham guaranteed that one would be a child of God, but rather a purpose to "call" a true Israel (9:6b) into being by choosing some Israelites and not others "before they were born or had done anything good or evil" (9:11). It is this Israel for whom the promises are valid. The unconditional election of Isaac and Jacob over Ishmael and Esau (whether to eternal destinies or only to historical roles) reveals the *principle of God's freedom in election* which is the ultimate explanation why many of Paul's kinsmen according to the flesh are accursed and cut off from Christ. As he says in Romans 11:7, "the elect obtained it [salvation], but the rest were hardened." For this reason it cannot be said that God's expressed purpose has fallen (9:6a).[30]

Piper, more than anyone else I have read, emphasizes that Paul is dealing with the Jewish thinking that, by being a member of the Covenant Seed of Abraham through Jacob, Jews were guaranteed the unconditional promise of eternal life. If a person does not keep this in mind when he studies Romans 9, he will not be able to get to the heart of what Paul is arguing in this chapter.

In the summary of Paul's thought in Romans 9:1-13 given above, it is obvious that Piper thinks the answer is found in the view that God unconditionally elects individuals for salvation. The Jews believed in unconditional election too. The difference was that the Jews believed in the unconditional election for salvation of all of the Covenant Seed of Abraham through Jacob. This election was corporate election, but it guaranteed the salvation of each individual member of the Covenant Seed of Abraham.

This meant there was a serious conflict, up front, with Paul and the Jews. The Jews thought all Jews were saved. Paul thought that a large portion of the Jews were lost. The only ones who were saved were those who believed in Jesus as their Messiah, Savior, and Lord. Paul also thought that was the only way those who were lost could be saved.

According to Piper, Paul's approach to showing the Jews that not all Jews were saved was to show them that only those who are unconditionally elected as individuals are saved. Paul did this by showing that God unconditionally chose Isaac rather than Ishmael and Jacob rather than Esau. The major part of Piper's argument that Paul was advocating unconditional individual election is based on the choice of Jacob rather than Esau. On this subject Piper comments:

> Paul's purpose in referring to God's choice of Jacob over Esau is to show that there is no way to evade the implications of God's unconditional election here. Unlike Isaac and Ishmael, Jacob and Esau had the same parents who were both Jews ("From *one* man Rebecca became pregnant" (Rom. 9:10c). Also unlike Isaac and Ishmael, when the determining promise was made concerning Jacob and Esau (Rom. 9:12c = Gen. 25:23), both were yet unborn and had done nothing good or evil (Rom. 9:11ab). Moreover they were twins in the same womb at the same time, and by all human standards, the elder Esau should have received the blessing of headship over his brother. Here there are no loopholes. God's choice of Jacob over Esau cannot be due to any human distinctive possessed by birth (like Jewishness) or action (like righteousness). It is based solely on God's own free and sovereign choice.[31]

Having concluded that 9:12 settled in no uncertain terms that God chooses individuals by an unconditional election, Piper considers that he has shown the fallacy of Jewish thinking that all Jews were guaranteed salvation simply by being the Covenant Seed of Abraham through Jacob. Verse 12, in Piper's thinking, supports the unconditional election of Jacob and the unconditional rejection of Esau. He supposes that this would have been met with an objection from the Jews. He supposes that the Jews would have thought that the unconditional election of Jacob and the unconditional rejection of Esau would have shown God to be unjust. This would particularly be true of the unconditional rejection of Esau. This understanding of what Paul had said up through verse 13 sets the stage for Piper's understanding of the rhetorical question that Paul raises in verse 14.

An Evaluation of Piper's View

I have pointed out above that Piper understands the Jewish problem. The question is: Does he have the right answer? He finds the answer in the unconditional election of each individual for salvation and the unconditional rejection of others. While he thinks that the choice of Isaac over Ishmael illustrates unconditional election, he thinks that the wording of verses 11 and 12 in setting forth the choice of Jacob and the rejection of Esau makes unconditional election irrefutable.

I do not think that he has made his case for unconditional election. To support my position, I give the following reasons:

First, even if verse 11 were seen as dealing with election for salvation, the case is still not decided for unconditional election. There is certainly no problem with the election occurring before birth. I think it does. Individual conditional election by God in eternity past does not involve a logical contradiction.

Second, to say that election is not being based on works presents no problem for conditional election. Conditional election does not mean election based on works. I think that, in chapter 6, I have made it clear beyond question that nothing the Christian ever does is considered a part of the payment for his justification.[32] If what I have said (in points one and two) is true, even if these verses speak of individual election, there is no conflict between verses 11 and 12 and conditional election.

Third, the Calvinist would be wrong to claim that my view makes faith a human work and thus is to be considered as merit. This is true for two reasons: (1) Paul specifically contrasts faith with works in Romans 4:1-8. (2) Faith is a human act in both Calvinism and Arminianism. Faith is synergistic in both Calvinism and Arminianism.[33] If the exercise of saving faith is a human work and thus must be considered as merit for salvation, both Calvinism and Arminianism would be indicted. In both cases, the human personality exercises faith by divine aid. In Calvinism, the divine aid is regeneration by the Holy Spirit. In Arminianism, the divine aid is the drawing and assisting power of the Holy Spirit.

Conclusions Established by This Study of Romans 9:6-13

There are two things about this passage that seem to me to be unquestionably clear: First, Paul was showing that not all of the descendants of Abraham were a part of the Covenant Seed. He gives two choices that God made that confirmed this observation: (1) Isaac was chosen as the one through whom the Covenant Seed would descend, while Ishmael was set aside. (2) Jacob was chosen as the one through whom the Covenant Seed would descend, while Esau was set aside. The Jews readily accepted these conclusions. These observations make it unquestionably clear that no case, based on the Abrahamic Covenant, can be made for the viewpoint that every individual member of the Covenant Seed is saved. Second, this observation meant that no case could be made for the conclusion that because the Jews were the seed of Abraham all were given an unconditional promise of eternal life.

Paul's point was simply this. If there can be a *broad* and a *narrow* use of the expression "the seed of Abraham," there is no reason to reject the idea that in a similar way there can be a broad and a narrow use of the name Israel.

It must be remembered that the Jewish problem grew out of the significance that they gave to the claim that they were the seed of Abraham rather than that they were the descendants of Jacob (Mt. 3:9 and Jn. 8:33-40). Why? Because it was to the seed of Abraham that promises were made (Gen. 13:14-15 and 17:8).

I think we can safely conclude that the election referred to in verse 11 is not Jacob's election to salvation. My reason for saying so is not that I could not be comfortable with the idea that verse 11 could be speaking about election for salvation. Rather, it is because the context will not support it. I have shown that above.

What, then, is the bearing of verses 6-13 on the subject of election? It is simply this: The Jewish concept of *unconditional personal election* of all Jews as the Covenant Seed of Abraham *must be discarded.* That means that, so far as Israel is concerned, election must shift from the *corporate election* of all Jews to *individual election* or salvation for Jews.

Up to this point in the passage, the question of conditional or unconditional election has not been decided.

It is my understanding that, up through verse 13, Paul argued that the choices of Isaac rather than Ishmael and of Jacob rather than Esau should help the Jews see that they are not to interpret the promise of eternal life given in Genesis 13:14-15 and 17:8 to guarantee the salvation of every individual Jew. Paul feels that he has adequately dealt with this concern. So, in verse 14, Paul gets to the heart of the matter, because this would affect the righteousness or justice of God.

The Question Concerning God's Justice in Verse 14

In verse 14 Paul says, "What shall we say then? There is no injustice with God, is there? May it never be!" (NASB).

My Interpretation of Romans 9:14

As we continue our interpretation of Romans 9, it is important that we keep in mind that Paul is dealing with Jewish concern. He is striving with his whole being to get them to see that believing and trusting in Jesus as Messiah, Lord, and Savior is the only way for them as individuals to be saved. No one ever put his whole being into anything more than Paul did in this chapter.

Paul is not trying to settle a Calvinist-Arminian debate on election. What he says may make a contribution to the question of whether election is conditional or unconditional, but that is not the aim and burden of Paul's heart in this chapter.

It is important we realize that in this verse Paul is harking back to verse 6 where he said, "But it is not as though the word of God has failed" (NASB). If God had promised the salvation of all the Jews as the Covenant Seed of Abraham, God would have failed if all Jews had not been saved. If God had failed to keep His promise, He would have been unrighteous or unjust. That cannot be!

Paul has shown that there is no basis for the idea that all Jews, as the Covenant Seed of Abraham, are saved. God has never made such a promise. Therefore, He cannot be charged with being unrighteous by not bringing it to pass.

Calvinism and Romans 9:14

Those who believe in unconditional election take this verse to be dealing with an objection to the unconditional election of Jacob and the reprobation of Esau with the emphasis being on the suggestion that God was unjust in the way He treated Esau. (See earlier quotations from Haldane, Harrison, Plumer, and Shedd.) The question is: Does this view fit the context?

First, let me say that I have already shown that Paul did not settle whether individual election for salvation was conditional or unconditional in verses 6-13. If that is true, Paul could not be dealing with objections to unconditional election of individuals in verse 14.

Piper, as I said above, has a good grasp on the fact that Paul is dealing with a Jewish concern. Whose concern is Paul dealing with in verse 14? Let me quote a statement from Piper. He explains, "When Paul said that God chose to bless Jacob over Esau apart from any basis in their actions but simply on the basis of his choice (*ek tou kalountos*, Rom. 9:12), his opponent objected that this would call God's righteousness into question (9:14)."[34]

The opponent to which Piper refers would have been a Jew. In Piper's view, in answering the Jew, Paul would have explained that the Jews were mistaken in their thinking that all Jews were saved. In God's choice of Jacob over Esau, God was saying that election was on an individual basis and thus was not corporate election. Also, in his choice of Jacob over Esau before they were born and before they had done anything either good or bad, God was saying that the choice was unconditional. The concern of the Jewish opponent was supposed to be that it was unrighteous or unjust for God to accept Jacob unconditionally and to reject Esau unconditionally. Special concern was supposed to be on the rejection of Esau.

I would make four observations: First, the Jews had no difficulty with unconditional election as such. They believed in their own unconditional election. Second, there is no evidence that the Jews had any difficulty with the rejection of Ishmael and Esau. This is true whether the concern was with the unconditional election of the individual for salvation, or with the exclusion of Ishmael, Esau, and their descendants from the Covenant Seed of Abraham. Third, the Calvinistic interpretation of verse 14 is based on a Jewish concern that the Jews did not have. Fourth, Paul's concern at the beginning of the chapter was to get the Jews to see that God had not promised salvation to all Jews. His burden was to get them to see that the only way a Jew could be saved would be for him or her to have faith in Jesus as the Messiah, Savior, and Lord. It would have brought no relief to Paul for him to be able to get the Jews to exchange belief in unconditional election for all Jews for a view that: (1) God had unconditionally elected certain Jews, and (2) God had unconditionally chosen the others for eternal damnation.

The Jewish Conclusion

The only trouble the Jews of Paul's day had with unconditional election was that, according to Paul, God had not unconditionally elected all Jews as they had thought. If God did unconditionally elect all Jews and Christianity denied that this was the case, Christ and Christianity would be written off without further investigation. The concern that the unbelieving Jew would have with God's righteousness or justice was that God's failure to follow through with the unconditional election of all Jews would mean that God had not kept His Word. For God to fail to keep His Word would mean that He would be unrighteous or unjust. Such a conclusion was unthinkable.

The only hope of getting Jews to acknowledge Jesus as the Messiah must be connected with evidence that God had never said that all Jews were unconditionally elected. If they could see this, they could look at the question of their own salvation in the light of the reality that not all Jews are saved. If, in fact, God never said that all Jews would be saved, Christ and Christianity should not be written off without a hearing. Paul had, from a brief look at their patriarchal history, shown them that no case could be built for the idea that God had unconditionally chosen all of them for personal salvation.

M. R. Vincent manifested good insight into Paul's question in verse 14 when he said:

> If it be asked therefore, "Is there unrighteousness with God? Does God contradict Himself in His rejection of unbelieving Israel?—it must be answered, "No!" If there was no unrighteousness in the exclusion of Ishmael and Edom from the temporal privileges of the chosen people, there is none in the exclusion of the persistently rebellious Israelites from the higher privileges of the kingdom of heaven. If not all the physical descendants of Abraham and Isaac can claim their father's name and rights, it follows that God's promise is not violated in excluding from His kingdom a portion of the descendants of Jacob. Descent cannot be pleaded against God's right to exclude, since He has already excluded from the messianic line without regard to descent. This choice Israel approved and cannot, therefore, repudiate it when the same choice and exclusion are applied to unbelieving Israel.[35]

Paul had shown that no case could be built for the idea that God was unrighteous in not saving every Jew, because He had never made such a promise. He had done this by reviewing their patriarchal history with them. He will now proceed in his appeal to "his kinsmen according to the flesh" by showing that election is individual, not corporate. If Paul can get the Jews to see that election is individual instead of corporate, it will make it much easier for him to help individual Jews to see that the only way to be saved is by faith in Jesus as the Messiah, Savior, and Lord.

Paul's Appeal to the Jews to See That Election Is Individual, Not Corporate

I do not think that verses 6-13 deal with individual election; neither do they settle the question of whether election is conditional or unconditional. The way had been prepared for the focus to change beginning in verse 15.

Before Paul finishes this chapter, he will deal with both the question of individual election and the question of whether election is conditional or unconditional. He will show that election is of individuals and that it is conditional. Again, it is important to keep in mind that Paul is dealing with a question of Jewish concern, not a Calvinist-Arminian debate. Since he deals with universal truth, we will find that what he says is helpful in dealing with the questions raised by Calvinists and Arminians.

Romans 9:15 and Individual Election

Since verse 15 is introduced by "for," we naturally expect a reason or proof to follow. However, such is not the case here. It is obvious that what follows does not take on the form of an argument defending the righteousness (or justice) of God in not saving all Jews. As Lenski explains, "The *gar* is not to prove the statement that there is no justice [The author obviously meant "injustice."] on the part of God in these promises; for what follows is not proof . . . . *Gar* is at times used simply to confirm; it does so here: 'yea.'"[36] The question of whether God could be unrighteous (or unjust) was not debatable between Paul and the Jew. One would reject such an implication as quickly as the other. The difference came in applying the truth of the righteousness of God to the question of whether all Jews were saved.

What follows in verse 15 is not evidence that God is not unrighteous. That was settled by an emphatic denial. What follows is an illustration from Scripture of how the action of God, who can do no wrong, supports the principle that some, but not all, from among Israel are chosen for salvation. That Paul is appealing to the authority of Scripture rather than building an argument in verse 15 finds broad agreement.[37]

In the quotation from Exodus 33:19, God said to Moses, "I WILL HAVE MERCY ON WHOM I HAVE MERCY, AND I WILL HAVE COMPASSION ON WHOM I HAVE COMPASSION" (NASB). My first observation is that the Greek for "whom" (*hon an*) is singular. This places the emphasis on the choice of the individual rather than on corporate election, as the case would be if God had chosen to save all of the Covenant Seed of Abraham. As Picirilli explains, "Even in the wilderness, when we might think all the nation was automatically entitled to His favor, He said: 'I will show mercy on whom I will show mercy.'" God wanted to establish clearly that "neither Moses nor Israel had any special claims on Him that took away His sovereign right to act as He chose. Nor will He show mercy to all of them just because they were Israelites in the flesh."[38]

As it relates to Paul's treatment of individuals in Romans 9:15-21, Thomas R. Schreiner calls attention to the use of the singular in these verses. He explains that *hon*, the word for *whom*, is singular. Thus, the passage is speaking of "specific individuals upon whom God has mercy." Schreiner also notes that the singular occurs "in the reference that Paul draws from Romans 9:15, in 9:16. God's mercy does not depend on 'the one who wills, nor the one who runs.' The conclusion to all of 9:14-17 in 9:18 utilizes the singular once again: 'God has mercy on whom he wants to have mercy, and he hardens whom he wants to harden.'" Paul continues this thought in Romans 9:19 and 21: "'Who (*tis*) resists his will?' [9:19.] And Paul uses the singular when he speaks of one vessel being made for honor and another for dishonor (9:21)."[39] This militates against exegetes who argue that Paul is using corporate rather than individual language to speak about election in Romans 9.

I strongly agree with Schreiner that the election in these verses is speaking of individual election. I agree with all that he says in the above quotation, yet I do not join him on unconditional election. However, that question is not settled up to this point in the chapter. It will not be settled until we get to verses 30-33.

ROMANS 9:15 AND WHETHER ELECTION IS CONDITIONAL OR UNCONDITIONAL

Some take the assertion of verse 15 that God shows mercy and compassion to whomever He chooses as proof of unconditional election. It seems to me to be involved in the very concept of God that He would be the one who decides who will be saved and who will not be saved.

However, I do not believe that such an observation decides on the side of unconditional election.

In Jeremiah 18:1-4, Jeremiah observed the work of the potter. The potter had control over the clay to make it into a vessel as it seemed good to the potter to do so. After he made this observation, God said, "'Can I not, O house of Israel, deal with you as this potter does?' declares the LORD. 'Behold, like the clay in the potter's hand, so are you in My hand, O house of Israel'" (18:6, NASB). God was saying to Israel, "You are in my hands. I can do with you what I choose." The exercise of this right on the part of God did not mean that He would not take into consideration anything done by Israel in deciding what He would do with Israel. That He would take Israel's action into account in deciding what to do with Israel is clear in the context of Jeremiah 18:6; see verses 7-10.

It should be obvious from Jeremiah 18:1-10 that the divine prerogative to exercise His right to do as He chooses with people does not mean that His decisions must always be unconditional choices. When we read that God will do as He chooses, it will help if we ask a simple question: What does God choose to do? When God told Jeremiah that He could do with Israel what He chose just as the potter could with the clay, He followed that observation by telling them what He wanted to do.

When we read in Romans 9:15 that God will have mercy and compassion on whomever He wills, it behooves us to ask: On whom does God will to show mercy and compassion? Once it is decided that the mercy and compassion under consideration is that shown in salvation, the answer is easy.

We certainly do not have to list an array of references from the New Testament in order to identify those to whom God wishes to give the mercy of salvation. Consider, for example, the answer given by Paul and Silas to the question: "Sirs, what must I do to be saved?" So they said, "Believe on the Lord Jesus Christ, and you will be saved, you and your household" (Acts 16:30-31).

God is choosing whom He wills when He chooses to show His mercy in salvation toward the one who believes in Jesus as his or her Lord and Savior. Such decision can in no way be viewed as a decision that God is forced to make. The whole idea of salvation was God's idea from the outset. He could have chosen to have left the whole human race in sin without offering salvation. Rather, He planned to provide and offer salvation to lost mankind long before (in eternity past) man felt the pangs of being lost. It was not even in response to man's pleading (much less his demanding) that God chose to offer redemption.

The whole plan of salvation from beginning to end is the work and plan of God. God is in charge. When salvation is offered on the condition of faith in Christ, that in no way weakens the words, "I WILL HAVE MERCY ON WHOM I HAVE MERCY, AND I WILL HAVE COMPASSION ON WHOM I HAVE COMPASSION" (NASB). God's sovereignty is fully in control in this view. I have given extensive attention in the previous chapter to the viewpoint that God is free to exercise His will and that He does it according to the influence and response model.

THE QUESTION OF WORKS

Paul explains, "So then it does not depend on the man who wills or the man who runs, but on God who has mercy" (verse 16, NASB). In order to see the meaning of this verse, we must see what the converse would be. What would it mean if it were of him that wills and runs rather than of God who shows mercy? It would mean that a person would merit or earn salvation. It would mean that his merit would obligate God to save him.

Such a concept is foreign to all Christianity stands for. Man was shut off from God by his own sin. God was under no obligation to save him or even provide a way of salvation. It was out of God's love that He sent the Holy Spirit to woo us to Christ. It was out of God's love that He has commissioned believers to tell unbelievers about Christ. God has offered salvation on the condition of faith. We must distinguish between the "condition" and the "ground" of salvation. Salvation is *grounded* solely in the death and righteousness of Christ provided by atonement (as indicated in the satisfaction view of the atonement) and imputed to the believer's account in justification. It is *conditioned* on the response of faith in Christ alone.

God has taken the initiative in providing what man needs for salvation. He has set the condition for salvation. He sends the messenger with the gospel. He woos through the Holy Spirit. The personal response of faith as the condition for salvation can in no way be considered in conflict with or in violation of "So then it does not depend on the man . . . who runs, but on God who has mercy."

Romans 9:16 and Whether Election Is Conditional or Unconditional

Those who believe in unconditional election seem to be quite certain that this verse strikes a deathblow to conditional election. Piper sees a parallel between the "willing" and the "running" and "working" of Philippians 2:13. He explains that divine mercy "determines man's willing and running." Since these words refer not to evil works but to the "obedience of faith," Piper argues, Romans 9:16 "cannot be limited to only some kinds of willing and running. For these reasons Rom. 9:16 should be construed so as to sweep away forever the thought that over against God there is any such thing as human self-determination in Pauline anthropology."[40]

I think the real question that Piper needs to face is: How is he using the expression "self-determination"? If he means that man's action is not the *cause* or *ground* of his salvation, I could not agree more. On the other hand, if he means that man's action in believing cannot be a deciding factor in God's bestowal of salvation on the one who believes and the withholding of salvation from the one who does not believe, I cannot agree. Such a view is in conflict with the obvious and direct teaching of Scripture (Jn. 3:16, 18, 36; Acts 16:31, etc.).

Faith as a *condition* (as distinguished from a *cause* or a *ground*) does determine on whom God bestows salvation. God is the one, not man, who has decreed that faith is the condition of salvation. When a person responds in faith, it is not *he* who is obligating God to save him. Rather, it is *God* who *has obligated Himself* by His very righteous commitment to His promises, *to save the person who believes.* When properly understood, there is not the remotest possibility that such a view can rightly be understood as salvation by works.

Piper is aware of the place of faith in salvation but attempts to make it fit with his concept of unconditional election. He observes, "Faith is indeed a sine qua non [the necessary] condition of salvation; Rom. 9:16, therefore, necessarily implies that the act of faith is ultimately owing to the prevenient grace of God."[41] I have no quarrel with his statement, "The act of faith is ultimately owing to the prevenient grace of God." The problem is how it is interpreted. If we say that, without the work of the Holy Spirit (Jn. 6:44), no one will ever believe in Christ, I would agree. However, such a statement, as I understand it, still leaves room for the individual's response of belief or unbelief.

As I perceive it, this is not Piper's interpretation of the statement. The work of the Holy Spirit "guarantees" or "causes" the response of faith. For a person to be *caused* to believe violates what it means to be a person. Faith is a personal experience. *It is a choice.* Divine *assistance* and *influence*, yes. Divine cause, no.

I have given considerable attention to the fact that the words *cause* and *effect* are not appropriate in describing personal relationships. *Influence* and *response* are the words to use in describing interpersonal relationships. There is no such thing as a person doing something without having a genuine involvement in the action. (See my discussion under "*Cause* and *Effect* or *Influence* and *Response*? An Arminian Answer.")

The Jewish Concern

To this point, our look at verse 16 has dealt more with current concerns as it relates to election. However, the concern that Paul was dealing with was a Jewish concern. As I stated earlier, in the New Testament we see two seemingly contradictory views concerning the Jewish concept of their own salvation: (1) They were unconditionally saved because they were the Covenant Seed of Abraham. (2) They were depending on their own righteousness.

Up through verse 15, Paul had dealt with their view that all Jews were unconditionally elected. In verse 16, he turns attention to their idea that they were saved by their own righteousness. He denies such a view. The divine choice for salvation is not based on any merit growing out of the "willing" or "the running" of the Jew. This would rule out any appeal to corporate righteousness on the part of the Jews.

ROMANS 9:18 AND THE PROBLEM OF DIVINE HARDENING

Having given such extensive treatment to the positive side of election, I must be brief in my treatment of divine hardening. However, I do want to make a few comments. Paul says, "So then He has mercy on whom He desires, and He hardens whom He desires" (NASB). My first observation is that "mercy" and "hardening" are not exact opposites. Mercy in this context refers to the bestowal of salvation. "Hardening" in this context does not refer to the infliction of penal wrath. If it did, it would simplify matters for my position. All I would need to do would be to ask, On whom does God desire to inflict penal wrath? The answer is, on those who do not believe in Jesus Christ (Jn. 3:18, 36).

In my opinion, the word *harden* is carefully chosen in this context. Those who were saved among the Jews were already experiencing the saving mercy of God. Those who were lost were not already experiencing the penal wrath of God. That is reserved for the eschatological future.

I think there would be general agreement that "blinded" in 11:7 would have essentially the same meaning as "harden" in 9:18. At the moment of Paul's writing, the Jews who had not already received the saving mercy of God would be considered "hardened" or "blinded." It is important to observe that Paul did not consider all Jews who were at that time hardened or blinded to be hopelessly locked by God in that state. The burden of Paul's heart was for their salvation (9:1-3; 10:1; 11:11-14, 28-32).

Some Calvinists seem aware that the word *harden* is not well suited to their purposes. The following quotation from Hendriksen shows how he is struggling to make *harden* suit his purpose. He explains, "There is no reason to doubt that the hardening of which Pharaoh was the object was final. It was a link in the chain: reprobation—wicked life—hardening—everlasting punishment. This does not mean that divine hardening is always final. See on 11:7b-11."[42]

Piper is dealing with the same difficulty when he says, "Must we not conclude, therefore, that the hardening in 9:18 has reference, just as the hardening in 11:7, to the action of God whereby a person is left in a condition outside salvation and thus prepared for destruction?"[43] Piper acknowledges in note 31 of chapter 9, "This does not imply that the condition sometimes called hardness of heart (Eph. 4:18) or mind (2 Cor. 3:14) cannot be altered by the merciful revivifying act of God (Eph. 2:1-4)."[44]

John Brown, in defense of the Calvinistic position, shows the problem even more clearly:

> The introduction of the idea of judicial hardening seems to destroy the antithesis. *Hardening* is not the natural antithesis of showing mercy. Had it been, "whom He wills He melts into penitence, and whom He wills He hardens into impenitence," the antithesis would have been complete; but the one time in the antithesis, being showing mercy, the other must correspond to it—He does not show mercy; He relents in reference to one, He does not relent in reference to another.
>
> I am therefore disposed to concur with those interpreters (and they are distinguished both for learning and judgment) who consider, the word rendered "harden," as equivalent to "treat with severity" in withholding favors and inflicting deserved punishment.[45]

I think it should be quite obvious that the concept of divine hardening in verse 18 does not aid the cause of those who believe in either unconditional reprobation, or those who say that God simply failed to include some in His plan of unconditional election. However, the word does require some explanation, and it does not submit to easy explanation.

That God does work in such a way that spiritual blindness or hardness results is clear. That this is a judicial work is clear. What we do not know is how to explain this to our fullest satisfaction in keeping with human responsibility or the nature of God. Yet we know that from God's perspective these concepts are consistent with one another.

The unbelieving Jews in Paul's day were blinded or hardened. When they were encountered by the message of God's grace, the majority resisted and were hardened. God could not reward this attitude. In a sense, it can be said that God hardened them. In a sense it can be said that they hardened themselves.

Hardness, while not to be taken lightly, does not necessarily imply that a person is in a hopeless condition. Paul himself was hardened before his conversion. Many other Jews were saved out of hardness. A proper understanding of how Romans 9 relates to election begins with a proper grasp of the problem Paul is dealing with. That problem is the Jewish concern mentioned above—that Paul does not go along with the Jewish belief in the corporate salvation of all Jews as the Covenant Seed of Abraham.

ELECTION: INDIVIDUAL AND ETERNAL (ROM. 9:19-24)[46]

Romans 9:19 reads: "You will say to me then, 'Why does He still find fault? For who has resisted His will?'" If God chooses whom He wills for salvation and if He hardens whom He wills, and if Pharaoh was unable to interfere with God's purposes, then the question arises, Why does He still find fault [or charge with blame]? For who has resisted His will? The word for will (Greek *boulemai*) means *purpose*.[47] The verse does not suggest that a person cannot resist in the sense of *opposing* God's purpose. Rather, no one can *defeat* God's purposes. A person can disobey God and will be held responsible for his disobedience. However, God has purposes that are carried out in spite of disobedience (Gen. 50:19-20).

Verse 20 reads: "But indeed, O man, who are you to reply against God? Will the thing formed say to him who formed it, 'Why have you made me like this?'" The maker has rights over that which he has made. (See Is. 29:16 and 45:9.) This does not mean that the rights of the Creator include arbitrary rights or rights that ignore right and wrong. Rather, the very nature of God is such that He cannot do otherwise than right. Henry C. Thiessen has well said that, in God, we have "purity of being before we have purity of willing. God does not will the good because it is good, nor is the good good because God wills it; else there would be a good above God or the good would be arbitrary and changeable. Instead, God's will is an expression of his nature, which is holy."[48] God is absolutely sovereign. For that reason, we need to find out what He has said and submit to it rather than argue with Him.

In verse 21, Paul goes on to say, "Does not the potter have power over the clay, from the same lump to make one vessel for honor and another for dishonor?" There can be no doubt that Paul had in mind Jeremiah 18:1-10. (See also Wisdom of Solomon 15:7.) In my comments above on verse 15, I think I made it very clear that if we ask the simple questions—Whom does God want to save? and Whom does God choose to condemn?—we will find that God wants to save those who believe in Jesus Christ as Lord and Savior. He chooses to condemn those who do not believe in Jesus Christ as Lord and Savior. For a more complete development of these thoughts see the comments under "Romans 9:16 and Whether Election Is Conditional or Unconditional."

Verses 22-23 read: "What if God, wanting to show His wrath and to make His power known, endured with much longsuffering the vessels of wrath prepared for destruction, and that He might make known the riches of His glory on the vessels of mercy, which He had prepared beforehand for glory. . . ." We have two points of concern with the phrase "What if God, wanting" (KJV, "willing"): (1) How is Paul using this word (Greek *thelō*)? (2) What is the significance of the form of the verb he uses (a Greek participle)? Concerning the meaning of *willing*, Shedd is correct when he avers that this passage is not discussing God's "mere permission" nor

His purpose. Both these, Shedd argues, "would require *Bouleuon*." Rather, he explains, the passage is describing the "deep and strong desire: a will that was so profound and intense as to require that self-restraint which is denominated the patience and long-suffering of God (2:4)." He goes on to explain that the phrase "willing to shew his wrath" regards the "spontaneity of the divine holiness, 'the fierceness and wrath of Almighty God' against sin (Rev. xix.15), which is held back by divine compassion, upon the ground of the hilasterion [3:25]."[49]

The participle "willing" or "desiring" might be rendered either "because desiring" (Greek: causal participle) or "*although* desiring" (Greek concessive participle). "Although desiring" seems to be preferred.

Although God strongly desired to show His wrath toward those who were "vessels of wrath prepared for destruction," He "endured with much longsuffering" these "vessels of wrath" (objects of wrath, not instruments of wrath) "that He might make known the riches of his glory." If God had released His wrath immediately, the human race would have been taken immediately into eternal punishment. In this case, there would have been no vessels of mercy (those who are saved by God's grace). However, instead of immediately releasing His wrath, God through longsuffering withheld His wrath to give people time to repent (Rom. 2:4 and 2 Pet. 3:9). This was done so that there would be those who respond to the gospel. Thus God can "make known the riches of His glory on the vessels of mercy, which He had prepared beforehand for glory."

It is generally agreed in Calvinistic commentaries that the language of the expression "vessels of wrath prepared (kjv, "fitted") to destruction" does not imply unconditional reprobation. (See Harrison,[50] Hodge,[51] Murray,[52] and Shedd.[53])

Piper, however, would interpret the reference as an unconditional *fitting* for destruction of the vessels of wrath by God. He develops his argument from the point of view that Paul has been dealing with double predestination in chapter 9. He explains:

> It seems to me that, after the clear and powerful statements of double predestination [unconditional election or predestination of who was to be saved and unconditional predestination to reprobation of who would be lost] in Rom. 9, it is grasping at a straw to argue that the passive voice of *katertismena* proves that Paul denied divine agency in fitting men for destruction . . . . And since Paul's inference from the Pharaoh story is that "God hardens whom he wills" (9:18), the most natural suggestion from the context is that "fitted for destruction" (9:22) refers precisely to this divine hardening.[54]

I think it has been conclusively shown, in commenting on Chapter 9 up to this point, that it is misconstruing what Paul is saying to interpret it to support either unconditional election or unconditional reprobation. As far as verses 22-23 are concerned, I am not acquainted with anyone who would insist that these two verses apart from the rest of that chapter must be interpreted in the Calvinistic framework.

I might say with reference to Piper's double predestination, I am not averse to double predestination as such. What I reject is *unconditional* double predestination. I believe in conditional double predestination. On the condition of foreknown faith in Christ, God has predestinated believers to eternal life. He has on the condition of foreknown sin and unbelief predestinated unbelievers to eternal damnation. Apart from such predestination, we cannot assure the believer of eternal life or the unbeliever of eternal damnation. I do not reject predestination. I reject the Calvinistic interpretation of predestination.

The words *prepared beforehand* are from the Greek *proetoimazo*. In one sense, all of God's decisions are eternal. Based on His foreknowledge, He knows who will believe in Christ and has chosen them in Christ (Eph. 1:4). The *condition* for being chosen for the application of the benefits of atonement is faith in Christ. The *ground* for being chosen is being in Christ. Those who were foreknown have been prepared in eternity past for glory. For them, things have been prearranged. As Picirilli says, "They are headed for Heaven, 'prepared for glory.'"[55]

Verse 24 reads, "Even us whom He called, not of the Jews only, but also of the Gentiles?" While God is, through longsuffering, withholding His wrath from the vessels of wrath, He is withholding it to give an opportunity for salvation for both Jews and Gentiles. It is important to keep in mind that, while Paul is deeply concerned that so many of his fellow Jews were unsaved, he was keenly aware, and wanted others to know, that Jews were being saved.

Verse 23, along with verse 24, clearly shows that *election* is eternal and *individual*.

Old Testament Evidence That Not All Jews Are Saved (Romans 9:25-29)

Romans 9:25-26 read: "As He says also in Hosea: 'I will call them My people, who were not My people, And her beloved, who was not beloved. And it shall come to pass in the place where it was said to them, "You are not My people," There they shall be called sons of the living God.'" Commentators widely agree that, while in Hosea the "not My people" who are called "the sons of the living God" refers to Israel (directed by Hosea to the 10 northern tribes), Paul is using it to refer to the Gentiles. If this were demanded by the context, I could accept it, but it appears that such is not the case.

It is very clear that verses 27-29 refer to Israel and call attention to the fact that Scripture should prepare Jews to understand that not all of them are saved. To Paul, the position that not all Jews were saved was not merely academic preservation of theological accuracy. It tore at his heart. He wanted the Jews to know that their belief in unconditional election of all Jews in connection with Abraham was false. That was the only way they would entertain the idea of being saved through faith in Jesus Christ.

It is true, of course, that Paul, as the apostle to the Gentiles, was deeply concerned about the conversion of Gentiles. It is also true that he had just indicated that there were Gentiles as well as Jews among the vessels "prepared beforehand for glory" (verses 23-24). However, that is not the burden of chapter 9.

The burden of chapter 9 is to get the Jews to see that they had misunderstood God's promise to Abraham. They were not unconditionally saved. Salvation was conditioned on faith in Jesus as the Messiah.

Out of this burden, Paul calls attention to the words of Hosea. These references clearly show that Hosea emphasized that there were Israelites who would come from an unsaved state into a saving relationship with God. This reference should put away once and for all the idea of the unconditional election of all Israelites. Of all the commentaries that I have researched, Lenski's comes the nearest to the position that I have set forth. He applies the fulfillment to the 10 tribes rather than the Gentiles.[56]

Verses 27-28 state: "Isaiah also cries out concerning Israel: 'Though the number of the children of Israel be as the sand of the sea, The remnant will be saved. For He will finish the work and cut it short in righteousness, Because the Lord will make a short work upon the earth.'" It is evident that Isaiah would not have been surprised (disappointed, but not surprised) that large numbers of Jews were not saved (verse 27). Verse 28 sheds light on why only a remnant would be saved. The longsuffering that Paul mentioned in verse 22 will not be extended forever. The Lord will finish His work. He will "cut it short in righteousness." This means that many will have waited until it is too late.

Paul goes on to say in verse 29: "And as Isaiah said before: 'Unless the LORD of Sabaoth had left us a seed, We would have become like Sodom, And we would have been made like Gomorrah.'" He is saying here that only by the mercy of God was a remnant of Israel even surviving. Certainly, the Old Testament is opposed to the concept of the unconditional election of all who descended from Abraham through Jacob!

The Reason Many Jews Were Not Saved (Romans 9:31-33)

Paul asks in verse 30, "What shall we say then? That Gentiles, who did not pursue righteousness, have attained to righteousness, even the righteousness of faith." His answer, in verses 31-33, is as follows: "But Israel, pursuing the law of righteousness, has not attained to the law of righteousness. Why?

Because they did not seek it by faith, but as it were, by the works of the law. For they stumbled at that stumbling stone. As it is written: 'Behold, I lay in Zion a stumbling stone and rock of offense, And whoever believes on Him will not be put to shame.'" Up to this point in Chapter 9, Paul had made it clear that the Jews as a whole could not lay claim to salvation by claiming they were unconditionally elected as the Covenant Seed of Abraham. He did not give as his reason that God had unconditionally elected *some* rather than *all*. Based on Exodus 33:19 he was telling the Jews that salvation was *individual* rather than *corporate*.

When Paul brought the unbelieving Jews face to face with why so many were not saved, he said that it was, "Because they did not seek it by faith, but as it were, by the works of the law. For they stumbled at that stumbling stone." That stumbling stone was Jesus the Messiah.

The reason that so many Jews were not saved is not based on the idea that God unconditionally elected *some* rather than *all* Jews. Rather, it is because they had failed to meet the condition of faith in Christ. If salvation is conditional, there is every reason to believe that election is conditional.

This is one of the primary passages that is thought to teach that the Jews believed in salvation by works. As I have pointed out in my discussion above, there is not a complete harmony in Jewish thought. Some statements can be found in Jewish writings that may sound as if Jews believed in salvation by works. However, the theme that God had unconditionally saved all Jews is so strong in their thinking that it overrides their thinking about works as a condition for remaining in the covenant. The only exception to "all Jews being saved" would be rare cases of apostasy.

Another factor that must be kept in mind in assessing Jewish thought is their belief in corporate salvation. For that reason, the works that would be under consideration would be corporate works, not individual works.

A Review of the Way Paul Develops His Case in Appealing to the Jews

Paul's viewpoint on election is seen in how he develops his case for the idea that not all Jews are saved. Step one is to show that since not all of the descendants of Abraham make up the Covenant Seed of Abraham (verses 6-13), there is no reason to believe that all of the Covenant Seed are saved. In step two, Paul appeals to Exodus 33:19 to show that election is individual rather than corporate. In step three, Paul gives the reason that not all Jews are saved. It is "Because they did not seek it by faith, but as it were, by the works of the law" (verse 32). In other words, not all Jews are saved, because salvation is conditioned on faith, and not all Jews have met the condition. This is the bottom line: *salvation is conditioned on faith. And conditional salvation calls for conditional election.*

This is grounded in the Abrahamic Covenant. It was said of Abraham, "And he believed in the LORD; and he accounted it him for righteousness" (Gen. 15:6). The Abrahamic Covenant is the basic redemptive Covenant. The hope of the Jew and the hope of the Gentile is the same hope. Paul cries out to them: "For the Scripture says, 'Whoever believes on Him will not be put to shame.' For there is no distinction between Jew and Greek, for the same Lord over all is rich to all who call upon Him. For 'whoever calls on the name of the Lord shall be saved'" (Rom. 10:11-13).

I started with Romans 9 since it is the major passage used to support unconditional election. I believe that my treatment of Romans 9:1-29 has shown that it does teach that election is *individual* and that it is eternal. But it does not settle the question of whether election is conditional or unconditional. However, the most natural interpretation of 9:31-33 is that justification is *conditional.* It is conditioned on faith in Jesus Christ as Messiah, Lord, and Savior. If justification is *conditional*, election is *conditional.*

The only hope left for unconditional election is to find another passage (or passages) that will unquestionably and irrefutably teach unconditional election. If that should be the case, the Calvinists could go to Romans 9:30-33 and say that the "whoever" of verse 33 is limited to those whom God has unconditionally chosen and regenerated. They are the only ones who can give the faith response to God's offer and be saved. If such an approach is taken, Romans 9 could be shown to be consistent with unconditional election. However, by such an approach, Romans 9 would no longer be *foundational for unconditional election*. I believe that Calvinism is in trouble in Romans 9. Calvinism is in trouble *without* Romans 9.

---

[1]In this treatment of Romans 9, I am drawing heavily from my paper, "Election in Romans 9: Conditional or Unconditional?" This paper drew heavily from my Romans commentary, F. Leroy Forlines *Romans* in the *Randall House Bible Commentary* (Nashville: Randall House, 1987). I read this paper at the Southeastern Regional Meeting of the Evangelical Society at Temple University in Chattanooga, Tennessee (ca. 1990). I also read it at the Theological Symposium meeting at Hillsdale Free Will Baptist Bible College (1997). In this paper, I used the NASB and will make many references to that translation here.

[2]Robert Haldane, *An Exposition of the Epistle to the Romans* (London, 1952; reprint, McLean, Virginia: MacDonald Publishing Co., 1958), 467.

[3]Everett F. Harrison, *Romans in The Expositor's Bible Commentary*, vol. 10 (Grand Rapids: Zondervan Publishing House, 1976), 106.

[4]William S. Plumer, *Commentary on Romans* (New York: Anson D. F. Randolph & Co., 1870; reprint, Grand Rapids: Kregel Publications, 1979), 473.

[5]William G. T. Shedd, *A Critical and Doctrinal Commentary on the Epistle of St. Paul to the Romans* (Charles Scribners, 1879; reprint, Grand Rapids: Zondervan Publishing House, 1976), 288.

[6]John Piper, *The Justification of God: An Exegetical Study of Romans 9:1-23* (Grand Rapids: Baker Book House, 1983), 100.

[7]Adam Clarke, *The New Testament of Our Lord and Savior Jesus Christ*, Vol. 6: Romans-Revelation (T. Mason & G. Lane, 1837, reprinted, Nashville: Abingdon-Cokesbury Press, n.d.), 111-112.

[8]F. L. Godet, *Commentary on the Epistle to the Romans*, trans. A. Cusin (Funk and Wagnall, 1883, reprinted, Grand Rapids: Zondervan Publishing House, 1956), 350-351.

[9]William Sanday and Arthur C. Headlam, *A Critical and Exegetical Commentary on the Epistle to the Romans*, in *The International Critical Commentary*

fifth edition, eds., S. R. Driver, A. Plummer, and C. A. Briggs (1895, reprinted, Edinburgh: T. & T. Clark, 1960), 245.

[10]Shedd, *Commentary on Romans*, 285.

[11]Charles Hodge, *Commentary on the Epistle to the Romans* (First published in 1835, reprinted from the 1886 revised edition, Grand Rapids: William B Eerdmans, 1983), 306-307, 312.

[12]William Hendriksen, *New Testament Commentary, Exposition of Paul's Epistle to the Romans* (Grand Rapids: Baker Book House, 1982), 323, 24.

[13]John Murray, *The Epistle to the Romans*, vol. 2. in *The New International Commentary on the New Testament*, F. F. Bruce, gen. ed. (Grand Rapids: William B. Eerdmans Publishing Co., 1982), 15-19.

[14]Piper, *Study of Romans* 9:1-23, 48-52.

[15]2 Esdras in *The Apocrypha of the Old Testament*, Revised Standard Version (New York: Thomas Nelson and Sons, 1957), 23.

[16]When I was doing research for my commentary on Romans, I visited an Orthodox Jewish Rabbi. I said to him, "When I study about the Jewish view of salvation, I get the idea that they believe that when God called Abraham He unconditionally saved all Jews." He said, "Yes." I then said, "I also get the idea that Jews believed in salvation by works." He said, "Yes." The seeming contradiction did not appear to bother him.

[17]E. P. Sanders, *Paul and Palestinian Judaism* (Philadelphia: Fortress Press, 1977), 120.

[18]Charles Hodge, *Commentary on the Epistle to the Romans* (First published in 1835, reprinted from the 1886 revised edition, Grand Rapids: William B. Eerdmans, 1983), 70-71.

[19]Douglas J. Moo, *The Epistle to the Romans in The New International Commentary on the New Testament*, Gordon D. Fee, ed. (Grand Rapids: William B. Eerdmans Publishing Company, 1996), 573.

[20]Ibid., 46-47.

[21]"Resurrection" in *The Jewish Encyclopedia*, vol. 10, Isidore Singer, managing ed. (Funk and Wagnalls, 1907; reprinted by Ktav Publishing House, Inc., 1964).

[22]Phillip Birnbaum, *A Book of Jewish Concepts* (New York: Hebrew Publishing Co., 1964), 609-610.

[23]Sanders, *Paul and Palestinian Judaism*, 180.

[24]Ibid., 75.

[25]Ibid., 147.

[26]Ibid., 33-59.

[27]This paragraph and the one prior to it are adapted from Forlines, *Romans*, 173-74.

[28]This paragraph is adapted from Forlines, *Romans*, 249.

[29]Piper, *Study of Romans 9:1-23*, 33.

[30]Ibid., 136.

[31]Ibid., 44.

[32]I think that my treatment of "Justification According to the Penal Satisfaction View of Atonement" in Chapter 6 shows that a person cannot successfully charge me with believing in salvation by works. I believe that I have shown in Chapter 2, under the heading "An Answer to the Third Assumption of Calvinism" that a person can believe in conditional election without it being based on works.

[33]See the treatment of saving faith under the heading "The Question of Synergism," Chapter 7.

[34]Piper, *Study of Romans 9:1-23*, 100.

[35]M. R. Vincent, *Word Studies in the New Testament* in one volume, second edition (New York, 1888; reprinted at Wilmington, Delaware: Associated Publishers and Authors, 1972), 732.

[36]R. C. H. Lenski, *The Interpretation of St. Paul's Epistle to the Romans* (Minneapolis: Augsburg Publishing House, 1961), 606-607. In the book, the word is "justice" rather than "injustice," but it is obvious that Lenski meant injustice.

[37]H. P. Liddon, *Explanatory Analysis of St. Paul's Epistle to the Romans* (1892; reprinted, Grand Rapids: Zondervan Publishing House, 1961) 162-63. See also Shedd, *Commentary on Romans*, 288.

[38]Robert Picirilli, *The Book of Romans* (Nashville: Randall House Publications, 1975), 183.

[39]Thomas R. Schreiner, "Does Romans 9 Teach Individual Election unto Salvation?" in *The Grace of God, the Bondage of the Will*, vol. 1, eds. Thomas R. Schreiner and Bruce A. Ware (Grand Rapids: Baker Books, 1995), 99.

[40]Piper, *Study of Romans 9:1-23*, 133-34.

[41]Ibid., 137.

[42]Hendriksen, *Commentary on Romans*, 326.

[43]Piper, *Study of Romans 9:1-23*, 159.

[44]Ibid., 275.

[45]John Brown, *Analytical Exposition of the Epistle of Paul the Apostle to the Romans* (Robert Carter and Brothers, 1857; reprinted, Grand Rapids: Baker Book House, 1981), 338.

[46]The material on verses 19-29 is adapted from my commentary on Romans. Forlines, *Romans*, 275-279.

[47]Ralph Earle, *Word Meanings in the New Testament*, vol. 3, Romans (Kansas City: Beacon Hill Press, 1974), 194.

[48]Henry C. Thiessen, *Introductory Lectures in Systematic Theology* (Grand Rapids: William B. Eerdmans Publishing Company, 1949), 129.

[49]Shedd, *Romans*, 298.

[50]Harrison, *Romans in The Expositor's Bible Commentary*, vol.10, 107.

[51]Hodge, *Commentary on the Epistle to the Romans*, 321.

[52]Murray, *The Epistle to the Romans*, vol. 2., 36.

[53]Shedd, *Romans*, 299.

[54]Piper, *Study of Romans 9:1-23*, 194.

[55]Picirilli, *The Book of Romans*, 187.

[56]Lenski, *Romans*, 627.

[57]The material on these verses is adapted from my commentary on Romans. Forlines, *Romans*, 239-241.

CHAPTER 4

Proof Texts for Unconditional Election: Other Texts

I will now turn attention to other passages that Calvinists think teach or support unconditional election. I do not think that it will be necessary for me to be as thorough with these other passages as I have been with Romans 9. The main thing that I need to do is to show that these passages do not contradict conditional election. Attention will first be given to the other passage in Romans that Calvinists use to support unconditional election.

ELECTION AND ROMANS 8:30

Paul further clarifies his view of election by an examination of Romans 8:30, in which he states: "Moreover whom He predestined, these He also called; and whom He called, these He also justified; and whom He justified, these He also glorified." The phrase "whom He predestined" is a reference to those whom "He also predestined to be conformed to the image of his Son" (verse 29). I will wait until it fits into the discussion in the next chapter before I deal with verse 29. Verse 30 refers to the order of events as they occur in the ministry of redemption. This is generally agreed upon in commentaries. Therefore, we need not give further attention to this fact.

Calvinists make a point of saying that whenever the call is mentioned in the epistles, it only refers to believers. But that is because believers are being addressed. Paul likes to use the word *called* in referring to believers to stress that our personal redemption owes its existence to God, who took the first initiative. We are not intruders into this salvation that is ours through Jesus Christ.

On the Calvinist's limitation of the word *called*, I would make two observations: First, to refer to believers as being "called ones" does not mean that the call has not been extended to any one else. A speaker at a special occasion may address the audience as "invited guests." The only thing that he is affirming is that those who are present have been invited. They are not intruders. It does not mean that no one else was invited. When believers are referred to as called, it is not necessary to conclude that others have not been called. Second, while the word *called* may not be used in the epistles to refer to those who have not responded, the concept of a call is seen where the word is not used. There is no plainer reference to this than Paul's statement when he says, "Truly, these times of ignorance God overlooked, but now commands all men everywhere to repent" (Acts 17:30). Paul's use of "whoever" in Romans 10:11-13 implies a call that extends to all men. It makes no difference whether a reference to God's calling sinners to salvation appears in the epistles in connection with the word *call*. The concept is undeniably there.

No one is justified who was not first called. There can be no question that Paul is referring to those cases where the call has had its desired effect. That is not the same as saying that the call is irresistible, nor that it has succeeded in every case. This simply cannot be read out of the language.

When the person responds in faith, God justifies him. In due time the one who is justified will be glorified. It will be observed that "called," "justified," and "glorified" are all in the past tense (the Greek aorist tense). The believing recipients of Paul's epistle had been called and justified, but not glorified. There has been some question about the use of the past tense with reference to "glorified," because glorification is yet future. The explanation commonly given is that it refers to the certainty of this future glorification. (See Bruce,[1] Hedriksen,[2] and Meyer.[3])

Murray points out that calling, justification, and glorification are solely the acts of God. He explains, "It is contrary to this emphasis to define any of these elements of application of redemption in any other terms than those of *divine actions*."[4] I find no problem with Murray's statement. The very nature of a call means that it is the activity of the one who extends the call. Justification is a divine act in which God declares us righteous based on the death and righteousness of Christ. The foundation of our justification is solely the merits of Christ rather than our own. But if Murray wants to insist that there is no involvement of the human personality in meeting the condition of faith as it relates to justification, then I must differ with him. However, this verse says nothing about faith. I concur with Godet when he says, "If his intention had been to explain the *order of salvation* in all of its elements divine and *human*, he would have put *faith* between calling and justification and glorification."[5]

I certainly have no quarrel with the statement that future glorification will be bestowed on us by divine action. It is quite clear that verse 30 speaks only of divine action. At the same time, it is quite clear that it is not an exhaustive treatment of the doctrine of salvation. Paul approached the verse in terms of divine action because he was still giving reasons for believing that God will be with us under any and all circumstances, as set forth in verse 28.

Concerning why Paul moved from justification to glorification without mentioning sanctification, I think Bruce is correct when he argues that sanctification and glory are different in degree but not in kind. Citing 2 Corinthians 3:18 and Colossians 3:10, he rightly sees sanctification as "progressive conformity to the image of Christ here and now." Glory, Bruce contends, is "perfect conformity to the image of Christ there and then. Sanctification is glory begun; glorification is sanctification completed."[6]

Calvinists have sometimes thought that this verse guarantees that everyone who is called will respond, everyone who is called will be justified, and everyone who is justified will be glorified. I find myself in agreement with John Wesley when he says:

> St. Paul does not affirm, either here or in any other part of his writings, that precisely the same number are called, justified, and glorified. He does not deny that a believer may fall away, and be cut off between his special calling and his glorification, Romans 11:22, neither does he deny that many are called who are never justified. He only affirms that this is the method whereby God leads step by step toward heaven.[7]

There is a parallel with words of Jesus when He said, "For the earth yields crops by itself: first the blade, then the head, after that the full grain in the head." (Mk. 4:28). The process that is followed from the appearance of the blade until the grain is fully developed is stated, but Jesus does not guarantee that, once the blade appears, in every case all of the other steps follow. In some cases, the stalk of grain dies before reaching full development.

While the wording of Romans 8:30 could fit the idea of an effectual call followed by justification of all the called and glorification without exception of all who are justified, it is not necessary to interpret it so. Such a view would require support from some other source. I do not believe that such a source can be found.

The Question of Unconditional Election and the Gospel of John

In deciding between unconditional election and conditional election, a biblical, systematic theologian must find what he considers to be irrefutable biblical proof of one position or the other. When, to his satisfaction, he has accomplished that, his next responsibility is to show how he would interpret passages of Scripture that would be used by those who have chosen otherwise.

In actual experience, I established my position of conditional election and then worked my way through how I would deal with the passages thought to teach unconditional election. However, in this treatment, I have thought it was better to first show how I would deal with passages thought to teach unconditional election. I deemed it wise to start with Romans 9.

I gave a rather thorough treatment to Romans 9. I believe that Calvinism is in trouble in Romans 9. If that is the case, I do not think it will be necessary for me to be as thorough with the other passages.

If I agreed that unconditional election was taught in Romans 9, I would give a Calvinistic interpretation to several verses in the Gospel of John. Or, if there were some other passage that I thought unquestionably taught unconditional election, I would feel as though unconditional election was behind much of what Jesus said in the Gospel of John. I do not believe that unconditional election is taught elsewhere in Scripture. I will show in the next chapter that the Bible teaches conditional election. The only obligation that I have in John is to show that what is said could fit in with conditional election and the *influence* and *response* model of God's sovereign relationship with human beings.

The Jewish Context

While dealing with Romans 9, I pointed out that the prevailing view among Jews was that in connection with the call and the covenant that God made with Abraham, He unconditionally saved all Jews. In support of that position, I gave quotations from, John Piper, Charles Hodge, and Douglas J. Moo. Support was also given from *The Jewish Encyclopedia*. In Jesus' ministry, He would have encountered the same viewpoint. It will be very interesting to keep this in mind when we examine the teachings of Jesus.

John 1:12-13 and the Question of Election

John 1:12-13 state: "But as many as received him, to them gave he power [*exousia*, authority or the right] to become the sons [*teknon*. The plural is better translated children.] of God, *even* to them that believe on his name. Which were born, not of blood, nor of the will of the flesh, nor of the will of man, but of God" (KJV, brackets mine). For verse 13, the NIV gives an interpretive reading that helps us understand the verse. It reads, "children born not of natural descent, nor of human decision or a husband's will, but born of God."

Robert W. Yarbrough, in defense of unconditional election, says:

> Divine election receives sharp emphasis in John 1:13, the identity of "all who received him" in 1:12. That is, those who savingly received the Messiah for who he truly was (1:12) did so because they were "born of God" (1:13)—and not vice versa. More specifically, they cannot ultimately attribute their saved status, if they possess it, to "natural descent," their Jewishness or descent from Abraham (cf. John 8:33). [8]

I agree that regeneration is a work of God. It is *monergistic*, not *synergistic*. However, there is nothing in verses 12 and 13 that would make them suggest that the "regeneration" of verse 13 took place prior to the "believing" in verse 12. The natural reading of the verses suggests that the "believing" of verse 12 precedes the "regeneration" of verse 13. The only person who would read it otherwise would be a person who comes to these verses with a prior commitment to unconditional election.

The Teachings of Jesus in the Gospel of John and the Question of Election

The teachings of Jesus that we will examine were directed to the Jews. It is important that we keep in mind that the prevailing view among the Jewish audiences that Jesus was addressing would have been that all of the Jews were already saved because of their relationship with Abraham. They would have believed in corporate election (or salvation). This presented a special challenge to Jesus.

There is a place for questions to be settled by detailed exegesis. It is especially incumbent upon us to use that approach at times. However, Jesus, as the God-man, avoided that kind of conflict with His Jewish audience. The Pharisees specialized in quibbling over minute details. Jesus did not want to quibble. He did not need to quibble. He spoke as "one having authority, and not as the scribes" (Mk. 1:22). The authority of the scribes was a documented authority. They passed on the Oral Tradition. They quoted the famous Rabbis. Jesus had authority. He spoke from Himself. His miracles were signs showing that He had the Father's stamp of approval (Acts 2:22; Jn. 20:30-31). Jesus, in speaking to the Jews said, "But I have greater witness than that of John [the Baptist]: for the works which the Father hath given me to finish, the same works that I do, bear witness of me, that the Father hath sent me" (John 5:36, KJV). The "works" that Jesus spoke of were His miracles.

Another thing that we must keep in mind is that some of the Jews who heard Jesus had been saved as Old Testament saints, and were saved prior to the time that they met Jesus. These people would have believed in Jesus when they were confronted with His miracles and His teachings. They became His followers.

With these observations in mind, we can move on and examine the teachings of Christ regarding their bearing on the subject of election. Since God is the same yesterday, today, and forever, we can assume the decisions God made in eternity are in perfect agreement with the decisions He makes in time. Based on that, we can reason back from what we learn in time to the kind of decisions that God made in eternity. Since the audience in John was Jewish, we need to see what Jesus was trying to get across to His Jewish audience.

Salvation (Election) Corporate or Individual

Those of us who have been brought up in a church where the Bible was taught and preached automatically look at people as saved or lost. That is not the way in which the Jews being addressed by Jesus were accustomed to thinking of themselves as Jews. Jesus had to address them in such a way that they would recognize that salvation was individual, not corporate. It was necessary for Him to get them to see the truth of His words, "I am the way, the truth and the life. No man comes to the Father except through Me" (14:6). Keeping in mind the things that I have mentioned about the Jewish concept of corporate election will not change our understanding of the universal truth taught in the Gospel of John. Yet it will give us a different understanding of how Jesus' Jewish audiences saw and understood Him.

The first encounter recorded in John emphasizing that salvation must be experienced by each individual is Jesus' meeting with Nicodemus. Nicodemus had seen the miracles that Jesus had performed (3:1). They had gotten his attention. He knew that there was something different about Jesus. He knew that God was with Him. His deep desire to see Jesus was apparently coupled with fear. So he went at night to see Him.

Jesus did not discuss the subject of corporate election of Jews. Yet what He said dealt with the problem in a way that could not be missed. He said to Nicodemus, "Unless one is born again he cannot see the kingdom of God." Again he says to him, "Unless one is born of water and the Spirit, he cannot enter the kingdom of God." (3:3, 5, NASB). It is clear that Jesus is telling Nicodemus that salvation must be experienced *individually*. It is impossible for us to imagine what this ruler of the Jews must have felt when he heard these words. He had not only heard these words. He had also seen Jesus' miracles. He also heard Jesus say: "And as Moses lifted up the serpent in the wilderness, even so must the Son of Man be lifted up, that whoever believes in Him should not perish but have eternal life" (verses 14-15).

There is a question over whether John 3:18 was spoken by Jesus, or whether it was added by John. John was still battling the problem of corporate election, just as Paul had in Romans 9. What is said in this verse is clearly in conflict with the corporate election of all Jews. "He who believes in Him is not condemned; but he who does not believe is condemned already, because he has not believed in the name of the only begotten Son of God." Verse 36 carries the same message. In John 5:24, Jesus said: "Most assuredly, I say to you, he who hears My word and believes in Him who sent Me has everlasting life, and shall not come into judgment, but has passed from death into life." Later in this chapter, we read the words of Jesus, "But you are not willing to come to Me that you may have life." (verse 40).

These words have a message of hope, for anybody, anywhere, at any time who will turn to Him. There is also a message of judgment for those who will not. But they had a special significance to the Jewish audience. We could add John 4:14; 6:25-29, 35, 51; 7:37-39; 10:7-11, 27-30, and 14:6.

I would like to call attention to one more passage. One of the times when Jesus used the strongest language in talking with the Jews is in chapter 8. There were apparently some who thought they believed in Jesus. Yet when He said, "If ye continue in my word, *then* are ye my disciples indeed; and ye shall know the truth, and the truth shall make you free" (verses 31-32, KJV), they did not like the suggestion that they were not already free. "They answered him, We be Abraham's seed, and were never in bondage to any man: how sayest thou, Ye shall be made free?" (verse 33, KJV). Jesus said to them:

> I know that ye are Abraham's seed; but ye seek to kill me, because my word hath no place in you. I speak that which I have seen with my Father: and ye do that which ye have seen with your father. They answered and said unto him, Abraham is our father. Jesus saith unto them, If ye were Abraham's children, ye would do the works of Abraham. But now ye seek to kill me, a man that hath told you the truth, which I have heard of God: this did not Abraham. Ye do the deeds of your father. Then say they unto him, We be not born of fornication; we have one Father, even God. Jesus said unto them, If God were your Father, ye would love me: for I proceeded forth and came from God; neither came I of myself, but he sent me (verses 37-42, KJV).

In verse 44, Jesus went on to tell them, "Ye are of *your* father the devil, and the lusts of your father ye will do" (KJV). These Jews went on in verse 48 and charged Jesus with being a Samaritan and being demon possessed. It was extremely clear that Jesus rejected any concept of the corporate election of all Jews. It was also clear that salvation was experienced on an individual basis. If salvation is experienced on an individual basis, it follows that, because God is the same yesterday, today, and forever, election in eternity past would have been on an individual basis.

In the discussion above, along with showing that salvation for the Jews is individual rather than corporate, a great deal of evidence was given that would show that faith in Jesus as Messiah, Lord, and Savior is the condition of salvation. I do not need to go into any depth on this point. I will just say that a reading of the verses used above under "Salvation (Election) Corporate or Individual?" leaves no doubt that salvation is conditioned on faith in Jesus Christ as Lord and Savior.

Calvinists do not deny that justification is conditioned on faith in Christ. Is not justification required for election? If faith is the condition of justification now, why would it not be viewed that way in eternity past?

The Occurrences of the Word *Eklegomai*

Eklegomai occurs five times in John (6:70; 13:18; 15:16, 19). Each of these times, it is translated "chosen." It is the verb form of the word for "elect." In each of these cases the reference is to the Twelve Apostles. The reference is to the fact that Jesus had chosen them to be His apostles. There is no problem for conditional election if it did include election to salvation.

A problem might be supposed by some from the reading of "You did not choose me, but I chose you." It seems apparent that this is a reference to being chosen to be an apostle. But the wording presents no problem if it applies to salvation. The provision of salvation, the offer of salvation, the drawing to salvation all originated with God. Any response on the part of any individual is a response to divine initiative. The only difference between unconditional election and the view of conditional election set forth by Classical Arminianism is *the difference in the divine activity that makes faith possible.* In both Calvinism and Arminianism, *the individual does make a choice.*[9] There is no such thing as human personality changing from unbelief to faith without making a choice. Calvinism has not won its case by the wording of 15:16.

The wording of 15:19, "I chose you out of the world," while referring to the apostles, may embrace election for salvation since they were chosen out of the world. What I have said in the previous paragraph will show that if it is election to salvation, there is no necessary conflict with conditional election.

Didomi and *Helkuo* in Regard to Salvation

Yarbrough takes the position that the Gospel of John gives strong support for unconditional election. In opening his treatment of "Divine Election in the Gospel of John," he explains, "Divine election in this chapter refers to God's determinative initiative in human salvation."[10] By tying election to "God's determinative initiative," Yarbrough is, of course, taking the position of unconditional election. In commenting on the Hebrew word *bāhar*, which is used in the Old Testament for "choose" or "elect," he explains, "The word 'indicates God's prerogative in deciding what shall happen, independent of human choice.'"[11] Having made it clear that his use of the word *election* is to be understood as a reference to unconditional election, he avows, "John's Gospel implicitly and explicitly asserts God's choosing, his election, of lost sinners to eternal life."[12] While he sees his support in other verses in John, he sees nine verses in 1:19–12:50 as being key verses. To get these before us, I will quote the pertinent part of these verses. The key Greek words in the verses in question are *didōmi* and *helkuō*. I will indicate where these words occur. To make it simpler to deal with, instead of taking each verse in the order in which it occurs in the book, I will group them together according to the problem they present.

Eklegomai

In 6:70, Jesus said, "Did I Myself not choose you, the twelve, and yet one of you is a devil?" (NASB). I have already dealt with this verse above under the previous heading "The Occurrences of the Word *Eklegomai*." I need not say more about it here.

Helkuo

No one can come to Me, unless the Father who sent Me draws [helkuō] him (6:44).

> *And I, if I be lifted up from the earth, will draw [helkuō] all men to Myself* (12:32, NASB).

It is important for us to keep reminding ourselves of the audience that Jesus is addressing. The clash between the concept of corporate election and salvation on an individual basis presented Jesus with a unique challenge. The challenge before Him was to get the Jews to see that salvation was on an individual basis and that it required faith in Him as the Messiah. This was not going to take place simply by making statements and giving explanations.

There were two big problems. One of the problems was the power of depravity that works to keep people away from God. This problem is common to all human beings. The other problem was unique to the Jewish people as a result of the way their thinking had developed by the time of Jesus. As they understood it, they did not come into salvation by individual decision. This was decided for them when God called Abraham and made the Abrahamic Covenant with him.[13] For them, salvation was *automatically* bestowed on them as the Covenant Seed of Abraham.

The burden of Jesus' ministry was to show those who thought that salvation was automatically bestowed on them that such was not the case. It is bestowed on individuals one at a time. God, who is sovereign, decides who will be saved. He has decided that those who place their faith in Jesus as Messiah, Savior, and Lord are the ones whom He wills to save (Jn. 3:16, 18; 5:24; 6:35, 37, 39-40; 8:51-52; 10:27-29; and 14:6). Those who do not place their faith in Jesus as Messiah, Savior, and Lord are the ones whom God decides to condemn (Jn. 3:18; 6:40; 8:24; and 14:6).

Even though Jesus made salvation available for everyone on the condition of faith in Jesus Christ, it was necessary for God to go a step further. He must send the Holy Spirit to draw them to Christ. Depravity is of such a nature that no one will come to Christ unless the Holy Spirit draws him. While this is true of all human beings, it was particularly important for this point to be driven home to the Jews. They needed to see that they did not have automatic salvation. There was no corporate salvation for them to experience. Salvation happened to people as individuals. Each person had to experience salvation or remain under condemnation. In John 6:44, Jesus was talking about individuals. No individual could come to Christ without being drawn.

There is certainly no contradiction between the drawing spoken of in John 6:44 and the drawing spoken of in Classical Arminianism. Classical Arminianism recognizes that a strong work of the Holy Spirit is necessary before any person can respond to Jesus Christ in faith.

According to Yarbrough, the word *helkuō* describes an irresistible drawing. He explains that the word appears only one place outside of John's gospel, in Acts 16:19 ("they seized Paul and Silas and dragged them into the market place," [NASB].) The Gospel of John uses *helkuō*, Yarbrough argues, "to speak of persons being drawn to Christ (12:32), a sword being drawn (18:10), and a net full of fish being hauled or dragged to shore (21:6, 11)." Furthermore, Yarbrough argues, *helkō*, a related word, "appears in Acts 21:30 ('they dragged him from the temple') and James 2:6 ('Are they not the ones who are dragging you into court?'). It is hard to avoid the impression that John 6:44 refers to a 'forceful attraction' in bringing sinners to the Son."[14]

I think the evidence Yarbrough presents does suggest that the drawing of John 6:44 is strong. I have no problem with the idea that the drawing spoken of in John 6:44 is a "strong drawing." But I do have a problem with speaking of it as a "forceful attraction." A word used literally may have a causal force when dealing with physical relationships. However, we cannot require that that word have the same *causal* force when it is used metaphorically with reference to an *influence* and *response* relationship. John 6:44 speaks of a personal *influence* and *response* relationship.

For John 6:44 to aid the cause of unconditional election, it must be understood in terms of *cause* and *effect*. The verse plainly says that no one can come to Christ without being drawn by the Father. But there is nothing in the word *helkuō* that would require that it be interpreted with a causal force. In fact, if we keep in mind that the relationship between God and man is a personal relationship, the use of *helkuō* in this verse is best understood in terms of *influence* and *response* rather than cause and effect.

When we go to John 12:32, the natural meaning of the verse is to understand *helkuō* in terms of *influence* and *response* rather than *cause* and *effect*. When Jesus said, "And I, if I be lifted up from the earth, will draw [*helkuō*] all men to Myself" (12:32, NASB), He definitely did not mean that He would drag every human being to Himself. He meant that there would go out from Him a drawing power that would make it possible for any person who hears the gospel to come to Him. It is strained exegesis to suggest as Yarbrough does that the likely meaning of "'all men' in John 12:32 refers to all—both Jew and Gentile—that the Father has given to the Son."[15]

If a person is going to interpret *helkuō* in John 6:44 and 12:32 to be an irresistible drawing, he must first find a passage elsewhere that irrefutably teaches that there is such an irresistible drawing. Then, he might suggest that as the meaning in John. These verses cannot be used as a part of a person's arsenal of irrefutable proof of an irresistible calling.

Didomi

John uses the word *didōmi* in the following verses:

All that the Father gives [didōmi] Me will come to Me, and the one who comes to Me I will by no means cast out" (6:37).

No one can come to Me unless it has been granted [didomi] to him by My Father (6:65).

And I give [didomi] eternal life to them, and they shall never perish; and no one shall snatch them out of My hand" (10:28, NASB).

My Father, who has given [didomi] them to Me, is greater than all; and no one shall snatch them out of the Father's hand (10:29, NASB).

I am separating my treatment of John 10:28 from the rest of the verses because the others refer to *those given to the Son by the Father*. This verse refers to the fact that the *Son* gives eternal life to those who are His. There is no way that this verse can have any bearing one way or the other on the question of whether election is conditional or unconditional.

It seems to be obvious that the use of *didōmi* in John 6:37; 6:65; and 10:29 refers to the end result of the Father's "drawing." Those who come as a result of the Father's drawing are considered to be "given to Jesus by the Father." This point seems to be very clear when we take John 6:44, "No one can come to Me unless the Father who sent Me draws [*helkuō*] him" and compare it with, "No one can come to Me unless it has been granted [*didōmi*] to him by My the Father (6:65). "Granted" here could be translated "given." *Didōmi* (granted or given) in 6:65 is interpreted by comparison with 6:44 to be the same as *helkuō* (draw). If that is the case, what I said above about drawing shows that there is no way that the word *given* in John's Gospel lends any support to unconditional election.

In one sense, all sinners are being held hostage by sin. It takes a work of God to break through, convince them of their sins, convince them that Jesus can save them, convince them that Jesus is the only way, and then lead them to Christ. However, there are different approaches that sin takes in holding sinners captive. For some, it has been the allurements of sin; for others, it has been the outright unbelief of secular modernism. Many today are held hostage by the moral, cultural, and religious relativism of postmodernism.

The situation that Jesus was facing, and the early church continued to face, was the Jewish misunderstanding of the idea that they were corporately and automatically saved as a result of the call and the covenant that God made with Abraham. Many of the Jews were held hostage by the false assurance that they were automatically and corporately saved. If we are going to understand the way Jesus dealt with the Jews as it is set forth for us in the Gospel of John, we will have to keep these observations in mind when we study the passages we have been looking at. I believe Classical Arminianism is on solid ground in the Gospel of John.

The Question of Why Many Jews Did Not Believe in Jesus

> *He who is of God hears the words of God; for this reason you do not hear them, because you are not of God (8:47, NASB).*

> *But you do not believe, because you are not of My sheep (10:26, NASB).*

Perhaps the best way to answer this question is first to answer the following question: Why did many of the Jews believe in Jesus? As I said above, many who were living when Jesus came were already saved. Their heart was right with God. They were submissive to God. When they met Jesus, saw His miracles, and heard His teachings, they believed in Him. It was this kind of people that Jesus had in mind when He said in John 7:17, "If any man is willing to do His [the Father's] will, he shall know of the teaching, whether it is of God or *whether* I speak of Myself" (NASB). There were those who already were of that disposition. These people responded and believed. Others as they saw the miracles and heard the teachings of Jesus responded to the drawing power of the Holy Spirit and believed (7:40-43).

Those who were referred to in John 8:47 and 10:26 were those who were not in a right relationship with God before they met Jesus. At the time these words were spoken to them they were still resisting. There is nothing to suggest that it was impossible for them to believe and be saved at a later date. There is no indication that God had made an unconditional choice to leave them out of His plan.

An Argument Based on Analogy

> *For just as the Father raises the dead and gives them life, even so the Son also gives life to [or makes alive] whom He wishes (5:21, NASB).*

Concerning this verse, Yarbrough remarks, "Here is a powerful analogy: As corpses depend on God's vivifying voice to resurrect them, so recipients of 'life,' or salvation, depend on the Son's good pleasure to give it."[16] True, this is a "powerful analogy," but within itself it sheds no light on whether the Son gives life *conditionally* or *unconditionally*.

A Preliminary Conclusion

I believe our examination of the evidence in the Gospel of John shows that there is no conclusive or foundational support in the Gospel of John for unconditional election. Any tying of the Gospel of John with unconditional election depends upon finding it somewhere else first. I think I have shown that such foundational support cannot be found in Romans 9. Before concluding this chapter, I will examine Acts 13:48.

Acts 13:48

> *And when the Gentiles heard this, they were glad, and glorified the word of the Lord: and as many as were ordained to eternal life believed* (KJV).

Of all of the verses in the Bible, this is the one that has taken me the longest to discover what, to me, provides a satisfactory interpretation, corresponding with conditional election. On the surface, it sounds as if these people had been elected to believe. Then, it seemed to follow that all who had been elected to believe believed on that occasion.

As I pointed out in the study of John above, there were those who were already saved prior to the coming of Jesus Christ. They believed in the redemptive message revealed in the Old Testament. They had a personal, trusting relationship with God. Probably most of these true believers lived in Palestine. Since Jews had migrated to others parts of the world, some of these true believers would have lived in other parts of the world as well. Since our concern in this passage is with what took place in Antioch in Pisidia, I think we could safely say that there were some in Asia Minor who were saved by believing the Old Testament redemptive revelation prior to Paul's first missionary journey. They were already saved by faith, but they had not come in contact with the message of Jesus Christ.

Along with the spread of the Jews, there was the spread of the influence of Jewish monotheism, the way of life set forth in the Old Testament, and the redemptive revelation that was intended to be a message of hope for all mankind. Many Gentiles were influenced by the Jews as they went forth.

Proselytes (Acts 2:10 and 13:43) were Gentiles who embraced the Jewish faith including circumcision of the males.[17]

F. F. Bruce says that the "simple monotheism of Jewish synagogue worship" and Jewish ethics attracted many Gentiles who were not ready to become full proselyte Jews. Some of these Gentiles went to synagogue and became very familiar with Jewish prayers and readings from the Septuagint. Others even observed Sabbath and abstained from certain foods. Thus Bruce argues, "That the first Gentile to hear and accept the gospel should be a God-fearer is the more significant because, as we shall see later in Acts, it was such God-fearers who formed the nucleus of the Christian community in one city after another in the course of Paul's missionary activity."[18]

These Gentiles who were influenced by Jewish thought, but chose not to become proselytes, are referred to as *devout men* or *God-fearers*. If some of the Jews were saved by faith before the coming of Jesus, it follows that some of the Gentile proselytes and God-fearers were also saved by faith. I think that any serious study of Acts must keep this observation in mind. I am not suggesting that all of these God-fearers were saved prior to hearing that Jesus the Messiah had come. There would have been some who would not have taken matters that seriously. However, I do believe that some were saved by believing the redemptive revelation of God given in the Old Testament before they heard the gospel message. That possibility no longer exists. But it did exist during this transition period.

The Gentiles who had been influenced by the Jews as they had migrated to different parts of the Roman Empire would not have found the concept of individual salvation as distinguished from corporate salvation as objectionable as the Jews did. I think this could account for much of the early success in reaching Gentiles with the gospel.

Now, let us see how this viewpoint helps us understand Acts 13:48. Verse 43 mentions "proselytes." They were among those who were persuaded by Paul and Barnabas "to continue in the grace of God." On the next sabbath day "almost the whole city came together to hear the word of God" (verse 44). The Jews were envious of the success that Paul and Barnabas were having and spoke against them (verse 46). Paul and Barnabas, then, turned to the Gentiles. When this move was made to the Gentiles, it is said, "And as many as were ordained to eternal life believed" (verse 48, KJV). The Greek word for "ordained" is *tassō*. It means "to ordain," "to appoint," "to allot," or "to assign." The form of the word that appears in verse 48 is *tetagmenoi*. It is a perfect passive participle form of *tassō*. It is preceded by *ēsan* which is the imperfect form of the Greek word *eimi* (*to be*). The expression *ēsan tetagmenoi* is what is called in the Greek a periphrastic pluperfect construction. The literal meaning would be "as many as were having been appointed to eternal life believed." Or in a less literal way, it would be "as many as had been appointed to eternal life believed."

The "had been appointed to eternal life" or the "appointment to eternal life" had occurred before they heard and believed the gospel that was presented by Paul and Barnabas. However, the wording does not require that this appointment to eternal life must be a reference to eternity past. I think what the verse is telling us is that all of those who had been saved prior to their hearing the New Testament gospel subsequently believed when they heard the gospel being presented by Paul and Barnabas. At the moment of their salvation in the past, they were appointed to eternal life. When they heard about the redemptive work of Jesus the Messiah, they believed and became New Testament believers.

I believe that what I have given is the most likely interpretation of this passage. If this is the case, this passage would present no problem for the position of conditional election. I would also like to point out that, in so far as the wording is concerned, it could be possible for Acts 13:48 to refer to an appointment made in eternity past. However, there is a problem for those who hold that position. The verse says, "As many as had been appointed to eternal life believed." If it is a reference to an unconditional appointment in eternity past, it would then mean that of the group present that day "as many as" or "all among them" that would ever be saved were saved on that occasion. I would doubt that those who believe in unconditional election believe that. It is hard to believe that, of that group, from among those who did not get saved on that occasion no one ever got saved later.

My Final Conclusion

Except for Ephesians 1, I have dealt with the verses most commonly used to support unconditional election. I believe I have shown that *none of these passages require unconditional election to be true*. In fact, I think *Romans 9 supports conditional election*. The reason I did not deal with Ephesians 1 in this chapter is that I cover it in the next chapter when building my case for conditional election. I will show that it also does not support unconditional election.

---

[1]F. F. Bruce, *The Epistle of Paul to the Romans, Tyndale New Testament Commentaries* (Grand Rapids: William B. Eerdmans Publishing Co., 1963), 177.

[2]Hendriksen, *Exposition of Paul's Epistle to the Romans*, 285.

[3]August Wilhelm Meyer, *Meyer's Commentary on the New Testament*, vol. 10, *Critical and Exegetical Handbook to the Epistle to the Romans*, Timothy Dwight, ed.; William P. Dickson, trans. and ed. (T & T Clark, 1883; reprinted, Winona Lake, Ind.: Alpha Greek Publications, 1980), 377.

[4]Murray, *The Epistle to the Romans*, vol. 1, 320.

[5]Godet, *Commentary on the Epistle to the Romans*, 327.

[6]Bruce, *The Epistle of Paul to the Romans*, 178.

[7]John Wesley, *Explanatory Notes Upon the New Testament*, vol. 2 (reprinted, Grand Rapids: Baker Book House, 1981) pages not numbered.

[8]Robert W. Yarbrough, "Divine Election in the Gospel of John," *The Grace of God, the Bondage of the Will*, eds. Thomas R. Schreiner and Bruce A. Ware (Grand Rapids: Baker Books, 1995), 49.

[9]Forlines, *The Quest for Truth*, 260.

[10]Yarbrough, "Divine Election in the Gospel of John," 47.

[11]Ibid.

[12]Ibid., 47-48.

[13]It appears that some of the Jews thought that it was possible for a person to repudiate his Jewish faith and become an apostate. It seems that some of the Jews were trying to say that Jesus was an apostate. (See Mt. 12:24; 26:65; Mk. 3:22; 14:62-64; Lk. 11:15; and Jn. 8:48.)

[14]Yarbrough, "Divine Election in the Gospel of John," 50, footnote 10.

[15]Ibid., 52.

[16]Ibid., 50.

[17]See Bruce, *Commentary on the Book of Acts* (Grand Rapids: William B. Eerdmans, 1955), 63-64, for the requirements of being a Jewish proselyte.

[18]Ibid., 216.

CHAPTER 5

Scriptural Support for Conditional Election

In chapter 2, I dealt with the theological problems that must be dealt with in a study of election. Unconditional election and conditional election were defined. Attention was given to decrees, determinism, the sovereignty of God, the meaning of free will, and so forth. Two differing models for understanding the way God carries out His sovereign purposes with human beings were explained. These were the *cause* and *effect* model and the *influence* and *response* model. The *cause* and *effect* model best serves unconditional election. The *influence* and *response* model best serves conditional election.

The ultimate question for a biblical, systematic theologian to try to answer is: Which view of election is taught in the Bible? I think I have shown in the previous chapter that the passages that have been thought to teach unconditional election do not require that interpretation. In fact, Romans 9, which has been considered to be the bedrock of Calvinism, is best understood as teaching election that is *individual, eternal,* and *conditional.* The first problem that I need to deal with in this chapter is the meaning of predestination in the New Testament.

THE NEW TESTAMENT USE AND MEANING OF PREDESTINATION

The Greek word for *predestinate* is *proorizō*. It means to predetermine that a particular thing will take place. It is found six times in the New Testament (Acts 4:28; Rom. 8:29-30; 1 Cor. 2:7; Eph. 1:5, 11).

Acts 4:28

Acts 4:28 uses *proorizō*: "to do whatever Your hand and Your purpose determined before to be done." In this verse, *proorizō* refers to what happened at the cross as having been predetermined by God. God had predetermined that Jesus Christ would be crucified and in connection with that event He would suffer the full wrath of God and make atonement for the sins of the human race.

1 Corinthians 2:7

First Corinthians 2:7 reads: "But we speak the wisdom of God in a mystery, the hidden wisdom which God ordained before the ages for our glory." In this verse, it is the revelation of the New Testament gospel ("the wisdom of God in a mystery") that Paul speaks of as being determined by God. God had predetermined that at the appropriate time, which to God was a specific time, the New Testament gospel would be revealed.

While Acts 4:28 and 1 Corinthians 2:7 do indeed indicate that God has predestinated or foreordained that certain things will take place, they do not address the subject of the election of believers. The remaining verses where *proorizō* occurs are pertinent to the question of individual election. The question that demands our attention is: Does the use of *proorizō* in any of these verses tell us that God has predetermined or predestinated that a particular person will believe?

Romans 8:29-30

In Romans 8:29–30, Paul states: "For whom He foreknew, He also predestined to be conformed to the image of His Son, that He might be the firstborn among many brethren. Moreover whom He predestined, these He also called; whom He called, these He also justified; and whom He justified, these He also glorified." It is obvious that the aim of predestination in verse 30 is the same as it is in verse 29. In verse 29, the aim of predestination is for those whom God foreknew "to be conformed to the image of Christ."

I understand that there is a problem surrounding the meaning of *foreknow* and *foreknowledge* in the New Testament. I will address that later when I look at the occurrences of the words for foreknowledge. It is quite clear that these verses do not say that the people under consideration were predestinated to believe. Rather, it is saying that those who do believe are predestinated to be conformed to the image of Christ.

Ephesians 1:5

Ephesians 1:5 reads: "having predestined us to adoption as sons by Jesus Christ to Himself, according to the good pleasure of His will." The "us" of the verse is a reference to those who had been chosen in Christ. I will comment on that verse later when I look at the verses where the Greek word for *election* occur. The word that is translated "adoption as sons" is *huiothesia*. The literal meaning of the word is "son placing." The defining passage for the meaning of *huiothesia* is Galatians 3:19–4:10. It is in Galatians 4:5 that the word occurs. But a study of 3:19–4:10 is necessary in order to grasp what is meant.

In this passage, Paul is telling us that in the Old Testament God viewed His believing children as being in a state of immaturity. The Mosaic Law with its civil and ceremonial laws was adapted to immaturity. Paul is telling us that, in connection with the coming of Christ, God has placed His believing children in the position of adult sons.

Paul spoke of the Law as being a *paidagōgos* (Gal. 3:24). In wealthy Greek and Roman families, a young boy was placed under a *paidagōgos* from ages 5 or 6 until 16 or 17. The *paidagōgos* was a trusted slave. This slave would go with the young boy for his protection and to instill the family values in the young boy. The KJV translates *paidagōgos* as schoolmaster.

That translation might have been useful when the KJV was translated,[1] but that is not the case now.

We do not have an exact parallel in our culture to the *paidagōgos* of Paul's day. Probably, the nearest parallel would be a *nanny*. The words *tutor* or *guardian* pick up the meaning somewhat. It is impossible to understand what Paul is saying about the *paidagōgos* without being assisted by a knowledge of the Greek and Roman culture of Paul's day.

An understanding of the word *paidagōgos* is necessary before we can understand Paul's use of the word *huiothesia*. The time of *huiothesia* (adoption) refers to the time when the parents released the young man from the *paidagōgos*. This took place when the young man was about 16 or 17. It was the time when he was released from a childhood method of treatment to one in keeping with the maturity of adulthood. Galatians 3:19–4:7 teaches us that in connection with the coming of Christ, God released His children from the *paidagōgos*. The use of *paidagōgos* in Galatians 3:24 is a metaphorical reference to the Mosaic Law with its civil and ceremonial laws.

Adoption (*huiothesia*) in the New Testament does not refer to the legal process of taking one who was not born to parents and making him or her a member of the family. Rather, it refers to taking one who is a member of the family and making him or her a *huios*. *Huios* is the Greek word for "son." It refers to one who is a legal heir of legal age. The one so adopted has the privileges of an adult heir. The first privilege to be bestowed is the release from the *paidagogos*. That means the release from the responsibility of living by the civil and ceremonial laws of the Mosaic Law.

The predestination Paul spoke of in Ephesians 1:5 was the predestination of us as New Testament believers to *huiothesia* (adoption) as explained above. Again, we see that it does not say that certain ones are predestinated to believe. Rather, this predestination was that of New Testament believers who would be adopted and, thus, delivered from the Mosaic Law as the *paidagōgos*. I realize that the meaning of adoption needs much more explanation than I have given here.[2]

Ephesians 1:11

Ephesians 1:11 reads: "In Him also we have obtained an inheritance, being predestined according to the purpose of Him who works all things according to the counsel of His will." The phrase "we have obtained an inheritance" is a translation of *eklērōthēmen*, which is the first person plural, aorist passive indicative of *klēroō*. The question to be decided is whether believers were "made an inheritance of God" or whether believers were "given an inheritance." Were we predestinated to be God's inheritance or we were predestinated to receive an inheritance from God? Either of these would be true statements. For support for the idea that believers may be viewed as God's inheritance, see Deuteronomy 32:8-9. The only pertinent question then is: What is the meaning here?

For our present purposes, we do not need to decide which of these is meant. No matter which of these meanings is the true meaning, it will not present a problem to conditional election. It is clear that it is not saying that people are predestinated to believe.

Conclusion

This study of *proorizō*, the Greek word for *predestinate*, has not settled for or against either conditional election or unconditional election. While it has not settled the question, it has not done damage to conditional election. Those who believe in conditional election have as much right to the word *predestinate* as those who believe in unconditional election. We do have a different understanding of the terminus of *predestination* as it relates to the act of faith. But as it relates to believers, we see predestination as having the same terminus that Calvinists do.

Those who believe in unconditional election believe that God has unconditionally chosen certain ones to believe and be saved. He predestinates those whom He has chosen to believe. In this case *faith* is the terminus of predestination. The Classical Calvinist approach works on the *cause* and *effect* model in producing faith in the individual. In the Classical Arminian approach, God works on the *influence* and *response* model in getting the response of faith from the individual. This difference in the understanding of the nature of the divine contribution in bringing a person to saving faith is the great continental divide between Classical Calvinists and Classical Arminians.

As it relates to the terminus of predestination in the verses that I have examined, the terminus, as it is believed by Classical Arminians and Calvinists, would be the same. There would, of course, be a difference in how God would achieve these goals.

The terminus of predestination in Romans 8:29 is clearly *that believers would be conformed to the image of Christ*. Classical Arminians and Classical Calvinists would agree that God has predestinated believers to be conformed to the image of Christ.

In Ephesians 1:5, the terminus of predestination is *adoption*. Classical Calvinists and Classical Arminians would agree that God predestinated New Testament believers to be adopted. Differences on the interpretation of adoption would have nothing to do with whether a person is a Calvinist or an Arminian.

In Ephesians 1:11, if the true meaning is that believers are predestinated *"to be God's inheritance,"* that would not present a problem to either Calvinism or Classical Arminianism. If the true meaning is that believers are predestinated *"to have an inheritance,"* that would not present a problem to either Calvinism or Classical Arminianism.

Predestination is just as essential for Classical Arminianism as it is for Calvinism. If there is no predestination, there is no gospel. Our gospel says that God has predestinated salvation for everyone who believes in Jesus Christ and He has predestinated that all who do not believe in Jesus Christ will be condemned to eternal death (Jn. 3:16, 18, 36; 5:24; 14:6; Acts 4:12; 16:31; Rom. 6:23; Rev. 21:8; and others). It is the fault of Arminians that we have almost forfeited the word *predestination* to the Calvinists. As Arminians, we need to reclaim the word *predestination*.

The New Testament Use and Meaning of *Foreknow* and *Foreknowledge*

The Greek word *proginōskō* (to foreknow) occurs five times in the New Testament. It is found in Acts 26:5; Romans 8:29; 11:2; 1 Peter 1:20; and 2 Peter 3:17. The Greek word *prognōsis* (foreknowledge) is found only twice in the New Testament—Acts 2:23 and 1 Peter 1:2.

2 Peter 3:17

The Apostle Peters says in 2 Peter 3:17: "You therefore, beloved, since you know this beforehand, beware lest you also fall from your own steadfastness, being led away with the error of the wicked." In this verse, *proginōskō* refers to human knowledge. Peter was saying that, since they know the damage that has been done by these false teachers, they should be on their guard lest they be led astray. They already knew (knew beforehand) the end result of those false teachers.

Acts 26:5

Acts 26:5 reads: "They [the Jews who accused Paul] knew [Greek, *proginōskō*] me from the first . . ." In this verse, *proginōskō* refers to the knowledge that a person has before the present moment which is *fore[before] knowledge.* We would say "prior knowledge." In 2 Peter 3:17, a person is in possession of a knowledge that makes him aware of the consequences that a particular thing will bring.

Divine foreknowledge as we will see it used in the other verses is different from what is mentioned in Acts 26:5 and 1 Peter 3:17. It refers to a knowledge that God had of events in eternity past. This kind of knowledge is knowledge of an event before it occurs.

Acts 2:23 and 1 Peter 1:20

Acts 2:23 speaks of "Him [Jesus of Nazareth], being delivered by the determined purpose and foreknowledge of God, you have taken by lawless hands, have crucified, and put to death." Calvinists believe these verses confirm their idea that the Greek words for *predestination*, *election*, and *foreknowledge* are essentially synonymous. They take the use of the word *foreknowledge* (*prognōsis*) in "being delivered by the determined purpose and the foreknowledge of God" to be *efficacious.*

I believe as strongly as any Calvinist that the crucifixion of Jesus Christ was prearranged and predetermined. The determined purpose of God and the foreknowledge of God prearranged and predetermined the crucifixion of Christ. I do not believe that this verse requires us to understand the word *prognōsis* (foreknowledge) to be *efficacious,* thus making it synonymous with *predetermined* or *predestinated.*

I believe that the proper understanding of *prognōsis* in Acts 2:23 is *instrumental.* The foreknowledge of God enabled Him to see the future as if it were present. I do not believe that everything was or is *present* to God. But He saw the *future* as fully and completely as He does the present.

It is important to realize that God did not foresee the future as a passive observer. He did not simply raise the curtain of time and look at a future that was already fixed before He looked. He planned the future. But when He planned the future with regard to human beings who were made in His image and thus were personal beings with a mind, heart, and will, He chose to work with them in accord with the *influence* and *response* model. He has a *cause* and *effect* relationship with the material universe, but such is not the case with human personality.

The cross of Christ was a predestinated event. At the same time, numerous human beings were involved in one way or another in the effecting of the event. Since human beings with free will were involved in the crucifixion event, we must understand the role of God's foreknowledge in predestinated events. It is important for us to keep in mind the observations made in the previous paragraph as well as what was stated in Chapter 2.

It is the kind of God that I have just attempted to describe (a God who was not a mere spectator) who foresaw the future from all eternity. As He foresaw the future, He saw it as it would progressively unfold from: (1) the result of His creative activity and His divine influence; (2) the result of the devastating influence of sin; (3) the result of the response that human beings would give as a result of the redemptive work of Jesus Christ, the ministry of the Holy Spirit, the ministry of the Word of God, and the ministry of the redeemed; (4) the result of all of the influences that would come from all sources outside Himself; (5) the result of all the influence that He would bring on people through His power and His infinite wisdom. He saw, then, everything that He sees and is doing now. He is the same God now that He was then. Everything that He is doing now is just as real as it would be if He had not known it in advance.[3]

God's omniscience and wisdom furnished Him with all the information and the "know how" that was needed for Him to arrange the death and suffering of Jesus Christ as the means of atonement for the sins of the world. With the aid of His infinite knowledge and wisdom, the determinate counsel was able to predetermine the crucifixion of Christ in eternity past. In this arrangement, foreknowledge was aiding, but foreknowledge as foreknowledge did not bear a causal relationship to the plan for the crucifixion to occur. Without foreknowledge, the determinate counsel could not have prearranged and predetermined the plan.

I think I have shown that there is no necessity whatever to give *foreknowledge* in Acts 2:23 a *causal* force with the result that it would be synonymous with *predestination*. I have read the comments on the use of *proginōskō* and *prognōsis* in several commentaries on Acts 2:23 and 1 Peter 1:20. I have tried to understand the reason that Calvinists consider it a valid and necessary conclusion to understand *predestination, election,* and *foreknowledge* to be essentially synonymous. I have also read the explanations given in several lexicons and theological dictionaries on these words. Most of what they say is based on the usage of *proginōskō* and *prognōsis* in Acts 2:23 and 1 Peter 1:20.

The verb *proginōskō* occurs three times in the Septuagint (Wisdom 6:13; 8:8; and 18:6). The meaning of *proginōskō* in the apocryphal *Book of Wisdom* is "to foreknow" or "to know in advance." The noun *prognōsis* is found in the apocryphal book Judith in 9:6 and 11:9. The use in 11:9 is understood as foreknowledge. The only use of the word *prognōsis* outside the New Testament that I have found is used to support the view that foreknowledge is an equivalent of predestination is found in Judith 9:6. Paul Jacobs and Hartmut Krienke give the meaning "of God's foreknowledge decreeing the fall of the Egyptians."[4] They take "foreknowledge" in Judith 9:6 to be the equivalent of "decreeing." *The Theological Dictionary of The New Testament* is in agreement. On *prognōsis*, it reads, "It is found in the LXX at Jdt. 9:6 with reference to the predeterminative knowledge of God."[5] It will be helpful to look in Judith 9:5-6:

> For thou hast done these things and those that went before and those that followed; thou hast designed the things that are now, and those that are to come. Yea, the things thou didst intend came to pass, and the things thou didst will presented themselves and said, 'Lo, we are here'; for all thy ways are prepared in advance, and thy judgment is with foreknowledge (*prognōsis*).[6]

I have found no defense given for the understanding that in Judith 9:6 *foreknowledge* is synonymous with *predestination*. It is true that predestination is spoken of in verses 5 and 6. But there is no reason to believe that *foreknowledge* has the same meaning as *predestination*. I think the meaning is that God's judgments were made in eternity past with the aid of His foreknowledge.

Peter says in 1 Peter 1:20 that Christ, as the lamb without blemish and spot, "indeed was foreordained before the foundation of the world, but was manifest in these last times for you." The word translated "foreordained" in 1 Peter 1:20 is *proginōskō*. The RSV translates it as "destined." The NIV has "chosen." The NEB translates "predestined." The NASB settles for "foreknown." I believe that the words *foreordained, destined, chosen*, and *predestined* are all appropriate words to apply to the fact that the atoning work of Christ on the cross was prearranged, preplanned, and predetermined in eternity past. God was not caught off guard by the fall of the race into sin. The plan of redemption was already made and determined before the fall of Adam and Eve took place in the chronological order of events. What was planned and determined in eternity past took place when Jesus died on the cross. What was in the mind of God in eternity past was "manifested for us in these last times."

When properly understood, I do not have any trouble with the words *destined, chosen, prearranged, preplanned, predestined,* and *predetermined.* Not only do I not have trouble with these words; I am as convinced of their truth as any Calvinist is. I do have a problem with translating *proginōskō* "predestined," or "chosen," or any words with a similar meaning.

Even if the true meaning in 1 Peter 1:20 is "predestined," it should be translated "foreknown." "To foreknow" is the proper translation of *proginosko.* To give it the meaning "foreordained," "destined," "chosen," or "predestined" is an interpretive translation. The Greek word *proginōskō* and the English word *foreknow* have exactly the same possibilities of meaning foreordained. When *proginōskō* is translated as "foreordination" or some word that is equivalent, the translator has become an exegete. He is giving a debatable meaning of *proginōskō* as the translation. Exegesis should be found in commentaries, not translations. If *proginōskō* means foreordained, it is the responsibility of the exegete to defend the interpretation with evidence. I am not aware of any strong defenses of the idea that "predestined" is one of the established meanings of the word *proginōskō.* The translation "foreordained" shows an influence of Calvinism to make *foreknowledge* synonymous with *predestination.* When this twist is given to the word foreknowledge, in the end predestination becomes the foundation for foreknowledge. God knows the future because He has predestinated it.

Whatever should be taken from 1 Peter 1:20 can be properly understood by taking *proginōskō* to mean "foreknown." The plan of God to provide atonement through the death of Christ was foreknown by God in eternity past. For this to have been foreknown meant, of course, that Jesus was chosen for the purpose of providing atonement by His death and that it was preplanned, predetermined, and prearranged. All of these concepts, while true, are true by necessary inference from the nature of God and from the direct teachings of Acts 2:22 and 4:28, not by the meaning and use of *proginōskō*.

Calvinism's insistence that *proginōskō* and *prognōsis* are to be taken as synonymous with predestination is without foundation from both biblical and extrabiblical usage.

Romans 8:29

Paul says in Romans 8:29, "For whom He foreknew, He also predestined to be conformed to the image of His Son, that He might be the firstborn among many brethren." The ones that are referred to by "whom he foreknew" are "those who are the called according to His purpose" in verse 28. Those who have now been called according to His purpose were foreknown by God in eternity past.[7]

From the standpoint of conditional election, there are two possible ways to understand foreknowledge as it is used in 8:29. Meyer explains: "God has fore-*known* those who would not oppose to his gracious calling the resistance of unbelief, but would follow its drawing; thereafter He has fore-ordained them to eternal salvation; and when the time had come for the execution of His saving counsel, has called them, etc." (ver. 30).[8]

Godet offers the same view, worded somewhat differently, "There is but one answer: foreknown as sure to fulfill the condition of salvation, viz. faith; so foreknown as His by faith."[9]

Lenski takes a somewhat different approach concerning the word know (Greek *ginōskō*). The meaning is "to know with affection and with a resultant affect." He goes on to say that to add the prefix "fore" (Greek *pro*) "dates this affectionate knowing back to eternity."[10]

If there is any doubt where Lenski stands on election, the following statement from him should settle the issue: "If it be asked why God did not foreknow, foreordain, call, justify the rest, the biblical answer is found in Matt. 23:37 and similar passages: God did not exclude them, but despite all that God could do *they* excluded themselves."[11]

Lenski's view is probably the correct view. "Whom he foreknew" speaks of knowing persons rather than simply knowing something about them. God foreknew the elect with affection, or He foreknew them as being His. There is no conflict whatsoever with this understanding of foreknowledge and conditional election.

What Meyer and Godet say about foreknowledge as referring to foreknowledge of faith is a necessary inference. To know a person implies a time of getting acquainted with that person. If God foreknew the elect as being His, it is necessarily inferred that this foreknowledge presupposes the person's belief in Jesus Christ as his Lord and Savior.

Romans 11:2

Romans 11:2 states that "God has not cast away His people whom He foreknew." In this verse, the reference is to the *affectionate foreknowing* of Israel as the Covenant People of God. The emphasis in this verse is the knowledge of corporate Israel as the people of God. It would be interesting to develop the concept of foreknowledge in this verse further, but that would involve a discussion of the place of Israel in the redemptive plan of God. That would lead us away from our present concern, which is how God's foreknowledge fits in with individual election and predestination. Romans 11:2 illustrates for us the use of foreknowledge as God's affectionate *foreknowing*. But it does not add additional light on foreknowledge and individual election.

1 Peter 1:2

First Peter 1:2 speaks of those who are the "elect according to the foreknowledge of God the Father. . . ." If we were to understand *prognōsis* (foreknowledge) as meaning predestination here, that would mean that election would be grounded in predestination. I think I have shown up to this point that there are no grounds for believing that foreknowledge is synonymous with predestination. This verse merely tells us that election is according to foreknowledge. It does not tell us what in foreknowledge formed the basis of election. It does not settle whether election was conditional or unconditional.

The New Testament Use and Meaning of Election

The word *eklegomai* occurs 21 times in the New Testament. *Eklektos* occurs 23 times. *Eklogē* occurs seven times. Many of the occurrences of these words do not have any bearing on the New Testament doctrine of election. However, I will examine every occurrence that has a bearing on this study.

The Word *Eklegomai*
The Gospel of John

This word *eklegomai* is found in John 6:70; 13:18; 15:16, 19. I have already dealt with these verses in Chapter 4 under the heading "The Occurrences of the Word *Eklegomai*."[12] *Eklegomai* is the verb form of the word for "elect." In the occurrences in John, it is translated "chosen." In each of these cases, the reference is to the Twelve Apostles. The reference is that Jesus had chosen them to be His apostles. There is no problem for conditional election if it did include election to salvation. For additional comments, see the treatment referred to above in the previous chapter. Of the occurrences of this word in the New Testament, the only other place that would help shed light on the doctrine of election is Ephesians 1:4.

Ephesians 1:4

Ephesians 1:4 reads: "just as He chose us in Him before the foundation of the world, that we should be holy and without blame before Him in love." This verse is probably the most important verse in the Bible on the subject of election. It makes very clear that believers were chosen in Christ before the foundation of the world. In no uncertain terms, it puts election in eternity past.

From the context of Scripture, it seems to me that the "us" is to be taken as a group of individuals who were chosen *individually*. Paul makes it very clear in Romans 9 that election is *individual*, not *corporate*. For a more thorough discussion, I would refer the reader to my comments in Chapter 3 under the heading, "Paul's Appeal to the Jews to See That Election Is Individual, Not Corporate." To support my case that election is individual, I will once again give the quotation that I gave in Chapter 3 from Thomas R. Schreiner which relates to Paul's treatment of individuals in Romans 9:15-21. Schreiner calls attention to the use of the singular in these verses. He explains:

> The word *whom* (*hon*) is singular, indicating that specific individuals upon whom God has mercy are in view. The singular is also present in the reference that Paul draws from Romans 9:15, in 9:16. God's mercy does not depend on "the one who wills, nor the one who runs." The conclusion to all of 9:14-17 in 9:18 utilizes the singular once again: "God has mercy on whom he wants to have mercy, and he hardens whom he wants to harden." In the same vein 9:19 continues the thought: "*Who* (*tis*) resists his will?" And Paul uses the singular when he speaks of one vessel being made for honor and another for dishonor (9:21). Those who say that Paul is referring only to corporate groups do not have an adequate explanation as to why Paul uses the singular again and again in Romans 9.[13]

What is of particular importance in Ephesians 1:4 is that Paul says, "He has chosen us in him." We are chosen in Christ. He does not say that we were chosen *to be in Christ*. At this point, I believe that Calvinism is in trouble. According to Calvinism, the elect were chosen by God as His very own *before* the decree to provide atonement. They were His at that very moment. In both Supralapsarianism and Infralapsarianism, the decision to elect some and reprobate others *precedes* the decree to provide atonement.[14]

Calvinism contends that this verse means, "chosen by God as His very own before the provision of atonement." Following this election, according to Calvinism, God decreed to provide atonement for those who were elected.

Then He decreed that those who were elected would be regenerated. This would guarantee that they would be efficaciously brought to exercise faith in Christ. It was decreed that, upon the experience of this efficaciously guaranteed faith, the person would be justified and placed in Christ.

This puts Calvinism in serious contradiction with Paul. Calvinism says that the elect were chosen by God as His very own before the decree to provide atonement. Paul says, "The elect were chosen in Christ."

Arminius was right when he said, "God can 'previously love and affectionately regard as His own' no sinner unless He has foreknown him in Christ, and looked upon him as a believer in Christ."[15] Arminius goes on to make a very insightful statement: "For, if God could will to any one eternal life, without respect to the Mediator, He could also give eternal life, without the satisfaction made by the Mediator."[16] Arminius puts his finger on what is probably *the most serious problem in Calvinism*. For the most part, Calvinists have been advocates and defenders of the satisfaction view of atonement. For election to precede, in God's plan, the provision of atonement violates the foundation on which the satisfaction view of atonement rests.

The satisfaction view of atonement insists that the holiness of God requires that *the guilt problem must be solved* before God can enter into fellowship with a fallen member of the human race. The only way that can happen is for a person to have the death and righteousness of Christ applied to his or her account. That takes place when a person places his faith in Jesus Christ and is placed in union with Christ.

It is not the prerogative of sovereign grace to enter into a personal relationship with a person *apart from the application of the death and righteousness of Christ* to his account. If that is the case, it was not the prerogative of sovereign grace in eternity past efficaciously and affectively to know or elect a member of the human race apart from foreknowing him or her to be in Christ.[17] Calvinism is harmed rather than helped by Ephesians 1:4.

THE WORD *HAIREOMAI*

Paul says in 2 Thessalonians 2:13, "But we are bound to give thanks to God always for you, brethren beloved by the Lord, because God from the beginning chose you for salvation through sanctification by the Spirit and belief in the truth." *Haireomai* occurs only three times in the New Testament. The other two places (Phil. 1:22 and Heb. 11:25) refer to choices by human beings. The related word *haritizō* is used only one time in the New Testament. It is found in Matthew 12:18 in a quotation from Isaiah 42:1. In this use, it is said by God the Father to the Son, "Behold my servant, whom I have chosen."

There does not seem to be any special significance in the use of *haireomai* rather than *eklegomai* in 2 Thessalonians. There is some thought given to the view that "from the beginning" refers to "the beginning of Paul's ministry among them." Others take "from the beginning" to refer to eternity past. Neither view presents a problem for conditional election. The salvation spoken of was experienced by "belief of the truth."

The Word *Eklogē*

This is the noun form. It refers to those who are chosen or elected. It is important that we remember that election refers both to our election by God in eternity past and to the election of God in time. When the New Testament speaks of a person (or persons) as being among the "elect" or "chosen," it means that God has chosen them already. People whom God foreknows to be people who will be saved in the future are not referred to as elect.

The use of the word *eklogē* in the following references assumes that the people under consideration have already been saved: Matthew 24:22, 24, 31; Mark 13:20, 22, 27; Luke 18:7; Romans 8:33; 16:13; Colossians 3:12; 2 Timothy 2:10; Titus 1:1; 1 Peter 1:2; 2:9; and Revelation 17:14. It is true that those who are saved in time were chosen by God in eternity past. But no person is designated as being "elect" or "chosen" unless he has already been saved.

The only use of the noun *eklogē* that is helpful in formulating the doctrine of election in eternity past is 1 Peter 1:2. It occurs in the plural form. The meaning is "elect ones" or "chosen ones." Peter goes on to tell us that this election took place in accordance with *foreknowledge*. While it clearly tells us that this election took place in eternity past, it does not address the subject of whether this election was conditional or unconditional.

The Question of Whether Election Was Conditioned on Faith

It is true that the Bible does not specifically say that foreknown faith was the condition of election in eternity past. The Calvinist is correct when he says that the Bible does not tell us why God chose the elect. However, silence on why God chose the elect gives no support for unconditional election. To recognize that God did not spell out for us in the Bible why He chose the elect is not the same as saying that we cannot know whether there was a condition and what that condition was. God's being the same yesterday, today, and forever means that if we know why God chooses people now, we can reason back to why God chose the elect in eternity past.

As Arminius has said well:

> Hence, God acknowledges no one, in Christ and for Christ's sake, as His own, unless that person is in Christ. He who is not in Christ, can not be loved in Christ. But no one is in Christ, except by faith; for Christ dwells in our hearts by faith, and we are ingrafted and incorporated in him by faith. It follows then that God acknowledges His own, and chooses to eternal life no sinner, unless He considers him as a believer in Christ, and as made one with him by faith.[18]

In commenting on "the conformity to Christ" that is predestinated in Romans 8:29, Arminius explains:

> Therefore, no one is predestinated by God to that conformity, unless he is considered as a believer, unless one may claim that faith itself is included

in that conformity which believers have with Christ—which would be absurd, because that faith can by no means be attributed to Christ, for it is faith in him, and in God through him; it is faith in reference to reconciliation, redemption, and the remission of sins.[19]

It is abundantly clear that salvation is by faith now. I do not think I need to give further development for the case that if salvation is conditional now, it necessarily leads to the conclusion that election in eternity past was conditional. The burden of proof is on those who think otherwise.

A Clarification on the Question of Ground and Condition

Our study of atonement and justification distinguished between the *ground* of justification and the *condition* of justification.[20] The same distinction must be made in election. The ground of election is that God foreknew us as being in Christ (in union with Christ). Thus, He chose us *in Christ*. That is what Ephesians 1:4 tells us. Since the condition for being in Christ is *faith in Christ*, it is necessarily implied that God foreknew that the person would meet the *condition* of faith in Christ.

The Extent of the Offer of Salvation
Where the Word *Called* Is Used or Implied

In Matthew 22:14, Jesus said, "For many are called, but few are chosen." In Acts 17:30, Paul said, "Truly, these times of ignorance God overlooked, but now commands all men everywhere to repent." It is generally agreed, even by Calvinists, that there is a general call that makes the gospel available to all people.

Some attention needs to be given to the use of the word *called* in the epistles. Calvinists make a point of saying that whenever the call is mentioned in the epistles, it refers only to believers. My response is that to refer to believers as being "called ones" does not mean that the call has not been extended to anyone else. A speaker at a special occasion may address the audience as invited guests. The only thing that he is affirming is that those who are present have been invited. They are not intruders. It does not mean that no one else was invited. When believers are referred to as "called," it is not necessary to conclude that others have not been called.[21]

The Appeal to "Whoever Will"

To understand the thrust of "whoever will," we need to remind ourselves again that, among the Jews in New Testament times, the prevailing view was that the Abrahamic Covenant automatically saved all Jews. We must keep this in mind when we consider how a Jewish audience (Jn. 3:15–16) would have understood an appeal to "whoever will believe in Jesus." It certainly means more than a simple, "Salvation is offered to anyone and everyone who will believe and receive it." The design is to break through the concept of corporate election or salvation and let them know that salvation is on an individual basis. It is for whoever will and only whoever will. The emphasis on only is strong because it is intended to bring an end to the concept of unconditional corporate election or salvation. The aim is to show that salvation is on an individual basis instead of a corporate basis.

John 4:13–14 is spoken to the Samaritan woman. In view of the conflict between the Jews and the Samaritans, the "whoever" in this verse is meant to assure the Samaritan woman that the life-giving water Jesus was offering was for her too.

Romans 9:33 comes at the end of a chapter in which Paul had poured out his heart to the Jews who had been blinded by the idea of a corporate election wherein all Jews were automatically saved. He desperately wanted to see his kinsmen saved. The "whoever" of this verse is intended to show that the salvation offer was for the Jews, but also to emphasize that it was made only to whoever would believe in Jesus as Messiah, Lord, and Savior.

In Romans 10:11-13, "whoever" is intended to make known that the offer extends to Greeks (Gentiles) as well as Jews. But when the reference is made to Jews, the intent is to make known that, while it was a genuine offer of salvation, it was also intended to emphasize that only "whoever," among the Jews, would believe in Jesus Christ as Messiah, Lord, and Savior would be saved. It was also making the claim that there was no difference between the way the Gentiles would be saved and the way of salvation for the Jews.

The contexts of these passages do not give the slightest hint that this "whoever will" is only offered to a "select few." Neither Jesus nor Paul inferred that, though this offer was to everyone, it had no real possibility of being received by anyone except those whom God had already unconditionally chosen. There is no suggestion that the only hope of a positive response rested on a person first being regenerated.

THE EXTENT OF THE ATONEMENT

Classical Calvinists are either Supralapsarians or Infralapsarians. Both Supralapsarians and Infralapsarians believe in limited atonement. They believe that the decree to elect preceded the decree to provide atonement. The decree to provide atonement was made specifically for the purpose of providing atonement for the elect. From their viewpoint it is better to speak of the *intent* of atonement than to speak of the *extent* of atonement. But either way it is stated, Jesus died only to make atonement for the elect.

Sublapsarian Calvinists believe that God decreed the provision of atonement for all mankind.[22] This was followed by the decree to elect some unconditionally for salvation. Sublapsarian Calvinists reject that point of Classical Calvinism referred to as limited atonement. These are referred to as Four-Point Calvinists. Some who have advocated this position say that God provided salvation for everybody, and nobody responded. Then God decreed to elect some unconditionally.

In the first edition of his theology text, Henry C. Thiessen adopted a modified form of Sublapsarianism. He explains: "We believe that the decrees are in this order: 1. The decree to create, 2. The decree to permit the fall, 3. The decree to provide salvation for all, and 4. The decree to apply that salvation to some, to those who believe."[23] Thiessen's "modified form of Sublapsarianism" is consistent with Arminianism. I accept it as my own.

It is interesting that many who believe in unconditional election think that the case for unlimited atonement is so compelling that they accept it. However, it seems to me that limited atonement fits more logically with unconditional election and the Calvinistic scheme.

I do not deem it necessary to give a thorough defense of the doctrine of unlimited atonement. The case must be strong and obvious because there are many who believe in unconditional election and yet they part with Classical Calvinism and adopt unlimited atonement. This is the position of Augustus Hopkins Strong[24] and Millard J. Erickson.[25] Henry C. Thiessen[26] is one who believes in both conditional election and unlimited atonement, although he joined the Calvinists on the doctrine of perseverance. Robert E. Picirilli, a Classical Arminian, gives an excellent and more thorough treatment of the subject of the extent of atonement in his book *Grace, Faith, Free Will*.[27]

Another reason I will not give an extensive treatment of unlimited atonement is that no one will ever become a Calvinist because he was first convinced of limited atonement and then embraced the other points of Calvinism. Even when he is convinced of other points, he will have some difficulty with limited atonement.

I will now give a very brief rationale for unlimited atonement.

John 3:16

John 3:16 states: "For God so loved the world that He gave His only begotten Son, that whoever believes in Him should not perish but have everlasting life." The only way anyone would ever question that *world* in this verse meant anything other than every human being is that he comes to the verse with a theological conviction that will not allow him to believe that. In this case the burden of proof is on the person who wants to place a restriction upon the scope of the word *world*.

1 Timothy 2:6

Paul says in 1 Timothy 2:6 that Jesus "gave Himself a ransom for all, to be testified in due time." The only possible reason for understanding "a ransom for all" any other way than that Jesus' death was a ransom paid for the sins of the whole race is that the person has a conflict between that interpretation and some other doctrine. This verse occurs in a context where Paul says, "Who [God] will have all men to be saved" (verse 4). The ransom was provided for "all." The "all" of verse 6 is the same as the "all" of verse 4.

Hebrews 2:9

Hebrews 2:9 reads: "But we see Jesus, who was made a little lower than the angels, for the suffering of death crowned with glory and honor, that He, by the grace of God, might taste death for everyone." The burden of proof is on the person who would place a restriction upon "everyone." The only natural reading of Hebrews 2:9 is that Jesus died for every human being.

1 John 2:2

The Apostle John in 1 John 2:2 says that Christ is "the propitiation for our sins: and not for ours only, but also for *the sins* of the whole world" (KJV). No one should deny that the most natural way to understand this verse is to reckon that the propitiatory sacrifice was intended to make atonement for the sins of the whole world. The only people who would think otherwise are those who believe in either Supralapsarianism or Infralapsarianism. The only reason for taking a verse whose meaning is apparent, and applying a strained interpretation (i.e., trying to make it fit the idea of limited atonement) would be their belief that the decree to elect preceded the decree to provide atonement. In such thinking, God decided whom He would save. Then, He decided to make atonement for those He had elected.

THEOLOGICAL ARGUMENTS AGAINST UNLIMITED ATONEMENT

Classical Calvinists believe that to hold to the satisfaction view of atonement precludes the possibility of unlimited atonement. They claim there are two insurmountable problems for those who believe in a satisfaction view of atonement if they at the same time reject limited atonement: (1) The only logical alternative to limited atonement for one who believes in the satisfaction view of atonement would be universal salvation. (2) If, as described by the satisfaction view of atonement, Christ died for those who are never saved, it would mean double payment with respect to those who spend eternity in hell.[28]

UNIVERSAL SALVATION OR UNLIMITED ATONEMENT A NECESSARY RESULT

Calvinists argue that, if Jesus paid the full penalty for the sins of the whole race, all for whom Christ died must of necessity be saved. This is true since His death settles their account and therefore forms the necessary basis for their forgiveness. Either Christ died for everybody and everybody would be saved, or He died only for the elect and only the elect will be saved, or so the argument goes. It is thought that for one who believes in the satisfaction view of atonement that the only way to escape universal salvation is to believe in limited atonement.

The answer is found in the kind of substitution involved. Christ died for the whole world in a *provisionary* sense. He suffered the penal wrath of God for sin, but that fact alone does not place His death on everybody's account. It is effectual for the individual only as it is placed on a person's account. It can be placed on a person's account only as a result of a union with Christ. Union with Christ is conditioned on faith.

The Calvinist may want to insist that the objection is valid and that Christ died only for the elect. The only way this argument could have any validity would be to deny the possibility of provisionary atonement. If there can be no provisionary atonement, it does follow that if Christ died for a person *his justification is never provisionary but always real.*

In explaining the view of limited atonement, Louis Berkhof comments: "The Calvinists teach that the atonement meritoriously secured the application of the work of redemption to those for whom it was intended and their complete salvation is certain."[29]

A close look at what Berkhof said will show that it does not rule out the provisionary principle in atonement. He says that the atonement "makes certain" the salvation of those for whom it was intended. He did not say that the atonement automatically saved everybody for whom it was intended. Calvinists do not teach that the elect are justified before they experience faith. They teach that the person for whom Christ died will of a certainty be justified, but they do not consider a person justified until he experiences faith as the condition of justification. Thus, atonement is provisionary until the time it is applied. The only way to deny the provisionary nature of atonement is to consider *all* people for whom Christ died to be justified *before* they experience faith.

Once we accept that atonement is *provisionary*, we invalidate the objection that penal satisfaction either leads to universalism or limited atonement. Provisionary atonement applied on the condition of faith and on the grounds of a union with Christ answers this objection and sustains the penal satisfaction view.

DOUBLE PAYMENT WITH REGARD TO SINNERS WHO GO TO HELL

The discussion above about provisionary atonement and union with Christ answers this objection. The death of Christ is not on the sinner's account who goes to hell. His account does not show a double payment. It is true that his sins were paid for *provisionally*, but there is no problem with justice which forbids collection of double payment as long as there is no double entry on the person's account.

The Desire of God and the Salvation of Sinners

I believe we are to conclude that God deeply desires His message of salvation to go out to all people, and He desires a positive response from all who hear this message. There are two passages that speak particularly of this concern of God. These are 1 Timothy 2:1-4 and 2 Peter 3:9.

1 Timothy 2:1-4

1 Timothy 2:1–4 reads, "Therefore I exhort first of all that supplications, prayers, intercessions, and giving of thanks be made for all men, for kings and all who are in authority, that we may lead a quiet and peaceable life in all godliness and reverence. For this is good and acceptable in the sight of God our Savior, who desires all men to be saved and to come to the knowledge of the truth." The only limitations on how many and which people are saved are: (1) our failure to confront people with the gospel and (2) the failure of people who hear the gospel to respond properly to the gospel. Verse 4 is not telling us that God has *planned* that all people be saved. Rather it tells us that it is His desire that all men be saved. The thought that it means anything other than that God has a desire for all people to be saved would never come up unless a person approaches these verses with a theological bias against this view. Nothing in these verses suggests that God does not desire that all people be saved.

2 Peter 3:9

2 Peter 3:9 states: "The Lord is not slack concerning His promise, as some count slackness, but is longsuffering toward us, not willing that any should perish but that all should come to repentance." In 2 Peter 3:4, Peter reminds us that there would be scoffers who would say, "Where is the promise of His coming? For since the fathers fell asleep, all things continue as they were from the beginning of creation." These scoffers misunderstand the delay of Christ's return. In verse 9, he tells us that we are not to consider that this delay means that Jesus is not coming again. Rather, the delay is

an indication that God is giving sinners time to repent. When Peter says that God is "not willing that any should perish," the word for "willing" (*boulomai*) means "to intend," or "to purpose." It is not God's purpose to plan unconditionally to bring about the eternal death of anybody. He does not unconditionally and sovereignly choose some for damnation.

CONCLUSION

I recognize that there are many Calvinists who are very strongly committed to evangelism and worldwide missions. I respect them for this, and I appreciate it. At the same time, I think Calvinism most surely dulls the concern of many. Clearly, in the teaching of unconditional election, obedience or lack of obedience to the Great Commission will not change who or how many people are saved.

As Arminians, we should feel rebuked by those Calvinists who are faithful in their obedience to the Great Commission. If conditional election is correct, and I believe it is, we must get under the burden of reaching lost people for Christ. We must feel deeply about it. We must feel convicted about it. And we must do better.

---

[1]According to the *Oxford English Dictionary* one of the obsolete meanings of the word schoolmaster was "a private tutor." That was one meaning of the word in 1611 when the KJV was translated.

[2]See a more complete explanation in Appendix 2, "Legalism in the Book of Galatians," in *The Quest for Truth*.

[3]See Chapter 2 under "Divine Foreknowledge of Free Human Choices and Acts Not Based on a Spectator Role."

[4]Paul Jacobs and Hartmut Krienke, "Foreknowledge, Providence, Predestination," In the *International Dictionary of New Testament Theology*, vol. 1, Colin Brown, ed. trans. from the German, *Theologisches Begriffslexikon Zum Neuen Testament*, 1967-1971 (Grand Rapids: Zondervan Publishing House, 1975), 692-93.

[5] *Theological Dictionary of the New Testament*, vol. 1, Gerhard Kittle, German ed., Geoffrey W. Bromiley trans. and ed. from *Theologisches Wörterbuch Zum Neuen Testament*, 1933-1973 (Grand Rapids: William B. Eerdmans Publishing Company, 1964-1974), 716.

[6] *The Apocrypha of the Old Testament*, Revised Standard Version (New York: Thomas Nelson, 1957).

[7] The explanation that I will give of "foreknow" (*proginōskō*) on this verse is taken from my commentary on Romans (Forlines, *Romans*, 236).

[8] Heinrich August Wilhelm Meyer, *Critical and Exegetical Hand-Book to the Epistle to the Romans*, 5th ed., John C. Moore, B. A. and Edwin Johnson, trans.; William P. Dickson, ed.; Timothy Dwight, American ed.; *Meyers Commentary on the New Testament*, vol. 5 (Clark, 1884; reprinted, Winona Lake: Alpha Publications, 1979), 337.

[9] Frédéric Louis Godet, *Commentary on the Epistle to the Romans*, trans. A. Cusin (Funk and Wagnalls, 1883; reprinted at Grand Rapids: Zondervan Publishing House, n. d.) 325.

[10] Lenski, *The Interpretation of St. Paul's Epistle to the Romans*, 557.

[11] Ibid., 562.

[12] See Chapter 4 under "The Occurrences of the Word *Eklegomai*."

[13] Thomas R. Schreiner, "Does Romans 9 Teach Individual Election unto Salvation?" in *The Grace of God, the Bondage of the Will*, vol. 1, eds. Thomas R. Schreiner and Bruce A. Ware (Grand Rapids: Baker Books, 1995), 99.

[14] See Chapter 2 under "The Order of Decrees in Calvinism."

[15] James Arminius, *The Writings of James Arminius*, James Nichols and W. R. Bagnall, trans. (Grand Rapids: Baker Book House, 1956), 3:314.

[16] Ibid.

[17] See the comments in Chapter 2 under "An Inconsistency in Calvinism" and "The Question of Sovereign Grace."

[18] Arminius, *The Writings of James Arminius*, 3:314.

[19] Ibid., 3:315.

[20]See the discussion in Chapter 6 under the heading, "The Ground of Justification."

[21]This paragraph is adapted from Forlines, *Romans*, 239.

[22]See Chapter 2.

[23]Henry C. Thiessen, *Introductory Lectures in Systematic Theology* (Grand Rapids: William B. Eerdmans, 1949), 344.

[24]August Hopkins Strong, *Systematic Theology*, 771-773.

[25]Millard J. Erickson, *Christian Theology* (Grand Rapids: Baker Book House, 1985), 829-835. For those who would like a more thorough defense of unlimited atonement than I will give, I would recommend Erickson's treatment.

[26]Thiessen, *Introductory Lectures in Systematic Theology*, 329-330.

[27]See Chapter "Calvinistic Arguments for a Limited Atonement," Chapter "Arguments for a Universal Atonement," and Chapter "New Testament Evidence for Universal Atonement" in Robert E. Picirilli, *Grace, Faith, Free Will* (Nashville: Randall House, 2002).

[28]I deal with this in Chapter 6. For the convenience of the reader I am using that treatment with modifications made to suit the use here. See Chapter 6 under "Universal Salvation or Limited Atonement a Necessary Result" and "Double Payment With Regard to Sinners Who Go to Hell."

[29]Berkhof, *Systematic Theology*, 393.

CHAPTER 6

The Nature of Atonement and Justification

Of all the events in the experience of Christ, His birth, His life, His death, His resurrection, and His return, His death stands central. As important as the other events are, both in themselves and in relation to His death, the death of Christ remains central, because apart from atonement there would be no forgiveness of sins. Christianity would be nonexistent. It is the birth that makes the death of Christ possible, but it is the death that makes the birth important. It is the resurrection that makes possible the application of the benefits of His death. It is the death that makes His resurrection important and makes the one who has been restored to life the Redeemer.

It is of utmost importance that we maintain a sound doctrine of atonement. The study of atonement must be done with the whole personality, not just the rational mind. While a study of atonement is fascinating in its logical consistency, it must go much deeper than that to be comprehended. It must grip the heart also. There is nothing that sheds light on the seriousness of holiness and sin like the atonement that God provided to bring forgiveness of sin. A proper view of atonement puts seriousness into the whole study of theology. Any system of ethics that does not read from atonement the seriousness of sin and the understanding of God's holiness and God's love that is seen in atonement will be grossly inadequate. Any view of grace that is not grounded in the understanding of sin, holiness, and the high regard for law that is manifested in atonement will be empty, shallow, and shot through with the tendencies of antinomianism.

It is not enough to proclaim the statement: Jesus died to save sinners. That statement must be grasped in its essential meaning before it is the gospel. That statement could be made by either a liberal or a fundamentalist, but with drastically different interpretations growing out of drastically different views of the authority of Scripture.

Most preaching falls short of giving a developed view of atonement. I hope this will be corrected. We need preaching and teaching that give a developed view of the need and the nature of atonement and how it is applied in justification. We need to preach and teach this truth often enough that our hearers will have an intelligent understanding of what Jesus Christ did on their behalf. Underdeveloped views of atonement run the risk of being replaced by false views. It is with a realization that our task is serious that we enter our study of atonement and its application in justification.

The major attention of this chapter will be taken up with contrasting the satisfaction view of atonement and the governmental view of atonement and the resulting views of justification. Some attention will be given to the moral influence view of atonement as advocated by liberalism.[1]

The Penal Satisfaction View of Atonement
Basic Assumptions

The penal satisfaction view of atonement rests on five basic assumptions: (1) God is sovereign. (2) God is holy. (3) Man is sinful. (4) God is loving. (5) God is wise. It is from a development of the inherent principles in these basic assumptions that we see the necessity, the provision, and the nature of atonement.

Lest we fall into the trap of mechanical versus personal reasoning, it is important for us to remind ourselves that atonement is designed to settle a conflict between persons—God and man. We must see sovereignty as personally administered by one who thinks, feels, and acts. God is capable of feeling joy, satisfaction, sorrow, and holy wrath. To deny God the ability to feel is to deny the integrity of His personality. As Henry C. Thiessen explains, philosophers often say that God does not feel things, that feeling would require "passivity and susceptibility of impression from without." They argue that this is incompatible with divine immutability. However, as Thiessen rightly argues, "immutability does not mean immobility. True love necessarily involves feeling, and if there be no feeling in God, then there is no love of God."[2]

Holiness is not an abstract principle, but an attribute of personality. It is not simply an attribute. It is an experience of the divine personality. It involves the principles and attitudes by which the divine personality operates. The same observations that have been made about holiness can also be applied to love and wisdom. These are experiences of the divine personality.

Man is personal. Sin is an experience of the human personality in conflict with a personal God. Atonement is designed to resolve this conflict and to form the foundation for restoring holiness as the experience of the human personality.

The Necessity of Atonement

The necessity of atonement draws on the first three of the previously given basic assumptions. God as Sovereign is both Lawgiver and Judge of the universe. This places man in a position of accountability before God. God cannot lay aside His responsibility as Judge, and man cannot escape his accountability before God—the Supreme Judge of the universe.

If there were no responsibility on God's part and no accountability on man's part, there would be no need of atonement, but this relationship is inescapably bound up in the nature of the case. Having established this responsibility-accountability relationship, there is still no necessity of atonement except as that necessity grows out of the holy nature of God. It is the holy nature of the One who is Sovereign, Lawgiver, and Judge that makes atonement necessary to resolve the conflict between man and God, since God has placed man under condemnation.

The Necessity for Sin to Be Punished

From the forewarned judgment against sin in Genesis 2:17 to the Great White Throne Judgment in Revelation 20:11-15, the Bible repeatedly reminds us of God's attitude toward sin. The culmination of God's attitude toward sin is seen in the eternal condemnation of the wicked (Mt. 25:45; Mk. 9:43-48; Rom. 6:23; Rev. 21:8).

Why is there such a dreadful penalty against sin? No principle of expediency for divine government could ever justify taking such a strong measure against sin apart from absolute necessity. Our whole being abhors the idea that God would take such a drastic step as eternal punishment apart from an absolute necessity existing within the nature of God. Such a step would be a violation of both the holiness and love of God. Our confidence in God tells us that He would not have taken such a step as eternal punishment if it had not risen from a necessity in the divine nature.

God's law issues from and is an expression of His holy nature. For holiness to be holiness, it not only differs from sin, but it is also intolerant of sin. This intolerance manifests itself in a penalty against the violation of the moral law of God. As J. Oliver Buswell, Jr., remarks, "The punishment of all that violates, or is contrary to the holy character of God is a logical implication and a necessary consequence of God's holiness. If God is holy, it must follow that He will vindicate His holiness as against all sin and corruption which is contrary thereto."[3]

The holy law of God pronounces a penalty on the person who violates that law. It is the work of divine justice to execute the penalty of the law and thus protect the holiness of God. The justice of God will not tolerate any attempt to set aside or diminish the penalty of the broken law of God. There can be no forgiveness of sin without a full satisfaction of the justice of God in the payment of the penalty.

Romans 3:26 declares that the design of propitiation was to make it possible for God to maintain His justice, while at the same time justifying the sinner who comes to God believing in Jesus. The implication is that for God to justify sinners without atonement would compromise the justice of God. This cannot be. It is clear that in this passage Paul is telling us that justice required atonement before there could be forgiveness.

A proper of view of both the necessity and the nature of atonement arises out of the absolute necessity for God to punish sin. This necessity comes from His holiness.

The Necessity for Absolute Righteousness

In Romans 2 and 3, Paul builds a strong case that our justification before God demands nothing less than absolute righteousness. In 2:1–3:8, Paul is particularly concerned with the Jews who have not believed in Jesus as their Messiah. He wants them to understand that they are not prepared to stand justified before God. He wants them to understand that merely being a descendant of Abraham through Jacob will not prepare a person to stand before God and receive the eternal inheritance promised to the seed of Abraham in Genesis 13:14-15 and 17:8.

The general consensus holds that Paul is addressing Jews in Romans 2. There are different opinions on what Paul is trying to say in verses 6-13. The problem centers around what Paul is trying to tell us will happen in "the day of wrath and revelation of the righteous judgment of God" (verse 5). He speaks of judgment according to deeds (verse 6). Patient continuance in "doing good" is what will be rewarded. Those who do not obey the truth will be under the wrath of God (verses 8-9). Those who do good will receive "glory, honor, and peace." In verse 12, he says that those who have sinned without the law (Gentiles) will perish. Those who have the law (Jews) and sin will be judged by the law (verse 12). In verse 13, he says emphatically that to have been the recipients of the law, as the Jews were, would carry no weight at the righteous judgment of God. Only those who are doers of the law will be justified.

These words have puzzled commentators. Thus, a variety of interpretations have been given. Most have concluded that verses 6-13 refer to the good works of Christians. This passage would be telling us that good works are essential evidence of being a Christian.

There are two problems with this interpretation. The first problem is that it does not fit the context. In Romans 1:18–3:20, it is clear that Paul is building a case for the argument that the whole world, including both Jews and Gentiles, stands condemned before God. No good reason can be given why Paul would depart from that theme in chapter 2 to talk about Christians doing good works as evidence of salvation. The second problem is that the works of which Paul speaks are absolute. In building his case, Paul states it from both the positive side and the negative side. On the positive side, he speaks of continuing in well doing. On the negative side, the presence of sin means judgment. In verses 12 and 13, there is no room for interpreting the "doing" to be anything less than "doing without exception."

Another view interprets the good works as "faith." Support for this interpretation has been sought from Jesus' words when He said, "is the work of God, that you believe in Him whom He sent" (Jn. 6:29). The problem with this view is that it does not fit the context.

A third view is that Paul is speaking hypothetically. If it were possible for a person to render absolute obedience to God, such a person would be justified. But, of course, such obedience is impossible for human beings.

I agree with those who hold the hypothetical view in saying that Paul's aim is to get the unbelieving Jew to see that, as a law violator, he is under condemnation. Where I differ is that I do not see it as hypothetical. Paul is not simply telling the law violator that he is condemned; he is telling him what is required of anybody who will ever be justified in God's sight.

The only way that any person can ever be justified before God is to have absolute righteousness (or to say it another way, to be considered a doer of the law). Briefly put, in 2:6-13 Paul is saying that a person must have absolute righteousness. In 3:10 he points out, "There is none righteous." In

3:20 he points out that "by the deeds of the law no flesh will be justified in His sight."

We must have absolute righteousness (2:6-13). We do not have absolute righteousness (3:10). We cannot produce absolute righteousness (3:20). The only hope of justification for either Jew or Gentile is to have absolute righteousness provided for us. There are two things that the justice of God will not permit a departure from: (1) Sin can under no circumstances go unpunished. (2) Under no circumstances will a person stand justified in God's presence without absolute righteousness.[4]

There are two things that the justice of God will not permit a departure from: (1) Sin can under no circumstances go unpunished. (2) Under no circumstances will a person stand justified in God's presence without absolute righteousness.

The Nature of Atonement

Sinful man is in a predicament for which he has no remedy of his own. He is under the condemnation of eternal death. The justice of God requires that the penalty be paid. Nothing less will be accepted.

I am not suggesting that an actual council, as I will describe, took place, but I am saying that what follows illustrates the principles involved. The justice of God demanded that the penalty of sin be paid. The love of God was interested in saving man, but it had to submit to the justice of God. The wisdom of God came forth with a plan that would satisfy both holiness and love. Through the incarnation of Christ and the substitutionary death of Christ, love could fulfill its desire to save, and holiness could hold to its insistence that sin be punished.[5]

There are two aspects of atonement: active obedience and passive obedience. Active obedience of Christ refers to the idea that He lived a life of absolute obedience to the Father. He lived an absolutely righteous life. Passive obedience refers to the death of Christ. He submitted to the wrath of God for our sins. Most of the discussion centers around passive obedience because it involved the payment of the penalty for our sins. A complete accounting of atonement also embraces the righteous life Christ lived on our behalf which was His active obedience.[6]

The Passive Obedience of Christ

What happened in the passive obedience of Christ? The Bible is quite clear on the basic principles involved. Isaiah 53:6 tells us, "the Lord has laid on Him the iniquity of us all." First Peter 2:24 reads, "who Himself bore our sins in His own body on the tree." Galatians 3:13 tells us, "Christ hath redeemed us from the curse of the law, being made a curse for us." Second Corinthians 5:21 says, "For He made Him who knew no sin to be sin for us."

When Jesus Christ went to the cross, all the sins of all the world that ever had been committed, ever were being committed, and ever would be committed were laid on Him. With our sins upon Him, He took our place under the righteous wrath of God. God poured out His wrath upon Him as if He were guilty of all the sins of the whole race. We read in Isaiah 53:10, "Yet it pleased the LORD to bruise Him; He has put Him to grief." In a very real and literal sense, Jesus took the place of every sinner.

It is a mistake to restrict the sufferings of Jesus Christ to that which the Roman soldiers inflicted on Him. The death Jesus Christ suffered by crucifixion was the least part of His suffering. His own Father inflicted the greatest suffering that was inflicted on Him. He took the place of sinners before God and drank the cup of wrath that was due sinners. He suffered as much on the cross as sinners will suffer in an eternal hell. He experienced separation from the Father. He who had enjoyed unbroken fellowship with the Father in eternity past uttered these words on the cross, "My God, My God, why have You forsaken Me?" (Mt. 27:46). This was a cry of agony rather than a cry from lack of understanding.

When Jesus finished suffering for the sins of the world, He said, "It is finished" (Jn. 19:30). When these words were uttered, He was telling us that He had finished paying for our sins. The same One who had a short time before uttered the words, "My God, My God, why have You forsaken

Me?" was now able to say, "Father, 'into Your hands I commit My spirit'" (Lk. 23:46).

When Jesus uttered the words, "Father, 'into Your hands I commit My spirit,'" this was the greatest reunion the universe has ever known. The One whose fellowship with God had been interrupted by having our sins placed upon Him had paid the penalty and removed the obstacle that separated Him from the Father. The way for His reunion was open. In opening it for Himself, He opened it for us. He identified Himself with our broken fellowship that we might be identified with His fellowship. He identified Himself with our sin that we might be identified with His righteousness.

Payment of the penalty through a qualified substitute was the only way God could save man. As William G. T. Shedd explains:

> The eternal Judge may or may not exercise mercy, but he must exercise justice. He can neither waive the claims of the law in part, nor abolish them altogether. The only possible mode, consequently, of delivering a creature who is obnoxious to the demands of retributive justice, is to satisfy them for him. The claims themselves must be met and extinguished, either personally, or by substitution . . . . And this necessity of an atonement is absolute not relative. It is not made necessary by divine decision, in the sense that the divine decision might have been otherwise. *It is not correct to say, that God might have saved man without a vicarious atonement had he been pleased to do so. For this is equivalent to saying, that God might have abolished the claims of law and justice had he been pleased to do so.*[7]

How was Christ able to pay the full penalty for our sins in a short time on the cross? It will help to elaborate on the penalty of sin. As the penalty of sin is related to man, it is called eternal death. The sinner will be paying it forever. Why is this so? I will suggest the following explanation. The penalty for sinning against a holy and infinite Person is an infinite penalty. Man is infinite in only one dimension of his being: his duration. Man will exist forever. The only way a human being can pay an infinite penalty is to pay it forever. Therefore, hell must be eternal.

As this relates to Christ, because of His divine nature, He is infinite in capacity. He can suffer an infinite penalty without it going into infinite time. Apart from this fact, there could have been no salvation. The only qualified redeemer is one who is the incarnation of deity. Our Redeemer had to be *man* to have the *right* to redeem. He had to be *God* to be *able* to redeem.

I am not saying that Jesus suffered the identical penalty that man would have suffered. I am saying that He suffered an equivalent penalty. If we say that Jesus went to hell for us when He paid our penalty, we are not meaning that He went to the lake of fire. We are meaning that He was subjected to equivalent punishment.

The Active Obedience of Christ

In the discussion on the necessity of atonement above, I pointed out that, through Romans 3:20, Paul had developed a case for saying that, if we were going to stand justified before God, it was necessary for us to have absolute righteousness. For us, that was bad news. We did not have absolute righteousness (Rom. 3:10), nor could we produce absolute righteousness (Rom. 3:20). So far as our own standing on our own merits is concerned, the trial was over. We were condemned. We were helpless, but not hopeless.

Just as surely as Paul, up through 3:20, sets forth our need, in 3:21-26 he proclaims a provision of absolute righteousness by Christ to meet our need. As human beings we must be "doers of the law." In Christ we have His righteousness which, so far as our justification is concerned, makes us "doers of the law." Christ's obedience becomes our obedience. It can be seen that to be doers of the law (or to have absolute righteousness) is not a requirement that is set aside by grace. Rather, the requirement, which we could not meet, was met for us by Jesus Christ.[8]

Romans 1:18–3:20 paints a very dark picture. In 3:21 the picture changes. The same God who declared the whole world as fallen short of the standard required by His holiness has made a provision that will stand under the scrutiny of the Supreme Judge of the universe. Paul says, "But now . . ." Now at this point in human and divine history, "the righteousness of God without the law has been manifested" (3:21). This righteousness is a "God-provided righteousness." This righteousness is "without works." It in no way takes into account our law-keeping or our failure to keep the law. It is the righteousness of Christ.

The Propitiatory Work of Christ in Atonement

The word *propitiation* is the most inclusive term in the New Testament denoting atonement. The key passage for understanding propitiation is Romans 3:25-26. It is not necessary to become involved in all the controversies about how to translate the word. Personally, I think *propitiation* or *propitiatory sacrifice* translates the word properly.[9]

The word *propitiation* means, in the biblical setting, to turn away the wrath of God and restore a person to favor with God. The word for *propitiation* is translated "mercyseat" in Hebrews 9:5, where it refers to the lid on the Ark of the Covenant. The lid on the Ark of the Covenant was the place of propitiation in the Old Testament Tabernacle. An understanding of what happened at the place of propitiation in the Tabernacle will help at this point.

The Ark of the Covenant was located in the Holy of Holies where the high priest went only once a year on the day of atonement. The Ark of the Covenant had within it the tables of the law (the Ten Commandments). The tables of the law represented the demands of the law which were: (1) absolute righteousness and (2) a penalty against sin in case of disobedience. When the high priest slew the goat on the day of atonement and took his blood into the Holy of Holies and sprinkled it on the mercyseat, it was as if he were saying to the Law, "This symbolizes the meeting of the demands that you require from sinners."

The animal *without spot* or *blemish* symbolized righteousness. The *slain* animal symbolized the payment of a penalty through a substitute. The satisfaction of the law was symbolized. This satisfaction included both the payment of the penalty and the provision of righteousness.

From the above discussion, we would observe that at the place of propitiation the law is satisfied. This, of course, tells us what the design of propitiation was. It was designed to satisfy the penal demands of the law, thus making it so God can turn away His wrath from the sinner who believes in Christ and at the same time maintain His justice. It was also designed to satisfy the demand for righteousness, thus giving positive grounds for God to view favorably the sinner who believes in Jesus and at the same time maintain His justice.

What the Old Testament sacrifice did in symbol on the day of atonement, Jesus Christ did in reality. He lived a completely holy life, thus fulfilling the demand for absolute righteousness. He paid the full penalty for sin, thus fulfilling the demand for a penalty. Propitiation, to sum it up, is the full satisfaction of the demands of the law, for righteousness and the payment of a penalty, by Jesus Christ. This makes it possible for God to turn His wrath from the sinner who believes in Jesus, and to view him with favor, yet remain a God of justice.

The Revelation of the Holiness and the Love of God

In the atoning work of Jesus Christ, we have the highest revelation of God's holiness and God's love. The holiness of God is seen in its refusal to approve a way of forgiveness that did not meet every demand of the moral law of God. The highest honor ever paid to God's holiness was paid by the Son of God when He fully satisfied the demands of the law to make possible our salvation. The highest possible regard for God's holiness is manifested in the atonement.

The love manifested at the cross is the highest possible manifestation of love. It will forever remain the unparalleled example of love. The sinless Son of God, on behalf of those who had sinned against Him, suffered the full wrath of God for their sins that they might be forgiven of their sins. The cross, as no other point in history or in the future, demonstrates the supremacy of holiness and the submission of love to holiness. While the cross is the foundation of grace, it is also the foundation of the highest interest in holiness on our part.

As McDonald explains: "In the atonement God's holiness is present in penal action and God's love is present in paternal grace. The cross is the place of a judgment on sin that God cannot withdraw and of a divine love for sinners that he will not withhold."[10]

Justification According to the Penal Satisfaction View of Atonement

The full view of atonement cannot be developed without also embracing the doctrine of justification. It is for this reason that I am treating justification here rather than in a later chapter. There are two aspects of justification. There is the negative aspect, which deals with the remission of the penalty for sin. There is the positive aspect, which deals with restoration to favor with God.

The Ground of Justification

Our justification is based on the imputation of the atoning work of Christ to our account. The chart below will help us see what takes place in justification.

Debits	THE SINNER	Credits
Absolute Righteousness		No payment
Eternal Death		No payment
	CONDEMNED	

Debits	THE BELIEVER	Credits
Absolute Righteousness		Christ's Righteousness
Eternal Death		Christ's Death
	PAID IN FULL JUSTIFIED	

We have already looked at how atonement was accomplished. Now the question: How do the death and righteousness of Christ come to be placed on our account? The condition for having the death and righteousness of Christ placed on our account is faith in Christ (Rom. 3:28; 4:1-25; Gal. 2:16; 3:1-18). Since there will be an elaboration on faith as the condition of salvation in a later chapter, I will not elaborate further at this time.

While *faith in Christ alone* is all that is involved on our part to receive the death and righteousness of Christ, there is more involved in the imputation of the death and righteousness of Christ to our account. The *ground* of the imputation of Christ's death and righteousness is the union of Christ and the believer. The substitutionary work of Christ for us was not substitution pure and simple. It was a substitution of the kind that in its application made it so that the believer can say, "I have been crucified with Christ" (Gal. 2:20).

Union with Christ and the Imputation of the Death of Christ to the Believer

The Scriptural evidence is clear that it is through union with Christ that the benefits of Christ's atonement, by which we are justified, are applied to us. Paul tells us: "Likewise you also reckon yourselves to be dead indeed to sin, but alive to God through Jesus Christ our Lord" (Rom. 6:11). "Through" in this verse translates the Greek preposition *en*. It is better to translate "in." It is "in Christ Jesus" that we are to consider ourselves to be dead to sin and alive to God. Again Paul says, "There is therefore now no condemnation to those who are in Christ Jesus" (Rom. 8:1). The ground for "no condemnation" is being "in Christ Jesus."

Romans 6:1-11

In Romans 6:3-4 and Galatians 3:27, baptism is used as a metonymy. A metonymy is a figure of speech in which one word is used for another which it suggests, such as the cause may be given for the effect or the effect for the cause. An example of this is, "For He Himself [Christ] is our peace" (Eph. 2:14). The meaning is that Christ is the cause or source of our peace.

The container may be given for that which is contained. An example of this is referring to the contents of the cup as the cup in the Lord's Supper (1 Cor. 11:25). The symbol is given for the thing symbolized. I believe an example of this is baptism in the verses under study.

In Romans 6:3, Paul says, "Or do you not know that as many of us as were baptized into Christ Jesus were baptized into His death?" This verse is designed to tell us how the believer's death to sin referred to in verse 2 was accomplished. By being baptized into Jesus Christ, we were baptized into His death. It was in this manner that His death became our death. It also tells us what kind of death is referred to. It is Jesus' death. The only kind of death that He died to sin was a penal death.

In saying that baptism is a metonymy in this passage, we are saying that the wording credits water baptism with what actually belongs to that which is symbolized. Water baptism does not baptize a person into Christ. It only symbolizes baptism into Christ. It is baptism by the Holy Spirit (1 Cor. 12:13) that baptizes the believer into Christ. In this baptism, we are united with Christ. In this union, His death becomes our death.

That Paul is saying that a union with Christ is accomplished by this baptism into Christ is made clear in verse 5. The word *sumphutos*, which the KJV translates "planted together," is a horticultural term. It is better translated "grown together." Conybeare and Howson give the translation, "For if we have been grafted into the likeness of his death." In a footnote they explain, "Literally, have become partakers of a vital union [as that of a graft with the tree into which it was grafted] *of the representation of his death* [in baptism]."[11] Many modern translations translate it "united with." The meaning is that by union with Christ we have the likeness of His death. As a rule, it is simply said that we died with or in Christ. In this case, likeness is used to stress that we have the credit for His death but did not experience the pain and agony of it.

That we received Jesus' death as our death in this union is further developed in this passage. In verse 6, which is given to explain verse 5, we are told, "Our old man was crucified with Him." Our old man here is our pre-salvation self or person, not our sinful nature. When we became a new man in conversion, what we were before that time became our old man because we are now a new person.

That the crucifixion of our old man was the penal death we died with Christ is clear from verse 7 where this death results in justification. The word that is translated "freed" is *dikaioō* and should be translated "justified." Only a penal death justifies. The only penal death that can justify us is the death of Christ.

Death by identification is further developed in verse 8, "Now if we died with Christ." If there has been any lack of clarity about having died by our union with Christ, verse 11 should remove all doubt. Paul plainly tells us that it is "in Christ Jesus" that we are to consider ourselves to be dead to sin and alive to God.

Three things are very clear in this passage: First, Paul talks about union with Christ. Second, this union identifies us with Christ's death. Third, this death is a penal death.

I am aware that most people understand the death to sin in this passage to be ethical rather than penal. In research for a thesis dealing with the believer's death to sin, I became firmly convinced that Paul was referring to a penal death. Support for this position was found in commentaries on Romans by David Brown, Thomas Chalmers, Robert Haldane, James Morrison, H. C. G. Moule, and William G. T. Shedd.[12] Some would insist on the ethical interpretation, because Romans 6 deals with sanctification. I will show how the penal death relates to sanctification in the chapter on sanctification.

Galatians 2:19-20

We are not dependent on Romans 6:1-11 alone. The penal death interpretation fits the context of Galatians 2:20. This death becomes the believer's death by being "in Christ." With reference to Galatians 2:19-20, Ellicot states:

The meaning is: "I died not only as concerns the law, but as the law required." The whole clause, then, may be thus paraphrased: "I, through the law, owing to sin, was brought under its curse; but having undergone this curse, with, and in the person of, Christ, I died to the law, in the fullest and deepest sense: being both free from its claims, and having satisfied its course."[13]

Shedd explains that "some commentators explain St. Paul's crucifixion with Christ, to be his own personal sufferings in the cause of Christ. But St. Paul's own sufferings would not be the reason he is 'dead to the law.' Christ's atoning suffering is the reason for this."[14]

Other Passages

After referring to 2 Corinthians 5:15-16 and 2 Timothy 2:11, Shedd concludes: "These passages abundantly prove that the doctrine of the believer's unity with Christ in his vicarious death for sin is familiar to St. Paul, and is strongly emphasized by him."[15]

Shedd and Walvoord on Union With Christ

William G. T. Shedd and John F. Walvoord shed light on the question of union with Christ. Shed calls the union between Christ and the believer a "spiritual" and "mystical" union. He explains that this mystical union provides the foundation for the "legal" and "federal" union between Christ and His people. It is because of their spiritual, vital, eternal, and mystical oneness with Christ that "his merit is imputable to them, and their demerit is imputable to him." Thus, Shedd rightly argues that "the imputation of Christ's righteousness supposes a union with him. It could not be imputed to an unbeliever, because he is not united with Christ by faith."[16]

John F. Walvoord makes synonymous the concepts of union with Christ and identification with Him. The believer is identified with Christ, Walvoord argues, "in his death (Rom. 6:1-11); his burial (Rom. 6: 4); his resurrection (Col. 3:1); his ascension (Eph. 2:6); his reign (2 Tim. 2:12); and his glory (Rom. 8:17)." Yet, he explains, this identification is limited. Through

His incarnation, Christ identifies with all humanity. However, "only true believers are identified with Christ." As a result of this identification, some of the "aspects of the person and work of Christ" are attributed to the believer, but not the "possession of the attributes of the Second Person, nor are the personal distinctions between Christ and the believer erased. Taken as a whole, however, identification with Christ is a most important doctrine and is essential to the entire program of grace."[17]

Summary Comments

Identification by union makes that which was not actually a part of a person's experience his by identification. For example, prior to the time that Hawaii became a part of the United States, a citizen of Hawaii could not have said, "We celebrate our day of Independence on July 4." Immediately upon their becoming a state, the same person who formerly could not make the statement could say, "We celebrate our day of Independence on July 4." What happened on July 4, 1776, became a part of their history. The history of the United States became the history of Hawaii, and the history of Hawaii became the history of the United States.

Prior to the union of Christ on the condition of faith, a person could not say, "I died with Christ." Immediately upon union with Christ, a person can say, "I died with Christ." The history of the cross became his history, not in the experiential sense but by identification, so that he received full credit for that death. At the same time, the history of our sins became Jesus' history, not in the sense that His character was affected, but so they would come into contact with the penalty He had already paid for them. He took the responsibility for them, but it was a responsibility He had already assumed on the cross. It is this side of the truth which Shedd was addressing in the quotation given earlier when he said, "And their [believers'] demerit is imputable to him."

Union With Christ and the Imputation of the Righteousness of Christ to the Believer

Attention has been given thus far to the imputation of the death of Christ to the believer. Let us now turn our attention to the imputation of Christ's righteousness. As Loraine Boettner has argued, most of the theological discussions of church history have focused on Christ's passive obedience at the expense of His active obedience. This has resulted in a situation in which many believers who eagerly recognize that Christ died for them "seem altogether unaware of the fact that the holy, sinless life which He lived was also a vicarious work in their behalf, wrought out by Him in His representative capacity and securing for them title to eternal life."[18]

In speaking of the righteousness of Christ that is imputed to us, it may be that we should understand righteousness to mean "that which is required to make one right or righteous before God." And, that would include both the penal death (passive obedience) and the righteous life of Christ (active obedience). I am inclined to agree with Robert Haldane when he says:

> No explanation of the expression, "The righteousness of God," will at once suit the phrase and the situation in which it is found in the passage before us [Rom. 3:21], but that which makes it that righteousness, or obedience to the law, both in its penalty and requirements, which has been yielded to it by our Lord Jesus Christ. This is indeed the righteousness of God, for it has been provided by God, and from first to last has been effected by His Son Jesus Christ, who is the Mighty God and the Father of eternity.[19]

Whether or not the righteousness of God that was provided for us includes the death of Christ, it would most certainly include the righteous life of Christ.

Paul says in 2 Corinthians 5:21, "That we might be made the righteousness of God in him" (KJV). In Philippians 3:9, Paul says, "And be found in Him, not having my own righteousness, which is from the law, but that which is through faith in Christ, the righteousness which is from God by faith." Both the NASB and NIV also translate *ek* as "from." In these verses, righteousness is ours "in Christ." Philippians 3:9 makes it clear that Paul is talking about a righteousness that is not his own in the sense of having personally produced it, but a righteousness that is from God.

In Romans 1:18–3:20, Paul had talked about man's need for righteousness. In and of himself, man did not and could not have righteousness. In Romans 3:21, Paul came through with a message of hope for those who were helpless. He spoke of a God-provided righteousness that was apart from personal law-keeping. It was provided by God on the condition of faith (3:22). In Romans 4:6, Paul spoke about the imputation of righteousness without works. In Romans 5:17, he spoke of the gift of righteousness. In Romans 10:3, he spoke of a righteousness that is not established by our own efforts but is submitted to. By taking all of this evidence together, we conclude that the righteousness that justifies is the righteousness of Christ placed on our account, given as a gift on the condition of faith.

Justification on Real Righteousness, Not Simply Declared Righteousness

On the condition of faith, we are placed in union with Christ. Based on that union, we receive His death and righteousness. Based on the fact that Christ's death and righteousness became our death and righteousness, God as Judge declares us righteous.

Some give great stress to the word "declare." They say that we are declared righteous, but we are not righteous. I beg to differ. Based on the death and righteousness of Christ becoming ours, we are righteous. The righteousness on which this declaration is made is a real righteousness. It is true that in our own persons we are not absolutely righteous, but we are not declared to be righteous in our own persons. We are declared to be righteous on the basis of a real righteousness, the righteousness of Christ. As will be seen later, the stress on the word *declared* belongs not to the satisfaction view but the governmental view.

Justification the Work of God as Judge

It is important to observe that justification is the work of God as Judge. God, as Judge, will not justify us in any way other than that which protects His own holiness and shows an interest in our holiness. The moral concerns of God are fully protected and are clearly manifested in God's provision of atonement and justification.

A shallow look at an account balanced by a gift of the death and righteousness of Christ leads to a cheap view of grace and has serious moral consequences. It has traces of antinomianism, which lacks appreciation for the moral responsibility of the believer.

It is true that justification is by grace, which is an unmerited favor. That fact must never be compromised. It must never be corrupted. There is a right way and a wrong way to approach grace. Grace must be understood in *the context of moral law*, not moral law in the context of grace. By this I mean that we start with law, and *grace conforms to the requirements and interests of law*. We do not begin with grace and make law conform to grace. We do not begin with the gospel and then move on to law. Rather, we begin with law and then proceed to the gospel. It is only when people see how they stand before God's law that they are ready to give proper attention to the good news of God's grace. In the last half-century or so, much harm has been done in the evangelical church world by preaching grace in such a way that the interests of law and holiness are not properly dealt with. The most open example of this has been those who have advocated the view that a person can receive Jesus as Savior without receiving Him as Lord.

In Romans 3:31, Paul says, "Do we then make void the law through faith? Certainly not! On the contrary, we establish the law." The provision of grace operates within the framework of the highest regard for law. Man was condemned by the holy law of God because of his sin. The holiness of God would not tolerate a plan of redemption that did not pay full respect to the law of God. We are not talking about arbitrary law. We are talking about law as the expression of the holy nature of a personal God. We are not talking about playing around with a legal technicality as sometimes goes on in our legal system. We are talking about truth. The only plan of atonement that God would approve was one that gave full satisfaction to the holiness of God by meeting all the demands of the law. Justification must be the work of God as Judge. As Judge, He sees to it that the fullest interest of the law is maintained. No person is justified apart from the complete satisfaction of the law. The full protection and the sure manifestation of God's moral concern is clearly seen by the way in which God provided atonement and justification. For God to be so determined to protect the interest of His holiness in atonement and then, by justification, to open the way for a Christian experience in which holiness is something we can take or leave would be absurd.

When we begin with grace or try to build grace on a weak moral foundation, we corrupt both grace and law. The hasty conclusions that are drawn in such a manner are both false and dangerous. It is reasoned that while moral responsibility might be good, it is optional. Since Jesus satisfied the demands of the law and the only condition of salvation is faith, it is felt by some that it is conceivable that a person can be a Christian and at the same time live in any degree of sin. We need to be careful in combating this error *lest we corrupt grace*; at the same time we must combat it lest we *corrupt both law and grace*. We combat it not by changing the nature of atonement and justification, but by having a view of sanctification that is an appropriate accompaniment of justification. This we will propose to do in the chapter on sanctification.

Reconciliation the Result of Justification

Atonement and justification were designed to resolve a conflict between God and man. The guilt of man closed the door of fellowship with man from God's side. Justification opened that door. It prepares the way for reunion and fellowship with God.

Full reconciliation involves reconciliation on our part. This involves repentance and regeneration which will be discussed later. As a result of all of this we are restored to fellowship with God. The functioning personal relationship with God that we so drastically need becomes a reality in salvation. The foundation for it all rests upon atonement and justification. The logical consistency and adequacy of atonement and justification meet the needs of our mind. The forgiveness of sins and restoration to favor and fellowship with God meet the needs of our hearts.

The Governmental View of Atonement

The majority of theologians who view the Bible to be an objective, divine revelation have adhered to the basic ideas of the penal satisfaction view of atonement. There have been some who have held to the governmental view. This view was first introduced by Hugo Grotius (1583-1645). Adherents of this view since Grotius have included Charles Finney, James H. Fairchild, John Miley, and H. Orton Wiley. In order to avoid some of the criticisms that have been given to this view, some have modified the governmental view, but have still held to most of the essentials. The basic assumptions of the governmental view are: (1) God is sovereign. (2) Man is sinful. (3) God is loving. (4) The end of God's sovereignty is the happiness of man.

The Necessity of Atonement

One of the basic principles of the governmental view is the rejection of the absolute necessity that sin be punished. John Miley, the nineteenth-century Wesleyan theologian and strong advocate of the governmental view says, "While thus asserting the intrinsic evil of sin, Grotius denies an absolute necessity arising therefrom for its punishment. The punishment of sin is just, but not in itself an obligation."[20]

Sin requires punishment only as it is necessary to secure the ends of God's government. Fairchild explains the interpretation of the end of government as it is perceived by those who advocate the governmental view:

> And when we speak of detriment to God's government, we should mean harm to the great interests of his rational and dependent universe. We sometimes speak of the necessity of protecting God's honor as a ruler,

or of magnifying the law of God, and or meeting the claims of justice. These terms have a limited significance; but all essential facts implied are summed up in the comprehensive idea of securing the wellbeing of God's rational creatures, the subject of his government. This is the sole end of government; and when this is secured the honor of God, and of the law, and of justice, will all be safe. Atonement is adopted to secure these ends.[21]

Since it is not an absolute necessity that sin be punished, the penalty can be set aside and never be paid either by the person or a substitute as long as another means can be provided that will protect the interests of government. It is concluded that atonement is necessary to protect the interests of government because forgiveness too easily granted would present problems.

Miley explains concerning Grotius's view: "Forgiveness too freely granted or too often repeated, and especially on slight grounds, would annul the authority of the law, or render it powerless for its great and imperative ends. Thus he finds the necessity for an atonement—for some vicarious provision—which, on remission of penalty, may conserve these ends."[22] The necessity of atonement rests in the need of a means by which sin can be forgiven without loss of respect for government. When this is achieved, the penalty can be set aside and sins can be forgiven.

It can be seen that there is a drastic difference between the necessity of atonement in the satisfaction view and the governmental view. That difference in the necessity of atonement results in drastically different views on the nature of atonement.

The Supremacy of Public Justice

In the governmental view of atonement, public justice, not retributive justice, is satisfied. It is not *the holy nature of God* that is satisfied, but *the public good*. Charles G. Finney, as an advocate of the governmental view of the atonement, believed that the divine exercise of public justice requires the "promotion and protection of the public interests, by such legislation and such an administration of law, as is demanded by the highest good of the public." Public justice demands that legal penalties be meted out when a divine precept is violated, "unless something else is done that will as effectually serve the public interests." When the latter is done, public justice demands that "the execution of the penalty shall be dispensed with, by extending pardon to the criminal. Retributive justice makes no exceptions, but punishes without mercy in every instance of crime. Public justice makes exceptions, as often as this is permitted or required by the public good."[23]

The Place of a Penalty in Public Justice

In serving the need of public justice, a penalty is a *moral force to discourage disobedience.* The death of Jesus Christ is not a penalty for sin. Occasionally some who hold to the governmental view use the word *penalty* in a loose sense but never in a technical sense. The death of Jesus Christ is a substitute for a penalty. It takes the place of a penalty and serves the same purpose as a penalty.

According to Miley, Grotius viewed the death of Christ as a penal example. "And he makes a very free use of the term penal substitution. Yet he does not seem to regard the sufferings of Christ as penal in any very strict sense—certainly not as a substitutional punishment of sin in the satisfaction of a purely retributive justice."[24]

Fairchild explains concerning the governmental view of the death of Christ: "*The theory presented does not present that Christ suffered the penalty of the law . . . .* In a very proper sense *the death of Christ takes the place of the penitent sinner's punishment, as a moral force in the government of God;* and thus it is that the Scriptures represent that Christ died for us; that "he bore our sins in his own body on the tree."[25] The suffering of Christ made the punishment of the penitent unnecessary.

The Moral Force of the Death of Christ

It may be asked what it is that constitutes this moral force in the death of Christ and thus makes atonement possible? Fairchild answers this question accordingly:

> *It is an exhibition of God's estimate of sin*, in that no arrangement less significant than the coming of the Emmanuel, and his patience and obedience unto death, could be devised, to counteract the mischief of sin, and deliver men from ruin. . . .
>
> Again, it is to be observed *that in the death of Christ sin has made an exhibition of itself* . . . . Sin never so displayed its malignity and hatefulness, as in that infamous deed; and the sight of the cross from that day to this, has tended powerfully to make the world ashamed of sin . . . .
>
> *It exhibits the beauty of holiness*, even more impressively than the odiousness of sin. The character and consecration of the Savior is the highest exhibition of goodness and unselfish devotion that the world has seen . . . .
>
> Again, *the cross is an exhibition of the love of God*, in the sense of sympathy and compassion for sinners . . . . *The goodness and the severity of God are united in the great lesson of the cross.*[26]

The value of Christ's death in the governmental view is revelational. It reveals God's attitude toward sin, that sin is odious, the beauty of holiness, and the love of God.

Justification According to the Governmental View of Atonement

Just as there is a drastic difference between the satisfaction and governmental views of atonement, there is also a drastic difference in the views of justification that grow out of these differing views of atonement.

No Imputation of Either the Death or the Righteousness of Christ to the Believer

One obvious result of the governmental view of atonement is that it denies the imputation of Christ's death and righteousness to the believer. Fairchild, for example, argues that theologians who teach the imputation of human sin to Christ and Christ's righteousness to human beings "treat justification as a judicial act, a pronouncing of the sinner just before the law. . . . The simpler and more reasonable view is, that *there can be no transfer, or imputation, either of guilt or of righteousness.*"[27]

Faith Imputed for Righteousness

Thus, in the governmental view, the penalty is set aside in the light of atonement when the sinner exercises faith in Christ. The chart below will help us see what takes place in justification according to this view.

Debits	THE SINNER	Credits
Absolute Righteousness		No payment
Eternal Death		No payment
	CONDEMNED	

Debits	THE BELIEVER	Credits
Absolute Righteousness		Faith in Christ
~~Eternal Death~~		
	JUSTIFIED OR PARDONED	

Those who hold the governmental view agree that absolute righteousness is what God required of the sinner, and eternal death is the penalty for disobedience. However, in view of faith in Christ, God sets the *penalty aside.* The same consideration that would have been given to absolute righteousness is given for *faith.* Faith is not absolute righteousness, but it is counted "for" or "as" righteousness. Fairchild says, "*Faith is another word for the righteousness which the law requires.*"[28] The exact meaning of "faith counted for righteousness" is understood with some variations among governmentalists, but all concur in denying that there is any imputation of the death or righteousness of Christ to the believer. These variations do not have any essential effect on the view.

Since justification, in the governmental view, declares the person to be righteous without this declaration being based on an absolute righteousness, it can be seen that it is appropriate to give stress to the word *declare*. The believer is declared to be righteous, but he is not righteous. This is supposed to be the way grace works. The satisfaction view does not admit this interpretation of *declare*. The believer is declared righteous because the righteousness of Christ, which is a real righteousness, is his.

Justification the Work of God as Sovereign

The judge must go by the law and uphold the law. He can declare a person righteous only as he is righteous by the standard of the law. A ruler has more latitude. This can be seen in the right of a governor to pardon.

In the governmental view, God as Ruler declares the believer righteous not by the strict standard of law but in a manner that is designed to protect the public good. This is what allows Him to set the penalty aside. The justice administered is not *retributive* justice but *public* justice. Finney explains:

> Courts never pardon, or set aside the execution of penalties. This does not belong to them, but either to the executive or to the lawmaking department. Oftentimes, this power in human governments is lodged in the head of the executive department, who is generally at least, a branch of the legislative power of government. But never is the power of pardon exercised in the judicial department. . . .
>
> It consists not in the law pronouncing the sinner just, but in his being ultimately governmentally treated as if he were just; that is, it consists in a governmental decree of pardon or amnesty—in arresting and setting aside the execution of the incurred penalty of law.[29]

The Technical Use of the Words *Pardon* and *Justify*

If we would be technical in the use of language, the governmental view should speak of "pardon" and the satisfaction view would speak of "justification." In the satisfaction view, God, as Judge, declares the believer *justified* because, in Christ, all of the requirements of the law have been met. In the governmental view, God, as Sovereign Ruler, declares the believer righteous and pardons the believer because, in view of the revelational influence of Christ's death, no violence is done to the interest of God's government.

Since we are not always technical in our use of language, *justification* and *pardon* will continue to be used interchangeably. Another factor that will keep the word *pardon* alive is that it lends itself more easily to use in poetry than the word *justify*.

Criticism of the Governmental View of Atonement and Justification

While the governmental view has many important differences that distinguish it from the moral influence theory of liberalism,[30] it has some dangerously close parallels. (1) Both views deny that there is any principle in the divine nature that requires satisfaction in atonement. (2) Both deny that it is absolutely necessary to inflict a penalty on sin. (3) Both views consider the value of Christ's death to be revelational.

Those who have believed in the governmental view have historically believed in the doctrine of hell for those who do not receive Christ by faith. Liberalism believes in universalism. There is no penalty against sin in the strict sense of the word. In liberalism, the emphasis in the revelational value of the death of Christ stresses the love of Christ. It is God's love on the one hand assuring the sinner that there is no obstacle to his return. On the other hand, God's love is a moral force to bring about moral transformation in the sinner. The great love of God manifested in sending Jesus to die is meant to show us that God loves us and serves as a heart-moving revelation designed to bring about moral change. In the governmental view, the death of Christ reveals the holiness of God, the seriousness of sin, the love of God, and God's interest in maintaining His government.

In the discussion of the satisfaction view, I set forth the reason for believing that it is an absolute necessity for sin to be punished. God's holy nature requires it. If the holy nature of God requires that sin be punished, it is a very serious matter to deny that truth. The governmental view proposes to emphasize the importance of holiness and the seriousness of sin. As weighed against the importance of God's holiness and the seriousness of sin in the satisfaction view, the governmental view falls far short. In the satisfaction view, holiness is so important and sin is so serious that nothing short of a full satisfaction of God's law can make atonement for sin. Nothing less would permit God in His capacity as Judge to declare the believer to be righteous. In the governmental view, God in His capacity as Ruler can set aside the penalty of sin and declare the believer to be righteous, who is in fact not righteous.

All of the valid principles that the governmental view proposes to uphold are done better by the satisfaction view. The satisfaction view more successfully shows the importance of holiness and the seriousness of sin. It gives a much higher view of the love of God. It creates a more solid foundation for respect for God's government.

While the satisfaction view does reveal the importance of holiness, the seriousness of sin, and the wonder of God's love, what it reveals is *not* what makes atonement. Atonement is based on full satisfaction of the demands of the law. God uses atonement as an instrument of revelation, but revelation is not a means of atonement. This revelation of God is used by God to bring people to Christ and promote holiness and love among believers.

While important differences can be pointed out in the revelation principle in the governmental view and the liberal view, I do not believe these differences are adequate to give the needed protection against liberal influence. Though I have not researched the subject to see, I am inclined to believe that history would show there had been a loss among governmentalists in this direction.

The most important thing that can be said for the governmental view is that its advocates have held to a serious view of Scripture. They have proposed their view to be the Scriptural view. The advocates of the moral influence view have had a low view of Scripture. Whatever protection the governmentalists have from taking up the liberal view rests far more upon their respect for Scripture than upon logical arguments to maintain the governmental view as opposed to the moral influence view.

One of the important distinctions between the satisfaction view and the governmental view is the ends they propose to serve. The governmental view is *man-centered*. It seeks to protect the welfare of mankind. The satisfaction view is *God-centered*. It seeks to vindicate the divine nature.

In my opinion, the governmental view is seriously inadequate. It is dangerously close to liberalism's view. Once a person denies the absolute necessity of the punishment of sin, there is no logical barrier that prohibits the slide into the moral influence theory. Whatever safety there is lies in the commitment to Scripture rather than a safety in the logic of the case.

Objections to the Penal Satisfaction View as Raised by the Governmental View

Penal Satisfaction Not Necessary

For a general development of the necessity for penal satisfaction, see my treatment of "The Necessity of Atonement." At this point I want to discuss the importance of having a proper view of the necessity of atonement in order to maintain the integrity of Christian thought.

The Importance of a Proper View of the Necessity of Atonement

A person's view of the *necessity* of atonement determines his *view* of atonement. When we speak of the necessity of atonement, we mean that atonement was necessary if a way of salvation were to be provided. The provision of atonement is not a necessity. There was no provision of atonement for fallen angels.

A person's view of atonement and his view of hell must be consistent with each other. If eternal punishment is an absolute necessity, it follows that penal satisfaction by one who is both God and man would be the only means of making the forgiveness of sin possible. If penal satisfaction did not occur in atonement, *eternal punishment in hell* (the only way a *finite* person can pay an *infinite* penalty) is not a divine necessity.

In particular individuals, ideas may be held without adhering to systematic coherence. But in the community of human experience, ideas have a way of moving toward logical consistency. A particular person may believe that eternal punishment of sinners in hell is an absolute necessity and yet not believe in the penal satisfaction view of atonement. However, when minds join together to promote that approach, given enough time the inconsistency will surface. It will be seen that one cannot speak consistently of the necessity for the punishment of sin on the one hand, and on the other hand deny penal satisfaction in explaining atonement. Belief in the absolute necessity of the punishment of sin will move in the direction of the penal satisfaction view of atonement.

A particular person may not believe in the penal satisfaction view of atonement and may believe that eternal punishment of sinners in Hell is an absolute necessity. However, in the community of Christian experience, the inconsistency of such an approach will surface. If rejection of the penal satisfaction view persists, in time, there will also be a rejection of the *absolute necessity* for the punishment of sin. If there is an absolute necessity that sin be punished, it follows that if Jesus Christ made atonement for our sins, it was necessary for Him to pay the penalty for sin.

There can be no satisfactory way to *maintain* the doctrine of an eternal Hell while at the same time rejecting the absolute necessity of the punishment of sin in atonement. Some may want to suggest that the problem would be eased if we would take the approach of the annihilation of the wicked rather than the view of eternal punishment. My first answer is that it is not our responsibility to look for ways that are more acceptable than that which is given in the divinely inspired Word of God. I would also say that annihilation would not be an act of kindness. It could be tolerated morally only if it were an absolute necessity. If it were an absolute necessity, how could Jesus Christ, as our substitute, make penal satisfaction? Whatever else we might say, He certainly was not annihilated!

Emil Brunner believed in annihilation, and also believed in the penal satisfaction view of atonement.[31] However, he made no attempt to explain how Jesus Christ satisfied the penal demand for annihilation. I can understand how infinite suffering by the One who was both God and man could be equivalent to eternal suffering on the part of a finite person. I cannot understand how anything that Jesus did would be considered equivalent to annihilation. If there was any absolute necessity of any kind of punishment for sin, it would be an absolute necessity for satisfaction to be made by a *qualified substitute*. Otherwise it would not be an absolute necessity to punish sin. Our deep inner being will not tolerate the idea that God would pronounce the penalty of eternal death on any other basis than that it was an absolute necessity growing out of His holy nature.

The power with which postmodernism conditions individuals today seriously diminishes the way people feel about sin. Even Christians do not feel as deeply about sin as they did prior to the rise of postmodernism. Relativism and deep feelings about sin do not go together.

Even people who would check the right answers on a questionnaire on basic matters about right and wrong do not feel as deeply about sin as people did 40 or 50 years ago. This makes it harder for the Holy Spirit to bring conviction of sin to people's hearts. It makes it much harder for people to think of sin as being so serious that it deserves the penalty of an eternal hell. If people do not feel deeply about sin, judgment, and hell, they certainly will not feel deeply about the need of an atonement for sin that would require Jesus Christ to suffer the full wrath of God for sin. All of this makes it much harder than it once was to convince people that they need a salvation that can be provided only by Jesus Christ.

Postmodernism has contributed to a troubled and mixed-up society. That problem is a deep Christian concern. But as important as it is to help people with mixed-up lives, that is not what made it necessary for God to require atonement. It was the guilt of our sins that demanded a holy God to require atonement before He could forgive sin. Atonement is of tremendous importance for those whose lives are filled with hurting, but Jesus did not have to go to the cross because we were hurting. Rather, He went to the cross because we were guilty.

If people were hurting, and there was no problem of guilt before a holy God, a case might be made for the helpfulness of the incarnation. But there would be no case for the need of atonement. The *need* of atonement rests on human guilt and the necessity of the divine nature to punish sin—*that and that alone.*

Penal Satisfaction Through a Substitute Not Possible

There are two types of punishments meted out by the judicial system—pecuniary punishment and penal punishment. Pecuniary punishment is the punishment that takes the form of a fine. It is possible for a substitute to pay a fine for a person. Penal punishment involves a punishment of the person. The person goes to jail, to prison, or is put to death. In our judicial system there is no substitution in the area of penal punishment. The punishment of sin is not pecuniary, but penal. Therefore, it is argued that there can be no substitution for us.

This objection does bring up a valid concern. *Substitution* pure and simple, whereby one person does something for or in the place of another, *would be invalid in atonement.*

The answer to this objection is found in the union of Christ and the believer as was discussed in connection with the satisfaction view. By identification with Christ the believer can say, "I died with Christ." The action can be considered to be his, not simply an action that was performed for him. As a result of this union with Christ, God can view the death and righteousness of Christ as *being the death and righteousness of the believer.*

In our judicial system, we cannot have penal substitution because there is no way it can be said that a person went to jail without actually going. In

Christ, we can say we died with Him without actually going through this experience. Therefore, penal substitution is possible. For a more thorough discussion of how union with Christ makes it so that Christ's death and righteousness are made a part of the believer's history, see the discussion on "The Ground of Justification."

Universal Salvation or Limited Atonement a Necessary Result

Calvinists argue that all for whom Christ died must of necessity be saved since His death settles their account and therefore forms the necessary basis for their forgiveness. Either Christ died for everybody and everybody would be saved, or He died only for the elect and only the elect will be saved, the objection states.

Again, the answer is found in the kind of substitution involved. Christ died for the whole world in a *provisionary* sense. He suffered the penal wrath of God for sin, but that fact alone does not place His death on everybody's account. It can be efficacious only as it is placed on a person's account. It can be placed on a person's account only as a result of a union with Christ. Union with Christ is conditioned on faith.

The Calvinist may want to insist that the objection is valid and that Christ died only for the elect. The only way this argument could have any validity would be to deny the possibility of provisionary atonement. If there can be no provisionary atonement, it *does follow* that if Christ died for a person, his justification is *never provisionary* but always *real*.

In explaining the view of limited atonement, Louis Berkhof comments: "The Calvinist teaches that the atonement meritoriously secured the application of the work of redemption to those for whom it was intended and their complete salvation is certain."[32]

A close look at what Berkhof said will show that it does not rule out the provisionary principle in atonement. He says that the atonement "makes certain" the salvation of those for whom it was intended. He did not say that the atonement automatically saved everybody for whom it was intended. Calvinists do not teach that the elect are justified before they experience faith. They teach that the person for whom Christ died will of a certainty be justified, but they do not consider a person justified until he experiences faith as the condition of justification. Thus, atonement is provisionary until the time it is applied. The *only way* to deny the provisionary nature of atonement is to consider all people for whom Christ died to be justified *before* they experience faith.

Once it is accepted that atonement is *provisionary*, the objection, which states that penal satisfaction leads to either universalism or limited atonement, is seen to be invalid. Atonement is provisionary until it is applied. It can be applied only on the condition of faith and on the grounds of union with Christ. When applied, atonement becomes efficacious. Then and only then is atonement efficacious. The objection that the penal satisfaction view requires either universalism or limited atonement fails.

Considerable biblical evidence supports the truth that Christ died for every person, thus provisionary atonement was made for all people. Hebrews 2:9 makes it clear that Jesus tasted death for every man. John tells us that "And He Himself is the propitiation for our sins, and not for ours only but also for the whole world" (1 Jn. 2:2). In 1 Timothy 2:6, Paul tells us that Christ Jesus "gave himself a ransom for all." In 1 Timothy 4:10, Paul tells us that Jesus "is the Savior of all men, especially of those who believe." This provisionary atonement is applied to whoever will meet the condition of faith (Jn. 3:16; Acts 17:30; Rom. 10:13; 1 Tim. 2:4; 2 Pet. 3:9; and Rev. 22:17). The fact that many Calvinists have accepted the view of unlimited atonement tells us that the biblical case for unlimited atonement must be strong and convincing.[33]

Double Payment With Regard to Sinners Who Go to Hell

The discussion above about provisionary atonement and union with Christ answers this objection. The death of Christ is not on the sinner's account who goes to Hell. His account does not show a double payment. It is true that his sins were paid for provisionally, but there is no double payment as long as there is no double entry on the person's account. No person will go to hell with the death and righteousness of Christ on his account.

Antinomianism the Logical Result

Some Arminians argue that, if we receive the death of Christ and the righteousness of Christ, the way is open for license to sin. If the account has been completely settled by Christ, they argue, a person can live as he pleases.

If we think of justification *apart* from sanctification, we have *antinomianism*. However, when we understand that justification is always accompanied by sanctification, we see that the antinomian charge is invalid. It is the nature of sanctification that *disallows* antinomianism. The evidence that sanctification nullifies the charge of antinomianism will be seen in the development of the doctrine of sanctification in the next chapter.

We should not be surprised when our doctrine of atonement and justification causes us to be accused of giving license to sin. Paul was accused of the same thing (Rom. 3:8; 6:1). We should be concerned if we cannot answer the charge. We do not answer the charge by tampering with the doctrine of justification, but by setting forth the doctrine of sanctification.

Necessarily Lead to the Conclusion "Once Saved, Always Saved"

It is not hard to see why this objection would be raised, but it is easily answered. If we had actually experienced what Jesus did on the cross, it would follow that we could never be called on to pay the same price again. It is true that *as long as we have the death and righteousness of Christ we are saved. As long as we are in union with Christ, we are as safe from the wrath of God as He is.*

Is it possible for us to forfeit our salvation and be lost again? The death and righteousness of Christ are ours by identification. They remain ours only as we remain identified with Him. The identification with Christ is ours as long as we remain in union with Him. The union is ours conditionally. It is conditioned on faith in Christ. If we make shipwreck of our faith, the union will be broken. We will lose our identification with Christ. His death and righteousness will no longer be ours.

John 15:2 teaches that we can be taken out of Christ. It is the branch "in Me" that "He takes away." I will give further discussion of this subject in the chapter on perseverance. I mentioned it here only to answer the objection raised against the satisfaction view of atonement.

Infant Salvation

In the history of the church, there have been those who have thought that infants who died without being baptized were lost. However, the tendency has been for theologians to look for some hope that those dying in infancy are spared from eternal condemnation. An article entitled "Infant Salvation" in The *New Schaff-Herzog Encyclopedia of Religious Knowledge* states that "with the Calvinist the heart is stronger than logic. Dr. Charles Hodge teaches emphatically the salvation of all infants who die in infancy, and asserts that this is the 'common doctrine of Evangelical Protestants' (Systematic Theology, I, 26)."[34] Arminians have always taken the position that those dying during infancy went to be with Christ. The tendency is for most people to believe that those dying in infancy are either safe or saved.

Scriptural Grounds for Believing in Infant Salvation

The Bible does not address the subject of infant salvation directly. We go on the basis of implications. When the young son of David died, in explaining to his servants why he ceased to fast after the child died, David said, "But now he is dead; why should I fast? Can I bring him back again? I shall go to him, but he shall not return to me" (2 Sam. 12:23). It is inferred that David and the child would meet each other after death. The implication is that the child will be with God in eternity.

In Matthew 18:10, Jesus said, "Take heed that you do not despise one of these little ones, for I say to you that in heaven their angels always see the face of My Father who is in heaven." The reference to "their angels" implies that they are in a favorable relationship with God. To me the implications involved in these passages give a solid foundation for rejecting the idea that infants will go to hell.

While I believe in infant salvation, I do not believe as Wesleyan theologians Summers, Fletcher, Pope, and Wiley do that infant salvation is taught in Romans 5:18-19.[35] Romans 5:18 says "the free gift came to all men, resulting in justification of life." Romans 5:19 says that "by one Man's obedience many will be made righteous." If the "all" of 5:18 is taken to refer to all who would make up the human race, it would be teaching universal salvation, which is not what these men taught. I think the "all" refers only to those who are identified with Christ.

There is no hint in the context that Paul would be specifically dealing with the question of infant salvation. Up to this point, Paul had said that the action of One Person formed the basis of salvation of all who would believe. That sounded too good to be true. An objector might ask: How could the righteousness of one person be the basis for salvation for many (all who would believe)?

When the occasion calls for it, Paul makes use of the *a fortiori* argument. This argument seeks to move from something that is harder to believe to the easier to believe. This is the kind of argument used in 5:8-10. In verses 12-29, Paul shows that it is easier to believe that Christ, One Person, can be the cause of the justification for many than it is to believe that Adam could be the cause of condemnation for many.[36]

If a case can be made for the view that infants are identified with Christ, that would form a basis for infant salvation. In such a case, it would be an inferred meaning, not the direct meaning of the passage. These verses do not address the question of *infant salvation*. It should be restated here that the position I am taking is infant salvation. I disagree with those who base the safety of the infant on the innocence of infants. According to such a view, infants are *safe*, not *saved*.

The Problem of Faith as the Condition of Salvation

The reason there is a problem in thinking about infant salvation is that faith is the condition of salvation. Infants are not capable of exercising faith. If they cannot exercise faith, how can they be saved?

The requirement of the condition of faith is God's way of dealing with us as persons—those who think, feel, and act. God will not transgress our personality. In requiring faith, God treats us as persons and requires a response from us. Failure to require a response in which we choose Christ would be a failure to treat us as persons. This problem does not exist with the infant. He or she is a person, but is not fully developed so as to enable the individual to exercise all the rights and privileges nor to assume all the responsibilities of being a person. There is no transgression of the individual's personality or will if God should remove his racial guilt since he is not capable of saying either yes or no. This approach may be all that needs to be said, but I will give more thoughts on the subject in the following discussion.

The Difference Between Racial Guilt and Personal Guilt

Racial guilt belongs to us simply by our being members of the human race—descendants of Adam. Personal guilt is ours because of our own personal sins. It should not seem strange if the application of atonement would be approached somewhat differently for forgiveness of racial guilt than from forgiveness of personal guilt.

Our personal sins were laid on Jesus on the cross. We receive forgiveness for them when we exercise faith in Christ and are placed in union with Him on an individual basis.

The Identification of Christ With the Race in the Incarnation and Infant Salvation

When Jesus Christ became incarnate, He became a member of the race. He identified Himself with a race that was under racial condemnation because of Adam's sin. In the incarnation, He became man and became identified with our racial guilt. Identification by union is a two-way street.[37]

In our personal union with Christ, our guilt was transferred to Christ and His death and righteousness were transferred to us.

The identification of Christ with the race in the incarnation[38] is a two-way street. Racial guilt was transferred to Christ. When He died and paid for racial guilt, there was an automatic transfer of that payment to the account of the race. This could be done because He was identified with the race. Personal guilt could not be taken care of automatically because the incarnation, as such, did not identify Him with our personal guilt. The transfer of personal guilt to Christ and the transfer of His death and righteousness for personal guilt requires a union between Christ and the individual person.

Certain points need to be made clear. First, Jesus did not have a depraved nature. The miraculous conception of His human nature sanctified His human nature. Second, Jesus did not actually sin in Adam. He simply became identified with Adam's sin. It did not change His character any more than it did when our personal sins were laid on Him. He no more actually sinned in Adam than we actually died in Christ. Third, the identification of Christ with the race, while not changing His character, did place Him in a position in which He could assume the responsibility for racial sin and pay the penalty for it.

If we accept this view, we believe that guilt and condemnation passed on the race from Adam. If it had not been for Christ, the whole human race would have been lost, including infants. Because of the atoning work of Christ, racial guilt has been lifted from everyone. If a person goes to hell, he will go because of his own personal failure to measure up to God's standard of absolute holiness. Those who die in infancy will not escape hell because the guilt of Adam was not imputed to them, but because the atoning work of Christ is applied to them.

The Age of Accountability

This approach to infant salvation does not open the way for a person to reach the age of accountability having lived a righteous life and not need to be saved. Depravity (or original sin) is not static. The operational base of the depravity is the subconscious mind. While the subconscious mind operates below the level of consciousness, it is not passive. It is characterized by attitudes, inclinations, dispositions, drives, and passions. These traits are active. They are ready to manifest themselves in overt acts of sin. They are culpable before God. These traits stand condemned by God as traits before they are manifested in *actions*. Romans 8:7-8 assures us that depravity will manifest itself in acts of sin.

I am inclined to believe that racial guilt involves more than the guilt imputed from Adam. Depravity or original sin is not passive in those who have not reached the age of personal accountability or responsibility. Depravity manifests itself even in infants. A temper tantrum on the part of an infant is not consistent with the holiness of God. Depravity manifests itself in sinful activity before a child reaches the age of personal accountability. All sin that precedes the time of personal accountability is racial sin. All racial sin is covered because the One who went to the cross was identified with the race. The transfer of His death and righteousness was automatic. It was built into the nature of the case.

When the child reaches the age of accountability, he or she reaches that point in life as one who is already sinful. The one who is already sinful racially immediately becomes one who is sinful personally. From that moment, the only hope is from a personal union with Christ conditioned on personal faith in Christ.

The Meaning of the Age of Accountability

The Bible is addressed to those who are personally accountable. It does not deal with the question of the age of accountability. Whatever we say in this regard is in some measure speculative.

Children have some sense of right and wrong before they reach the age of accountability. In my opinion, we must distinguish between the feeling of guilt on the part of the child in relation to his or her parents and guilt in relation to God. The age of accountability is reached when the child has some realization that he or she has sinned against God.

I am of the opinion that, while general revelation alone is adequate to bring an individual to the age or time of accountability, that point is reached more quickly where children are taught from the special revelation of God in the Bible. Adequate teaching of the Bible to children, I would think, would bring a child more quickly to the time of accountability than would be the case where there is little or no biblical knowledge. The gospel would be involved in bringing the child to the time of accountability. In such a case, it would be possible for the child to be saved at that time. Those who do not have these opportunities would reach the age of accountability at a later point in life.

Those who are severely handicapped mentally would be dealt with the same way infants would. There is good reason to believe that the people who never have anything but general revelation would not reach the age of accountability as soon in life as those who have the benefit of special revelation. However, in the light of Romans 1:18-32, especially verses 19 and 20, we must believe that at some point along the way those who reach adulthood do become accountable.[39]

Erickson's View of the Status of Infants

Millard J. Erickson argues that all humanity is involved in Adam's sin. Thus, all people receive both Adam's post-fall "corrupted" nature and his "guilt and condemnation." Yet he explains that, as with the imputation of the righteousness of Christ, human beings must engage in "conscious and voluntary decision." Without this, in his view, only a "conditional imputation of guilt" exists. This means that there is "no condemnation" until a human being reaches an age of "responsibility." If death occurs before a child is capable of such conscious and voluntary decision, then "there is only innocence, and the child will experience the same type of future existence with the Lord as will those who have reached the age of moral responsibility and had their sins forgiven as a result of accepting the offer of salvation based upon Christ's atoning death."[40]

Erickson explains what happens when we reach the age of responsibility and how we become guilty of Adam's sin. He contends that human beings become "responsible and guilty" when they "accept or approve" their depraved nature. At the point in people's lives at which they gain awareness of their "tendency toward sin," they may reject their sinful makeup. However, he says, if individuals "acquiesce" in their "sinful nature," they give their "tacit approval" to Adam and Eve's sin in the Garden of Eden. In effect, Erickson argues, "We become guilty of that [original] sin without having to commit a sin of our own."[41]

It will be observed that Erickson does not use the term "infant salvation." The term used in his "Author and Subject Index" is "Infants, status of." He sets forth the position of a conditional imputation of Adam's sin. At the age of responsibility, when a person approves or takes sides with the corrupt nature that he or she received from Adam, each person becomes guilty of Adam's sin. That act of approval would cause each of us to be guilty before God "without having to commit a sin of our own." If a child dies prior to that time, "there is only innocence, and the child will experience the same type of future existence with the Lord as will those who have reached the age of moral responsibility and had their sins forgiven as a result of accepting the offer of salvation based upon Christ's atoning death."

Evaluation of Erickson's View

Deep within, we cannot bear the thought that those dying in infancy will spend eternity in hell. Even Calvinists try to avoid such a conclusion. At the same time, we speak with hesitation when we try to explain why we think that is the case. We do not want to leave the impression that we have a weak view of sin or the fall of man into sin. We certainly do not want to be labeled Pelagian or Semi-Pelagian. We almost find it easier to pass over the subject and say nothing about it rather than to invite misunderstanding and accusations that may grow out of misunderstanding. It is obvious that

Erickson was struggling with his thoughts and his words when he sought to set forth his view on the status of infants. This is evidenced when he introduced his discussion with these words: "The current form of my understanding is as follows." Whatever we may say about Erickson's view, he did not back off from the subject.

Erickson's hope of eternal life for the one who dies before reaching the age of responsibility is "innocence." Based on this innocence, the one dying before the age of responsibility has the same future with God as those have who have placed faith in the atoning work of Christ. Adam's guilt is not imputed to the one who dies before reaching the age of responsibility. The imputation of Adam's guilt to the individual is conditional. It is imputed when the individual at the age of responsibility acquiesces and approves the corrupt nature inherited from Adam. At that point the individual becomes guilty of Adam's sin and his or her own acts of sin that are committed from that point on.

It seems to me that, because the race was in Adam when he sinned, the very nature of the case means that his sin was necessarily imputed to the race, including infants. Erickson sets forth a conditional imputation of Adam's sin. Through that means he seeks to protect the innocence of infants and ensure their eternal life that way. It seems to me much better and more in keeping with Scripture to recognize that the nature of the case required the imputation of Adam's sin and then believe in infant salvation as I explained it above.

Erickson tries hard to distance himself from the view that says we inherit depravity from Adam, but not Adam's guilt. But when he resorts to the conditional guilt to be imputed only upon approval of the corrupt nature at the age of responsibility, it seems that he has, in fact, distanced himself from the natural headship view of the imputation of Adam's sin to the race. While that seems to be the logic of the case, on the page prior to the one the quotations above come from, he clearly commits himself to the natural headship view. In summarizing, he explains that he espouses the Augustinian or natural headship view of the imputation of sin to the human race. Therefore, all human beings were "present in undifferentiated form in the person of Adam, who along with Eve was the entire race. Thus, it was not merely Adam but man who sinned. We were involved, although not personally, and are responsible for the sin."[42]

When we look at all of Erickson's thoughts on the subject of the effect of Adam's sin on the race and the question of whether those who die in infancy are lost, we are convinced that he does not believe that those who die in infancy are lost. We are sure he believes that we inherit a corrupt nature from Adam. However, we are left a bit confused on the question of the imputation of Adam's guilt. On one page, he says, "We were actually present within Adam, so that we all sinned in his act. There is no injustice, then, to our condemnation and death as a result of original sin."[43] On another page, he speaks of conditional imputation of Adam's guilt. We become guilty of Adam's sin only after we approve of the sinful nature that we receive from Adam.[44] That happens when we reach the age of responsibility. In such a case, it seems that Adam's sin is not imputed to us because we were in Adam, as taught by the natural headship view, but because we personally choose sides with the sinful nature received from Adam.

James Leo Garrett concludes that though Erickson "espoused" the natural headship view, by the way he dealt with the question of infants he "abandoned realism [the natural headship view] and instead opted for . . . the Placean theory of the imputation of depravity."[45] The Placean theory is the theory of the mediate imputation of Adam's sin as distinguished from the immediate imputation of Adam's sin.

Erickson supports his conclusion with regard to infants by suggesting that there is a "parallelism between our accepting the work of Christ and that of Adam."[46] I think we can understand why he makes this suggestion. But I think there is an important difference which makes his suggestion invalid. We were in Adam at the time of his sin. It is the fact of being in

Adam that forms the basis for the imputation of Adam's sin. Being *in Adam* makes it so the imputation of his sin was required. If it was required, it could not be conditioned on some personal approval that we would give upon reaching the age of responsibility.

As it relates to our personal sins, we were not in Christ at the time of His death. The union with Christ that identifies us with Christ and makes His death ours took place at the time we placed our faith in Jesus Christ as our Lord and Savior. Being in Christ does not just make it *merely possible* for His death and righteousness to be imputed to us. Being in union with Christ *requires that His death and righteousness be imputed to us*. It cannot be otherwise as long as we are in union with Christ. If that be true, if we were in Adam at the time of his sin, it was necessary that the guilt of his sin would be imputed to us. When identification by union is present, imputation is not optional with God. I pointed out in my treatment of the imputation of sin that the principle involved in imputation of something from one to another is *identification by being in or in union with the person*. This is true whether it be sin or whether it be righteousness. The Scripture knows of no other way that the action of one person can be imputed to another. This is the principle involved in the imputation of the death and righteousness of Christ to the believer.[47]

The nature of the case means that we were in Adam when he sinned. It also means that the incarnation has identified Christ with the race. In the incarnation, there was an automatic identification of Christ with racial guilt. That identification meant that when Christ made atonement, since He was identified with the race, there was an automatic application of the benefits of atonement for racial guilt to the race.

As it relates to our personal sins, it was different. They were laid on Christ (Is. 53:6). The benefits of atonement for personal sins can be applied only when there is a personal union with Christ. When a person places his faith in Jesus Christ as Lord and Savior, he is baptized into Christ by the

Holy Spirit. At that point, he or she has the death and righteousness of Christ placed on his or her account.

---

[1]For those who are interested in a study of the various views of atonement that have arisen in the church, I would recommend the treatment given by H. Dermot McDonald, *The Atonement and the Death of Christ: In Faith, Revelation, and History* (Grand Rapids: Baker Books, 1985).

[2]Thiessen, *Introductory Lectures* (1949), 131.

[3]J. Oliver Buswell, *A Systematic Theology*, 2:114.

[4]Much of the above three paragraphs is adapted from Forlines, *Romans*, 55.

[5]I learned the essence of this illustration of a council between the attributes of God from reading "The Priesthood of Christ" by James Arminius. I read it in the 1951-1952 school year while taking a course on Arminian theology taught by Dr. L. C. Johnson, founding president of Free Will Baptist Bible College. The reading of this message by Arminius greatly helped me develop my understanding and acceptance of the penal satisfaction view of atonement. I was convinced then, and I still am, that Arminius believed in the penal satisfaction view of atonement. [In various editions of *The Writings of James Arminius*, the material is differently. In the set that I have (published by Baker Book House in 1956), "The Priesthood of Christ" is found in volume 1, pp. 2-51. The "Priesthood of the Believer" was "Delivered on the Eleventh day of July, 1603, by Arminius, on the occasion of receiving the Degree of Doctor of Divinity" (p. 2). The illustration of the council between Justice, Mercy, and Wisdom is found on pp. 28-31.]

[6]The course on Arminian theology mentioned above was the occasion of my first struggle with exactly what Christ did that made atonement for my sins. It challenged my thinking more than any course that I have ever had. During this time of struggling with the thought of the atonement, I realized that Jesus, to be our Redeemer, must satisfy the demands of the Law for perfect obedience and the requirement of the payment of an infinite penalty. It was at that time that I discovered the book by Loraine Boettner, *Studies in Theology*, 2nd. ed. (Grand Rapids: Eerdmans Publishing Company, 1951), 299-300. This book used the terms active and passive obedience of Christ, providing the terminology for my developing idea.

[7]William G. T. Shedd, *Dogmatic Theology* (1889; reprint, Grand Rapids: Zondervan Publishing House, Classic Reprint Edition), 2:436-437. Italics mine.

[8]This paragraph is adapted from my commentary on Romans. Forlines, *Romans*, 55.

[9]Leon Morris, "Propitiation," *Evangelical Dictionary of Theology*, Walter A. Elwell, ed., (Grand Rapids: Baker Books, 1984), 888.

[10]McDonald, *The Atonement and the Death of Christ*, 345.

[11]W. J. Conybeare and J. S. Howson, *The Life and the Epistles of St. Paul* (reprint, Grand Rapids: Eerdmans Publishing Company, 1978), 511, note 5. Brackets in original.

[12]Leroy Forlines, "A Study of Paul's Teachings on the Believer's Death to Sin and Its Relationship to a New Life" (unpublished M.A. thesis, Winona Lake School of Theology, 1959).

[13]Charles J. Ellicott, *A Commentary, Critical and Grammatical, on St. Paul's Epistle to the Galatians* (New York: Wiley, 1860), 61.

[14]William G. T. Shedd, *A Critical and Doctrinal Commentary upon the Epistle of St. Paul to the Romans* (New York: Scribner, 1879), 149.

[15]Shedd, *A Critical and Doctrinal Commentary on the Epistle of St. Paul to the Romans*, (1879; reprint, Grand Rapids: Zondervan Publishing House, 1967), 148-149.

[16]Shedd, *Dogmatic Theology*, 2:534.

[17]John F. Walvoord, "Identification with Christ," *Evangelical Dictionary of Theology*, 542.

[18]Loraine Boettner, *Studies in Theology*, 299.

[19]Robert Haldane, *An Exposition of the Epistle of Romans* (1852; reprint, McLean, Virginia: McDonald Publishing Company, 1958), 131-132.

[20]John Miley, *Systematic Theology* (New York: Hunt and Eaton, 1894), 2:162.

[21]James H. Fairchild, *Elements of Theology* (Oberlin, Ohio: Pearce and Randolf Printers, 1892), 224.

[22]Miley, *Systematic Theology*, 163.

[23]Charles G. Finney, *Finney's Lectures on Systematic Theology*, rev. ed., James H. Fairchild, ed. (1878; reprint, Grand Rapids: Eerdmans Publishing Company, 1953), 259.

[24]Miley, *Systematic Theology*, 163.

[25]Fairchild, *Elements of Theology*, 229. Italics mine.

[26]Ibid., 227-228. Italics mine.

[27]Ibid., 277.

[28]Ibid., 278.

[29]Finney, *Finney's Lectures on Systematic Theology*, 383-384. It is interesting to note that Hugo Grotius, the founder of the governmental view of atonement, was a lawyer. In fact, he holds the distinction of being the father of International Law. Charles Finney was also a lawyer. The governmental view of atonement and justification is developed by drawing an analogy between the way a governor of a state works in granting a pardon and the way God works.

[30]For a treatment of the moral influence theory of liberalism, see Albert C. Knudson, *The Doctrine of Redemption* (New York: Abingdon-Cokesbury, 1933). I dealt with Knudson's moral influence theory of atonement in "The Need of Atonement According to Representative Theologians" (unpublished B.D. thesis, Northern Baptist Theological Seminary, 1962).

[31]In the thesis mentioned in the note above, I dealt with Emil Brunner's view of atonement. Concerning the question of annihilation, Paul Jewett says: "In His eternal hope, Brunner seems to have given up the doctrine of hell in favor of annihilation of the wicked. A negative decision against Christ in this life will not be changed in the world to come, but it will be terminated." (Paul K. Jewett, *Emil Brunner: An Introduction to the Man and His Thought* [Chicago: InterVarsity Press, 1961], 23.) Brunner says, "Without detracting from his Holiness, God could make an end of sinful man." (Emil Brunner, *Dogmatics*, vol. 1, "The Christian Doctrine of Man," trans. Olive Wyon [Philadelphia: The Westminster Press, 1950], 274).

[32]Louis Berkhof, *Systematic Theology*, 393.

[33]Millard J. Erickson, *Christian Theology* (Grand Rapids: Baker Book House, 1985), 825-841. See also Charles Ryrie, *Basic Theology* (Wheaton: Victor Books,

1987), 318-323. For more discussion of the extent of the atonement, see Chapter 2 of this book.

[34]"Infant Salvation" in *The New Schaff-Herzog Encyclopedia of Religious Knowledge*, Samuel Macauley Jackson, ed. (1907; reprint, Grand Rapids: Baker Book House, 1950), 491.

[35]H. Orton Wiley, *Christian Theology* (Kansas City, Mo.: Beacon Hill Press, 1952), 2:132.

[36]This paragraph is adapted from my Romans commentary. Forlines, *Romans*, 130.

[37]In a quotation given earlier from Shedd, with regard to the union of Christ and the believer, he explains, "Because they are spiritually, vitally, eternally, and mystically one with him, his merit is imputable to them, and their demerit is imputable to him" (Shedd, *Dogmatic Theology*, 2:534). I believe this same reasoning can be applied to the identification of the Christ with the race in the incarnation.

[38]In the quotation from Walvoord given earlier in the chapter, he says, "Christ is identified with the human race in incarnation, but only true believers are identified with Christ" ("Identification with Christ," *Evangelical Dictionary of Theology*, 542.) He makes the observation that the incarnation identified Christ with the race. If that is true, there should be some theological implications derived from this identification. I believe that those implications are pertinent to salvation.

[39]See my comments on general revelation in *The Quest for Truth*, Chapter 3, 32-33.

[40]Millard J. Erickson, *Christian Theology*, unabridged one vol. ed. (Grand Rapids: Baker, 1985), 639.

[41]Ibid.

[42]Ibid., 638.

[43]Ibid., 637.

[44]Ibid., 638.

[45]James Leo Garrett, Jr., *Systematic Theology* (Grand Rapids: Eerdmans Publishing Company, 1990), 1:487.

[46]Ibid.

[47]This is taken from Chapter 1.

CHAPTER 7

The Condition of Salvation

I have chosen to discuss the nature of salvation first and then come to a discussion of the condition of salvation. As a rule, it is done the other way around. I have chosen to do it this way because I believe we can get a better understanding of the condition of salvation this way.

REPENTANCE AND FAITH: ONE CONDITION OR TWO?

The Problem Set Forth

As a rule, we say that there is only one condition of salvation. That condition is faith. However, we frequently say that repentance is a condition of salvation. In discussions of repentance and faith, it frequently sounds as if there are two conditions of salvation. How many conditions of salvation are there?

Numerous times in the New Testament, faith is presented as the only condition of salvation (Jn. 1:12; 3:16, 18, 36; Acts 16:31; Rom. 3:22, 28; 4:1-25; 5:1; Gal. 2:16; 3:1-18; Eph. 2:8-9; and 1 Jn. 5:13). There are also places where repentance, without the occurrence of the word faith, is mentioned as the condition of salvation (Lk. 24:47; Acts 2:38; 3:19; 5:31; 11:18; 17:30; 26:20; 2 Tim. 2:25; Heb. 6:6; and 2 Pet. 3:9).

What conclusion should we draw from this? If we draw the conclusion that repentance and faith make up two conditions of salvation, there would be only three places in the New Testament where both conditions would be mentioned in the same passage (Mk. 1:15; Acts 20:21; and Heb. 6:1). Would we conclude that these are the only three places where a person is told how to be saved in one passage? Would we have to pick up one condition in one place and one in another if we did not use one of these verses?

If we want to make repentance and faith two conditions of salvation, what do we do with the fact that the words *repent* and *repentance* do not occur in the Gospel of John nor in 1, 2, and 3 John? Do we conclude that these books do not have the complete requirement for salvation?

It would be strange if the condition(s) of salvation were found in only three places in the Bible. The preferred conclusion is to believe that there is only one condition of salvation if we can support that conclusion. There is a problem involved in trying to make a choice between repentance and faith for the condition because both are presented in the Scripture as the condition of salvation. The answer is found in looking at repentance and faith as one condition because both are presented in the Scripture as the only condition of salvation. They both speak of the same experience.

The Meaning of Repentance

The Greek word *metanoeō* which is translated "repent" means to change one's mind. So far as the Greek word is concerned, in its usage, it could refer to a change of mind, whether for good or for bad. R. C. Trench says, "Plutarch (Sept. Sap. Conu. 21) tells us of two murderers, who having spared a child, afterward 'repented' (*metenoēsan*), and sought to slay it." Trench goes on to say: "It is only after *metanoia* has been taken up into the uses of Scripture, or of writers dependent upon Scripture, that it comes predominantly to mean change of mind, taking a wiser view of the past."[1]

To change the mind in repentance refers to the change of the mind, heart, and will. One viewpoint is exchanged for another viewpoint. There is an appropriate change of attitude and behavior to go along with the exchange of viewpoint. It is a reference to a change of attitude and behavior that Paul has in mind in Acts 26:20. He preached "to the Gentiles, that they should . . . do works befitting repentance." (See also Mt. 3:8 and Lk. 3:8.) In repentance, there is a change of mind. There is a change of opinion, viewpoint, or conviction. In the repentance related to salvation, the question is: On what does the change focus? This question will be answered by an examination of the passages where repentance is used in connection with salvation.

The passages where the context clarifies the area of change in repentance are found in Acts. If we read these passages and translate *repent* "to change one's mind," it will help us to see what areas of thought the speakers had in mind. On the day of Pentecost, when Peter said to the Jews, "Repent" (Acts 2:38), in the context they were to repent of their unbelief toward Jesus Christ (Acts 2:23, 36). This would involve not only a change of opinion but of attitude and behavior. The same basic thought is seen in Acts 3:19 and 5:31. In Acts 17:30, on the negative side, they were to change their mind regarding idolatry (verses 22-29). On the positive side, they were to believe in Jesus Christ (verse 31).

The Relationship between Repentance and Faith

In repentance, there is a "from" and a "to." The exact nature of the "from" may vary from one person to another. Some need to change from a simple case of unbelief. Others need to change from false religion or paganism. Whatever the case may be about the nature of what a person may need to change his or her mind from, the "to" for all is the same. All are to change to faith in Jesus Christ.

While repentance includes a "from" and a "to," the stress of repentance is on the *to* instead of the *from*. Repentance is a forward-moving word. This is not to diminish the importance of the "from." It is to place primary focus on the "to." The "to" of repentance is identical with faith. In Acts 20:21 Paul speaks of "repentance *toward* God." In 2 Timothy 2:25, he speaks of "repentance *to* the acknowledging of the truth" (italics in these verses mine).

Faith and repentance are involved in each other. To exercise faith implies a change from unbelief, whatever the form of unbelief may be. Repentance terminates in faith. If we tell a person to repent, or if we tell him to believe, we are telling him to do the same thing. Repentance stresses that change is involved. Faith stresses the end to which change is directed.

We can illustrate the difference between repentance and faith this way. If we tell a man in Atlanta to leave Atlanta and go to New York, that would illustrate repentance. If we should tell the man in Atlanta to go to New York, that would illustrate faith. We would be telling the person to do the same thing no matter which approach we might choose.

A word needs to be said about sorrow and repentance. Some equate sorrow for sins with repentance. Sorrow is not repentance. It leads to repentance. Paul tells us that "godly sorrow produces a repentance leading to salvation" (2 Cor. 7:10).

Faith is the primary term because it is faith that describes the positive response in which repentance terminates. Repentance speaks of a change *from* something *to* something. Faith explains what the something is to which repentance is directed.

When we speak of repentance and faith in salvation, we are talking about one condition for salvation, not two. To experience repentance and to experience faith is to experience the same thing. Since faith is the primary term, we will now turn our attention to a discussion of saving faith.

THE NATURE OF SAVING FAITH

The Meaning of Saving Faith

Saving faith is the abandonment of all trust in self or anything else and a complete, confident trust in Christ for salvation. The problem that plagues us is: How do we avoid leaving the impression that salvation can be a superficial experience if faith is the only condition for salvation? Some try to cope with this problem by the way they explain the nature of faith. They try in some way to explain that faith, by definition, involves obedience. But at the same time they explain that faith is distinguished from works.

As I see it, we do not avoid the impression that salvation is a superficial experience by the way we define faith. Faith is not complicated. There are two elements of faith: (1) acceptance of redemptive truth, and (2) trust. In the history of God's people, the content of saving faith involved the redemptive truth with which God had confronted people at a given time in history. They were to accept this revelation to be true. For us, we are to believe the redemptive revelation of God as it is revealed in Jesus Christ. I can see how a person may have saving faith and have some misunderstanding of what the Bible says about Christ. I cannot see how a person can have saving faith and not believe what the Bible says about Jesus Christ. Faith believes what the Bible says about Jesus Christ to be true. In the trust element of saving faith, there is dependence on God for salvation. In the New Testament, this is dependence on Jesus Christ for salvation.

We do not safeguard ourselves from superficial Christianity by the way we define faith. It does not take some special knowledge of Hebrew or Greek to define faith so safeguards can be built in our definition. What we need is a correct definition of salvation. We believe "for salvation." Salvation is the goal for faith. There will be no superficial experience for the person who experiences salvation unless salvation is superficial. Salvation consists of justification and sanctification. The whole study of sanctification, especially the guaranteed results of sanctification, make it clear that sanctification cannot be superficial. We cannot believe for the forgiveness of sins without believing for a change in our experience with God and sin. If we receive salvation, we will receive forgiveness of sin and a change in our experience with God and sin. That will not be superficial.

Where the problem comes is when we tell people they can be forgiven and leave the impression that a change in experience is optional. This opens the way for a lot of professions in which there is no salvation. The tragedy is not that such people receive Jesus as Savior but not as Lord. The tragedy is that they receive Jesus as neither Lord nor Savior.

There can be no exercise of saving faith without at least some understanding of what salvation is all about. Saving faith is exercised by a person who realizes that salvation is designed to forgive people of sin and restore them to the experience of holiness. Such a person realizes that he or she is a sinner. He sees sin as serious. He sees himself as unworthy and condemned. He is under conviction. The problem of sin is real in his mind and in his heart. He wants something done about sin in his life. He wants to be forgiven. He wants to be changed. He understands that Jesus Christ has suffered on the cross and died to save him. He believes what God has said in the Bible about Jesus as Savior. He trusts in Jesus as Savior. In so doing, he trusts in Jesus to forgive his sins and to change his life. According to Christian theology, upon this act of faith, based on the atoning work of Christ, the person is justified and sanctified.

There is no saving faith except where a person has become aware of his or her sins and has a changed attitude toward sin and Jesus Christ. The termination of that change we call faith. The process of change including the termination of the process we call repentance. Both terms need to be used. *Faith* needs to be used to explain the real nature of the condition of salvation. *Repentance* needs to be used to make people aware that a deep change of mind, heart, and will is involved in the exercise of saving faith.

I like the way it is done among the Baptists in the former Soviet Union. When someone makes a profession of faith, they say, "He repented." When I asked Oleg, the interpreter who traveled with my wife and me when we were in the former Soviet Union, when he was saved, he said, "I repented in 1988." Christians are regularly referred to as believers. But they speak of the initial act of faith as repentance.

Faith and the Personality

The mind, heart, and will are involved in saving faith. With the mind, the truth about sin, Jesus Christ, and salvation is comprehended objectively. The content of the truth is grasped and understood.

With the heart, what is grasped objectively by the mind is grasped subjectively. The truth about sin becomes real. Conviction takes place. The truth about Jesus Christ and salvation becomes real. The reality of the truth conditions the heart for action to follow. The emotions are definitely involved in the experience of faith and the total Christian experience. We feel what we believe. We are not emotional blanks. Emotions are a part of the human personality by creation. Emotions need to be based on truth and disciplined by truth, but emotions must not be downgraded.

With the will there is the commitment of the personality to Jesus Christ. We receive Jesus Christ. The will can act only where there is a prepared mind and a prepared heart. The will, out of the prepared mind and heart, sets in action the response of faith. What is objectively perceived by the mind is subjectively felt by the heart, and subjectively appropriated by the will.

Faith as a Gift

Jesus said in John 6:44, "No one can come to Me unless the Father who sent Me draws him." There must be a move toward man on God's part before there will be any response on man's part. Not only is there a need for a divine invitation, but there is also a need for a divine drawing. The Holy Spirit must take the Word of God and work in the human heart and mind to prepare the heart and mind before there can be the response of faith from a sinner.

It does not belong within the framework of possibilities of the unsaved person for him to be able to respond to Jesus Christ apart from the work of the Holy Spirit. The Holy Spirit works as the Word is preached. The human heart can resist this work of the Holy Spirit, but where the Holy Spirit is allowed to work, He enlightens the mind concerning sin, Jesus Christ, and salvation. He produces conviction in the heart. The preparation of the mind and heart by the Word of God and the Holy Spirit creates a framework of possibilities in which a person can respond in faith to Jesus Christ. The response of faith is not guaranteed, but it is made possible. The person can say, "Yes," or he or she can say, "No."

Faith is called a gift because it cannot be exercised without the work of the Holy Spirit. At the same time, it is a response of the person in such a way that it is a response of his or her personality. It is in a real sense his own action. If a human being is to be treated as a person, in some real sense the action must be the person's own, regardless of how much divine aid may be given. Otherwise, a human being has been reduced to a subpersonal being.

Some have understood "the faith of the Son of God" in Galatians 2:20 and similar references to mean that saving faith is Christ's faith given to the person. It is a gift in that it is taking Christ's faith and giving it to the person.

In the expression "the faith of the Son of God," the genitive case in the Greek could be considered a subjective genitive and thus be understood as "faith belonging to Christ." It can also be considered an objective genitive and would mean "faith in Christ." While either interpretation would be possible so far as Greek grammar is concerned, only one is possible in the light of Scripture. The Bible addresses us and tells us to believe. We are nowhere told that Jesus is to believe for us. It is clear that "the faith of the Son of God" is not Jesus' faith, but it is our faith in Jesus.

Faith is not some substance that exists outside of us that is to be given to us. It is an experience that must take place within us. That is the only way we can have faith. Faith is a gift in the sense that God gives to us the aid that is necessary, without which we could not exercise faith. It is not a gift in the sense that it is not an exercise of our own personality.

Faith the Condition, Not the Ground, of Salvation

The difference between condition and ground could be illustrated this way. The condition for a chair supporting me is for me to sit in the chair. When I am sitting in the chair, the chair is the ground of my support. The ground of our salvation is Jesus Christ and His atoning work. The condition of our salvation is the response of faith.

Sometimes people make the mistake of focusing more on the condition than the ground. In looking for assurance, they examine their faith instead of Christ. If I want to have confidence that a chair will hold me up, I will examine the chair, not my confidence in the chair. As I examine the chair, if it is well built, my confidence will be made sure.

If I want my assurance of salvation to be strong, I should examine Christ—the ground of my salvation. In so doing, I will have a strong faith and confidence. If I examine my faith, I will tend to have doubts. It is not faith in faith that is the condition of salvation. It is faith in Christ.

Faith and Doubt

Sometimes, we get caught up in the reasoning that if salvation is by faith, a Christian cannot doubt his or her salvation because faith rules out doubt. At first thought, the definition of saving faith would seem to make it sound as if there is no room for doubt. Saving faith is a complete, confident trust in Christ for salvation. Doubt is not exactly consistent with a complete, confident trust.

How do we harmonize the possibility of doubt with saving faith? Definitions describe a thing in its ideal, healthy state. For example, a definition of a dog would include that a dog is a four-legged animal. Yet, I have seen dogs that had only three legs. A dog could be a dog with fewer than four legs, but it would not be a normal dog in full health. Saving faith in its healthy state does not include doubts. However, saving faith can and does exist where doubts also exist. As a rule, these doubts will clear up with a better understanding of doctrines of salvation. However, in some cases the difficulty is not cleared up this way. The problem is related to complications in the person's background.

The Difference Between Classical Arminianism and Classical Calvinism on Faith as a Gift

I make the reference here to Classical Calvinism because there are some trends in Calvinistic thought that would approach the question somewhat differently. I will deal with that kind of Calvinism later. Herein lies the bottom-line difference between Classical Arminianism and Classical Calvinism. Calvinism insists that regeneration, which is irresistible grace, precedes saving faith. Regeneration makes the "yes" answer of faith in Christ a guaranteed result. The "no" answer is not an option for the person who has been regenerated by the Holy Spirit. In such a case, we are dealing with *cause* and *effect*. Regeneration is the *cause*. Faith is the *effect*.

R.C. Sproul, in explaining the view of Augustine, points out that Augustine's view of grace as irresistible, really means that it is effectual. It is monergistic. It brings to pass what God wanted to bring to pass. "Divine grace changes the human heart, resurrecting the sinner from spiritual death to spiritual life. Formerly the sinner was unwilling and not inclined to choose Christ, but now he is not only willing but eager to choose Christ." Sproul rejects the concept that the sinner is "dragged to Christ against his will." He argues that Augustine's view is monergistic "*at* the initial point of the sinner's movement from unbelief to faith." Yet that does not mean that the "whole process is monergistic." Once God has given regenerating grace, Sproul says, "the rest of the process is synergistic. That is, after the soul has been changed by the effectual or irresistible grace, the person himself chooses Christ. God does not make the choice for him. It is the person who believes, not God who believes for him. Indeed the rest of the Christian life of sanctification unfolds in a synergistic pattern."[2]

Regeneration Monergistic in Both Classical Arminianism and Classical Calvinism

While there is an important difference between my view of regeneration and the view of Calvinism, the difference is not *monergism*. In both views, regeneration is solely the work of God. In Calvinism, the order is regeneration, faith, justification, and sanctification. In my view the order is faith, justification, regeneration, and sanctification.

The Work of the Holy Spirit in Faith

As I remarked above, Jesus makes it clear that it does not fall within the framework of possibilities for a sinner to respond to the gospel unless he is drawn by the Holy Spirit (Jn. 6:44). The influence of the Holy Spirit working in the heart of the person who hears the gospel brings about a framework of possibilities in which a person can say yes or no to the gospel. If he says yes, it is his choice. If he says no, it is his choice.[3] The work of the Holy Spirit in this case is solely a work of God and would thus be *monergistic*. It is not regeneration. It can be resisted.

In Calvinism, the only work of God that is capable of resulting in saving faith is regeneration. Regeneration so transforms the person that he or she will freely believe. It is irresistible. The "no" answer is ruled out.

The Question of Synergism

It is my contention that faith is *synergistic* in both Calvinism and Arminianism. Sproul says in the quotation given above, "Once the operative grace of regeneration is given, the rest of the process is synergistic. That is, after the soul has been changed by the effectual or irresistible grace, the person himself chooses Christ. God does not make the choice for him."

It seems to be evident that *Sproul considers faith to be synergistic*. If there is any doubt in anyone's mind, Sproul removes the doubt. In another source he says, "Faith is not monergistic."[4] Sometimes it sounds as if Calvinists are saying that faith is *monergistic*. But the nature of the case makes that impossible. By definition, faith is a human act of believing. Active participation in faith on the part of the believer means that it cannot be otherwise than *synergistic*. In my view, we are dealing with influence and response. The person can say, "yes" only by the aid of the Holy Spirit. But under this circumstance, he can say, "yes" or "no." Human participation *cannot* be ruled out of faith in either Calvinism or Arminianism.

An Inconsistency in Calvinism

In Calvinism, it is impossible for a person to believe unless he or she is first regenerated. There is also another impossibility. It is impossible for sanctification to take place *prior to* justification. Robert Haldane explains that, as long as people are under sin's guilt, God cannot have "friendly intercourse" with them, for "what communion hath light with darkness? But Christ having canceled his people's guilt, having redeemed them from the curse of the law, and invested them with the robe of his righteousness, there is no longer any obstacle to their communion with God, or any barrier to the free ingress of sanctifying grace."[5]

Following through with this reasoning, justification must be *prior to* regeneration. This is true since regeneration is the initial work of sanctification. In support of this conclusion, I will provide a quotation from Louis Berkhof, who states that "regeneration is the beginning of sanctification."[6] He goes on to quote A. H. Strong with approbation. Strong says, "It (sanctification) is distinguished from regeneration as growth from birth, or as the strengthening of the holy disposition from the original impartation of it."[7]

In his discussion on justification, Berkhof points out that there have been those who advocated the idea that the elect were justified from eternity. He would place antinomians and some Reformed theologians in this category. He goes on to give a thorough refutation of this view.[8] He explains, "The elect are not personally justified in the Scriptural sense until they accept Christ by faith and thus appropriate His merits."[9]

According to Berkhof, one of the arguments that has been used in support of eternal justification is: "The sinner receives the initial grace of regeneration on the basis of the imputed righteousness of Christ. Consequently, the merits of Christ must have been imputed to him before his regeneration." Berkhof's response is: "But while this consideration leads to the conclusion that justification logically precedes regeneration, it does not prove the priority of justification in a temporal sense. The sinner can receive the grace of regeneration on the basis of a justification ideally existing in the counsel of God and certain to be realized in the life of the sinner."[10]

Berkhof recognizes the problem of having regeneration prior to justification. He does not reject the conclusion that regeneration is dependent on justification. He recognizes that justification is logically prior to regeneration. But he says that "it does not prove the priority of justification in a temporal sense." His only answer is, "The sinner can receive the grace of regeneration on the basis of a justification ideally existing in the counsel of God and certain to be realized in the life of the sinner."

If indeed it is true that regeneration is "the beginning of sanctification" (Berkhof, a major Calvinist theologian), and if indeed it is true that God cannot enter with His sanctifying grace until the guilt problem is solved by justification (Haldane, one whose Calvinistic credentials are not in question), then Calvinism is in trouble with its view of having regeneration prior to justification.

Unless someone can come up with a better answer, the validity of Calvinism's insistence that regeneration precedes faith hangs on the fragile thread of the suggestion that Berkhof gave of "justification ideally existing in the counsel of God and certain to be realized in the life of the sinner." That fragile thread will not hold!

I have no quarrel with the idea that in some sense all of God's decisions are eternal. But His decisions are based on a prior knowledge of what He will do. He has not performed an act until He actually does it. I have no quarrel with the idea that whatever God knows He will do He will certainly do. However, such knowledge was a knowledge of what God would do. He knew from eternity who would believe and whom He would justify and when He would justify them. In both Calvinism and Arminianism, a person is not justified in the sight of God until he believes.

To speak of "justification ideally existing in the counsel of God and certain to be realized in the life of the sinner" is not the same as saying that the person is already justified. There can be no divine actions that require justification as a grounds until the person is in fact justified. If that is the case, Calvinism is in trouble with its own theology when it places regeneration prior to justification.

In his refutation of "the doctrine of justification from eternity," Berkhof makes it clear that justification cannot be considered a reality until it takes place in time. One of the arguments used by the advocates of justification from eternity that Berkhof cites is, "Justification is an immanent act of God, and as such must be from eternity." His response is:

It is hardly correct, however, to speak of justification as an *actus immanens* in God [an immanent act, or an act inherent in God Himself]; it is rather an *actus transiens* [a transitive act, or an act originating in God but acting upon an object, an act which is not complete until the object exists], just as creation, incarnation, and so on. The advocates of justification from eternity feel the weight of this consideration, and therefore hasten to give us the assurance that they do not mean to teach that the elect are justified from eternity *actualiter* [actually or really], but only in the intention of God, in the divine decree. This leads us back to the usual distinction between the counsel of God and its execution. If this justification in the intention of God warrants our speaking of a justification from eternity, then there is absolutely no reason why we should not speak of a creation from eternity as well.[11]

Later Berkhof explains: "Justification is one of the fruits of Christ's redemptive work, applied by the Holy Spirit. But the Spirit did not and could not apply this or any other fruit of work of Christ from eternity."[12] Berkhof would be in agreement with my statement: "He [God] has not performed an act until He actually does it." I think Berkhof has successfully refuted the validity of his own statement, "The sinner can receive the grace of regeneration on the basis of a justification ideally existing in the counsel of God and certain to be realized in the life of the sinner."

There can be no divine action based on justification that has not already occurred. If this is true, regeneration cannot precede faith. Regeneration is not an act of God that prepares the way for redemption. It is a redemptive act. I commend Calvinism for upholding the satisfaction view of atonement and the imputation of the death and righteousness of Christ as the ground of justification. Yet Calvinists need to reexamine the question of whether the redemptive act of regeneration can be performed on a person before the death and righteousness of Christ is actually imputed to his account.

The Question of Sovereign Grace

Classical Calvinists have been champions of the satisfaction view of atonement. But they speak of election as being based on sovereign grace.

Sovereign grace would be a divine right growing out of God's sovereignty rather than a provision made possible by atonement. This seems to be what John Piper, in his book on Romans 9, is saying when he remarks: "We can say God's glory and his name consists fundamentally in his propensity to show mercy and his sovereign freedom in its distribution, or to put it more precisely, it is *the glory of God and his essential nature mainly to dispense mercy (but also wrath, Ex 34:7) on whomever he pleases apart from any constraint originating outside his own will. This is the essence of what it means to be God. This is his name.*"[13]

The question that I am concerned about is not whether some constraint is imposed on God outside His will. I do not believe that is the case either. The question is whether His own holy nature forbids Him to choose anyone for salvation apart from Christ. Does not His own holy nature forbid Him to choose a person for salvation apart from the application of atonement? Will not His holy nature forbid Him from performing a redemptive act on a person before the death and righteousness of Christ is imputed to him? I think it will.

The Difference Between Classical Arminianism and Erickson's View

Erickson agrees with Calvinism on unconditional election, but differs with Classical Calvinism on the logical order of regeneration and faith. As Erickson points out, Scripture supports the idea that conversion precedes regeneration: "Various appeals to respond to the gospel imply that conversion results in regeneration. Among them is Paul's reply to the Philippian jailer (we are assuming that regeneration is part of the process of being saved): 'Believe in the Lord Jesus, and you will be saved, you and your household' (Acts 16:31)."[14] Erickson correctly observes that faith must precede regeneration because regeneration is a part of salvation, which is conditioned on faith.

While Erickson rejects the view that regeneration precedes faith, he sides with Calvinism on the view that God's call is irresistible. He observes that God's "special calling" is an "intensive and effectual" work of the Holy Spirit.

"It is not the complete transformation which constitutes regeneration, but it does render the conversion of the individual both possible and certain. Thus the logical order of the initial aspects of salvation is special calling—conversion—regeneration."[15]

Earlier in his treatment of the subject, Erickson compared his view with the Arminian view. He explains:

> Special or effectual calling, then, involves an extraordinary presentation of the message of salvation. It is sufficiently powerful to counteract the effects of sin and enable the person to believe. It is also so appealing that the person will believe. Special calling is in many ways similar to the prevenient grace of which Arminians speak. It differs from that concept, however, in two respects. It is bestowed only on the elect, not upon all humans and it leads infallibly or efficaciously to a positive response by the recipient.[16]

I think Erickson has correctly analyzed the difference between his view and the Arminian view as I hold to it. R. C. Sproul's description of Lewis Sperry Chafer would suggest that Chafer's view is similar to Erickson's.[17]

Since Erickson has God electing people *to be* in Christ rather than electing people *in Christ* as taught in Ephesians 1:4, it follows that the divine choice of election was based on sovereign grace rather than grace made possible through atonement. In any view of unconditional election, the divine decision to elect the person of necessity preceded the divine decision to apply the benefits of atonement and justification to the person. The person is elected to have the benefits of atonement applied. I am referring here to those divine decisions as they were made in eternity past.

Faith Not a Work

Arminians believe that faith is the condition of justification. Calvinists also believe that faith is the condition of justification. The problem comes, as we have seen, in Calvinists' claim that regeneration must precede faith and give birth to faith. Since Arminians believe the sinner can believe without first being regenerated, the Calvinists tend to view faith in Arminianism as being a work. Thus they have charged that Arminians believe people are justified by works.

Based on the place of faith in justification in the governmental view of atonement and justification, it can at least be understood why this charge would be made against the Arminians who hold this view. Let me reproduce here the chart from Chapter 6 on the governmental view of justification:

Debits	THE BELIEVER	Credits
Absolute Righteousness ~~Eternal Death~~		Faith in Christ
	JUSTIFIED OR PARDONED	

In this view of justification, it is recognized that faith in Christ is not absolute righteousness, but it gets the same consideration before God that absolute righteousness would receive. Faith in Christ is counted as righteousness. It can be seen why this approach could be accused of considering faith as a work. I am sure that those Arminians who believe in this approach to justification by faith would deny that this means they believe in justification by works. They would deny that faith is a meritorious act that earns their salvation. They would say that for God to treat faith in Christ as if it were absolute righteousness would be a gracious act of God. Calvinistic works that have criticized Arminianism have been based on this approach to Arminianism rather than the kind of Arminianism that I have set forth in this book. I am persuaded that my views are in essential agreement with those of Jacob Arminius. But that is not the reason I believe my view. It is because I believe it is based on Scripture.

In Classical Arminianism, the ground of justification is the imputation of the death and righteousness of Christ to the believer's account. The condition of justification is faith in Jesus Christ. Faith in no way whatever gets any consideration as any form of merit that would form the smallest part of the ground of my justification. The only ground of my justification before God is the penal death of Christ and His life of absolute obedience to the Father.

If when I stand before God He should ask me, "What is your hope of acceptance based on?" I would not mention anything that I have ever done or not done. I would say, "My hope is built on nothing less and nothing more than the death and righteousness of Christ." I would not even say, "I had faith in Christ." When I declared that I was basing my hope of acceptance on the death and righteousness of Christ—that and that alone would be a manifestation of my faith. Until the time when I stand before God, my song is to be found in the words of that great hymn written by Edward Mote:

My hope is built on nothing less
Than Jesus' blood and righteousness;
I dare not trust the sweetest frame,
But wholly lean on Jesus name.

His oath, His covenant, His blood
Support me in the whelming flood;
When all around my soul gives way,
He then is all my hope and stay.

On Christ, the solid Rock, I stand;
All other ground is sinking sand,
All other ground is sinking sand.
When darkness seems to hide His face,
I rest on his unchanging grace;
In every high and stormy gale,
My anchor holds within the vale.

When He shall come with trumpet sound,
Oh, may I then in Him be found;
Dressed in His righteousness alone,
Faultless to stand before the throne.

On Christ, the solid Rock, I stand;
All other ground is sinking sand,
All other ground is sinking sand.[18]

The words of the Apostle Paul destroy forever the possibility that faith can rightly be called works. He says: "For what does the Scripture say? 'Abraham believed God, and it was accounted to him for righteousness.' Now to him who works, the wages are not counted as grace but as debt. But to him who does not work but believes on Him who justifies the ungodly, his faith is accounted for righteousness" (Rom. 4:3-5).

The Meaning of "Faith Counted for Righteousness"

Those who subscribe to the governmental view of atonement believe that in the statement, "Faith is counted for righteousness" (Rom. 4:3, 5, Gal. 3:6), they find solid support for their position. It must be admitted that, so far as this expression is concerned, the governmental view is grammatically possible. (See 2:26 where uncircumcision is counted "for" circumcision.) The big question is: Does it fit the context of Scripture as it relates to atonement and justification? Of immediate concern is: How does such an interpretation fit what Paul has already said in Romans? To answer this question, we must go back to what Paul said about the necessity of atonement.

There are three very important truths set forth in Romans 2:1–3:20. (1) God's requirement for justification is absolute righteousness (2:1–16: see notes on 2:13). (2) No human being has produced righteousness (3:10). (3) No human being by his own activity can produce absolute righteousness (3:20).

The big question before us now is: Is it universally and unchangeably true that "God requires absolute righteousness for justification?" If this is true, the governmental view and all similar views cannot be considered valid interpretations of atonement and justification. The same principle that eliminates the governmental view establishes the satisfaction view. What God requires has been provided by Christ. He provided for us and offers to us nothing less than absolute righteousness.

If the satisfaction view is true, how do we understand "his faith is counted for righteousness?" There are two possibilities. The first is to keep the translation as it is and to understand it to mean "faith, embracing its object which is Christ," is counted as righteousness.[19] The meaning would be similar to Jesus' statement to the woman in Luke 7 when He said, "Your faith has saved you" (Lk. 7:50). It is quite obvious that it was Christ who saved the woman. This being true, it was faith embracing its object. The One embraced by faith saved her. In this instance, faith would be a metonymy.

There is another view that seems more likely. A distinction is made between "the imputation [or counting] of faith" (v. 5) and the "imputation of righteousness" (v. 6). A further point of clarification comes from the meaning of "for" (Greek *eis*). While "for" is a proper translation, there are other possibilities. A very common translation is "unto." It is also translated "toward."

By translating it as "toward," it would read, "his faith is counted toward righteousness." Faith, then, is counted (or imputed) toward the receiving of righteousness."[20]

CONCLUSION

I believe that I can say, "Justification is by faith alone" with as much conviction and as much confidence as any Calvinist or Lutheran can. But I would like to go further and make a distinction between the condition of justification and the ground of justification. When it comes to the ground of justification, I would say, "Justification is by Christ alone." My hope in built on nothing less and nothing more than the death and righteousness of Christ—that and that alone. The death and righteousness of Christ are placed on my account on the condition of faith alone. By God's help, I believed and He freely justified. To put it briefly, "Justification is grounded in Christ alone. It is bestowed on the condition of faith alone."

---

[1] Richard Chenevix Trench, *Synonyms of the New Testament* (1854; reprint, Grand Rapids: Associated Publishers and Authors, Inc., n. d.), 242.

[2] R. C. Sproul, *Willing to Believe: The Controversy Over Free Will* (Grand Rapids: Baker Books, 1997), 73.

[3] See chapter 1.

[4] R.C. Sproul, *Chosen by God* (Wheaton: Tyndale House Publishers, Inc., 1986), 118.

[5] Robert Haldane, *An Exposition of the Epistle of Romans* (1852; reprint, McLean, Virginia: McDonald Publishing Company, 1958), 248-249.

[6] Louis Berkhof, *Systematic Theology*, 536.

[7] Strong, *Systematic Theology*, 536.

[8] Berkhof, *Systematic Theology*, 517-520.

[9] Ibid., 520.

[10] Ibid., 518.

[11] Ibid., 518-519. Translation by Dr. Darrell Holley, professor of Latin at Free Will Baptist Bible College, Nashville, Tennessee.

[12] Ibid., 519.

[13]John Piper, *The Justification of God* (Grand Rapids: Baker Book House, 1983), 67.

[14]Millard J. Erickson, *Christian Theology*, unabridged one vol. ed. (Grand Rapids: Baker, 1985), 932.

[15]Ibid., 933.

[16]Ibid., 931.

[17]Sproul, *Willing to Believe*, 189-202.

[18]Edward Mote, "The Solid Rock" in *Rejoice: The Free Will Baptist Hymn Book* (Nashville: National Association of Free Will Baptists, 1988), 419.

[19]Lenski, *The Interpretation of St. Paul's Epistle to the Romans*, 290.

[20]This and the preceding five paragraphs are adapted from my commentary on Romans. Forlines, *Romans*, 105.

CHAPTER 8

Sanctification

The two aspects of sin are *guilt* and *depravity*. Sin as guilt makes a person liable to punishment. Sin as depravity is a power in a person's life that causes him to commit sin. Two aspects of salvation are designed to deal with the two aspects of sin: *justification* and *sanctification*. Justification settles the problem of guilt. It changes our standing before God. Sanctification deals with the problem created by depravity. It changes our experience with God and with sin. It is very helpful in understanding the doctrine of salvation to get a clear understanding of the difference between justification and sanctification and the relationship between the two.

JUSTIFICATION	SANCTIFICATION
1. Positional (Standing)	1. Experiential (State)
2. Objective	2. Subjective
3. Right Standing With God	3. Conformity to the Image of Christ
4. Always Full and Complete	4. Moving Toward Completion
5. Christ's Righteousness	5. Personal Righteousness
6. Absolute Righteousness	6. Relative Righteousness Now— Absolute in the Life to Come

A review of this chart after studying this chapter will make it more meaningful. Presenting it here puts the mind on the alert so we can avoid confusing justification and sanctification. Let it be said here that while there are *clear distinctions between justification and sanctification*, the Bible knows of *no separation of the two*. We cannot receive justification without also receiving sanctification.

THE RELATIONSHIP BETWEEN JUSTIFICATION AND SANCTIFICATION

At conversion, we receive justification and sanctification simultaneously. While both are received at the same time, justification is logically prior to sanctification and makes sanctification possible. Sanctification is *dependent* on justification. Justification is *not dependent* on sanctification. Justification is dependent on the death and righteousness of Christ.

Finney's View of the Relationship Between Justification and Sanctification

Charles Finney's view on this point is an illustration of the errors that can grow out of the governmental view of atonement and justification. He remarks:

> Present sanctification, in the sense of present full consecration to God, is made another condition, not ground of justification. Some theologians have made justification a condition of sanctification, instead of making sanctification a condition of justification. But this we shall see is an erroneous view of the subject . . . . Sanctification is sometimes used to express a permanent state of obedience to God, or of consecration. In this sense it is not a condition of present justification, or of pardon and acceptance. But it is a condition of continued and permanent acceptance with God. It certainly cannot be true, that God accepts and justifies a person in his or her sins. The Bible everywhere represents justified persons as sanctified, and always expressly, or impliedly, conditionates justification upon sanctification, in the sense of present obedience to God.[1]

Sanctification—an Essential Accompaniment of Justification

I can appreciate Finney's concern for not separating justification and sanctification and thus allowing a person to be justified who is not sanctified. However, his approach confuses the doctrine of justification and places it in jeopardy.

Sanctification is always an *accompaniment* of justification, but it is *not a condition* or *ground* of justification. It is simply that the salvation "package" includes both, and the package cannot be broken to separate the two. We can no more have justification without sanctification than we can sanctification without justification.

The ultimate concern of God in redemption is to restore fallen human beings to favor and to a functional relationship with God. Justification is an absolutely essential step in the process of redemption. To bypass justification or to ground it on anything other than the death and righteousness of Christ is to do violence to the holiness of God and to grace. To break the package and allow justification without sanctification is to commit the following errors:

First, it is a serious misunderstanding of Scripture. I will deal with this later in this chapter. Second, it is to ground the satisfaction of the holiness of God in atonement and justification in a technical necessity in God rather than a personal necessity in God. If the satisfaction of holiness is a technical necessity, that interest can be set aside when the technicality is settled. It would be a formality required to uphold the letter of the law. If the satisfaction of holiness is grounded in God's personal experience of holiness and His attitude toward sin, that interest is just as strong once a person is justified as it was before. Justification is a step in the process of redemption that makes sanctification possible. A holy God will most definitely pursue His interest in holiness with the believer. Third, it opens the door to cheap easy-believism, which promises justification without sanctification—forgiveness without change. Such a view is not the gospel. It is another gospel.

For years we have operated with the rightful assumption that grace would become corrupted through a wrongful involvement of law—that it would in effect become another gospel. However, the reverse danger received, in most cases, no attention. It is true that a wrong involvement of law can corrupt grace so that we would be preaching another gospel. This is what Paul taught in Galatians (Gal. 1:8-9). It is also true that we can so abuse grace and void its interest in law that we would be preaching another gospel. This is what Paul was warning against in 1 Corinthians 6:9-11; Galatians 5:19-21; and Ephesians 5:3-7. The Book of James exposes this error. Particular interest is given to it in James 2:14-26. First John gives a clear warning against this error (1 Jn. 1:6; 2:3-4, 9-11; 3:3-10, 14-15; 4:20). The correction of this error does not change the nature of the doctrine of justification, but the correction must insist that justification is always accompanied by sanctification. *Forgiveness and change always go together.*

The Influence of Pseudo-Calvinism

A corruption of the Calvinistic doctrine of perseverance has been largely responsible for the spread of cheap easy-believism. It has talked about people being eternally secure who show no evidence of sanctification. This is a corruption of Calvinism. Historic Calvinism has taught the perseverance of the saints, not eternal security whether they persevere or not.

James Oliver Buswell, Jr., a Calvinist, calls this corruption of Calvinism pseudo-Calvinism. He explains:

> I have heard several pseudo-Calvinistic speakers in Christian college chapel exercises say, "Dear young people, there are two ways to go to heaven: The spiritual way and the carnal way. It is so much better to take the spiritual way!" I knew a certain young person who believed this false doctrine and said to the Dean, "I am a Christian, but I do not mind sitting in the bleachers. I choose to go to heaven the carnal way!"
>
> No! The carnal way is the way to eternal punishment. Those who practice things of this kind are not going to inherit the kingdom of God. (Galatians 5:21)[2]

Though I am not a Calvinist, I do think it is important that both non-Calvinists and Calvinists be aware of the difference between historic Calvinism and the corruption of Calvinism by pseudo-Calvinists. The pseudo-Calvinist reminds me of Ahimaaz. When Absalom was killed, he prevailed upon Joab to let him go and tell David. At first Joab denied the request and sent Cushi. Ahimaaz again prevailed upon Joab to let him go. With reluctance, Joab consented. With great zeal, Ahimaaz overtook Cushi and was the first to get to David. When Ahimaaz gave his report, he said, "I saw a great tumult, but I knew not what it was" (2 Sam. 18:29).

The pseudo-Calvinist has heard that salvation is free. It is a gift. It is by grace. Without thinking things through and getting things in perspective, he concluded that it meant that sanctification was optional. Off he goes with his half-truth. It is true that salvation is free, but it is not true that sanctification is optional. He goes off half-cocked, having a misunderstanding of both Calvinism and Scripture. The harm that this has done to the Church of Jesus Christ is beyond estimate. A morally drained society is being confronted by a morally anemic church.

It would be unfair to lay the spread of cheap easy-believism altogether at the feet of the pseudo-Calvinist. Many non-Calvinists have picked up the chant of cheap easy-believism with no significant modifications and have preached it. Cheap easy-believism is inherent in all weakening of the moral thrust of Christianity.

The tragedy of cheap easy-believism is that it leads to many false professions. It offers assurance to people who have never been saved. It is not the gospel. It is another gospel. It is as much a corruption of the gospel as is a wrong emphasis on law. There is less hope of leading people out of cheap easy-believism than there is from a corruption of the gospel by a wrong emphasis on law. The wrong emphasis on law corrupts grace but does not corrupt law. Cheap easy-believism corrupts both law and grace. By understanding neither law nor grace, it has weakened all points of appeal that could be used to bring about correction.

It is not easy to correct the view that corrupts grace through a wrong emphasis on law, but there is a possibility. By leaving law intact and in good shape, law can be used as a starting point from which to show a person that a proper understanding of grace satisfies, honors, and upholds the law.

How Justification Contributes to Sanctification

We need to elaborate now on how justification contributes to sanctification. Justification makes both a negative and a positive contribution to sanctification.

The Power of Sin Broken

On the negative side, the power of sin is broken. Paul says, "For sin shall not have dominion over you, for you are not under law but under grace." (Rom. 6:14). As we observed in the Chapter 6, Romans 6:7 should be translated, "For he that died is justified from sin." The death referred to is the penal death of Christ which belongs to the believer by union with Christ. Justification based on the identification of the believer with the penal death of Christ is given by Paul as the grounds for his statement "that henceforth we should not serve sin" (verse 6, KJV).

How does the penal death of Christ received in justification break the power of sin? David Brown explains: "As death dissolves all claims, so the whole claim of sin, not only to 'reign unto death,' but to keep its victim in sinful bondage, has been discharged once for all, by the believer's penal death in the death of Christ; so that he is no longer a 'debtor to the flesh, to live after the flesh.' (chapter 8:12)"[3]

Before the guilt problem is solved by the death of Christ, there is nothing to check the power of sin. Sin reigns unchecked. When the believer has the guilt problem settled by the death of Christ, the power of sin is broken. The believer is delivered from the sphere where sin reigned and is transferred into the sphere of grace. "So that as sin reigned in death, even so grace might reign through righteousness to eternal life through Jesus Christ our Lord" (Rom. 5:21).

The Entrance of God's Sanctifying Grace

On the positive side, the penal death of Christ received in justification opens the way for the entrance of God's sanctifying grace. Paul says, "For if we have been planted together [grown together or united] in the likeness of his death, we shall be also in the likeness of his resurrection" (Rom. 6:5, KJV). To be in the likeness of Christ's death is to have His death become our death so that we receive the benefits of it. This involves justification.

To be in the likeness of Christ's resurrection is to live a life of triumphant power over sin. In verse 4, Paul explains "just as Christ was raised from the dead" as being that which involves the "walk in newness of life." The likeness of Christ's resurrection manifests itself in newness of life. This involves sanctification. The likeness of Christ's death (justification) opens the way for likeness of Christ's resurrection (sanctification).

Our guilt stood as a barrier between us and the sanctifying power of God. God's holiness would not allow Him to enter into a personal relationship with us as long as our guilt was still upon us. When the guilt was removed by the justifying grace of God, the way was open for the entrance of God's sanctifying grace.[4] As the justifying grace of God is effective in forgiving our sins and restoring us to favor with God, so the sanctifying grace of God is effective in changing our experience with God and sin. It guarantees a change in our lives.

Justification Foundational for Sanctification

It can be seen that justification is foundational for sanctification. To interpret sanctification on the one hand to be a condition or ground of justification, or to interpret justification on the other hand as contributing to a weak view of sanctification, is to grossly misunderstand the biblical teaching on salvation.

God's Personal Interest in Holiness Maintained in Both Justification and Sanctification

In interpreting principles that apply to persons and to personal relationships, we tend to become mechanical. We cannot totally avoid the treatment of principles this way at times. We can and must offset the influence of this tendency, nonetheless, by constantly putting things in perspective by reconstructing the context in terms of persons and personal relationships. The requirement that holiness makes in atonement is grounded in God's personal concern for holiness. He is not simply protecting the letter of the law or some legal technicality. When the demands of holiness are put into the context of God's personal concern for holiness, that concern can neither be stopped nor depreciated by the satisfaction of the law involved in justification. It will manifest itself in a concern for sanctification that is consistent with the holy nature of God. The redemptive process is designed to restore us to favor with God and to restore the holiness that was lost in the fall. Justification is a step in that process by a personal God who is intensely interested in holiness. That interest will never be diminished.

The Meaning of Sanctification

To sanctify is to make holy. Holiness is more than a moral term. It also speaks of a relationship with God. There can be a measure of morality without dedication to God, but there can be no holiness without dedication to God. The person whom we refer to as a "good, moral" person who is not dedicated to God is unholy.

The first Table of the Law begins with "You shall have no other gods before Me," and goes through "Remember the sabbath day, to keep it holy" (Ex. 20:3-11). The second Table of the Law begins with "Honor your father and your mother," and goes through "You shall not covet" (Ex. 20:12-17). Obedience to the first Table of the Law constitutes *godliness*. Obedience to the second Table of the Law constitutes *righteousness. Holiness* embraces godliness (reverential living before God) and righteousness (conformity to God's moral standard). Disobedience to the first Table of the Law constitutes ungodliness. Disobedience to the second Table of the Law constitutes unrighteousness. Disobedience to any of the Ten Commandments constitutes a failure to be holy.

It is interesting in studying the prophetic writings to see which Table of the Law is receiving attention. For example, Hosea's main concern is with the violation of the First Table of the Law, while the main concern of Amos is with the violation of the Second Table of the Law.

The primary meaning of holiness is dedication to God, but we cannot think of the primary meaning as existing apart from the secondary meaning, which is separation from sin. To move toward God is to move away from sin as surely as to go north means to go away from south.

Positional Sanctification

Positional sanctification means to be positionally set apart for God. Positional sanctification has as its goal experiential sanctification. The thought here is similar to that of electing a person to be president of an organization. He is elected to serve. At the moment the former president's term expires, he is president positionally on the basis of being elected. He is president in experience only as he functions in the capacity for which he was elected. We are positionally set apart by God at conversion. We are experientially sanctified only as we practice holiness.

We can distinguish in fact between positional sanctification and experiential sanctification for purposes of definition, but we are not to think of the believer as being positionally sanctified without being experientially sanctified. From now on, all use of the word *sanctification* in this study will refer to experiential sanctification unless otherwise indicated.

Experiential Sanctification

We not only study the subject of sanctification where the word and related words are found, but we also study it anywhere the concept is found whether the word or related words appear or not.

Sanctification begins with conversion (2 Cor. 5:17). It is at that very moment that a person begins to experience holiness. A changed life is the essential fruit of conversion.

Sanctification continues to progress in this life by the process of growth (2 Pet. 3:18). Every challenge to dedication or separation from sin that is addressed to Christians is evidence that the New Testament treats sanctification as being progressive and involving growth.

Sanctification will not be completed until the resurrection. The spirit will be completely sanctified at death. At the resurrection, however, sanctification will be completed so far as the body is concerned. After death, we will be completely holy. We will never again have anything in our personality that will not be compatible with God and acceptable to God.

The Goal of Sanctification

Restoration of the Functional Likeness of God

This brings up again the subject of the image of God in man. As was observed earlier, at creation the image of God embraced the *constitutional likeness,* which embraced personhood, and the *functional likeness,* which embraced personality. All of the constituent parts of personhood remained after the fall, though they suffered damage. This damage reflects itself in man's personality. Man lost his functional likeness of God in the fall. He no longer thinks, feels, and acts in the likeness of God. It is the design of redemption to restore the functional likeness of God to man's personality. As Paul tells us in Romans 8:29, we are to be "conformed to the image of his Son [Christ]."

It is very important that our concept of the Christian life take into account that man is a person. God has made us persons who think, feel, and act. We are never more personal than when we are the closest to God—when our personality is most closely conformed to His likeness.

The Limitations of Illustrations in Examining Our Relationship With God

Mechanical terms and expressions can be used to illustrate as long as we do not take them too far. The control of a machine, the use of an instrument, the filling of a vessel, the molding of clay, and the control of a puppet may all be used to illustrate our dependence on God. However, we should recognize the limitations of these illustrations. There is one drastic difference. A person is one who thinks, feels, and makes choices. If this observation is not taken into account, the error can be serious. A puppet cannot refuse to obey the directions of its master; a person can. The actions of a person must reflect his or her own basic nature before they are his in the truest sense of what it means to be a person. If the actions of a being are not in some sense his own, he is not a person.

Influence and Response, Not Cause and Effect

We need to say again that we must not interpret the relationship between persons in terms of mechanical cause and effect. *Influence* and *response* are more appropriate terms. Also, the choice is not to be made between being either active or passive. Such a choice fits mechanical relationships but not personal relationships. In many decisions we are both active and acted upon. We are dependent, independent, and interdependent in our personal relationships.

Sanctification and the Subconscious Mind

If we are truly to be in the likeness of Christ, we must be in His likeness both on the conscious and subconscious levels of our personality. Thoughts, words, and actions take place on the conscious level, but they are expressions of our inner basic nature which exists on the subconscious level.

It is the design of sanctification to change our thoughts, words, and actions into the likeness of Christ and to so change our basic inner nature that these thoughts, words, and actions represent a real attitude of heart. Anything less than this fails to recognize the implications involved in the fact that man is personal. The view of redemption that makes man, in his highest dedication, a surrendered instrument or machine to be controlled by God, to the point that a Christian's decisions are in no real sense his own, fails to understand what is meant to be changed into the image of Christ. Such a view fails to comprehend fully that man is a personal being.

The church has always been plagued with the idea that there is no real redemption of the personality in this life. Man is pictured by some as being so totally wrecked by sin that he is beyond repair in this life, even by God. Salvation becomes a divine towing service for the wrecked human being. Nothing can be done to restore him in this life. Everything will be made all right when we are finally towed into the heavenly garage, but that will be in the next life.

The best thing, according to this view, is for a person to dwell on the idea of his or her own nothingness and worthlessness. He is to believe that he is doing nothing and cannot do anything worthwhile. God is doing everything. The best he can do is to keep from being a hindrance while God is towing His wrecked humanity into the heavenly garage. To despise himself would seem to be his highest virtue. To respect himself or to have anything like self-confidence is a sin.

Biblical Evidence for the Transformation of the Subconscious Mind

I appreciate the problems that many sincere Christians have that move them, to whatever extent, along the line of thought described above. However, the Bible clearly teaches that there is a basic change in the personality of redeemed people both on the conscious and subconscious levels that makes our actions in a real sense our own and a reflection of our inner nature.

In Romans 8:29, the word for "conformed" is the Greek word *summorphos*. Sanday and Headlam explain that this word "denotes inward and thorough and not merely superficial likeness."[5]

In 2 Corinthians 3:18, when Paul speaks about the process of being transformed into the image of the glory of the Lord, he uses a very interesting word. He uses a verb that is kin to the word used in Romans 8:29. It is the word *metamorphoō*. The word is made up of two words meaning "after" and "to form." The noun which comes from the same root is the word *morphē*. R.C. Trench calls attention to an interesting contrast between *morphē* and another Greek word *schēma*. He explains that *morphē* "signifies the form as it is the utterance of the inner life."[6] *Schēma* refers to outward appearance or fashion and can be superficial.[7] *Suschēmatidzō* is a verb which is made up of two words "with or together" and the verb form from the same root as *schēma* which means "to fashion." *Metamorphoō* refers to an internal change rather than a mere external change. *Suschēmatidzō* refers to an outward, superficial change.[8]

The choice of the word *metamorphoō* in 2 Corinthians 3:18 shows us that when Paul speaks of being changed into the image of the Lord, he is speaking about a deep, basic change in the inner nature of the Christian. It is a change of our personality on the subconscious level that manifests itself in conscious actions that are true reflections of the person.

In Romans 12:2 Paul says: "And do not be conformed to this world, but be transformed by the renewing of your mind." The Greek word for conformed is *suschēmatidzō*. The Greek word for transformed is *metamorphoō*. Trench correctly explains: "'Do not fall in,' says the apostle, 'with the fleeting fashions of this world, nor be yourselves fashioned to them (*mēsuschēmatizesthe*), but undergo a deep abiding change (*alla metamorphousthe*) by the renewing of your mind, such as the spirit of God alone can work in you' (cf. 2 Corinthians iii.18)."[9]

It is clear from the words used in Romans 8:29; 12:2; and 2 Corinthians 3:18 that Paul is referring to the fact that as Christians we experience a deep, basic, inner change.[10] The life of the believer is brought into the likeness of the life of Christ. The outward life is to be a manifestation of an inner reality.

Sanctification and the Total Personality

The New Testament teaches that conformity to the image of Christ extends to each area of the personality. It affects the way we think, feel, and act. Romans 12:2 proves to be very interesting at this point. Paul speaks about a basic, inner change taking place "by the renewing of your mind." Concerning the meaning of this expression, Barclay M. Newman and Eugene A. Nida explain: "The meaning is that the Christian confession demands that the entire bent of one's mind be changed. The entire clause may be rendered as 'permit God to change your inside by giving you a completely new mind' or 'by making your mind and your heart completely different.'"[11]

As I understand it, the renewing of the mind is not a process that somehow stands outside the basic inner change that brings it about. Rather, it is involved in the change. The renewing of the mind is involved in the basic inner change.

The important question here is: What is the mind? In the English language, the word *mind* means: (1) that with which we think and reason, (2) the mind (in the limited sense just referred to) plus the heart and the will. It is this use of the word *mind* that is reflected in the statement: "I have made up my mind to serve the Lord." We mean by this that our whole being—mind, heart, and will—is involved in the decision.

I believe the Greek word *nous* as Paul is using it embraces mind, heart, and will. Concerning the meaning of *nous*, J. H. Thayer gives as one of its meanings: "The mind, comprising alike the faculties of perceiving and understanding and those of feeling, judging, determining."[12] This use of the word *mind* is closely related to person or personality. We would be correct in saying that, in Romans 12:2 when Paul speaks of a change in our basic inner nature by the renewing of our mind, he was referring to a basic inner change in our total personality.

Persons, Not Puppets

We are told in Scripture that God said with reference to the New Covenant, "I will put My laws in their mind" (Heb. 8:10). The evidence that we have examined up to this point, the challenge to use our minds and our hearts in our relationship with God, and the challenges that are made to our will leave no doubt that, in a very real sense as Christians, our actions are to spring from the inner realities of our personality.

It is a misunderstanding of Scripture for us to reduce ourselves to instruments for God to use or channels for God to work through. These metaphors are all right if we do not press them too far. When we press them to the point that we are passively to yield ourselves to God with the idea that we are to do nothing and let God use us like puppets, we are overlooking the truth that God has made us as persons and treats us accordingly in His dealings with us.

In our relationship with God, we are both *dependent* and *independent*. We are dependent in the sense that we need His help and cannot be what we should be without His help. We are independent in the sense that, even though we cannot be what we should be without God's help, in a real sense, our actions are our own. God does not treat us like puppets. We have latitude for obedience and disobedience.

The Fruit of the Spirit: An Expression of Our Transformed Inner Nature

Let me illustrate by applying the basic principles of our discussion to the fruit of the Spirit in Galatians 5:22–23. Dependence is seen in that the various virtues listed are called the fruit of the Spirit. But when we talk about love, joy, peace, longsuffering, and so forth, we are not simply talking about divine activity in which we are used as channels. It may sound good to talk about God loving through us, but what about God having joy through us, or God having peace through us, and so on through the list? The Holy Spirit is helping us to be the kind of person who loves, experiences joy, peace, longsuffering, and so forth. As the Holy Spirit produces fruit in us, these virtues begin to characterize us and express our inner nature. In this work of the Holy Spirit, we are both active and passive. He is working in us as active *persons*, not as passive *puppets*.

I am not suggesting that our inner being is completely transformed in this life. I am not suggesting that there are no inner conflicts. I am, however, suggesting that, though there are inner conflicts, there are also inner realities.

Sanctification and a Proper View of Self-Worth

A proper view of redeemed man gives a foundation for a proper sense of self-worth, self-respect, and a good self-image. We were created in God's image. This gives a sense of self-worth. Sin made us unworthy of God's favor, but it did not render us worthless. God considered man worth (not worthy) what it cost to redeem him. Because of that, we are now sons of God. We belong to the family of God. This gives a sense of self-worth. We are being transformed into the image of God in our personalities. All of this runs counter to the idea of downgrading ourselves. We dare not downgrade the redemptive work of God in our lives.

It is no compliment to God for a Christian to grind himself or herself into the dust of nothingness so he can claim no credit for what he is and so he can give all the glory to God. It is no compliment to God for us to thank Him for making us "nothing." I think it brings far more glory to God for us to recognize the positive good He has done for us, to us, and in us and to thank Him for it and to give Him the glory for it. In a proper view of self-worth, a Christian is always cognizant that he or she owes his or her existence and everything that is worthwhile to God as Creator and Redeemer. This recognition gives rise to gratitude and humility.

Sanctification and the Self

Along the same line of thought, there seems to be a widespread confusion about "self." I can appreciate the difficulty of being exact and precise. Frequently, wrong terminology may be used, though one understands the right meaning, but to speak of crucifying self and to condemn loving oneself is wrong terminology and leads some people into confusion.

Let us reflect on the idea that a person should not love himself and see where such thinking would lead. Jesus said, "Love your neighbour as yourself" (Mt. 22:39). If I am to love my neighbor as myself, but I am not to love myself, that is a poor standard for loving my neighbor. It is all right for a person to love himself. (See Eph. 5:28-29.) But it must be done in the context of loving God and our neighbor. That is not the same as being in love with yourself. It is not narcissism.

The Bible does not speak of "crucifying self" nor "dying to self." The self is the real you. The only way to crucify self would be to bring about the annihilation of the self. This is impossible. Jesus taught self-denial, but that is not crucifixion of self; neither is it self-torture. In Luke 9:23, Jesus said, "If anyone desires to come after me, let him deny himself, and take up his cross daily, and follow me."

In the history of the church, there have been those who have been so obsessed with self-denial that they could not see that broader picture of Christian responsibility. They became ascetics. Such an approach to self-denial misses the focus of the verse. If an undue amount of time is spent in self-examination, the person has become self-centered regardless of what his or her motives are for this inward search. We need to be Christ-centered, not self-centered. The focus of the verse is on Jesus' words "follow me," not on "deny himself."

Self-denial is necessary to the extent that it requires us to set aside all plans and all personal interests that interfere with following Jesus. When self-denial causes us to set aside all of our desires and plans that would interfere with following Jesus, it has fulfilled its purpose. Self-denial is a tough assignment, but it does not call on a person to grind himself or herself into the dust of nothingness. A person who is truly following Jesus has practiced and is practicing self-denial, but this kind of self-denial is not an obsession.

"Self" is not some aspect of our being that gives us trouble. Self is the real you—the real person. Selfhood embraces our personhood and personality. A person does not need to crucify the self. He or she needs to surrender self and develop self. He or she needs self-improvement, not self-crucifixion.

I am sure many people mean essentially the same thing by the expression "crucifixion of self" as I suggest by my interpretation of self-denial, but many take it much further. It becomes a hindrance to the development of the personality of the Christian.[13]

Both Earthen Vessels and Vessels of Honor

It will help at this point if we will keep in mind that there are several different aspects or angles of the truth. If we develop our view from just one aspect or angle of a particular subject, we will fail to see it in proper perspective. Our thinking will not be properly balanced by the different angles of the truth.

In 2 Corinthians 4:7, Paul says, "But we have this treasure in earthen vessels, that the excellence of the power may be of God and not of us." In contrast to God, we see our weakness. We see our utter dependence upon Him. We give Him honor, glory, and praise. We see that without Him we would be nothing and could do nothing (Jn. 15:5). Paul refers to us as "earthen vessels" to stress this side of the picture.

If our total thinking of a Christian as a vessel is taken from 2 Corinthians 4:7, we can see the direction it would take us in our thinking. This is not all that Paul said about us as vessels. In 2 Timothy 2:21 he explains, "If himself from these, he shall be a vessel unto honour, sanctified, and meet for the master's use, and prepared unto every good work"(KJV). Here we see Paul talking about the Christian who separates himself or herself from iniquity as being a "vessel unto honour. . . meet [or fit] for the master's use, and prepared unto every good work." This represents true value. We must take both 2 Corinthians 4:7 and 2 Timothy 2:21 into account in arriving at a proper estimate of ourselves as Christians.

To have a sense of value carries with it a sense of responsibility. If a person has a sense of value, he wants to dress and act in a manner that is appropriate for that value. The practical application of the Christian value system is affected by whether we downgrade ourselves or whether we recognize a value that is given to us by creation and redemption.

True Humility

True Christian humility is not based on having a low sense of self-worth. It is based on a recognition that the Christian is indebted to God for his or her self-worth. When Christians recognize their dependence on God, they are thankful. They are not filled with a haughty spirit. They also recognize a sense of debt and gratitude to other people. Recognition of dependence and the feeling of gratitude leave no room for false pride.

Humility is not a marvel when expressed by a person who is characterized by self-degradation and poor accomplishments. It is a marvel when exercised by those who have achieved success and have a sense of self-worth. For such people to recognize their dependence on God and others and to express their gratitude to God and to others—we call this virtue. This is true humility.

The Righteousness of Sanctification

The righteousness in justification is the righteousness of Christ that becomes ours. It was not acted out or lived out by us. The righteousness of sanctification is our personal righteousness that is worked out in us by the Holy Spirit as we avail ourselves of the grace of God. This righteousness is sometimes called *imparted* righteousness as contrasted with the *imputed* righteousness of justification. The word *imparted* is misleading. It sounds as if righteousness were a substance that exists outside of us and is imparted to us. It is better to speak of it as a righteousness that is worked out in us or produced in us.

THE SCOPE OF SANCTIFICATION

The Four Basic Relationships

Sanctification is to extend to all of life's experiences. All of life's experiences involve one or more of the *four basic relationships*: (1) a person's relationship with God, (2) a person's relationship with other people, (3) a person's relationship with himself, and (4) a person's relationship with the created order. In sanctification, these relationships are to be lived out in subjection to God's authority as revealed in the Bible, the Lordship of Christ, and the leadership of the Holy Spirit.

The Four Basic Values

All morals and ideals are reducible to *four basic ethical values* (or virtues). The four basic values are the foundation for the guiding moral and ethical principles as we function within the framework of the four basic relationships. The four basic values are: (1) holiness, (2) love, (3) wisdom, and (4) ideals. Holiness is concerned with the question: Is it right or is it wrong? Love is concerned with the question: How can I show my concern? Wisdom is concerned with the practical side of truth. It asks the question: What is the best judgment? Ideals are concerned with the question: What is good, beautiful, and excellent? Because of holiness, we have convictions. Because of love, we are concerned. Because of wisdom, we exercise common sense, or good judgment. Because of ideals, we are challenged toward excellence.[14]

The influence of sanctification is to manifest itself in our total experience. It embraces our experiences both as a member of the church and a member of society. To believe in a unified view of knowledge, we must believe that our belief in God and Christian values have implications for the whole of life.

The Image of God in Man and the Scope of Our Sanctification

In determining the scope of sanctification, we need to go back to the meaning of being created in the image of God. We were designed to be in the functional likeness of God. This should be seen in the entire scope of human experience. All our experiences in every area of life are to be affected by the divine likeness that we are to manifest. The design of sanctification is to restore the functional likeness of God that was lost in the fall. We were designed to be in the moral likeness of God. When we speak of the moral likeness of God in this context, we are using the word moral in its broadest meaning. We are to be holy, loving, and wise because God is holy, loving, and wise. We are to be concerned about ideals, beauty, and excellence because God is the quintessence of the high and the lofty. This likeness of God is to be highly evident as we carry out the divine mandate to exercise dominion over the earth and its inhabitants, and as we obey the Great Commission.

REGENERATION AND SANCTIFICATION

Regeneration in Calvinism and Arminianism

In traditional Calvinism, regeneration precedes faith. Calvinists consider it to be impossible for a sinner to believe unless he or she is first regenerated. Arminians believe that it is absolutely necessary for the Holy Spirit to work in the heart of the person who hears the gospel in order for faith to be possible (Jn. 6:44). But to Arminians this work of the Holy Spirit is not regeneration. In Arminianism, faith precedes regeneration. In Calvinism, only the regenerate believe. In Arminianism, only believers are regenerated. Both believe that believers are justified.

Classical Arminianism believes in *conditional monergism* with regard to justification and regeneration. Justification and regeneration are solely the acts and the provisions of God. This means justification and regeneration are effects. God is the cause. The condition for justification is faith in Christ. Faith is a human experience that can take place only with divine aid. Justification is solely an act of God, as the Supreme Judge of the universe, in which the person who has the death and righteousness of Christ is declared righteous. Justification is the ground of sanctification. Regeneration is the first step in sanctification and forms the foundation for all growth and development that takes place in the process of sanctification. Without regeneration there could be no sanctification. Regeneration is solely the work of the Holy Spirit.

In making *regeneration* precede faith, Calvinism makes *sanctification* precede *justification*. By anybody's definition, regeneration is a life changing experience. Regeneration is the first step in sanctification. When Calvinism has regeneration preceding justification, it is on a collision course against its own theology. Calvinism correctly understands that sanctification is dependent on justification. Louis Berkhof, a major Calvinistic theologian, tells us that "regeneration is the beginning of sanctification." Only a few lines down on the same page he says, "Justification precedes and is basic to sanctification in the covenant of grace . . . . Justification is the judicial basis of sanctification."[15]

I think it is in order to restate a quotation given earlier from Robert Haldane. Haldane, whose Calvinism is not in question, explains:

> So long as the sinner is under the guilt of sin God can have no friendly intercourse with him; for what communion hath light with darkness? But Christ having canceled his people's guilt, having redeemed them from the curse of the law, and invested them with the robe of his righteousness, there is no longer any obstacle to their communion with God, or any barrier to the free ingress of sanctifying grace.[16]

It can be seen that what both Berkhof and Haldane say puts their theology in conflict with the concept that regeneration precedes faith. Calvinism correctly observes that sanctification is grounded in justification. This creates a problem when they say that "regeneration is the beginning of sanctification" yet place regeneration before justification.

The Necessity of Regeneration

Paul tells us that "the carnal mind is enmity against God; for it is not subject to the law of God, nor indeed can be. So then, those who are in the flesh cannot please God" (Rom. 8:7-8). For a person who is so enslaved by his or her inherited depravity, there can be no conformity to the image of Christ apart from regeneration. The Christian life would be impossible apart from regeneration.

The Means and Agency of Regeneration

Peter says that God "has begotten us again to a living hope through the resurrection of Jesus Christ from the dead" (1 Pet. 1:3). Regeneration is involved in partaking of the benefits of Christ's resurrection. By union with Christ, we share the benefits of His resurrection. We are identified with His life as well as His death (Rom. 6:4-5, 8, 11).

The Word of God as a life-giving Word is an instrument in our regeneration. James said, "Of his own will He brought us forth by the word of truth" (Jas. 1:18). Peter speaks of being "born again, not of corruptible seed but incorruptible, through the word of God which lives and abides forever" (1 Pet. 1:23).

The Holy Spirit is the agent who performs the work of regeneration (Jn. 1:33; 3:5-6; Tit. 3:5; Eph. 2:10). This means that regeneration is solely a divine work. Since it is solely the work of God it is monergistic. God is the cause. Regeneration is the effect.

The Nature of Regeneration

In regeneration we are made new creatures or a new creation (2 Cor. 5:17). We are given a new direction in life (2 Cor. 5:17 and Eph. 2:10). We have a different attitude toward sin and Jesus Christ. We have a basic desire in our heart to do right and to be right with God. This change is a basic change, not an *absolute* change. It puts a person on the side of God and right, but it does not eradicate all traces of sin.

The Results of Regeneration

As a result of the new birth we become children of God. We are restored to fellowship with God and have the ability to function morally and spiritually. To enter into the kingdom of God (Jn. 3:3, 5) does not refer to entering the kingdom of God after death. It refers to entering it now as a functioning citizen of that kingdom. We have to enter the kingdom of God now to be in it after death.

The new birth results in victorious living. John tells us, "For whatever is born of God overcomes the world. And this is the victory that has overcome the world—our faith" (1 Jn. 5:4). Since this will receive further development when I discuss the guaranteed results of sanctification, I will not give further development to it at this time.

The Guaranteed Results of Sanctification

The design of God to make us righteous is not a design that may or may not be effective. A measure of success is guaranteed. First Corinthians 6:9-

10; Galatians 5:19-21; and Ephesians 5:3-5 make it clear that those who are characterized by gross immorality can lay no claim to salvation.

John makes it abundantly clear in his first epistle that only those who are basically righteous have any right to claim to be a Christian. On the positive side, he says, "Now by this we know that we know Him, if we keep His commandments" (1 Jn. 2:3). On the negative side, he says, "He who says, 'I know Him,' and does not keep His commandments, is a liar, and the truth is not in him" (2:4). In 3:10 he says, "Whoever does not practice righteousness is not of God."

First John 3:9 is an unusually strong and clear verse on this subject. This verse refers to "whoever has been born of God." This means every Christian because every Christian is born of God. Concerning one who is born of God, John says he "does not sin . . . and he cannot sin." The meaning here, based on the Greek tense, is: "He does not go on sinning, and he cannot go on sinning." It does not mean that he never sins; but it does mean that sin is not the habit of his life, and it cannot be the habit of his life as long as it can be said he is born of God. I am inclined to believe that, in order to understand the meaning of this verse, we need to understand the distinction made between *sins of ignorance* and *presumptuous sins* discussed in Numbers 15:27-31. I am inclined to believe that the reference here is not to repeated failures that grow out of weakness, but a defiant, deliberate choice of sin. More attention will be given to this subject when I deal with the subject of perseverance.

It is quite clear that John would have had no hesitancy in saying that those who do not practice righteousness are not saved (1 Jn. 2:3-4, 15-16; 3:2-3, 10; 5:4). There can be no doubt about it. The Bible says that salvation changes the life (2 Cor. 5:17 and Eph. 2:10). There is an interest in righteousness in the heart of a Christian.

A Christian is one who has recognized his or her moral guilt and unworthiness. He has come to Jesus Christ desiring to be forgiven of his sin and wishing to have his experience with sin changed. He has received a new nature through the new birth. This new nature is interested in righteousness. He has declared war on sin. He may not win every battle, but he is a soldier fighting against sin. When he sins, it is the sin of one who is defeated in battle, not the sin of one who had not declared war on sin. When he does sin, there is a process that begins within him to work repentance.

The Christian is not and cannot be morally indifferent or unconcerned about sin. There is room for moral growth, but his or her heart is cultivable soil. Man fell from a state of holiness into a state of sin. Redemption is designed to bring man from the state of sin into a state of holiness. If there is no holiness, there is no redemption.[17]

I am fully aware that salvation is by grace, and that it is free and thus a gift. To insist that it must have the results that the Bible unquestionably ascribes to it is in no way to confuse or corrupt grace. We need simply to understand what it is that is free. It is salvation that consists of justification and sanctification. Justification guarantees forgiveness to the person who has it. Sanctification guarantees a changed life to the person who has it.

The fact that a thing is free has nothing to do with whether or not it will work. "Free" simply means that it does not cost anything. The giver of our free salvation has said that it will work. First John 3:9 says that the presence of the new birth prohibits the practice of sin. Galatians 5:17 says that, because we have the Holy Spirit, we cannot do the things that we would.

The freedom of the will is a freedom within the framework of possibilities. Unsaved persons and Christians do not have the same framework of possibilities. According to 1 John 3:9 and Galatians 5:17, it is not in the framework of possibilities for the Christian to practice sin. It is within the framework of possibilities for him to please God and to live right.

There is some latitude within this framework of possibilities. There is room for disobedience but not on an unlimited scale. Since there is room for disobedience, Christians must be challenged, exhorted, and admonished. There is also room for variations of growth and progress. Here, there is the need for challenge, exhortation, and encouragement.

Sanctification and Perfection

It is not my purpose here to involve myself in the controversies surrounding the subject of perfection. I will just set forth what I believe the New Testament teaches on the subject and support my case.

The Meaning of the Greek Word *Teleios*

In the majority of places in the New Testament where the word *perfect* is found, it is a translation of the Greek word *teleios* which has as its basic meaning "complete." This is obvious in 1 Corinthians 13:10. Paul says, "But when that which is perfect has come, then that which is in part will be done away." In this verse, the "perfect" is contrasted with the "part." It is obvious that the perfect is the whole or the complete.

In most cases, the completeness referred to is the completeness that is achieved through growth. Thus, the perfect is the mature. This meaning is obvious in Hebrews 5:14, where the Greek word for perfect is translated by the words "of full age." Translations such as the NASB and NIV translate "mature." The writer of Hebrews is telling us that strong meat belongs to those who through growth and development have reached maturity.

Maturity is obviously the meaning of *perfect* in Ephesians 4:13. A reading of verses 13 and 14 together shows that the "perfect man" of verse 13 is contrasted with "children" of verse 14. Both the NASB and the NIV translate "mature." The perfect or mature man has the steadfastness that goes with maturity in contrast to the instability that goes with immaturity.

In 1 Corinthians, 14:20 the Greek word for perfect (*teleios*) is translated "men" in the KJV and NKJV. The NASB translates "mature." The NIV translates "adult." Paul is telling us that in malice we should be like children. We are, in understanding, to be mature or adult. In the KJV and NJKV, "men" is used to mean adult.

The thrust of completeness seems to be a little different in Matthew 5:48. Jesus said, "Be ye therefore perfect, even as your Father which is in heaven is perfect" (KJV). Let us read the word complete in each of the places where the word perfect occurs. This will raise the question: In what way are we to be "complete, even as our Father which is in heaven is complete?" In the previous context beginning with verse 43, Jesus has been talking about two kinds of love. One was a love that only loves those who love us. This would be an incomplete love. The other was a love which embraced both those who love us and those who do not. This would be a complete love. The Father showed His love to both the just and the unjust by sending the rain and sunshine to both. This illustrates the complete or perfect love of the Father. We, like the Father, are to have a complete or perfect love that loves both those who love us and those who do not.

The Meaning of the Greek Words *Artios* and *Katartizmos*

In Ephesians 4:12 and 2 Timothy 3:17, Greek words with a different connotation are used. In 2 Timothy 3:17 the Greek word is *artios*. The meaning of the word for perfect is explained by the last part of the verse. The perfect man is "thoroughly equipped for every good work." He is a prepared person. He is equipped for service.

In Ephesians 4:12, the Greek word is *katartizmos*. The KJV translates "perfecting." The NKJV and NASB have "equipping." The NIV has "to prepare." This word is closely related to *artios* which was used in 2 Timothy 3:17. The meaning is "the equipping or preparing of the saints for the work of the ministry."

Summary of the New Testament View of Perfection

The idea of flawlessness is not the meaning of the Greek words for perfect. The reference in most places is to the complete in contrast with the incomplete, or the finished with the unfinished. An unfinished building would not be perfect even if the workmanship were flawless. The person who is mature physically is perfect even though he is not flawless. The child would not be perfect even if he were flawless in his physical body. It is also obvious that when perfect refers to "equipping," flawlessness is not the point of emphasis.

When we are challenged to be perfect in the New Testament, we are challenged to be mature, complete, and equipped. Certainly, this would call for moral concern and progress, but it does not entangle us with the depressing goal of moral perfection.[18]

---

[1]Charles G. Finney, *Finney's Lectures on Systematic Theology*, rev. ed., J. H. Fairchild, ed. (1878; reprint, Grand Rapids: Eerdmans Publishing Company, 1953), 391-392.

[2]James Oliver Buswell, Jr., *A Systematic Theology*, vol. 2, 146.

[3]David Brown, Acts–Romans, in *A Commentary Critical, Experimental and Practical on the Old and New Testaments*, vol. 3, Robert Jamieson, A. R. Fausset, and David Brown (1864–1870; reprint, Grand Rapids: Eerdmans Publishing Company, 1984), 226.

[4]Again, as Robert Haldane argued, as long as one is under sin's guilt, God "can have no friendly intercourse with him; for what communion hath light with darkness? But Christ having canceled his people's guilt, having redeemed them from the curse of the law, and invested them with the robe of his righteousness, there is no longer any obstacle to their communion with God, or any barrier to the free ingress of sanctifying grace." Robert Haldane, *An Exposition of the Epistle of Romans* (1852; reprint, McLean, Virginia: McDonald Publishing Company, 1958), 248-249.

[5]William Sanday and Arthur Headlam, *The Epistle to the Romans in the International Critical Commentary*, 5th ed. (1902; reprint, Edinburgh: T. & T. Clark, 1960), 218.

[6]Richard Chenevix Trench, *Synonyms of the New Testament*, (1854; reprint, Grand Rapids: Associated Publishers and Authors, Inc., n. d.), 245.

[7]Ibid., 243-244.

[8]Ibid., 246-247.

[9]Ibid., 247.

[10]Most commentaries agree with the difference noted between "conformed" (Greek *suschēmatidzō*) and "transformed" (Greek *metamorphoō*). (For discussions which agree, see Barclay 157-158; Hendriksen 405, note 338; and Sanday and

Headlam 353. For discussions that deny this distinction, see Barrett 232-233; and Cranfield 2:605, 608). [This is noted in Forlines, *Romans*, 321.]

[11]Barclay M. Newman and Eugene A. Nida, *A Translator's Handbook on Paul's Letter to the Romans* (New York: United Bible Societies, 1973), 235.

[12]Joseph Henry Thayer, *Thayer's Greek-English Lexicon of the New Testament* (1889; reprint, Grand Rapids: Zondervan Publishing House, 1962), 429.

[13]For a more complete discussion of the problem of a person's attitude toward himself see my book, *Biblical Ethics* (Nashville: Randall House Publications, 1973), 59-67.

[14]For a system of ethics based on the application of the four basic values to the four basic relationships, see my book, *Biblical Ethics*.

[15]Berkhof, *Systematic Theology*, 536.

[16]Robert Haldane, *An Exposition of the Epistle of Romans* (1852; reprint, McLean, Virginia: McDonald Publishing Company, 1958), 248-249.

[17]The material under "The Guaranteed Results of Sanctification" up to this point with slight modification is taken from my book, *Biblical Ethics*, 34-36.

[18]Most of the material under "Sanctification and Perfection" was taken from my book *Biblical Ethics*, 138-140.

CHAPTER 9

The Perseverance of the Saints

Τhe concern before us in this chapter is: Is it possible for a person who has once experienced the saving grace of God to once again be lost? I am going to take the position that it is possible for a person who has been saved to commit apostasy and become once again lost and under the wrath of God. While I will take the position that it is possible for a person to be lost after he has experienced the grace of God, the position that I will set forth, I believe, will stand up against any charge of salvation by works.

In order for us to develop a strong case for our position, we must understand why those arriving at the opposite conclusion do so. In dealing with their views, it is incumbent upon us to be fair and honest in our treatment.

There are basically two very different approaches used by those who take the position "once saved, always saved." *The first view,* and the one that has a longer history, *claims that those who are truly saved will continue in faith and holiness.* This is the view that is held by traditional or Classical Calvinism. *The second view is that once a person is saved, nothing that he or she could ever do would cause him or her to be lost again.* If a person should deny his faith, or if he should live in any imaginable degree of sin, he would never cease to be a child of God. While those who take such a view would admonish saved persons not to live in such a manner, they would admit that such could happen and that it would never alter a person's justification before God. Most of the people who hold this view would not likely hold to the other points of Calvinism,[1] especially unconditional election and irresistible grace. This view is what I would call the popular view. It is held more by popular preachers than by scholars.

As a point of clarification, I need to make it clear that there are those who accept only this point of Calvinism but do not accept the position that saved people could be in, and continue in, any imaginable degree of sin. They believe that those who are living such a lifestyle were never saved.

CLASSICAL CALVINISM'S VIEW OF "ONCE SAVED, ALWAYS SAVED"

It will be beneficial here to reiterate the essential tenets of Classical Calvinism. There are five major points in Classical Calvinism's soteriology: (1) total depravity, (2) unconditional election, (3) limited atonement, (4) irresistible grace, and (5) perseverance of all those who are saved.

The first point, total depravity, puts forth the idea that sin permeates the entirety of the human personality. The Calvinistic view of depravity is that the sinner is under the power of sin to such a degree that in order to exercise faith he or she first must be made alive. A spiritually dead person could not believe—only one who is made alive by regeneration could believe. How this fits into the Calvinistic system will be clearer as we explain the other points of Calvinism.

The most fundamental of all the points of Calvinism is its view of unconditional election. It is the Calvinist's view that, in eternity past, for reasons known only to God, God chose certain ones to be saved, and He chose not to save others. God will see to it that those whom He chose or elected will come to faith in Christ and be saved.

While there are some who believe in unconditional election and take the position that Christ died for everybody, the traditional position is that Christ died only for the elect. Thus, it is referred to as limited atonement. The intent and, thereby, the extent of atonement was only for the elect.

When Calvinists speak of irresistible grace (some prefer to speak of effectual grace), they mean that all whom God moves upon to bring to saving faith will certainly believe and be saved. In Classical Calvinism, the effectual call (or irresistible grace) of God is regeneration. In Calvinism, regeneration precedes faith. The person is regenerated and then believes and is justified. In Arminianism, the person believes and then is justified and regenerated. In Calvinism, a sinner cannot believe unless he is first regenerated. When Calvinists speak of faith as a gift, they mean that God is totally responsible for the person having saving faith. It was all of God. It can be seen that the first four points of Calvinism logically lead to the last point: the final perseverance of all who are saved.

The Case for Classical Calvinism's View of Perseverance

The basic foundation of the traditional Calvinistic view of "once saved, always saved" is the Calvinist's interpretation of God's sovereignty. Lewis Sperry Chafer argues that "the failure of one soul to be saved . . . whom God has ordained to that end means the disruption of the whole actuality of divine sovereignty." If God can fail in one thing, He can fail in anything, Chafer contends. "He ceases to be God and the universe is drifting to a destiny about which God himself could know nothing."[2]

As perceived by Calvinists, their view of unconditional election is the logical outgrowth of the doctrine of sovereignty. The doctrine of unconditional continuance in salvation is the logical result of unconditional election. James Oliver Buswell, Jr., explains, "If God has unconditionally elected to save people, and if He has provided atonement which makes their salvation certain, it follows by inevitable logic that those whom God has elected to eternal salvation will go on to eternal salvation." Buswell goes on to state unequivocally that "a denial of the doctrine of the perseverance of the saints is a denial of the sovereign grace of God in unconditional election."[3]

Millard J. Erickson concurs, arguing that God's election of particular individuals for eternal life, and His choice that His chosen "will necessarily come to receive eternal life" logically results in "a permanence to their salvation. If the elect could at some point lose their salvation, God's election of them to eternal life would not be truly effectual. Thus, the doctrine of election as understood by the Calvinist requires perseverance as well."[4]

Chafer, Buswell, and Erickson—all Calvinists—show the connection between unconditional election and final perseverance. It is unthinkable that God would unconditionally elect a person and draw him by irresistible grace, and not guarantee that he would remain in a state of grace.

The Popular View of "Once Saved, Always Saved"

As I said above, this view is held more so by popular preachers than by scholars. For a view to be held more so by popular preachers than by scholars does not make that view either right or wrong. But it does help us to know who it is that holds the view.

Again, according to this view, once a person is saved he could never do anything that would cause him to be lost again. If a person should deny his faith or if he should live in any imaginable degree of sin, he would never cease to be a child of God. One of the proponents of this view is Charles Stanley, who argues that, if abandoning faith or falling into sin "short-circuits salvation," then believers are able "to demonstrate unconditional love to a greater extent than God." In other words, If God attaches a condition to His relationship with believers, then He is not demonstrating unconditional love. "On the other hand," Stanley comments, "I know people who have demonstrated pure unconditional love to family members who were incredibly undeserving."[5]

In another place, Stanley asks, *Does the Scripture actually teach that regardless of the consistency of our faith, our salvation is secure?* [Italics his]. He then answers: "Yes, it does, through both proposition and illustration.

'If We Are Faithless . . .'

The clearest statement on this subject is issued by Paul's second letter to Timothy:

If we died with Him, we shall also live with Him;

If we endure, we shall also reign with Him;

If we deny Him, He also will deny us;

If we are *faithless*, He remains *faithful*;

for He cannot deny Himself.

—2 Timothy 2:11-13[6]

My main purpose at this point is to explain what Stanley and others are saying and why it is that they believe it. My answer to their thinking will come later. But since it will not fit in at a later point to deal with 2 Timothy 2:11-13, let me say a few words about it now. Stanley does not deal at all with the statement, "If we deny Him, He also will deny us." In fact Stanley is saying that a person who is a Christian could deny Him, and He will not deny that person.

With regard to the last part of verse 13, "If we are faithless, He remains faithful, for he cannot deny Himself," I would give the following explanation: If we become faithless, Christ will remain faithful to His character and will deny us. What I have said is in agreement with the explanation given by M. R. Vincent: "True to his own nature, righteous character, and requirements, according to which *he cannot accept as faithful one who has proved untrue to him*. To do so would be to deny himself."[7]

The Case for the Popular View of "Once Saved, Always Saved"

As we can see, this view is quite different from the view held by Classical Calvinists. It is also built on a different doctrinal foundation. Those who advocate the popular view think it is *a necessary consequence of their view of atonement and justification*. Stanley remarks: "If Christ took upon Himself every single one of your sins, what is going to cause God to reverse His verdict of not guilty? Hallelujah, not a thing."[8]

In order to understand this view, we need to understand the view of atonement and justification on which it is built. While I differ strongly with this view, it is not because I have a different view of atonement and justification. To put it briefly, the view of atonement is what is called the penal satisfaction view. I have explained this at length in Chapter 6 of this book and in my Romans commentary.[9]

The satisfaction view of atonement is based on the following ideas: (1) that Jesus Christ suffered the full wrath of God for our sins, thus paying their penalty, and (2) that Jesus lived a completely righteous life, thus rendering to God perfect obedience on our behalf. In so doing, Jesus completely satisfied the holy demands of God for us.

On the condition of our faith in Christ, God placed on our account the death of Christ and the righteousness of Christ. Christ's death and righteousness legally applied to our account fully satisfies God's requirement for our guilt (because of His death) and restores us to favor with God (because of His righteousness). Those who take this popular view believe that the nature of Christ's payment for our sins requires that nothing we could do could ever alter that fact. While I differ very strongly with this, I can see why some people believe it. When I present my view, I will explain why I think "once saved, always saved" is not a necessary result of the satisfaction view of atonement and justification.

In about the last 30 years or so, a position has received a lot of attention that would tend to go along with this approach. Its proponents are involved in the "Lordship Controversy." One side insists that, at conversion we must receive Christ as Lord and Savior. The other side insists that a person can receive Christ as Savior without receiving Him as Lord. Those who insist that a person can receive Christ as Savior without receiving Him as Lord would admit to the possibility of such things as Stanley suggests. Some scholars have taken this position. Among these is Zane Hodges.[10]

I should also point out that there are those who accept the logic of the popular view but try to avoid its abuses. They would accept the idea that nothing a person could ever do would cause him to cease to be saved, but they would insist that, if a person is saved, he or she would show evidence of salvation. They would tend to believe that those who did not show evidence were never saved. On the one hand, they believe that verses like John 10:28-30 teach that, once a person is saved, he or she will never be lost again. On the other hand, they believe that the change spoken of in 2 Corinthians 5:17 rules out the idea that a person could be saved and show no evidence of salvation.

The Conflict of Opinion Among Those Who Believe "Once Saved, Always Saved"

It is very important that we keep in mind that the view I have just presented as the "Popular View" is rejected by many Calvinists. In speaking of extreme views on the doctrine of continuance in salvation, William Wilson Stevens explains: "One [view] is held by those who say they believe in the doctrine (eternal security of the believer) but who have really perverted it, maintaining that one is justified and is eternally safe regardless of what he may become in his person and character."[11]

Buswell comments:

> In a young people's conference I once heard a Christian layman speak as follows: "I was once a member of a young people's gospel team. We were all saved, and we had some success in preaching the gospel. But one member of the team got into worldly company. He married a very worldly girl. He denied his Christian profession of faith, and he died a drunkard. Now you see, young people, he was a Christian; he went to heaven; but he was a "carnal Christian," and he did not have the reward of a "spiritual Christian." No wonder the Arminians are scandalized by what is falsely called Calvinism.[12]

Much of the popular preaching on this subject perverts Calvinism rather than setting forth the historic Calvinistic position. Such preaching has done great harm to the church. Both the traditional Calvinist and the Arminian are disturbed by this kind of preaching. I appreciate much of what some of these people do, but this area of their thought causes me great concern.

The historic position of Calvinism has held to the perseverance of the saints, not to a guarantee of their future salvation whether they persevere or not. As John H. Gerstner explains concerning the Calvinistic view, "Perseverance not only does not, but cannot, lead to antinomianism because, by definition, it means persevering in holiness and not unholiness."[13] Berkhof explains concerning this doctrine, "It is maintained that the life of regeneration and the habits that develop out of it in the way of sanctification can never entirely disappear."[14]

Arguments for "Once Saved, Always Saved" Based on Scripture

The cases given above are doctrinal in nature. Let us now turn our attention to passages of Scripture that are used to support the view "once saved, always saved." The exegetical proof would be about the same for most of these verses no matter which of the views set forth above are used. I will not make an exhaustive list of verses, but I will deal with the primary verses. Up to this point, I have given the views and why the proponents of these views believe them. At this point, I will give my reasons for believing that the verses do not require the conclusion "once saved, always saved." Later, I will explain why the cases given earlier are not valid.

John 10:28-29

There are three arguments found in these verses: the first, the words "eternal life"; the second, the words "they shall never perish"; the third, "neither shall anyone snatch them out of My hand."

I do not need to show that these verses teach that a person can be lost after he is saved. They do not. I will give support for that position later from other passages. The only thing I need to do is to show that to accept what these verses teach does not contradict the viewpoint that a person can be lost again after he or she has experienced saving grace. Let us examine these arguments and see if they state a truth that contradicts the idea that it is possible for a Christian ever to be lost again.

Let us consider the first one. It must be admitted that eternal life can be possessed only in the sense of potential. The believer certainly does not possess eternity. Some have taught that there is no past and future with God, but no one has ever said that of the believer. The eternal life of the believer is in the Son, as is taught in 1 John 5:11, "God has given us eternal life, and this life is in His Son." This life is the believer's by identification with Christ. Should that identification be broken (Jn. 15:2, 6), he would be severed from this eternal life, yet it would not alter the fact that he had possessed it. It should also be pointed out that Adam possessed the potential for eternal life before he fell, but he lost it with the fall. It is seen then that the loss of salvation does not contradict the words "eternal life."

The second argument is based on "they shall never perish." John 3:36 teaches that the converse is true of unbelievers when it says, "He who does not believe the Son shall not see life." No one says that, since it is said of the unbeliever that he shall not see life, he is permanently bound without hope in that condition. It is a fact that, as an unbeliever, he shall not see life, but if he becomes a believer, he will see life.

Now, if the words "shall not see life," which describe the unbeliever, are not contradicted when the unbeliever becomes a believer and sees life, where is the contradiction when it is said that a believer "shall not perish," but if he becomes an unbeliever, he will perish? The fact is that a believer, as long as he remains a believer, "shall not perish."

The third argument is based on the statement, "neither shall anyone snatch them out of My hand." The next verse adds a similar thought concerning the Father's hand. The teaching is simply this: The believer's relationship with God is a personal one between him and God. Though all of the powers of the universe were to combine against the believer, they could not take the believer away from God. Some would add, "Neither can the believer take himself out of the body of Christ." Yes, that is true. But, it is also true that he could not have placed himself into the body of Christ. However, upon his faith in Christ, the Holy Spirit placed the believer into the body of Christ (1 Cor. 12:13). If the believer renounces his faith, God will take him out (Jn. 15:2, 6). There is no contradiction between the statements "No one can take us out of Christ" and the statement "God the Father takes those people out of Christ who turn from Christ in unbelief."

Romans 8:35-39

It is my opinion that this passage does not deal with the question of whether a saved person can ever be lost again. Rather, it teaches that a person who is a child of God can never, at the same time, be separated from God's love. In other words, the believer is never to interpret hardship as meaning that God does not love him. Instead, he should recognize that God's love is still with him and should say with Paul, "Yet in all these things we are more than conquerors through Him who loved us" (Rom. 8:37). It was because of God's abiding love that Paul could say, "I have learned in whatever state I am, to be content" (Phil. 4:11).

While I think that Paul was telling the believers in Romans 8:35-39 that the trials and tribulations of life do not mean that God does not love us, I do not take that position as a means of escaping the view that the passage teaches "once saved, always saved." It presents no problem to me to say that the passage deals with the security of the believer.

Suppose the passage does deal with the matter of security. It would be explained the same way as the statement of Jesus when He said, "neither shall anyone snatch them out of My hand" (Jn. 10:28). Paul would be saying as emphatically as human language can make it that our personal salvation is a matter between the individual believer and God. He would be saying that neither tribulation, distress, persecution, famine, nakedness, peril, sword (verse 35), death, life, angels, principalities, powers, things present, things to come (verse 38), height, depth, nor any other created thing (verse 39) viewed collectively or singularly can take a believer away from Christ. I believe that. What Paul says in these verses in no way contradicts the viewpoint that, if a believer turns away from God in defiant, arrogant unbelief, God will take him out of Christ (Jn. 15:2, 6).

When I was in Russia, on more than one occasion when speaking on this subject, I said, "Communism put many in prison because of their faith and killed many because of their faith. But Communism did not take one person out of Christ." If all of the governments of the world voted that a person should be taken out of Christ, that would not and could not make it happen. For Russian Baptists, the possibility of losing salvation is very important. In the past, many of them could have avoided prison if they had been willing to deny their faith. Many of them filled a martyr's grave rather than deny their faith. When my wife and I were there in 1996, we could still feel the pain of the Stalin years as we moved across Russia.

Romans 11:29

Romans 11:29 reads, "For the gifts and the calling of God are without repentance" (KJV; NKJV: "irrevocable"). This means that, if God has made an *unconditional* promise, it will forever remain an *unconditional* promise. On the other hand, if He has made a *conditional* promise, He will never change the condition of that promise. This is the line of reasoning used by Paul in Galatians 3:15-18. The Abrahamic Covenant that had already promised justification on the condition of faith could neither be set aside nor have the condition changed when the law came. There is certainly no argument to prove that a promise could not be *irrevocable* and *conditional* at the same time.

Philippians 1:6

In this verse Paul says, "Being confident of this very thing that he which hath begun a good work in you will perform it until the day of Jesus Christ" (KJV). This is a confidence that we can have as believers. God will perform the work of salvation until the day of Jesus Christ in those who continue in faith. This is not a promise made to unbelievers. There is no contradiction if one who is a believer becomes an unbeliever and the promise no longer applies.

I have not dealt with every verse that is used by those who believe in "once saved, always saved," but the major verses have been given attention. I believe that what I have said about these verses will help a person understand other verses that may be introduced.

A Case for Believing It Is Possible for a Person to Be Lost Again After He Is Saved
The Doctrinal Foundation

What I have presented above shows the doctrinal foundations upon which the different approaches to "once saved, always saved" are based. Let us now turn our attention to the doctrinal foundation for believing that it is possible for a person who is saved to turn again to unbelief and again be lost.

The theological foundation that supports the possibility of becoming lost again after a person is saved is found in what it means to be made in the image of God. (See Chapter 1.) Being made in the image of God means that we are personal beings. We think, feel, and act. A person makes decisions or choices. Regardless of how much influence is brought to bear on the will or how much assistance is given, a person's actions are in a very real sense his own. That is what it means to be a person. While there is divine aid for the Christian, it is possible for him to resist this aid and make wrong choices. Among these wrong choices is the possibility of turning back to unbelief. God made us persons. In His relationship with us, He never violates our personhood. While I do not think the likelihood is high that a person who is saved will become an unbeliever again, I do believe that, because we are persons, the possibility remains open.

The terminology usually used in explaining what I have just said is "freedom of the will." While that is appropriate terminology, the real issue, as I have stressed earlier, is whether a Christian is a genuine, personal being. Does he think, feel, and make choices (both good and bad)? Freedom of will is involved in what it means to be a person.

The Teaching of Scripture

The ultimate question is what does the Scripture teach? I will now turn my attention to a biblical defense of the view that it is possible to be lost again once a person has been saved. Then I will show how this position is consistent with other doctrines.

It will not be my purpose to see how many verses I can set forth to support my position. Rather, I will deal with those that are most helpful and the ones that, so far as I am concerned, must be interpreted so as to fit the idea that a saved person could be lost again. *To say that a saved person could never be lost again would place us in contradiction, I believe, with what these verses irrefutably teach.*

Hebrews 6:4-6

Had these people been saved? In this passage, those under consideration have the following characteristics: (1) "once enlightened"; (2) "have tasted the heavenly gift"; (3) "have become partakers of the Holy Spirit"; (4) "have tasted the good word of God"; (5) have tasted "the powers of the age to come"; (6) have repented. (It is definitely implied that they had repented because it is said that it is impossible to renew them *again* to repentance.)

It would certainly seem obvious that the characteristics given above are descriptive of a saved person. However, some say this passage describes those who had only professed faith in Jesus but had not actually received Him as Savior. Herman Hoeksema takes this position. In commenting on Hebrews 6:4-6, he explains:

> But the author has in mind their former state, as they *appeared*, as they were known by men, as they used to be members of the church visible in the world. They were baptized. And they went through the *outward show of repentance*, and for a time walked in that repentance. But now they have definitely *fallen away even from the outward show*. They have become unbelievers. They have become wicked. They have become a part of the Antichrist. And the text says that it is impossible that those who so fall can ever again be renewed unto repentance. The case of these people is therefore hopeless. Their falling away is final. They can never return.[15]

Since there are those who take the position that this passage is dealing with individuals who made a profession of faith but were never saved, we will take a careful look at the passage to see whether it refers to those who had been saved or to those who had merely professed to have faith in Jesus Christ.

The word that is translated enlightened in verse 4 is *phōtidzō*. In Hebrews 10:32, it is translated "illuminated." The writer says, "But recall the former days in which, after you were illuminated, you endured a great struggle with sufferings." It sounds here as if he is referring to the conversion experience. Thayer says concerning this word that it means "to enlighten spiritually, imbue with saving knowledge . . . with a saving knowledge of the gospel: hence *photisthentes* of those who have been made Christians, Heb. vi. 4; x. 32."[16]

Some have argued that, since the word *taste* is used, they approached the very threshold of salvation, even to the extent of having partial acquaintance with what it is like to be a Christian, but they were not saved. Such an experience is without scriptural support; either a person is saved or he is not. By comparing the use of the word *taste* in other parts of the Scripture, we see that it can mean an experience. Examples are Matthew 16:28, Hebrews 2:9, and 1 Peter 2:3. We shall take particular notice of Hebrews 2:9 which says, speaking of Jesus, "that He, by the grace of God, might taste death for everyone." Surely this is referring to an actual experience with death.

It is my position that the word *taste* is one of the strongest words that could have been used. In tasting, there is always a *consciousness* of the presence of that which is tasted. There is always an *acquaintance* with the distinctive characteristics of that which is tasted. This is evidenced by 1 Peter 2:3. By tasting, the believer learned that one of the distinctive characteristics of the Lord is that He is gracious. There is also a matter of contact in tasting. In other words, tasting may be called *conscious acquaintance by contact*.

When we apply the previous observations to the subject under consideration, we learn that those mentioned here have had an experience in which they become *consciously acquainted by contact* with the heavenly gift. The heavenly gift either means Christ or salvation. In either case, it would mean that the person would be saved, because only a saved person has such an acquaintance with Christ or with salvation.

Now we go to the third expression: "have become partakers of the Holy Spirit." In Hebrews 3:14, we find a reference in which the same Greek word that is translated *partake* in Hebrews 6:4 is used. It reads: "For we have become partakers of Christ." This would certainly refer to a close relationship. The Greek word for partaker could be translated *a companion* or *one who goes along with*. When used of being made a partaker of the Holy Spirit, it carries with it the idea of a companion relationship—a going along with. To *go along with* means to *be in agreement*. The person is taught by and led by the Holy Spirit.

The fourth characteristic is: "have tasted the good word of God." These persons had gone further than the original enlightenment of the way of salvation, as mentioned in the first expression. They had an acquaintance with the Word of God. Such an understanding belongs only to Christians.

The fifth expression is that they had tasted "the powers of the age to come." This phrase seems to mean that they had entered into the joys of knowing that they were going to heaven because of their faith in Christ.

The sixth characteristic is that they had repented. Repentance[17] and faith both refer to the same experience, but from different angles. Therefore, we must conclude that they had experienced saving faith. (See my discussion on the relationship between repentance and faith in Chapter 7.)

Concerning the description of those referred to in the passage under study, J. D. O'Donnell correctly says that, if one who has such an experience is not saved, then "it is hard to imagine what it would take to describe a true believer. Even many securitists admit that a saved person is described but try to diminish the meaning of the passage by interpreting the full passage as a hypothetical situation that will never take place."[18] As Robert E. Picirilli comments:

> There is absolutely no doubt those lives refer to genuine Christian experience. If you wanted a better way to describe conversion, you could not find it! Any one of the four expressions cannot fail to represent real salvation. Take the third phrase for example: A "partaker," one who

partakes of, one who is in fellowship with. Now, only a real Christian is a partaker of the Holy Spirit of God.[19]

What had these people done? In interpreting these verses, we must remember that these Jews were in danger of forsaking Christ and going back into Judaism. These warnings were given to keep them from making this mistake.

In 6:6 it is said "they crucify again for themselves the Son of God." Let us note that this is a crucifixion in relationship, that is, to themselves. An example of crucifixion in relationship is found in Galatians 6:14 where Paul says, "By whom the world has been crucified to me, and I to the world." So far as reality was concerned, both Paul and the world were living and active; but so far as relationship was concerned, they were dead to each other. They had no relationship existing between them. The relationship of Christ to the unsaved is that of a dead Christ; but to the saved, He is a living Christ. A person could not crucify to himself the Son of God afresh unless he were in a living relationship to Him. Therefore, such could be committed only by a saved person.

If we will compare this verse with Hebrews 10:29, we will get a more complete picture of what is discussed. In this verse, the person has "counted the blood of the covenant by which he was sanctified a common thing." This would be the case of the Jewish believer who came to the point that he said that Christ's blood was no more than any other man's blood; it was not that blood which was typified by the sacrifices in the Old Testament; it possessed no saving power; Christ was not the Savior. When the person came to this point, he denounced his faith in Christ. He drove Christ out of his life. In relationship, Christ became a dead Christ; thus, he had crucified Christ to himself.

When this person denounced his former faith in Christ, he was saying that there was nothing to the experience he thought he had had with Christ. In so doing, he put Christ to an open shame.

What is the condition of the person who has fallen away by unbelief? The writer of Hebrews says that it is impossible to renew such a person again unto repentance. It is my understanding that this means he cannot be restored to faith. He cannot be saved again. Not everyone who interprets this passage to teach that loss of salvation is possible accepts the position that it is impossible for such a person to be saved again. It seems to me that "For it is impossible . . . to renew them again to repentance" admits to no other interpretation than that it is impossible for such a person to be saved again.

Some interpreters would say that it is impossible with man, but not impossible with God. There is nothing in the passage that would suggest this. The comments of I. Howard Marshall are insightful here. He believes that "the point at issue is not the question as to who might be able to restore the lapsed, but the fact that the lapsed cannot be restored. This is important because the passage gives us no right to assert that there may be a special intervention of God to restore those whom men cannot restore."[20]

Some interpreters have suggested that this statement means that it is impossible to renew them to repentance "while they are crucifying to themselves the Son of God afresh." They would suggest that they could repent and be saved again if they would stop crucifying the Son of God. That is about the same as saying that it is impossible to repent as long as they remain unrepentant. Or, they can repent if they repent. This kind of thinking reduces the statement to a mere truism.

Others agree that apostasy is without remedy, but a person could forfeit his salvation by an accumulation of sins (usually a vague concept) and could repent and be saved again. Some would object to saying he would be saved again (repeated regeneration). But if he or she did not repent, he would be lost if he died that way. I am of the conviction that the only thing that brings loss of salvation is apostasy or unbelief. The conviction that apostasy is without remedy does not depend on this passage alone. It is taught by other passages also, as we will see when we look at some other passages.

Once it is seen that apostasy is without remedy, we will be more cautious about what we think would cause a person to forfeit his or her salvation. Marshall speaks to this point when he says, "It is agreed on all hands that, if the passage does teach the impossibility of repentance, this is only in the case of a definite attitude of apostasy and not in the case of individual sins."[21]

Hebrews 10:26–29

Had the person been saved? In this passage, the person is qualified as having been sanctified (verse 29). The other references in the epistle in which the word *sanctify* is used are: 2:11; 9:13; 10:10, 14; 13:12. If the reader will examine these verses, he will find that each of these except for 9:13 has reference to sanctification that accompanies salvation in the New Testament. If the writer of the epistle were going to use sanctification in an entirely different sense here, does it not seem reasonable that he would have made it clear when using it in connection with such a drastic warning? Also, keep in mind that the sanctification referred to here was effected by the blood of Christ. Regardless of what the warning is in these verses, we must admit that it is to saved people. Verse 26 refers to the state of willful sin (or apostasy) that the person is in. Verse 29 explains how all of this got started. It refers to the initial act of apostasy that set in motion this state of apostasy.

What had this person done? The person referred to here had "counted the blood of the covenant by which he was sanctified a common thing" (verse 29). To count the blood of Christ as being no different than that of any other person's constitutes unbelief. It is apostasy or shipwreck of faith. As Marshall explains, "Such a sin is an act of total rejection of God. The sinner has become an adversary of God (Heb. 10:27), and he has rejected the very things which were the means of his salvation, the atoning blood of Christ and the Spirit of grace."[22]

What is the condition of the person who has fallen away by unbelief? In verse 26, we see that he is sinning "willfully." The Greek indicates that the reference is not to an act of willful sin, but a *process* of willful sin. Such willful sinning is not possible as long as a person is born of God. Verse 26 describes the state of the apostate, while verse 29, which is past tense, describes the first act of sin that started this state.

As a further point of clarification, verse 26 says of such a person, "there no longer remains a sacrifice for sins." There is no longer a sacrifice for sins. The apostate has sins but no available sacrifice for his sins. Having rejected the sacrifice made by Jesus Christ, there is no other sacrifice to which to turn.

Robert Shank has a concern at this point. He raises the question, "Is apostasy without remedy?" He then says, "Several passages of Scripture seem to affirm this."[23] After that, he goes to great lengths to build a case for saying that there is a remedy for apostasy. His chapter "Is Apostasy Without Remedy?" is devoted entirely to an attempt to prove that apostasy is remediable. Shank's basic approach is to show that even though there are some verses that seem to teach that apostasy is without remedy, in a number of other places, the New Testament seems to teach otherwise.

He illustrates with the case of the Apostle Peter. He explains:

> On the mount, with James and John, he beheld His glory—the glory of the only begotten of the Father—and heard the Voice out of the cloud, "This is my beloved Son" (Matthew 17:5). And yet, in the hour of trial, he denied even the remotest acquaintance with Jesus: "I do not know the man!"—as though He were quite an ordinary person, thus conceding that the judgment of His enemies was, in his opinion, entirely correct. How persistent he was in his denial—three times! And how deliberate and emphatic his denial! He cursed and swore under oath, "I know not the man."
>
> And yet, Peter found forgiveness. Is that not encouraging for us all, as we think of the many times and many ways we have so shamefully denied our Holy Saviour? Have we not sworn by deed and life, if not in word, "I know not the man"? Have we no need to go out and weep bitterly with Peter? But still He comes—the man of Sorrows, forever scarred—and gently asks, "Lovest thou me?"[24]

We cannot read Shank's words above without empathizing with the deep feeling of concern that he conveys. Shank conveys a sense of humility before God that we should deeply appreciate. However, I do not believe he has proved his case. I cannot, in this present treatment, give an in-depth critique of Shank's view. But I believe I can show that his view is flawed.

I believe he overlooked the connection between the sin of apostasy in Hebrews 10:26-29 and the presumptuous sins of Numbers 15:30-31. I do not think there is any doubt that the writer of Hebrews meant to say that the "willful sin" of Hebrews 10:26 was the same kind of sin as the presumptuous sin in Numbers 15:30-31. There was no sacrifice for the presumptuous sin. There is an obvious connection between the words "there no longer remains a sacrifice for sins" (verse 26) and the fact that there was no sacrifice for sins in the case of presumptuous sins in Numbers 15:30-31. In supporting his view, Shank ruled out the idea that there was any sin beyond forgiveness. Surely, we cannot keep Numbers 15:30-31; Hebrews 6:4-6; 10:26-29; and the teachings of Jesus on the unpardonable sin in mind and still sustain the position that there is no sin for which there is no remedy.

I have done extensive research that shows that the willful (*hekousiōs*) is to be equated with the presumptuous sin of Numbers 15:30-31 and Psalm 19:13.[25] I will give a brief treatment here to the ideas that are pertinent to our present concerns.

The LXX does not use *hekousiōs* to refer to presumptuous sins. However, *akousios* and *akousiōs* which mean "unwilling" are used several times to refer to sins of ignorance. *Akousios* is used to translate the Hebrew for sins of ignorance in Numbers 15:25-26; and Ecclesiastes 10:5. *Akousiōs* is used in Leviticus 4:2, 22, 27; 5:15; Numbers 15:24, 27-29; 35:11, 15; and Joshua 20:3, 5, 9. It can hardly be doubted that *hekousiōs* as it is used in Hebrews 10:26 was deliberately chosen as being in contrast with *akousiōs*.

The Old Testament makes a clear distinction between sins of ignorance and presumptuous sins. Sins of ignorance (also called "unintentional sins"[26]) were basically sins of weakness. The person who committed such a sin had better desires, but these desires were defeated. The one committing such a sin was to offer a sacrifice (Num. 15:27-29). Presumptuous sins were committed with a "high hand." They came from an attitude of arrogant, defiant unbelief. According to Numbers 15:30-31, there was no sacrifice for presumptuous sins. If, in fact, the sin of apostasy mentioned in Hebrews 6:4-6 and 10:26-29 is to be equated with the presumptuous sin of Numbers 15:30-31, that should settle forever the question of whether apostasy is without remedy.

It is important to observe that the writer of Hebrews is not introducing a new idea when he speaks of a sin for which there is no sacrifice. He is simply placing the sin of apostasy in the category of the presumptuous sin of the Old Testament. Those who are in a state of saving grace do commit sins, but they are the kind referred to in Numbers 15:27.

Once we see the distinction between presumptuous sins and sins of ignorance in the Old Testament, it is clear that this distinction comes over into the New Testament. It is evident that, when Jesus said, "Father, forgive them, for they do not know what they do" (Lk. 23:34), He was considering the sins of those who crucified Him to be in the category of sins of ignorance. In Acts 3:17, Peter said that the Jews had crucified Jesus through ignorance. For that reason they could be forgiven (Acts 3:19). In describing himself before his conversion, Paul said, "I was formerly a blasphemer, and a persecutor, and an insolent man." In explaining how it was that he could be forgiven, he said, "But I obtained mercy because I did it ignorantly in unbelief" (1 Tim. 1:13). It is clear that Paul was placing his sins of blasphemy and his persecution of the church in the category of sins of ignorance. It was for that reason that they could be forgiven.

If Paul's persecution of the church could be considered a sin of ignorance, surely Peter's denial of Christ on the night of the betrayal of Christ should be considered a sin of ignorance (or weakness). If that be true, the case of Peter would have no bearing on the question of whether there is or is not a remedy for apostasy. If we keep the Old Testament teaching on presumptuous sins in mind, and the teaching of Hebrews 6:4-6 and 10:26-

29 in mind, I do not think we will have any serious problems in maintaining the view that apostasy is without remedy.

A Matter of Concern

Any discussion of unpardonable sin runs the risk of causing some people ungrounded concern. Over the years, I have had a number of people to talk with me about their fears that they had committed the unpardonable sin. In my opinion, none of those who talked to me about their fears had come close to committing the unpardonable sin. Usually, these people were undergoing an extended period of some form of unhappiness. In their search for what may be the cause for this unhappiness, they came up with the idea that if they had committed the unpardonable sin that would be a big enough reason to explain their problems. Then, they became afraid that they might have committed the unpardonable sin.

My first observation is if a person is concerned about whether he or she has committed the unpardonable sin, I believe that we can confidently say that such a person has not committed apostasy or the unpardonable sin. When the Holy Spirit works a concern in a person's heart, it is to bring repentance, not to tantalize him. That being true, if the Holy Spirit produces a concern in a person, that person has not committed apostasy. Also, it is very important to realize that it is not just the act itself that makes the kind of sin mentioned in Numbers 15:30-31 a presumptuous sin. It is the attitude of arrogant, defiant, unbelief that is manifested in the sin.

The words of Peter will help us understand the finality of the apostate's situation, and will help us to see that those who come to us with their fears have not committed apostasy. He tells us:

> For if, after they have escaped the pollutions of the world through the knowledge of the Lord and Savior Jesus Christ, they are again entangled in them and overcome, the latter end is worse for them than the beginning. For it would have been better for them not to have known the way of righteousness, than having known it, to turn from the holy commandment delivered to them (2 Pet. 2:20-21).

Verse 10 of 2 Peter 2 sheds more light on the subject. In that verse, Peter describes these apostate teachers as *tolmētēs*. The KJV translates *tolmētēs* as "presumptuous." The NASB renders it as "daring." The NIV and NKJV translates it as "arrogant." *Tolmētēs* occurs only here in the New Testament. Concerning its use here, J. A. Motyer explains, "The single occurrence of the noun (*tolmētēs*) is clearly in the bad sense . . . , the arrogant man of 2 Peter 2:10 who brooks no restriction on self-will and recognizes no authority to which he will be answerable."[27]

It is clear that Peter is considering these false teachers to be guilty of the presumptuous sin of Numbers 15:30-31. The arrogant defiance of these apostates gives a finality to their action. Before they were saved, they did not have this finality about their lost condition. The presumptuous, daring, arrogant decision with which they committed apostasy means that it was done with finality. This puts them in worse condition than they were before they were saved.

I believe we can rest assured that the person who comes to us to talk about his or her fears of having committed the unpardonable does not fit the description of the people described in 2 Peter 2:20-21; Hebrews 6:4-6; and 10:26-29. If there is concern to be restored to a right relationship with God, such a person has not committed apostasy.

The people in the United States who have come to me with their fears have not said that, in their past, they had made a decision to denounce their faith in Christ. The situation in Russia and Central Asia presents a different problem. When I have spoken on this subject there, some real concerns have been expressed. In one discussion period, someone said that he had known someone who under persecution had renounced his faith in Christ. Later on the person had repented.

To evaluate a case like that, we need to keep in mind the distinction between presumptuous sins and sins of ignorance. It is not simply what a person does or says that determines the case. Attitude is a decisive factor. In explaining how he was able to get forgiveness for persecuting the church, Paul is certainly implying that if he had done what he did "presumptuously," there would have been no forgiveness.

We cannot imagine the suffering inflicted in times past on some people in Russia to force them to deny their faith. Death was merciful in the light of the severe torture to which some were subjected. I think we would have to say that it was certainly possible for the lips to utter the words of a denial of faith that did not represent an arrogant, defiant unbelief toward God. If that be the case, the words of denial that the person uttered would not be equivalent to apostasy or shipwreck of faith. It appears that there were some who spoke words of denial that did not in fact commit apostasy. But I do not believe that we can explain all cases that way.

We must be faithful to the teaching of the Bible. If we are convinced the Bible teaches that apostasy is without remedy, we must teach it. The same would be true of whatever we believe it teaches on the unpardonable sin. However, we should do so with compassion and caution. We should not choose to speak on it to draw a bigger crowd. We need to keep in mind the problems that such topics cause for some people. Also, based on my experience in talking with people, I would caution preachers about jumping too quickly to the conclusion that the person who talks with them about having committed apostasy has indeed done so. I think it would be better to take it as a plea for help.

A View Held by Many Calvinists

I pointed out above that Hoeksema takes the position that the people referred to in these passages were not saved. Probably, most Calvinists take the position that they were saved. A proponent of this view is Millard J. Erickson. He explains that, even though he believes that Hebrews 6 teaches that believers can apostatize, John 10 teaches that they will not. In other words, he posits a "logical possibility" that will never eventuate in reality. "Although they could abandon their faith and consequently come to the fate described in Hebrews 6, the grace of God prevents them from apostatizing. God does this, not by making it impossible for believers to fall away, but by making it certain that they will not." Erickson hastens to say that his emphasis on "can" and "will" is "not inconsequential," because it actually safeguards individual freedom. Though believers are able to renounce their faith, they will "freely choose not to" because of divine grace.

Erickson seeks to answer the question of why Scripture contains such warning passages if salvation is "so secure and certain." His answer is that such passages are God's means of making it certain that no believer will fall. "It is not that God renders apostasy impossible by removing the very option," he argues. "Rather, he uses every possible means of grace, including the warnings contained in Scripture, to motivate us to remain committed to him. Because he enables us to persevere in our faith, the term perseverance is *preferable* to *preservation*.[28]

In supporting his interpretation of Hebrews 6:4-6, Erickson explains:

> The meaning in cases like this must be determined on the basis of the context. The key element in the present context is found in verse 9. "Though we speak thus, yet in your case, beloved, we feel sure of better things that belong to salvation . . . ." Verse 9, however, is a statement that they will not fall away. They could, but they will not! Their persistence to the end is evidence of that truth. The writer to the Hebrews knows that his readers will not fall away; he is convinced of better things regarding them, the things that accompany salvation.[29]

It is important to observe that Erickson and those who say that these passages describe something that is only theoretically possible are admitting that the possibility of losing salvation is consistent with every doctrine except the sovereign, keeping power of God. Erickson actually says, "There is the logical possibility of apostasy."

This approach is admitting that there are no logical arguments that prohibit the possibility that a person could commit apostasy and be lost after he is saved. The position that a person who is saved will in no case ever commit apostasy and be lost again would depend solely on a commitment on God's part in which He says that He will keep such from ever happening. For this to be a necessary conclusion would require: (1) a promise from God that He would not allow a person who is saved to apostatize, or (2) that the doctrine of unconditional election would be true. In the case of unconditional election, the guarantee that apostasy would not happen would be implicit in the doctrine of unconditional election. If God gives a promise that He will not allow a Christian to commit apostasy, where is it?

Erickson's view is also dependent on the view that the only way that John 10:28-29 can be understood is as denying the possibility that a person can lose his salvation. I think I have shown in my treatment of these verses above that that is not the required interpretation of John 10:28-29.

Another important point in Erickson's case is his view that Hebrews 6:9 affirms the position that the writer was telling his readers that the danger he was describing had not and would not happen to them. I think we can safely say that the recipients of the epistle had not committed apostasy. But that is not the same as saying that no one had. The ones who had committed apostasy would have already left the church. Verse 9 is a statement of what was true of the recipients of the epistle at the time of the writing of the epistle, not a guarantee about the future.

The translation of the NASB of the first part of Hebrews 6:6 is, "And *then* have fallen away." This translation suggests that some had fallen away. It is a better translation of the Greek than the "if" translation of the KJV, NKJV, and NIV. The "if" translation requires that *kai* (the Greek for "and") be left untranslated. The *kai* is translated in the NASB as "and." That gives us a more accurate picture of what the Greek is saying.

Robert Shank's comments are to the point concerning the view that these are only warnings to help the believer avoid an apostasy that he most certainly will not commit. He explains:

> The folly of their contention is seen in the fact that, the moment a man
> becomes persuaded that their doctrine of unconditional security is correct,

the warning passages immediately lose the very purpose and value which they claim for them . . . . How can there be any "earnest warning" to the believer who is sufficiently "instructed" to understand that the "warning" is directed against an impossibility?[30]

2 Peter 2:20-22

Had these people been saved? The ones under consideration are qualified by two expressions: (1) "They have escaped the pollutions of the world." (2) They did it "through the knowledge of the Lord and Savior Jesus Christ." In the same epistle, in 1:4, the following expression occurs: "having escaped the corruption that is in the world through lust." It is associated with being made a partaker of the divine nature, which is a privilege only for Christians. The expression in 1:4 is practically the same as in 2:20. Surely they refer to the same thing. It is the only other such expression in the epistle. On what grounds does a person say that one text is referring to a saved person and the other text to one who has made a false profession of Christianity?

Let us examine the second expression: "through the knowledge of the Lord and Savior Jesus Christ." It will be observed that this knowledge was the basis of their having escaped the pollutions of the world. It will also be noted that, in 1:3-4, the following things are obtained through the knowledge of Christ:

1. "All things that pertain to life and godliness" (verse 3).
2. "Partakers of the divine nature" (verse 4).
3. "Escaped the corruption that is in the world through lust" (verse 4).

A careful study of 1:3-4 and 2:20 will show that, in both instances, the corruption of the world had been escaped through the knowledge of the Lord and Savior Jesus Christ.

When such evidence occurs within the bounds of the same epistle for considering those in 2:20 as being saved on the same grounds as those in 1:3-4, the question must be asked: For what reasons can a person deny that those referred to in 2:20 were saved while affirming that those in 1:3-4 were saved? Also, keep in mind that every expression such as "through the knowledge of our Lord and Saviour Jesus Christ" found in the epistle, without exception, refers those who are saved. Regardless of what we may interpret the warning to be, we must accept the fact that it refers to people who have been saved.

What is the warning about in this passage? In 2 Peter 2:20-22, it is made plain that the warning here is against forsaking the truth that is in Christ for a false system. This is made clear when we read the entire second chapter. The first part of the chapter makes mention of false teachers, and the last part warns against being led astray by them and tells what the consequences will be.

What will be the result if they fail to heed the warning? In this passage it is said, "The latter end is worse for them than the beginning . . . it would have been better for them not to have known the way of righteousness." The only way these statements could be true would be that they describe the same condition as the verses in Hebrews; therefore, we conclude that these could not be saved again.

Other Passages

The passages just treated, I think, are the basic passages, but they are by no means the only ones that exist. Let us examine a few more.

Colossians 1:21-23

In this passage, Paul is laying down a stipulation of continuance in the faith as a condition of one's being presented holy, unblamable, and unreprovable in His sight. Here it is definitely implied that to fail to continue in the faith would mean loss of salvation. It is also worthy of note that Paul is warning his readers not to become entangled with false teachers who were teaching things contrary to the true view of Christ.

John 15:2, 6

In verse 2, it is said the branch that bears no fruit is taken away. It has been objected that one should not press an analogy too far. Therefore, this passage must not be taken as proving that a person can be lost again after having been saved. The only thought that is being taught here is that of fruit bearing. I also believe in exercising great caution against pressing analogies too far. I believe that much injustice is done to the interpretation of Scripture by overworking analogies and figures. But we must keep in mind that Jesus Himself is drawing all of the analogies in this allegory;[31] therefore, when He says, "Every branch in Me that does not bear fruit He takes away; and every branch that bears fruit He prunes." I must make a distinction between "being taken away" and "being pruned." Also, "being taken away" requires an interpretation because Jesus draws the analogy Himself and says that there is a work which the Father does of taking away the unfruitful branches.

It is important to observe that there are two kinds of branches spoken of in verse 2: (1) one that bears no fruit, and (2) one that does not bear as much as it should.

A branch is not taken out because it fails to bear as much as it should. Such a branch is pruned so it will bear more fruit. The believer is not taken out of Christ because he or she is not bearing as much fruit as he should. Rather, God works with him to get him to bear more fruit. It is the one who bears no fruit that is taken away.

I think it will be very helpful if we tie this in with Hebrews 6:7-8. The result of the apostasy that is described in verses 4-6 is seen in verse 8. The apostate is bearing thorns and briers.

It is a point of interest here to note that verses 7 and 8 are speaking of the same piece of ground. At first it brought forth herbs, and later it brought forth thorns and briers. *The Amplified Bible* makes it clear that verse 8 is speaking about the same piece of ground as verse 7. It reads, "But if [that same soil] persistently bears thorns and thistles, it is considered worthless and near to being cursed, whose end is to be burned."³² [Brackets by translators].

By comparing our findings to John 15:2, we see the apostate as one who does not bear fruit; instead, he bears thorns and briers. Therefore, he is taken out as one who does not bear fruit.

John 15:6 is referring to the same things as verse 2, only looking at it from a different point of view. Here we see that, if a man abides not in Christ, he is cast forth as a branch.

First John 2:22-24 is helpful in determining just what is meant by *abiding* and *not abiding*, as used in John 15. In 1 John 2:22-23, John warns against those who have false views concerning Christ. In 2:24, he says, "Therefore let that abide in you which you heard from the beginning." In other words, instead of taking the view of Christ as presented to you by false teachers, continue to believe the correct doctrine of Christ that you have heard from the beginning. Then he goes on to say, "If what you have heard from the beginning [the correct doctrine of Christ] abides in you, you also will abide in the Son, and in the Father,"

The same Greek word that is translated *abide* in John 15 is translated *continue* in the verse just cited. In 1 John 2:24, the condition for abiding in Christ is to abide in the true doctrine concerning Christ. It is definitely implied that, if the reader of 1 John should choose to forsake the true doctrine of Christ, he would not remain in Christ.

Second John 9 gives proof of what we have just said, "Whoever transgresses and does not abide in the doctrine of Christ does not have God." This verse definitely proves that a person who does not believe in the true doctrine of Christ is not saved. Taken in its context, it seems to be a warning to the saved person not to be led astray by false teachings concerning Christ. To forsake the true doctrine in favor of the false would mean that the person would not have God.

Upon considering these references, it seems clear that for a person not to abide in Christ, as in John 15:6, would mean that he forsook the true teachings of Christ. Is it not also taught in the other references mentioned that to fail to continue in the true doctrine of Christ would mean rejection by God, which John 15:6 describes as being cast forth as a branch? The result of being cast forth is to be withered and burned. The same thing happens to the apostate of Hebrews 6 as is seen in the figure set forth in verse 8.

Up to this point, the following conclusions have been established: (1) The Bible teaches that a saved person can lose his salvation.[33] (2) Salvation continues on the condition of faith but will be forfeited by unbelief. (3) As long as a person remains saved, he has both justification and sanctification. (4) When a person does lose his salvation, he cannot be saved again.

---

[1]For a long time those who accepted only the last point of Calvinism called themselves "Calvinists." There is a trend among some to call themselves "Arminian." In fact, they are more Arminian than Calvinistic.

[2]Lewis Sperry Chafer, *Systematic Theology* (Dallas: Dallas Seminary Press, 1948), 3:316.

[3]James Oliver Buswell, Jr., *A Systematic Theology*, 2:145.

[4]Millard J. Erickson, *Christian Theology* (Grand Rapids: Baker Book House, 1985), 986-987.

[5]Charles Stanley, *Eternal Security* (Nashville: Thomas Nelson Publishers, 1990), 11-12.

[6]Ibid., 92.

[7]M. R. Vincent, *Word Studies in the New Testament*, 2nd ed. (1888; reprint, Wilmington, Delaware: Associated Publishers and Authors, 1972), 1059. [Emphasis mine.]

[8]Stanley, *Eternal Security*, 35.

[9]Forlines, *Romans*, 90-96.

[10]Zane C. Hodges, *The Gospel Under Siege: A Study of Faith and Works* (Dallas: Rendención Viva, 1981).

[11]William Wilson Stevens, *Doctrines of The Christian Religion* (Grand Rapids: William B. Eerdmans Publishing Company, 1967), 258.

[12]Buswell, *A Systematic Theology*, 2:146.

[13]John H. Gerstner, "Perseverance," *Baker's Dictionary of Theology*, 404.

[14]Berkhof, *Systematic Theology*, 404.

[15]Herman Hoeksema, *Reformed Dogmatics* (Grand Rapids: Reformed Free Publishing Co., 1966), 258.

[16]John Henry Thayer, *Thayer's Greek-English Lexicon of the New Testament*, (1889; reprint, Grand Rapids: Zondervan Publishing House, 192), 663.

[17]R.C. Sproul brings up an interesting observation about the use of *repentance* here. He explains: "I think the passage may well be describing true Christians. The most important phrase for me is 'renew again to repentance.' I know there is a false kind of repentance that the author elsewhere calls the repentance of Esau. But here he speaks of renewal. The new repentance, if it is renewed, must be like the old repentance. The renewed repentance of which he speaks is certainly the genuine kind. I assume therefore that the old was likewise genuine" [R.C. Sproul, *Chosen by God* (Wheaton: Tyndale House Publishers, Inc. 1986), 185].

[18]J.D. O'Donnell, *Free Will Baptist Doctrines* (Nashville: Randall House Publications, 1974), 78.

[19]Robert E. Picirilli, *Perseverance* [a booklet] (Nashville: Randall House Publications, 1973), 20.

[20]I. Howard Marshall, *Kept by the Power of God: A Study of Perseverance and Falling Away* (Minneapolis: Bethany House, 1969), 142.

[21]Ibid., 146.

[22]Ibid., 148.

[23]Robert Shank, *Life in the Son: A Study of the Doctrine of Perseverance* (Springfield, MO: Wescott Publishers, 1960), 309.

[24]Ibid., 328-329.

[25]This paper was presented at the Southeastern Region of the Evangelical Theological Society meeting in Charlotte, North Carolina, March 10, 1995. This material is found in *The Quest for Truth*, Appendix 1.

[26]A discussion on the appropriate name for these sins will be found in *The Quest for Truth*, Appendix 1.

[27]J. A. Motyer, "Courage, Boldness," in *The International Dictionary of New Testament Theology*, vol. 1, Colin Brown, ed. (Grand Rapids: Zondervan Publishing House, 1975), 365.

[28]Millard J. Erickson, *Christian Theology*, One vol. originally published in three vols, 994.

[29]Erickson, 993-994.

[30]Shank, *Life in the Son*, 164-165.

[31]John 15:1-8 is frequently referred to as "The Parable of the Vine and the Branches." This passage is more accurately called an allegory. A parable is an extended simile, while an allegory is an extended metaphor. A simile is a figure of speech introduced by "like" or "as." For example, "red like crimson" or "white as snow" are similes. A parable is an extended simile, e.g., "The kingdom of heaven is like. . . ."

On the other hand, a metaphor omits the like or as. For example, Jesus said, "I am the bread of life." When we make a distinction between allegories and parables, the Gospel of John is found to have no parables, only allegories. Since an allegory is an extended metaphor, Jesus words, "I am the vine, you are the branches" (Jn. 15:5), and His extended explanation of this statement is an allegory. The nature of allegories demands that more attention be given to interpreting their details than for a parable.

[32]*The Amplified Bible* (Grand Rapids, Michigan: Zondervan Publishing House, 1987), Heb. 6:7-8.

[33]Some who believe that it is possible for one who is saved to cease to be a Christian and once again be under the wrath of God object to the term "lose salvation." To them it seems that it would say that you could accidentally or without intention lose your salvation. I understand their concern. However, that is not the only meaning that lose can have. To "lose something" simply means to no longer be in possession of it.

The term "lose your salvation" is so commonly used that it is almost impossible to say much about the subject without using it. Even if a particular person avoids using the term, it will continue to be used.

CHAPTER 10

Apostasy and Assurance: Doctrinal and Practical Considerations

THE CONSISTENCY OF THE POSSIBILITY OF LOSS OF SALVATION WITH OTHER DOCTRINES

There are several questions that are yet to be answered in developing and defending the doctrine. The first problem is to show the consistency of this doctrine with other doctrines.

Consistent With God's Sovereignty

The Calvinistic view of continuance in salvation is the logical outgrowth of their interpretation of God's sovereignty. To show this connection, I will repeat a quotation given earlier in this book from Lewis Sperry Chafer. He explains:

> The failure of one soul to be saved and to reach glory whom God has ordained to that end means the disruption of the whole actuality of divine sovereignty. If God could fail in one feature, be it ever so small, He could fail in all. If He could fail in anything, He ceases to be God and the universe is drifting to a destiny about which God himself could know nothing.

Their interpretation of divine sovereignty is the foundation principle and the guiding principle in the thought of thoroughgoing Calvinists. There can be no question that "God must accomplish what He sets out to do if He is to be Sovereign." I fully concur with this statement. The question is *what has God set out to do*. Has He set out to include all divine

3

activity in a *cause* and *effect* relationship as distinguished from an *influence* and *response* relationship? Does God have the same sort of cause and effect relationship with persons that He has with the material universe?

If God works with cause and effect relationships in His relationship with human persons, the Calvinistic system has much to commend itself. By applying the cause and effect relationships to persons, I do not mean to infer that the nature of the object in personal relationships may not be taken into account, but it is cause and effect as long as *the cause guarantees the effect*. It cannot be otherwise. This must be true in both redemptive and nonredemptive matters. If not, God is not sovereign on Calvinistic premises. At least this would be true in Classical Calvinism. Those who choose the name Calvinist, but are not willing to follow through with the logical implications set forth above probably need to rethink whether they should call themselves Calvinists. The burden of proof is on them as to whether or not they can legitimately designate themselves as Calvinists.

The ultimate question in all of this is: What has God revealed to us in His Word concerning His sovereignty? The problem is that if a person goes to the Bible with the preconceived notion that the only way for God to be sovereign is for Him to perform all of His activity in the framework of cause and effect relationships, he will force that interpretation on all Scripture passages, regardless of what they say. Therefore, we need to give some attention to whether this is the only way in which an absolute Sovereign may act.

Is it impossible, in principle, for God to direct His sovereignty within the framework of influence and response when it comes to His relationship with persons? Is He incapable of working within this framework? Does He have to restrict Himself to cause and effect relationships to keep from losing His sovereignty? My answer to all these questions is no. I would think any person would think long and hard before he gave a yes answer to any of these questions. Yet, if the answer to these questions is no, there is no logical necessity for a person to believe that all of God's activity toward persons must be with the intent of a guaranteed effect. We do not have to study the Word of God with the predisposition that divine sovereignty demands a guaranteed effect.

I believe God accomplishes *all of His purposes*. He achieves *all of His goals*. The choice to create human beings as personal beings was His own choice. That choice meant He would deal with us as persons. He would work with us in the framework of influence and response. This meant man's responses could include both *obedience* and *disobedience*. God does not lose His sovereignty when man disobeys. We are not to assume that God desires man's disobedience. We should assume however that God desires that disobedience would be a real option for man, created as he is with personality. In the *cause* and *effect* relationship approach to sovereignty, it is rather difficult to see how disobedience ever entered the universe without either destroying God's sovereignty, if He disapproves of sin, or corrupting His holiness if He does not. It does not help very much to say that God's ways are inscrutable to us.

In the influence and response approach, God does not depend upon omnipotence alone to execute His sovereignty. He depends upon wisdom. It takes far more wisdom for God to be sovereign within the framework of influence and response than it does within the framework of cause and effect. I think the influence and response approach exalts the sovereignty of God far more than does the cause and effect approach. If we grant that God's sovereignty must work within the framework of cause and effect, unconditional election, irresistible grace or effectual call, and unconditional continuance in salvation all follow through with absolute precision of thought and logical necessity. It is a very simple system. It may be hard to believe, but it is not hard to understand. If we grant that God's sovereignty *could* work within the framework of influence and response whether it does or not, the Calvinistic system does not follow through as a logical necessity. We would be dependent upon revelation to tell us how God chooses to operate.

If we grant that God's sovereignty works within the framework of influence and response, Calvinism is either ruled out or one would be using influence and response simply as a disguised form of cause and effect. It requires more thought to comprehend personal relationships than it does cause and effect relationships. The simplicity of cause and effect relationships is not found in influence-response relationships. The operation of God's sovereignty within the framework of influence and response requires more thought to be appreciated and understood. This should not be surprising since we are dealing with personal relationships. There is much that is hard to explain about the function of personal relationships, even when speaking of exclusively human relationships.

My purpose in these observations has been to show that there is no logical necessity which requires that the Calvinistic system be true. I am quite certain that it is within the *framework of logical possibilities* for God to choose to use the approach of *conditional continuance in salvation* in dealing with man. There is *no logical necessity* for God to lose His sovereignty and the universe either fall apart or run on an uncertain course if a person should lose his salvation. This would be true only if God chose to operate within the framework of unconditional continuance in salvation, but failed to achieve His purpose.

If God says that every Christian is eternally secure and can under no circumstance ever lose his salvation, we would certainly judge God to be less than sovereign if anyone did lose his salvation. However, there is nothing in the nature of God's sovereignty to forbid Him to be able to work in a plan whereby He used the approach of conditional continuance in salvation rather than unconditional continuance. As Picirilli explains, "We believe in a Sovereign God; but a Sovereign God is just as free to make salvation conditional as any other way. And our God is big enough to handle a real contingency in His universe."[1]

Consistent With Atonement and Justification

Berkhof comments: "In His atoning work Christ paid the price to purchase the sinner's pardon and acceptance. His righteousness constitutes the perfect ground for the justification of the sinner, and it is impossible that one who is justified by the payment of such a perfect and efficacious price should again fall under condemnation.[2]

It is true that as long as a person has the death and righteousness of Christ he is justified. He cannot be lost and at the same time have the death of Christ. However, since he has the death and righteousness of Christ only by identification conditioned on faith, on the condition of unbelief the identification can be broken and the person would no longer have the death and righteousness of Christ. (For a more thorough explanation of this point, see the discussion under objections to the satisfaction view of atonement in Chapter 6.)

A Choice to Be Made by Calvinists

The Calvinist, to be logical, must decide between basing his view of unconditional continuance on *atonement* or on *the keeping power of God*. If atonement seals the security of the believer so that it cannot be undone, there is no place for being kept by the power of God, at least so far as justification is concerned. By the nature of the case, it could not be forfeited. The only place for the keeping power of God for those who base unconditional continuance in salvation on the nature of atonement and justification would be in the area of sanctification. The keeping power of God would have no bearing on continuance in justification since by the nature of the case justification could not be forfeited.

Either option that the Calvinist chooses is not without consequences. To ground unconditional continuance on atonement and justification means that it cannot be grounded in the power of God that is related to His sovereignty. To take the ground for unconditional continuance away from the keeping power of God creates a real problem for those who say the passages used to support conditional continuance are, instead, warnings that God uses as a means of helping those who are saved to persevere. Berkhof explains concerning the warnings:

> There are warnings against apostasy which would seem to be quite uncalled for if the believer could not fall away, Matt. 24:12; Col. 1:23; Heb. 2:1; 3:14; 6:11; 1 John 2:6. But these warnings regard the whole matter from the side of man and are seriously meant. They prompt self-examination, and are instrumental in keeping believers in the way of perseverance. They do not prove that any of those addressed will apostatize, but simply that the use of means is necessary to prevent them from committing this sin.[3]

To interpret these warnings, as Berkhof and many other Calvinists do, to be real warnings used to prevent apostasy on the part of believers means that, in principle, a person could lose his salvation were it not for the power of God. For this to be true, the loss of salvation would have to be consistent with every other doctrine except the promised keeping power of God. Yet, Berkhof, as quoted above, grounds unconditional continuance also in atonement and justification. It cannot be both ways. If the Calvinist chooses to ground unconditional continuance in atonement and justification rather than the power of God, he *cannot* interpret the passages referred to as warnings used by God to help the believer persevere. This would be true because, in principle, there would be no possibility of losing his salvation. There must at least be the *possibility* in principle, if not in fact, of a person losing salvation before warnings can be said to be used in helping a person to keep from losing his salvation. The warning is not a warning if it does not say to people that they would lose them salvation if a certain thing were to take place.

Those who ground unconditional continuance in salvation on atonement and justification must come up with some other interpretation of the warning passages. The other interpretation that is given for these passages is that they are warnings to professing Christians. Herman Hoeksema in dealing with Hebrews 6:4-6 in a quotation given earlier does not believe that these people had been saved. He takes the position that "they went through the outward show of repentance, and for a time walked in that repentance. But now they have definitely fallen away even from the outward show." Wayne Grudem takes the position that while it is possible to take what is given in this passage as a description of a saved person, the case is not decisive.[4]

My own treatment, and why I believe the people referred to in this passage had been saved, appears in Chapter 9. I will not restate my case here. I will simply say that, if we knew some who had made a false profession, I think we would spend our time trying to get them to make a genuine decision for Christ. We would do that rather than tell them that if they fall from that profession, they can never be renewed to that profession again. What those who merely profess need to know is that they are not saved. They need to be told how they can tell that their profession is empty. They need to examine themselves in the light of the guaranteed results of salvation.

When a person chooses to ground unconditional continuance in salvation in the power of God rather than grounding it in atonement and justification, he is admitting that in principle a person could lose his salvation, if not in fact. This means that unconditional continuance must either relate:

1. to logical necessity growing out of a *cause* and *effect* relationship view of sovereignty, or
2. God's promise of unconditional continuance. Either way, we expect to find a Scriptural basis for unconditional continuance that would take the form of a *promise*. I have already given my reasons for believing the Scripture teaches the contrary. Earlier I have dealt with the verses thought by some to make such a promise.

Consistent With the Imputation of Christ's Death and Righteousness

While the satisfaction view of atonement and justification are consistent with the possibility of losing salvation, it is not consistent with some patterns of thought in connection with the possibility of losing salvation. If we believe in the imputation of Christ's death and righteousness as the ground of our justification, we do not have room for a halfway state between being saved and being lost. If we are in union with Christ, we have

His death and righteousness and are justified. If we are not in union with Christ, we are not justified.

We can be in danger of losing our salvation. However, we have lost it only when the union is broken and we no longer have the death and righteousness of Christ.

Consistent With Union with Christ

Berkhof explains:

> They who are united to Christ by faith become partakers of His Spirit, and thus become one body with Him, pulsating with the life of the Spirit. They share in the life of Christ, and because He lives they live also. It is impossible that they should again be removed from the body, thus frustrating the divine ideal. The union is permanent, since it originates in a permanent and unchangeable cause, the free eternal love of God.[5]

There can be no question that as long as a person is in union with Christ he is saved. To be in union with Christ is to be saved. For one not to be in union with Christ means he is not saved. The question of whether this union can be broken is for God to decide. Our knowledge should come from His revelation. It is not for us to decide on the basis of what we think is logical necessity or what we consider to be unthinkable. Jesus has answered the question for us in clear terms, "Every branch in Me that does not bear fruit He takes away" (Jn. 15:2). I pointed out above that those who base their view of unconditional continuance upon the keeping power of God are admitting, in principle, that their view of union with Christ would not preclude believing a person could lose his salvation.

According to John 15:2, 6, if one turns back to unbelief, God will take that one out of Christ. Such a person will no longer be in union with Christ. He or she will no longer have the death and righteousness of Christ on his or her account. If what I am saying here is true, there are no grounds on which to build the popular view of "once saved, always saved" that is advocated by Stanley and others.

Consistent With Salvation by Grace Through Faith

Salvation by grace means that it comes by unmerited favor. It is a gift bestowed upon us that we do not deserve. It is something for which we in no way pay. Our justification is a gift from God. In no way did we participate in the ground of our justification. It is the death and righteousness of Christ that forms the grounds of our justification—not our obedience. This fact always remains unchanged. The act of baptizing us into Christ, regenerating us, and the indwelling of the Holy Spirit are all gifts of God grounded in the atoning work of Christ. These have all been applied to our account. Every loving move of God toward us is based on His grace which is grounded in Christ's atonement. Nothing that I have said about conditional continuance in salvation has at any point contradicted these observations.

There is nothing whatsoever about the nature of a gift that either keeps it from being rejected when offered or keeps it from being returned if received. It is inherent in the nature of a gift that as long as it remains a gift the recipient of the gift can in no way participate in the payment of the gift. The very nature of the requirement of justification along with the qualifications of a human being who has sinned, means that a human being can never participate in the payment for his own justification. He can provide neither absolute righteousness nor infinite sufferings.

The Bible plainly conditions salvation on faith. To insist that salvation is *kept on the condition of faith* no more contradicts the notion of free salvation than saying that it is *received on the condition*. It is surprising that anyone would think so. It is folly to charge that to require the continuation of faith for the continuation of salvation makes faith a work and thus puts salvation on the basis of works. The Bible itself clearly removes faith from the category of works (Rom. 4:3-5).

Faith would be a work if it were to be considered the *ground* of our justification instead of the *condition*. Faith contributes *absolutely nothing* to the ground of our justification. The ground of our justification is the death and righteousness of Christ on our account—nothing more and nothing less! When this distinction is made between *ground* and *condition*, there is no way that continued faith serving as the condition of continued justification could make a *work* out of faith.

Picirilli comments:

> Any time the Bible talks about believing for salvation, the verb "believing" is always in the tense in the Greek that means continuing belief . . . . Verses like John 5:24, "he that . . . *believeth*" always have the verb in the tense that denotes the action in process. In other words, we could well interpret John 5:24: "He that goes on believing in me shall not come into condemnation." So in this way too, the conditional nature of such promises is made clear.[6]

It would be helpful at this point to elaborate on what it means to say that a person has saving faith in Jesus Christ. It means more than saying that he maintains correct doctrine about Jesus, although it certainly involves that. When a person exercises faith in Jesus, he is recognizing Jesus as a Redeemer from sin. This includes both justification and sanctification. Faith in Jesus as Redeemer always implies that the person who is exercising this faith also wants redemption. He is trusting in Jesus both to forgive him and to make him the kind of person he should be. There is the desire and the expectation that God will be working to make the person into the likeness of Christ. We are not to suppose that people who are basically indifferent to moral and spiritual concerns have saving faith. This would contradict both the nature of saving faith and the nature of salvation.

Roads to Apostasy
Heretical Doctrine

One of the main roads to apostasy is through false doctrine. This is one of the reasons that the New Testament takes such a strong stand against heresy (Gal. 1:8-9; 1 Jn. 4:1-3; 2 Jn. 7-11; Jude 3-19; and others) and gives so much attention to grounding Christians in the faith.

This danger may be presented to the Christian by cults as well as various forms of liberal doctrine within many denominations. One of the tragedies of born again Christians attending liberal seminaries has been that many have lost their faith. As strange as it may seem, this was more of a problem 50 years ago than it is today.

The Influence of Modernism

In secular education, modernism seeks to build a worldview based on natural causes and effects. It has no place for divine revelation. The problem here centers to a large extent on the fact that many believers encounter naturalism when confronted by teachers who are far better trained than they are. In many instances, they do not know of anyone to whom they can turn who can explain the difficulties they are facing. They run the risk of being overcome by naturalism when they are unable to defend themselves. This is one of the reasons that Christian colleges should be provided for Christian young people where their faith will be strengthened rather than undermined. The greater danger now is from postmodernism. I mention modernism here because there are still many functioning according to the modernist paradigm.

The Influence of Postmodernism

The danger of postmodernism does not come from powerful rational arguments against Christianity. Postmodernism spells the death of Truth, the death of reason, the death of morals, and the death of a rational worldview. In Christian thought, belief in Truth, the proper use of reason, moral conviction, and a rational worldview are all foundational to the survival of Christian thinking. The conditioning power of postmodernism creates a postmodern mood which desensitizes people and undermines the concern in these areas that is necessary to Christian conviction. The brand of bigotry which is leveled against anyone who dares to believe that his or her view is true and someone else's view is wrong is more than some are prepared to cope with.

Tampering with Sin

A third road that leads to apostasy is tampering with sin. This can lead to a spirit of defeat and place one under the chastising hand of God (Heb. 12:7-11). God has determined that His people will be holy; thus, He places His people under chastisement when they sin. God's determination to make His people holy will bring a sinning Christian to a point in which he or she will either have to repent or forsake God altogether. If he should turn from God, this will mean turning from faith. He will make shipwreck of faith (1 Tim. 1:18-19).

A Prolonged Experience with Severe, Unresolved Problems

When a person goes through a period of severe difficulty, and he or she seems to find no answers to the problem he or she is facing, whatever belief-system (or worldview) he or she acknowledges will be seriously challenged. People are at higher risk of changing their belief-system when the view that they trust in proves to be inadequate to deal with the problems of life that they are facing.

I have made the above statement many times in classes that I have taught. I remember one occasion when, after I said that, a young man gave the class an illustration of what I had said. He said that he and his wife had lost a five-year-old daughter. His wife's father was an atheist. His atheism was unable to support him in his time of grief at the loss of his granddaughter. He gave up his atheism, which was inadequate for his need, and became a Christian. His daughter who was a Christian almost lost her faith. The pain she was experiencing placed a strain on the view she had believed and was trusting in. The student said that his wife had been able to find answers for her needs and that she had been able to deal with her doubts.

We will do well to keep in mind that the Book of Hebrews was written to believers who were suffering persecution. The writer refers to the book as "a word of exhortation" or "a word of encouragement" (Heb. 13:22). It was during a time of severe discouragement that some had chosen to forsake Christ and go back to the Old Testament sacrifices.

Suffering From Severe Persecution

With many of us in America, our belief in the possibility of apostasy is somewhat an academic matter. We have not been given the choice of prison or freedom if we would deny our faith in Christ. We have not been given the choice of life or death if we would deny our faith. As I traveled across Ukraine and Russia in 1996, I saw those who had chosen prison rather than deny their faith. In Kiev, Ukraine I had the privilege of meeting Georgi Vinns who spent eight years in prison for his faith before President Carter arranged for his release in connection with the release of two Russian spies.[7] I met those who had family members who chose death rather than to deny their faith. I saw those whose children were denied the right of higher education because they were Christians. I saw those who suffered all kinds of harassment from the KGB. To the Baptist in the Former Soviet Union, the doctrine of the possibility of shipwreck of faith is very real. Those living in areas of continued persecution need our prayers that they will keep the faith.

A Word of Caution to Arminians

When the impression is given that it would be very easy for a person to lose his or her salvation, many live their lives in the bondage of fear. Jesus said, "I have come that they may have life, and that they may have it more abundantly" (Jn. 10:10). There is no abundant life in living in the bondage of fear.

Any view of a biblical teaching that makes one live in the bondage of fear is faulty. It is not God's intent for people to be obsessed with the fear of losing salvation. An unhealthy fear leads one into over-introspection. As Christians, we are not to be given over to continuous introspection. Continuous introspection makes a person self-centered. As Christians, we are to be Christ-centered.

We need to have a healthy concern about the possibility of us losing our salvation. But it is not healthy when it causes people who are nowhere close to losing their salvation to be robbed of the joy of the Christian life.

We need to help people see that they are saved by Christ alone, on the condition of faith alone. They need to see that they are justified by the death and righteousness of Christ. They are justified by Christ's righteousness, not their own. They need to understand that the only thing that would cause them to lose their salvation would be a deliberate choice to turn from Him. That is my doctrine. I have assurance of salvation. I do not live in fear of losing my salvation.

Assurance of Salvation

No writing on perseverance is complete unless it is also discussed from the standpoint of assurance. Certainly the grounds of assurance are strong enough in the Scriptures that a child of God can enter into the blessings of assurance and not be constantly worried by the fear of falling.

When we stop and think what the new birth does for a person, surely we have strong grounds to believe that he will continue in the faith. By the new birth a person is made a new creature (2 Cor. 5:17) and possesses a new nature. This new nature within him is thirsting and hungering for the things of God. There is also a distaste for the things of sin. With this change wrought in his heart, the person who is born again will never be satisfied apart from a close walk with God.

The relationship which the indwelling Spirit has with the believer is another ground of assurance that the believer will continue in the faith. The Holy Spirit has a vital interest in us and works patiently and untiringly with the believer to get him to be an obedient child. He does this by producing a consciousness and conviction of sin in the heart of the Christian. He chastises the believer (Heb. 12:7-8, 11), making it so that he cannot enjoy life except when living in harmony with God. He teaches the Christian many wonderful truths about Christ that encourage him to live for Christ. Along with all else He does, He gives strength to the believer in his warfare against the flesh (Gal. 5:16-17). Thus, we see that the Holy Spirit seeks to lead the believer away from that which would ensnare him; He enables him to walk in this way and keeps him from enjoying walking any other way.

John 10:28-29 gives the Christian strong grounds on which to stand. In Christ, he has eternal life and will never perish. When a person is saved, he is baptized into Christ's body; and as long as he is in Christ, he has eternal life and will never perish. This is what we have in Christ, and we are also promised that no one can take us out of Christ. Salvation is a personal matter between the believer and Christ. No outsider can take the believer out of Christ. If he is ever taken out, it will be an act of God the Father as husbandman, as is set forth in John 15:2, and that only on the grounds of not abiding in Christ (Jn. 15:6). To be in Christ means to have eternal life, and no outside force or combination of forces can take us out of Christ.

Another ground of security is that God will not cast us out at the least little thing we do. We are saved by faith and kept by faith. We are lost, after we are once saved, only by turning from faith in Christ to unbelief.

The view as we have given it gives a person all the assurance he needs to have joy. It does not keep him in constant fear of falling; yet, at the same time, he is aware that it is possible to fall. It also keeps salvation on a faith basis instead of mixing it with works. This is not just a line of reasoning; it has the support of the Scriptures.

Some who hold to unconditional continuance in salvation seem to think that conditional continuance makes the continuation of salvation a matter that is so totally of man that God is out of the picture. This is not the case. God is working with the person to help him or her continue in faith and to grow in grace. The continued response of faith is not in a context where the Christian is totally independent. It is in a context where he is dependent on God. God is working in and through him. Yet, there is a sense in which his decisions are his own. It is possible for him to go contrary to God's leading not only before he is saved, but also afterward. Nevertheless, those who love God and understand the positive grounds for assurance do not live with fear that they will go contrary to God's leading and depart from the faith.

To warn Christians against apostasy is not intended to make people live in great fear. Let me illustrate. Suppose you were traveling down a road after a severe rainstorm and you discovered that a bridge was out and you put up a sign to warn people. You would not do that to create fear in people. You would do that to increase their safety. The warning signs on a road give me assurance as I travel. Since I know what the dangers are, I can avoid them.

As I travel the road of the Christian life, if there are warning signs along the way it helps me to know what the dangers are. It helps me avoid apostasy if I know what it is and what the result would be.

When many Calvinists interpret Hebrews 6:4-6, they say the same thing that I have just said. (See the quotation given from Erickson.) Calvinists, who take this approach, think it is a warning to help a Christian avoid something that he will not do. I think it is a warning to help a Christian avoid a sin that he could commit and in rare instances some people do commit. When I see these warning signs, they help me follow Peter's advice when he said, "Wherefore the rather, brethren, give diligence to make your calling and election sure: for if ye do these things ye shall never fall" (2 Pet. 1:10).

It also helps our assurance when we see that a Christian is not lost every time he commits a sin. Christians do commit sins of the kind mentioned in Numbers 15:27. The Christian desires to do right, but he does not always succeed. But Hebrews 6:4-6 and 10:26-29 are talking about something drastically different. When Christians commit the kind of sins referred to in Numbers 15:27, they feel bad about what they are doing and the Holy Spirit works to produce repentance. We have no right to offer assurance to people who sin and do not have any concern about it. Such people do not show evidence that they have been made new creatures as is spoken of in 2 Corinthians 5:17. In most cases like this, the people have never been saved. However, when people are chastised for their sins, that is evidence of salvation (Heb. 12:7-8).

Let me say here that assurance is not guaranteed by a person's theology. A person may believe any of the various forms of the doctrine of "once saved, always saved" and still doubt his or her salvation. It is possible for a person to believe that he cannot lose salvation and still not be sure that he has it. One of my professors told about a leading Calvinist theologian who lost the assurance that he was one of the elect and went insane. It is important for all of us to give attention to the assurance of salvation.

Justification and Sanctification Always Together

We must not conclude this study without stressing that salvation includes both justification and sanctification. To speak about continuing in salvation is to speak about continuing in both justification and sanctification. The package cannot be broken. We cannot have one without the other. The viewpoint that offers continued justification, whether conditional or unconditional, without sanctification has no support whatsoever in the Bible. It is also impossible to reduce sanctification to the point that it has no results in the believer's experience.

I have already dealt with this point in the chapter on sanctification. Let me give a summary restatement that holiness is not optional but is a guaranteed result of salvation. (1) Paul emphatically states that those who live in gross sin will not inherit the kingdom of God (1 Cor. 6:9-11; Gal. 5:19-21; and Eph. 5:3-7). (2) The writer of Hebrews says that without holiness no man shall see the Lord (Heb. 12:14). (3) From both a positive and a negative viewpoint, 1 John makes it clear that for a person to fail to practice righteousness means that he is not saved (1 Jn. 2:3, 4, 9-11; 3:3-10, 14-15; 4:20; and 5:4, 18).

These verses do not say that for a person to practice these sins would cause him or her to lose his salvation. That is not the reason given for saying that those practicing sin are not saved. The reason given for denying that people who practice sin are saved is that those who are born of God cannot practice sin (1 Jn. 3:9).[8] Practicing righteousness is neither the condition of receiving salvation nor is it the condition for its continuation. It is a result of salvation, or we might say it is a part of salvation.

The loss of salvation cannot come as a result of practicing sin, because a person who is born of God does not have practicing sin in the framework of his possibilities. (See "The Guaranteed Results of Sanctification.") This does not mean that he cannot commit acts of sin. The fact that acts of sin are an open possibility for the believer means that it is an open possibility that a person could commit an act of apostasy. This is so only if apostasy is a sinful act rather than being a process of practicing sin. While the initial act of apostasy is a single act, it will be followed by a practice of willful or defiant sin (Heb. 10:26). The single act of apostasy propels a person into the practice of sin.

Before Adam and Eve sinned, it was not in the framework of possibilities that they could practice sin, but it was within the framework of possibility for them to commit an act of sin. When they committed that act of sin, their nature was changed. With their change of nature they could practice sin. The sinner does not have it within the framework of possibilities for him to practice righteousness and to be able to please God. By the help of the Holy Spirit, it is within the framework of possibilities for the sinner to respond to the gospel and be saved. If he does respond, this introduces him to a framework of possibilities wherein he can practice righteousness and please God. Having done so, he can no longer practice sin.

It is within the framework of possibilities for a person to lose his salvation if the cause for it can be summed up in an act of departure. There would, of course, be some things that lead up to the act of departure. From the standpoint of reason, it is just as logical that a saved person could make this departure, so far as his own will is concerned, as it was for Adam and Eve to sin or for a sinner to respond to the gospel. It is also just as logical to believe that a Christian can depart from his faith, in the light of God's sovereignty, as it is to believe that Adam and Eve sinned in the light of God's sovereignty. The only thing that could make it more logical to believe that Adam and Eve could sin, in the light of God's sovereignty, but that the Christian cannot depart from faith, would be to believe that God wanted Adam and Eve to sin while He does not want the Christian to depart from his faith.

Some Practical Problems

Some people are hard for us to identify in the light of our theology. It seems as if they have definitely been saved at some time in the past. It seems that they have not committed apostasy or turned from their faith. Yet, it seems that they are living in sin or practicing sin. I would say that obviously one of our judgments is wrong. Either, the person never was saved, has lost his faith, or is not living in sin. I may not be able to decide what his real case is. I would certainly not offer assurances to such a person. I would not propose to give an official diagnosis of his case. I am sympathetic with those who may feel obligated to consider such people as neither exactly in nor exactly out, but I think the position that I have set forth which says that a person must be either in or out is more tenable.

I believe a person is either saved or unsaved, but I cannot pass judgment on all cases. It is my opinion that a similar position will have to be adopted in some cases regardless of what a person's view may be.

Some people prefer to limit their use of the word *apostasy* to a departure from the faith on theological grounds, i.e., trading the truth for heresy. I use the term *apostasy* to refer to shipwreck of faith in the broad sense. It is what a person leaves, not what he goes to that counts. Some may go to a clearly defined system of unbelief. Others may simply turn to unbelief.

There is a problem about the use of the word *backslider*. The question is often asked: Is the backslider saved? It depends on how the word *backslider* is used. The word does not appear in the New Testament. In the Old Testament, it is a very strong word. In every instance except one, the Hebrew word means to turn away or to turn back. The exception is Hosea 4:16 where it means stubborn or rebellious. If by backsliding, we mean a person has turned away from God, such a person is not saved. He has made shipwreck of faith.

In the common use of the word *backslide*, it has a variety of meanings. Some use it only of serious cases. Others use it to refer to lesser degrees of drifting. I prefer not to use the word *backslide* because of the various interpretations that people give to it. They invariably understand me according to their meaning of the word, not mine. To say that a backslider is *not* lost means to some people that a person could be saved and then fall into the worst conceivable state of sin and still be saved. This is absolutely false, whether a person believes in conditional or unconditional continuance in salvation.

Many careless words are spoken on the subject of security—sometimes in stating our own view and at other times stating the views of other people. A well-formulated doctrine of security requires much careful thought and study. The same is true if we are going to understand the other person. The subject of continuance in salvation is an important subject and should receive some of our most careful thought.

---

[1]Robert E. Picirilli, *Perseverance*, 22.

[2]Berkhof, *Systematic Theology*, 547.

[3]Ibid., 548.

[4]Wayne Grudem, "Perseverance of the Saints: A Case Study from Hebrews 6:4-6 and the Other Warning Passages in Hebrews," in *The Grace of God, the Bondage of the Will*, eds. Thomas R. Schreiner and Bruce A. Ware (Grand Rapids: Baker Books, 1995), 1:139-150.

[5]Berkhof, *Systematic Theology*, 548.

[6]Picirilli, *Perseverance*, 25-26.

[7]During the 1960s and 70s, Georgi Vinns was one of the most significant voices in the USSR for religious freedom. This cost him two terms in prison. He had spent eight years in prison when President Carter negotiated his release in 1979. He came to America and set up Russian Gospel Ministries in Elkhart, Indiana. On February 18, 1996, he and his wife visited an Autonomous Baptist Brotherhood Church in Kiev, Ukraine. He had been one of the pastors of this church prior to his imprisonment. This was the first time he had visited this church since his release from prison. Well over a thousand people packed into that church for a three-hour service. Many stood, some of them old people,

the entire time, while the much of the crowd filled other rooms in the church. Georgi Vinns died of an inoperable brain tumor January 11, 1998.

[8]In the light of the teaching of the Old Testament about presumptuous sins, it seems that 1 John 3:9 should be understood as saying that a Christian cannot choose sin as a lifestyle. It has reference to more than mere repetition of sin. It would be a deliberate choice of sin as a lifestyle. There is a very significant difference between being shamefully defeated by sin and choosing sin for a lifestyle.

Author, Subject Index

A

Abide, abiding: 30, 285, 295, 312, 332, 351

Abraham: 99-104, 107, 113-120, 122-127, 133, 135, 139-142, 144, 151, 152, 155, 158, 161, 203, 269

Abrahamic covenant: 105-107, 113-120, 122-127, 133, 135, 141-142, 158, 188, 313

Absolute determination: 41

Account: vi, vii, viii, 4, 15, 26, 84, 86, 117, 129, 131, 164, 184, 192, 193, 209, 211, 212, 218, 219, 233, 234, 235, 239, 246, 264, 267, 271, 282, 283, 290, 308, 338, 344, 345, 346

Accountability: 201, 240-241
Age of 239-241
See also Age of responsibility

Action(s), act(s), divine 14, 89, 149, 156, 263-264, 287

Active obedience: 205-206, 208, 217

Adam: 7-9, 14-15, 20-21, 25-34, 39, 51, 68, 73-74, 80-81, 84-85, 103, 179, 237-245, 311, 354

Adoption: 171-172, 174

Agency: 39, 41-42, 56, 138, 294
Personal: 56

Annihilation, annihilated: 230-231, 248, 289

Antichrist: 315

Antinomian, Antinomianism: 200, 219, 235, 262, 309

Apocrypha: 101, 144, 177-178, 196

Apostasy: vii, xii, 103, 108, 111-112, 141, 303, 319-328, 331, 342, 346-349, 351-352, 354-355

Ark of the Covenant: 209

Arminianism: iv, vii, ix, x, 21, 43-44, 46, 60-61, 67, 73, 89-90, 121, 156, 159, 161, 174, 190, 259-261, 263, 265-267, 293, 305

Arminius, Jacob or Jacobus: iv, v, vi, x, xi, 22, 33, 61, 63, 70, 74, 184, 186, 267

Artios: 299

Ashby, Stephen M.: ix, 10, 17, 34

Assistance, aid, divine: 132

Assurance: vi, vii, 161, 258-259, 264, 277, 337, 350-353, 355

Atheism: 58, 348

Atonement: iv, v, vi, vii, xi, 32-33, 36, 85-88, 109-110, 131, 138, 170, 177, 179, 183-184, 187, 189, 191, 193, 199-203, 206-212, 219-222, 224-225, 227-235, 238, 245, 265-266, 269-270, 275, 280, 305, 307, 340-343, 345
Day of: 209-210
Limited: 189-193, 233-234, 304
Unlimited: 37, 190, 192, 234
Provisionary: 192-193, 233-234
And apostasy Nature of: 200, 203, 205, 220, 222, 341
Extent of: 189-190
Penal Satisfaction view: iv, vii, 200, 211, 221, 230-231
Satisfaction view 83-84, 131, 184, 192, 200, 236, 264, 308, 341, 343
Governmental view iv, 200, 221-222, 224, 227, 267, 269, 274
Moral influence view: 200

Augustine of Hippo: 46

Augustine, Augustinian: v, 9, 33, 46, 61, 64, 83, 244, 260

Author of sin: 39

B

Backslide, backslider: 355-256

Bagnall, W. R.: 196
footnote only

Baptism: 212-213
Water 212-213
Into Christ 212-213

Basinger, David: 91-93
footnote only

Basinger, Randall: 91-93
footnote only

Beauty: 4, 19, 224, 292

Berkhof, Louis: 7, 15, 17, 34, 54, 75, 83, 92, 94, 95, 193, 197, 233, 248, 262-264, 271, 293-294, 301, 310, 334, 340-342, 344, 356

Biblical Ethics: 301
footnote only

Birnbaum, Phillip: 145
footnote only

Blind(ed): 55, 133, 135, 188

Blood: 151, 209,
Of Christ: v, 268, 318, 320

Boettner, Loraine: 41-43, 91, 217, 246, 247

Brown, David: 214, 278, 300

Brown, John: 134, 146

Bruce, F. F.: 144, 148-149, 164, 166-167

Brunner, Emil: 231, 248

Buswell Jr., J. Oliver: 40-41, 44, 74-75, 91, 94, 202, 246, 276, 300, 305-306, 309, 333-334

C

Call, Calling, Called: 23, 35, 59, 107, 117, 119, 139, 142, 144, 147, 148-151, 158, 161, 171, 180, 187-188, 313
General: 187
Special: 150, 265-266
Effectual: 35, 48, 150, 265-266, 305, 33
Irresistible: 35, 48, 148, 160, 265-266, 305, 339

Calvin, John: vi, xi, 46, 64

Calvinism: ix, x, xii, 21, 23, 29, 34, 36-37, 40, 43-49, 52, 60-61, 65, 67, 73, 83, 86-87, 89, 93, 97-99, 117, 121, 124, 143, 145, 151, 156, 169, 174, 179-180, 183-184, 189-190, 195-196, 259-261, 263-265, 276-277, 293-294, 303-305, 309, 333, 338-339

Care, caring
Of God 78

Carnal Christian: 309

Cause and effect: vii, 12, 21, 47-51, 58, 78-82, 97, 132, 159-160, 169, 173, 176, 260, 283, 338-340, 343

Cause, causality: 76

Certainty: 67, 76, 93, 95, 148, 193, 234

Chafer, Lewis Sperry: 266, 305-306, 333, 337

Chalmers, Thomas: 214

Cheap easy-believism: 275-277

Choose, choosing, choice: 6, 12, 19, 21, 22, 29, 37, 39, 41, 47-48, 50-54, 56-57, 61-63, 65-66, 68, 73, 76, 80, 89, 90, 94, 98, 117, 119, 120-124, 126-130, 132-133, 135-136, 156-157, 162, 185-186, 195, 238, 244, 252, 254, 260-261, 265-266, 276, 283, 296, 305, 314, 326-327, 332, 338-343, 349-350, 357
Of apostles: 156, 182
Free: 55-56, 61, 63, 66, 69, 73-75, 77, 88
chosen: 27, 29, 35, 41, 80, 99, 102, 107, 111, 118, 122, 125-127, 130, 133, 138, 142, 150, 156, 171, 173, 178-179, 182-187, 189, 271, 305, 334, 348-349

Christ, Jesus: v, x, 5, 48, 75, 78, 80, 82, 85, 87, 109, 112, 113-115, 129, 133, 136, 139, 142-143, 148, 156, 158-159, 163, 170-171, 174, 176-177, 181, 184, 189, 200, 206, 208, 210, 212-213, 217, 223, 230-231, 238, 245, 253, 255-258, 267, 277-278, 294-296, 308, 313, 315, 321, 324, 329-330, 346

Circumcision: 102, 104, 164, 269

Clark, Gordon H.: 15, 17, 34, 38, 40, 58, 90-92

Clarke, Adam: 45, 64, 99, 143

Classical Arminians, Arminianism: iv, vii, x, 46, 61, 156, 159, 161, 174, 259-260, 265, 267, 293

Coerce, coerced, coercion: 53, 65

Communion With God: 23-24, 261, 294, 300

Compassion: 114, 127-130, 137, 224, 326

Compatibilism: 42
See also soft: determinism

Conception: 14, 54, 64, 73-74, 239

Condemnation: 16, 26, 29-30, 32, 86, 102, 118, 159, 202, 204-205, 212, 236-239, 241, 244, 341, 346 See also judgment, hell

Condition of salvation: 86, 131-132, 156, 180, 212, 220, 238, 251-252, 256, 258-259
vs. Ground: 130-132, 138, 258-259

Conformity, conformed: 16, 80, 147, 149, 170-171, 174, 180, 186-187, 219, 273, 280, 282, 284-285, 294, 300

Constitution, moral: 18, 20

Contingency: 39, 76-77, 93, 95, 340

Continue, continuance, continuing: vii, 155, 164, 194, 203-204, 303-304, 309, 313, 330, 332-333, 337, 346, 350-351, 353
Conditional: 340-341, 345, 351, 356
Unconditional 305, 339-344, 351, 356

Control: 12, 56, 129, 282-283
Divine: 37-38, 63, 69, 79-80, 129-130

Conviction of sin: 20, 231, 350

Conybeare, W. J.: 213

Corporate election: vii, 124, 188
Of Jews: vii 102-104, 107, 119, 123-124, 127, 152-155, 158, 188

Cottrell, Jack: 63, 76, 79 93-95

"Counsel of His Will": 82, 173

Counsel of God: 262-264

Covenant: 14, 27-29, 101, 107-108, 110-111, 151, 161, 268, 286, 294, 318, 320

Covenant people: 100, 111, 181

Covenant seed of Abraham: 99-100, 103, 107, 114-119, 122-125, 127, 133, 135, 141-142, 158

Covenantal Nomism: vii, 110

Crabtree, J. A.: 37, 44, 53-54, 90-92

Craig, William Lane: 63-64, 71-73, 92-94

Create, creation: 3-4, 6-7, 9, 11, 14, 30, 36, 63, 70, 72-73, 81, 87, 89, 92, 190, 194, 257, 264, 282, 290, 295, 339

Creationist theory (of origin of soul): 14, 28, 30

Creator , God as: vii, 1-8, 11, 14, 62, 63, 70, 75, 78, 81, 136, 282, 288

Credits, in justification: 211, 267

Cross, the: iv, 170, 176, 178-179, 206-207, 210, 211, 216, 224, 224, 232, 235, 238, 240, 256,

Crucified, crucifixion: 23, 31, 88, 170, 175-177, 206, 212, 214-215, 289, 318, 323

Cultural mandate: 10

D

David, King: 70, 236, 277

Day of Atonement: 209-210

Dead, death: iv, v, x, 4, 11, 23, 25-29, 31-33, 35, 80, 84, 86, 88, 105, 131, 149, 154, 162, 174-175, 177, 179, 184, 191-193, 195, 199, 205-207, 211-219, 223-227, 231-236, 239-242, 244-247, 264-265, 267-268, 271,

274-275, 278-279, 282,
293-295, 308, 312, 316,
318, 326, 341, 343-347,
349-350
Spiritual: 23-24, 260,
304
In trespasses and sins:
23
To sin: 212, 214

Debits, in justification: 211,
225, 267

Decision(s): 12, 22, 30, 38,
44, 48, 52-53, 62, 66, 68,
72-73, 129-130, 138,
152-153, 158, 183, 207,
241, 248, 263, 266, 283,
286, 314, 325, 343, 351

Decrees: 35-37, 46, 87, 89,
97, 169, 190
Divine: 87, 97
Efficacious,
unconditional and
conditional: 87-88
To influence: 87-89
To permit: 87, 89
To create: 36, 89, 190
To provide salvation:
36, 90, 190

Depravity: vi, 14-15, 17-18,
20-21, 25, 27, 32, 34, 46,
83-85, 158, 240, 243-
244, 273, 294, 304
Total: 17, 45-46, 52, 83,
87, 304
Voluntarily
appropriated: 33

Descendants: 20, 99, 102-
103, 116-118, 122, 125-
126, 142, 238

Design of God as Creator:
2-4, 8-9, 13-14, 18, 49,
58, 178, 292, 295
Desire of God: 67-68,
71, 80-81, 133, 137,
194, 339

Determinism: vii, 37-39,
42-44, 47, 49-50, 54-57,
59-60, 64-69, 75, 79-81,
97, 169
Unlimited: 38, 43, 47,
60, 64-66, 69, 75, 80
Limited: 38, 47, 67-69
Hard: 57, 66
Metaphysical: 39
Soft: 42, 44, 57, 65-66
Scope of: 38
Philosophical: 39

Dichotomy, dichotomous:
75

Didomi: 157, 160-161

Die, died: 8-9, 33, 80, 150,
179, 189, 191-193, 200,
213-217, 223, 227, 232-
234, 236, 239, 242-244,
256, 278, 304, 307, 309,
319, 357
See also Death

Direct perception: 70

Disobedience: 29, 59, 81,
89, 110, 135, 209, 223,
225, 280, 287, 297, 339
Divine action(s), divine
act(s): 14, 89, 149, 156,
263-264, 287

Dominion of sin: 22, 278

Double payment: 192, 193,
234

Doubt: 259, 352

Drawing: 156, 159-161,
180, 331

By the Holy Spirit: 16,
24, 84, 86, 88, 121, 162,
257
Irresistible: 159-160

E

Earle, Ralph: 146 footnote
only

Edwards, Jonathan: 37-38,
64

Effectual call, calling: 35,
48, 150, 266, 305, 339

Efficacious: 176, 233-234,
341
Decrees: 87-89

Eklegomai: 156-157, 182,
185

Election: 35, 43, 46, 106,
114, 117, 119, 122-123,
128, 132-133, 135, 153,
157, 264, 266, 306, 352
Of apostles: 182
Proof Texts for
Unconditional: 97-143,
147-166
Unconditional: 29, 35,
37, 44-47, 64, 68, 86-87,
265-266, 304-306, 328,
339
Conditional: 35, 45-46,
68, 83, 87, 90
In Romans: 9 97-143
Scriptural Support for
Conditional: 169-195
Individual: vii, 100, 107,
120, 121, 123-124, 126-
128, 135, 139, 142, 153,
155-156, 169-170, 181,
183, 305
Corporate: vii, 102-104,
107, 119, 123-124, 126-
127, 142, 152-154, 156,
158, 183, 188

Of Jews: 102-104, 107, 110, 125, 139-140, 154-155, 188

Ellicot, Charles J.: 214

Equivalent punishment: 208

Erickson, Millard J.3: 36, 190, 241-244, 265-266, 305-306, 326-328, 352

Esau: 98-100, 116-125

Eternal Condemnation: 202, 236
See also judgment, hell

Eternal punishment: 137, 202, 229-230, 276
See also judgment, hell, condemnation

Eternity: 38, 41, 63, 70, 78, 153, 176-177, 180, 192, 217, 236, 242, 262-264, 310

Eternity past: 35, 77, 121, 130, 138, 155-156, 165, 175, 178-180, 182, 184-187, 206, 266, 304
Eve: 7-9, 14, 21, 33, 51, 68, 73-74, 80-81, 84-85, 179, 242, 354

Evil: 9, 11, 17, 20, 77, 80, 89, 98, 105, 119-120, 131, 221

Excellent, excellence: xii, 4, 19, 63, 76, 190, 290, 292

F

Fairchild, James H.: 221, 223-225

Faith: iv, vi, vii, ix, 11, 23, 31, 35, 43, 46, 48, 52, 61, 83-87, 101, 112-114, 116, 121, 125-126, 130-132, 138-142, 148-149, 156, 158-159, 163-164, 173-174, 180-181, 184, 186-187, 192-193, 212, 215-220, 227, 234-235, 238, 240, 243, 245, 251-266, 271, 293-295, 303-306, 308-309, 311-313, 315, 317-320, 325-327, 330, 333, 341, 344-351, 354-355
As a gift: 24, 36, 48, 257-260, 305
Counted for righteousness: 225, 269-270
Imputed for righteousness: 225, 270
Not a work: 204, 266-269, 346

Faith alone: vi, 85-86, 113, 271, 350

Fall of man: 10, 14-15, 242

Fallen man: 12, 16-18, 20-22, 45, 48-49, 51-52, 85-86

Falling away, fall away, fallen away: 150, 315, 319-320, 327-328, 342

Father: 12, 84, 101-103, 117, 126, 153, 155, 157, 159-162, 181, 185, 194, 205-207, 217, 236, 257, 268, 280, 298-299, 311, 321, 323, 331-332, 348, 351

Fear: 58, 154, 164, 324-325, 349
Of losing salvation: 349-352

Federal headship: 14, 27-29, 32

Federal union: 215

Feinberg, John S.: 37, 42-44, 65-66

Fellowship with God: 9, 16, 23-24, 86, 184, 206-207, 220-221, 295, 318

Finney, Charles: iv, 221-222, 226, 274-275

First parents (Adam and Eve): 33, 41

Force: 42, 47, 65, 111, 159-160, 177, 223-224, 227, 326, 338, 351

Foreknow, foreknowledge: vii, 57, 138, 171, 175-182
Arminianism and: 60-61
Divine (Of God): vii, 35, 43-44, 47, 57, 60-64, 67-78, 87-89, 138, 175-181, 184-185

Forgiveness: vi, vii, 19, 109, 192, 199, 202-203, 210, 221-222, 230, 233, 238, 255, 275-276, 297, 321-322, 325-326

Foreordination: 41, 43-44, 179

Forsake: 332, 348

Four-point Calvinism: x, 37, 189

Framework of possibilities: 21-22, 51, 257, 260, 297, 354

Free agency: 39, 41-42

Free knowledge: 72

Free salvation: 82, 297, 345

Free will: v, vii, 20, 37, 40-42, 50, 52, 54-58, 60-61, 63, 65, 68, 71, 73-75, 79, 81, 97, 169, 176
Denial of: 37, 40, 58, 69
And foreknowledge: 43, 48, 60, 63, 73-74

Free will theism: 61-62

Freed, freedom: vi, vii, 20-22, 39, 41-42, 44, 47, 50-54, 56, 59-63, 65-66, 71, 76-77, 79, 88, 106, 119, 214, 265, 297, 314, 327, 349

Freewillism: 40

Fruit bearing: 331

Fruit of the Spirit: 287

Future: vii, 10, 44, 60-64, 69-71, 74-78, 104-105, 133, 148-149, 176, 179, 185, 210, 241-243, 309-310, 328
Free decisions in: 62-63, 77

G

Garrett, James Leo: 244

Geisler, Norman: 37, 55-57, 70

Gentiles: 18, 101-102, 104, 109-110, 112-113, 139-140, 163-165, 188-189, 203-204, 253

Gerstner, John H.: 309

Gift: x, 33, 36, 45, 48, 59, 218-219, 237, 277, 297, 313, 315-316, 345

Faith as a: 23-24, 48, 257-258, 305
Justification as a: 86

Gill, John: 64

Glorification: 148-150

Glory: 10-11, 78. 136-139, 149, 170, 191, 203, 215, 265, 284, 288, 290, 321, 337

Glory of God: 10, 265

God-centered: 229

Godet, Frederic Louis: 45, 99, 149, 180-181

Gospel: 20, 22, 24, 51, 59, 61, 82, 85, 88, 112, 131, 137, 150-152, 154, 157, 159-161, 163-165, 170, 174, 182, 187, 194, 200, 219, 241, 252, 260, 265, 275-276, 277, 293, 309, 316, 354

Government, divine: 38, 202

Governmental view of atonement: iv, 200, 221-229. 267, 269-270, 274

Grace: v, vi, x, 23, 39, 48, 52, 86, 109, 184, 199, 208, 211, 216, 219-220, 226, 259-262, 264, 266, 268, 275-278, 297, 304-306, 310, 320, 323, 327, 339, 345, 351
Sanctifying: 84, 261, 263, 279, 294, 300
Of God: 22-23, 132, 135, 137, 164, 191, 219, 268, 279, 291, 303, 305, 316, 326
Divine: 265-266

Great Commission: 195, 292

Grotius, Hugo: iv, 221-223

Ground: 211-212, 233, 264, 267-269, 271, 274, 293, 341-343, 345, 350-351, 355
Of Salvation: 130-131, 258-259
vs. Condition: 86, 131, 138, 187, 258, 275, 279, 345-346

Grudem, Wayne: 343

Guilt: v, 19, 27, 29-30, 32-33, 65, 84-85, 109, 184, 220, 225, 232, 241, 243-245, 261, 263, 273, 278-279, 294, 296, 308
Racial: 238-240, 245
Personal: 11, 32-33, 238-240

H

Haireomai: 185

Haldane, Robert: 45, 83, 98, 124, 214, 217, 261, 263, 294

Happy, happiness: 2, 6, 19, 54, 221, 324

Hard determinism: 57, 66
Harden, hardening: 119, 128, 133-135, 138, 183

Harrison, Everett F.: 45, 98, 124, 137

Headlam, Arthur: 45, 99, 284

Headship: 120
Augustinian view: 240
Natural: 27-30, 32, 243-244

Federal: 14, 27-30, 32
Of Adam: 27

Heart: vi, 4-7, 9-10, 18, 21-
22, 24, 47, 51, 60-61, 67,
101, 105, 114, 119, 123,
133-134, 139, 162, 176,
186, 188, 199, 221, 227,
231, 236, 252, 256-257,
260, 283, 286, 293, 295-
297, 324, 350

Heavenly: 12, 284, 315-316

Helkuo: 157-161

Hell: 33, 87, 192-193, 197,
206-208, 227, 229-231,
234-235, 237, 239, 242,
248
See condemnation,
judgment, punishment

Hendriksen, William: 45,
134

Henry, Carl F. H.: 15, 17

Heretical doctrine: 346
And apostasy: 346

Hodge, Charles: 45, 64,
100, 102-103, 106, 137,
151, 236

Hodges, Zane: 308

Hoeksema, Herman: 315,
326, 342

Holiness: 4, 8, 16, 64, 81,
86, 137, 184, 199-203,
205, 208, 210-211,
219-220, 224, 227-228,
239-240, 256, 275, 279-
281, 292, 297, 303, 310,
339, 353

Holley, Darrell: 271
footnote only

Holy of Holies: 209

Holy Spirit: 24, 33, 46, 52,
78, 82-83, 85, 87, 121,
132, 159, 177, 213, 231,
246, 257, 260-261, 264-
265, 287, 291, 293, 295,
297, 311, 315, 317-318,
324, 345, 350, 352, 354
Drawing of: 16, 22, 24,
51, 84-86, 88, 121, 130-
131, 158, 162, 260
Influence of: 22, 51, 85

Howson, J. S.: 213

Human freedom: 39, 44,
59-61, 65, 71

Human nature 1, 12, 18,
21, 41, 51, 75, 239

Hyper-calvinism: 36

Hypothetical
contingencies: 77

I

Ideal(s): 4, 259, 291-292

Identification: 1-2, 28, 30-
32, 214, 245, 278
With Christ: 31, 215-
216, 232, 235-236, 238-
239, 311, 341

Illuminate(d), illumination:
vii, 316

Image of God: 1-6, 11, 13,
15-16, 18-19, 48, 85,
282, 288, 292, 314

Immanence: 61

Immaterial part of man: 14

Impassible, impassibility:
78

Imputation: vi, 211, 218,
225, 270
Of Christ's death: 28,

31-32, 84, 211-212,
217, 224, 245, 264, 267,
343
Of Christ's
righteousness: vii, 28,
31-32, 84, 212, 215,
217, 224, 241, 245, 264,
267, 343
Of depravity: 244
Of guilt: 32, 241, 243-
244
Of sin: 27-28, 31-33,
242-245

Inability: vi, 38-39, 48-49
Incarnation: 109, 205,
208, 216, 232, 238-238,
245, 264

"In Christ," "In Him" vi, 24,
31, 61, 82, 84, 86, 104,
113, 130, 131-132, 138,
141, 154, 156, 158, 162,
171, 173, 182-184, 186-
187, 190, 204, 208, 210,
212-214, 217-218, 225,
227, 235, 238-240, 245,
254, 258-259, 266-269,
271, 276, 293, 296, 304,
308, 311, 317-318, 325,
330, 332, 345, 347, 349,
351-352
See also Union with
Christ

Indeterminism: 44

Indifference, indifferency:
52-55, 60, 65, 67, 69,
79-82
Liberty of: 53-55, 60,
65, 67, 69, 79-82

Individual election: 120-
121, 123-124, 126-128,
170, 181
Of Jews: 123, 126

Individual salvation: 99,
109, 164

Indwelling of the Holy
Spirit: 345

Infants, infancy: 33, 241,
243-244
Salvation: 32, 236-239,
242-243
Baptism: 236
Depravity: 240
Dying: 32-33, 236, 239,
242, 244

Infinite penalty: 207-208,
230, 246

Influence and response: vii,
12, 21, 47-51, 57-59,
78-86, 97, 130, 132,
151, 159, 160, 169, 174,
176, 261, 283, 338-340

Infralapsarianism: 36, 183,
191

Inheritance: 103, 106, 173-
174, 203

Innocence, innocent: 8,
237, 241-243

Intend, intent, intention:
33, 55, 67, 110-111,
149, 163, 178, 188-189,
191, 193, 195, 233, 264,
304, 335, 338, 348, 351

Interpersonal relationship:
9, 47, 132

Intrapersonal relationship:
11

Irresistible
Drawing, call: 35, 148,
159-160, 265
Grace: 48, 52, 259-261,
304-306, 339

Isaac: 98-100, 103, 116-
123, 126

Ishmael: 98, 100, 116, 118-
123, 125-126

Israel: 38, 99, 101-105, 107,
110-111, 114-115, 117-
119, 122-123, 126-129,
139-140, 181

Jacob: 98-101, 103, 115-
124, 126, 140, 203

Jacobs, Paul: 178

Jewett, Paul: 248 footnote
only

Jews, Jew, Jewish, Judaism:
vii, 100-116, 118-127,
132-133, 135, 139-142,
151-156, 158, 160-165,
175, 183, 188-189, 203-
205, 253, 318, 323
Understanding of
salvation: vii, 100-112,
122-127, 132, 135
Paul's burden for: 112-
116, 118-120, 127, 132-
133, 135

Johnson, L. C.: iv, 246

Joseph: 38
And determinism: 38

Judge, God as: iv, vi, 86,
201, 207, 209, 218-220,
227-228, 293, 340

Judgment: 5, 11, 26, 65,
106, 134, 154-155, 178,
202-204, 211, 231, 292,
321, 355

Great White Throne: 202

Judicial: 134-135, 225-
226, 232, 294

Just, justice: iv, v, 40, 58,
102, 104, 123, 125, 127,
207, 210, 221-223, 2269
Divine: v, 202-203, 205

Justification, justified vi, vii,
xi, 15, 24, 31-32, 35, 84,
86, 88, 113, 121, 131,
142, 147-150, 156, 171,
184, 187, 192-193, 200,
203-205, 208, 212, 214,
218-221, 225-227, 233-
235, 237, 261-264, 266-
267, 269-271, 293-294,
304-305, 307, 309, 313,
340-346, 350
And apostasy: 354
And Sanctification: v,
vi, 83-84, 86, 149, 255-
256, 260, 273-276, 278-
280, 291, 293-294, 297,
333, 346, 353
Penal satisfaction view:
211
Satisfaction view: 83-
84, 308, 343
Governmental view:
224, 227, 267-268, 274

K

Katartizmos: 299

Keeping power of God:
327, 341-342, 344

Kingdom of God: 154, 276,
295, 353

Knowledge, of God: 8, 44,
60-61, 63, 68, 70, 72-75,
77, 175, 177, 181, 263,
Natural: 72-74
Middle: vii, 71-73
Free decisions in: 72
See also Foreknowledge

Knudson, Albert C.: 248
footnote only

Krienke, Helmut: 178

L

Law: iv, vii, x, 4, 10, 18, 64,
72, 84, 101-102, 104,
106, 108, 110, 113, 140-
142, 200, 202-207, 209-
210, 215, 217, 219-220,
222-223, 225-228, 246,
261, 275, 276-278, 280,
286, 294, 313
Mosaic (of Moses): 107,
171-172
Ceremonial: 171-172
"Doers of": 204, 208
Lawkeeping: 209, 218
Ten Commandments:
19, 209, 280
Tables of: 209, 280-281

Law of noncontradiction:
64

Lawgiver: 201

Legalism, Ethical: 106
Soteriological: 106

Lenski, R. C. H.: 45, 127,
140, 180-181

Liberalism, liberal: 200,
227-229, 347

Libertarian(ism): vii, 52, 55

Liberty
Of spontaneity: 53-55,
65, 69, 81-82
Of indifference: 53-55,
60, 65, 67, 69, 79-81

Liddon, H. P.: 145 footnote
only

Likeness: 3-5, 7, 19, 213,
279, 282-285, 292, 346
Divine, in man: 6, 15,
292
Rational: 3
Moral: 4, 292

Constitutional: 6-8, 16,
282
Formal: 6, 16
Functional: 6, 8, 16-17,
282, 292

Limited atonement: 189-
193, 197, 233-234, 304

Limited determinism: 38,
67, 69

Lord: 140, 142, 163, 185,
194, 206, 213, 241-242,
284-286, 316, 353
Jesus as: 48, 116, 119,
123, 125-126, 129-130,
136, 142, 156, 158, 181,
188-189, 212, 217, 219,
245, 255, 265, 278, 308,
324, 329-330

Lordship: 291, 308

Lose, loss, losing salvation:
313, 327, 342-343, 349,
353

Lost: 21, 23, 30, 52, 60,
100, 105, 109, 112-113,
119, 130, 133, 138, 153,
157, 195, 235-236, 239,
244, 280, 282, 292, 303,
306, 309-312, 314-315,
319, 325, 327, 331, 341,
343-344, 347-348, 351-
353, 355-356

Love, loving: 4, 155, 182
Divine: 62, 88, 130, 184,
190, 199, 201-202, 205,
210-211, 224, 227-228,
287, 299, 306, 312, 344
Human: 228, 287-288,
292, 299, 306, 351

Lutheran(s): 45, 71, 271

M

Man-centered: 229

Marshall, I. Howard: vii, ix,
319-320

Martyr, Justin: 103

Mature: 298-300

McDonald, H. D.: 211

Mediator: 184

Mercy: 106, 127-131, 133-
134, 136-137, 140, 183,
207, 223, 265, 323

Merit(s), meritorious: vi,
17, 36, 71, 107, 111,
121, 130, 133, 149, 193,
208, 215, 233, 262, 267-
268

Messiah: 112, 114, 16, 119,
123, 125-126, 140, 141-
142, 152, 156, 158, 164-
165, 188-189, 203

Methodist(s): 56

Metonymy: 212-213, 270

Meyer, August Wilhelm:
45, 148, 180-181

Middle knowledge: vii,
71-73

Miley, John: iv, 56, 59, 64,
221-223

Mind: 4-7, 10, 19, 21, 38,
47, 51, 60, 98, 134, 176,
199, 221, 252-253, 256-
257, 285-286, 194
Subconscious: 7, 240,
283-284

Ministry: 60, 78, 147, 151,
158, 177, 185, 299
Of the Word: 78, 177
Of the redeemed: 78,
177

Missions: 195

Molina, Luis de, Molinism: vii, 71-72

Monergism, monergistic: 24, 88, 152, 260-261, 295
Conditional: 293

Monotheism: 163-164

Moo, Douglas I.: 103, 151

Moral responsibility: 9, 219-220, 242

Morrison, James: 214

Mote, Edward: 268

Motyer, J. A.: 325

Moule, H. C. G.: 214

Muller, Richard A.: 38-40, 43, 67-68

Murray, John: 45, 100, 137, 149

Mystery, mysteries: 43-44, 59, 61, 67, 74, 170

Mystical Union: 215

N

Narcissism: 288

Nash, Ronald H.: 53-54

Natural headship: 27, 29-30, 32, 243-244

Natural knowledge: 72-74

Necessity: 22, 24, 30, 39, 53, 76-77, 84, 87, 109, 177, 192, 202-203, 221-222, 228-233, 266, 294, 338-340, 343-344
Of atonement: 200-203, 207-208, 221-222, 229-

230, 269, 275

New birth: 16, 20, 23, 86, 295, 297, 350
See regeneration

Newman, Barclay: 285

Nichols, James: x, 34, 93, 196 footnotes only

Nida, Eugene: 285

Nomism, covenantal: vii, 110

Noncontradiction, law of: 64

O

Obedience: 29, 59, 80, 89, 106, 108, 110-111, 131, 195, 204, 208, 254, 274, 280, 287, 339, 345
Christ's: vi, 29, 206, 208, 217, 224, 237, 246, 268, 308
Active: vi, xi, 205-206, 208, 217
Passive: vi, xi, 205-206, 217, 246

O'Donnell, J. D.: 317

Offspring: 100, 103, 116

"Old man": 214

Omniscience: 64, 69, 72, 77, 177

Once save(ed), always saved: 45, 235, 303-310, 312-314, 344, 352

Open theism: vii
See free will theism

Oral law: 106

Oral tradition: 106, 153

Order of Salvation (*ordo salutis*): 84, 149

Order of the decrees: 36, 89

Ordination, Of all things: 39

Ordo salutis (order of salvation): 84, 86, 149

Original righteousness: 8, 33, 84

Original sin: 8, 33, 240, 242, 244

Oxford English Dictionary: 8, 53

P

Paidagogos: 171-172

Pain: 64, 78, 213, 313, 348

Pardon
iv, vi, 223, 225-227, 267, 274, 340

Partake, partakers: 30, 213, 315, 317-318, 329, 344
Passive obedience: vi, xi, 205-206, 217, 246

Paul: vii, 4-5, 18, 23, 31, 58, 86, 98-104, 107, 109-133, 135-142, 147-150, 154, 159, 163-165, 170-172, 175, 180, 183-185, 187-189, 191, 203-204, 208-209, 212-215, 217-219, 234-235, 237, 253-254, 265, 269, 276, 278-279, 282, 284-286, 290, 294, 298, 306, 312-313, 318, 323, 326, 330, 353
Burden for Jews: 100, 112-133, 135-142, 183

Payment: v, 121, 192-193, 202, 205, 207, 209-211, 225, 234, 239, 246, 308, 341, 345

Pelagian: 22, 71, 242

Penal satisfaction view: 193, 229, 234, 308
Of atonement: iv, 200, 211, 221, 229-231,
See also Punishment

Penalty for sin: iv, 207, 210-211, 223, 230

Perception: 70

Perfection: vi, 298-300

Perish: 154, 160, 190, 194-195, 203, 310-311, 351

Perkins, William: 39

Permit, permission: 56, 63, 74, 87, 89, 136, 205, 228, 286
Of fall: 36, 89, 190

Perseverance: vi, vii, , 58, 190, 236, 276, 296, 303-306, 309, 327, 342, 350

Persistence: 327

Personal: 5-6, 12-13, 18, 21, 40, 48-49, 56, 62, 78, 85, 104, 109, 126, 131-132, 148, 159-160, 163, 176, 184, 200-201, 215-216, 218-219, 221, 239-240, 245, 273, 275, 279-280, 282-283, 289, 291, 311-312, 314, 338-340, 351
Agency: 56

Personal election: vii, 122

Personal guilt: 238-239

Personal sin: 32, 238-239, 245

Personality, person, personhood: 2-3, 6-7, 13, 15-16, 18-26, 28, 31-32, 41-42, 47-49, 52-53, 55-56, 65, 72, 85, 199, 201, 238, 256-258, 282-286, 289, 314, 339
Divine: 59, 201, 257
Human: 3, 59-60, 75, 121, 149, 156, 176, 201, 257, 304
and Free Will: 42-43, 50-51, 54-55, 65-66, 74
Total: 7, 15, 28, 285-286
Theology of: 47, 59

Pharaoh: 38, 134-135, 138
Hardening of heart: 134, 138

Pharisee(s): 106, 113, 152

Picirilli, Robert E.: ix, 45, 63, 66, 76-77, 127, 138, 190, 317, 340, 346

Pinnock, Clark H.: 61-62

Pinson, J. Matthew: 22-23, 33

Piper, John: 98, 100, 114, 118-121, 124, 131-132, 134, 137-138, 151, 265

Placean theory: 244

Plan, divine: 10, 14

Pleasure
God's good, Son's good: 58, 162, 171

Plumer, William S.: 45, 98, 124

Positional: 273, 281
Justification a: 273

Positional sanctification: 281

Possible individuals: 72-74

Possible worlds: 72-73

Postmodern, postmodernism: 161, 231, 347

Potter and clay: 129, 136

Preach, preaching, preached: v, 82, 153, 200, 219, 253, 257, 276-277, 304, 306, 309, 326

Predestination, predestinate, predestine: v, 38-41, 67, 73, 76-77, 88, 137-138, 147, 169-182, 186

Pre-existence: 14

Presbyterian(s): 45

Preservation: 139, 327

Prevenient grace: 132, 266

Priest, priesthood: iv, v, 209

"The Priesthood of Christ" (Arminius): iv, 246

Process theism: 61

Profess, professed, professing: 315, 342-343

Proginosko: 175, 177-180, 196

Promise: 80, 100, 103-104, 106-107, 110, 114-120, 122-127, 132, 140, 194, 203, 275, 313, 328, 342-343, 346, 351

Proof texts: 5, 97, 147

Proorizo: 170, 173

Propitiation: 191, 203, 209-210, 234

Proselyte(s) 164

Protestant(s) 71, 236

Provide, provision: 14, 20-21, 35, 51, 82, 191, 205, 208-209, 215, 217-219, 270, 293, 345
Of salvation: 36, 90, 130, 156, 189-190, 229, 231
Of atonement: 36, 85, 87-88, 131, 179, 183-184, 189, 191, 199-200, 219-220, 222, 229, 265, 305

Providence, providential: 39, 66

Provisionary atonement: 192-193, 233-234

Prune(d): 331

Pseudo-calvinism: 276-277

Psychology, psychological: 13, 40

Public good: 222-223, 226

Public justice: 222-223, 226

Punish, punishment: iv, v, 65-66, 102, 110, 134, 137, 202-203, 205, 208, 221-223, 228-232, 273, 276
See also Wrath
See also Judgment

Purpose(s): 10, 13, 19, , 56, 58, 67, 71, 80-82, 87, 97, 113-114, 117-120, 134-135, 137, 169-170, 173, 175-176, 179-180, 189, 195, 223, 281, 289, 298, 307, 315, 329, 339-340

R

Rabbi(s): 102, 105, 109, 144, 153

Racial guilt: 238-240, 245

Racial sin: 239-240

Ransom: 191, 234

Rationality: 3, 5

Reconciliation: 187, 220

Redeemer, redeem(ed): 28, 39, 48-49, 67, 78, 177, 199, 206, 208, 246, 261, 284, 287-288, 294, 300, 346

Redemption, redemptive: v, 3, 13, 47, 78, 80, 82, 84, 86, 114, 130, 142, 147-149, 163-165, 177, 179, 181, 187, 193, 219, 233, 255, 264-265, 275, 280, 282-284, 288, 290, 297, 338, 346

Reformation: x, xi
footnotes only

Reformed: iv, v, vi, vii, 38-41, 67, 262

Reformed Arminian: iv, v, vi

Regenerate, regeneration, regenerated: 24, 46, 48, 83-88, 121, 142, 152, 184, 189, 220, 259-266, 294-295, 304-305, 310, 319, 345
And Sanctification: 83-84, 260, 262-263, 293-294

Reid, J. S. K.: 39

Relationship, relationships: 2, 8, 12, 15, 24, 27, 30,

49, 58, 85, 89, 102, 107-108, 152, 159, 176-177, 253, 273-274, 283, 318, 338-340, 350
Four basic: 13, 291-292
To God: 8-9, 12, 23, 47, 50, 56, 62, 68, 71, 107-108, 111, 140, 151, 160, 162-163, 184, 201, 221, 236, 275, 279-280, 282, 286-287, 291, 306, 311, 314, 317-318, 325
To other people: 8-9, 12, 50, 279-280, 291
To the created order: 8, 10, 291
To himself: 8, 11, 291
Interpersonal: 9, 47, 49, 132
Intrapersonal: 11

Remedy: 205, 319-324, 326

Remission of sins: 187
Renew(ed): 3, 315, 319, 334, 343

Repent, repentance: vi, vii, xi, 23, 101, 110, 137, 148, 187, 194-195, 220, 251-254, 256, 297, 313, 315, 317, 319-320, 324-325, 334, 342, 348, 352

Reprobate, reprobation: 36, 64, 100, 124, 134, 137-138, 183

Resist, resistance: 24, 128, 135, 180, 183, 257, 261, 314

Response: vii, 7, 12, 21, 24, 46-52, 54, 57-59, 62, 78-88, 97, 110, 130-132, 142, 151, 156, 159-160, 169, 174, 176-177, 187, 189, 194, 238, 254, 257-258, 261-263, 266, 283, 338-340, 351

Responsibility: 9-11, 39, 42, 59, 106, 135, 172, 201, 216, 230, 239, 289-290
Age of, in children: 240-245
See also Age of Accountability Moral: 9, 106, 219-220, 242

Restoration: 211, 221, 282
Of Functional likeness Of God: 282

Resurrection: 104, 109, 116, 199, 215, 279, 282, 294

Retributive justice: 207, 222-223, 226

Revelational: 224, 227

Rice, Richard: 62

Righteousness: 4, 19, 21-22, 51, 82, 101, 120, 133, 140, 142, 209-210, 237, 278, 280, 291, 296-297, 300, 324, 330, 353-354
Original: 8, 33, 84
Of God: x, 98, 104, 123-125, 127, 209, 217-218, 308
Of Christ: vi, vii, x, xi, 28-29, 31-32, 35, 84, 86, 131, 149, 184, 207, 209, 211-212, 215, 217-219, 224, 226, 232-233, 235-236, 239-241, 245-246, 261-262, 264-265, 267-269, 271, 273-275, 291, 293-294, 308, 340-341, 343-346, 350
Imputed for righteousness: 217-218, 224-225, 241, 245, 261-262, 267, 270

Imparted: 291
Absolute: 82, 203-205, 208-211, 225-226, 267, 269-270, 273, 345

Risk(s)
God as taking: 62

Romans Commentary (Forlines): 143, 249, 308

Ryrie, Charles C.: 17

S

Sacrifice(s): iv, v, 62, 191, 209-210, 318, 321-323, 348

Salvation: vi, vii, ix, 17, 23, 32-33, 35-36, 47, 58, 67-68, 86, 90, 99, 129-132, 135, 139, 148-149, 152-159, 162, 165, 174, 180, 182, 185, 188, 190, 192-194, 204, 208, 210, 221, 229, 231, 233, 235-239, 242-243, 265-267, 273, 275, 279, 284, 296, 303, 305-306, 308-309, 311-313, 316-317, 319-320, 327-328, 330, 333, 335, 337, 339-344, 349-354, 356
By grace: 39, 45, 297, 345
By faith: 85-86, 130-132, 142, 156, 180, 187, 212, 220, 238, 254-259, 330, 333, 345-346, 351
Condition of: 86, 130-134, 140-142, 156-158, 180, 187, 212, 220, 238, 251-259, 333, 345
Ground of: 130-131, 258-259
Free, freeness: 45-48, 83, 86, 87, 277, 297

Of Jews: 100-135, 139, 141-142, 156, 158-159, 164, 188-189

Sanctification: vi, vii, 185, 214, 260, 277, 282-283, 285, 287-288, 291, 295, 298, 310, 320
And regeneration: 83, 262-263, 293-294
And justification: v, vi, 83-84, 86, 149, 220, 235, 255-256, 260-261, 273-280, 291, 293-294, 297, 333, 341, 346, 353-354
Guaranteed results: 295-297
Experiential: 281-282
Positional: 281
Scope of: 291-292

Sanctifying grace: 84, 261, 263, 279, 294, 300

Sanday, William: 45, 99, 284

Sanders, E. P.: vii, 102, 110-111

Satan, satanic: 84-85

Satisfaction view: 225-229, 270
Of atonement: iv, 83-84, 131, 145, 184, 192, 200, 222, 236, 264, 308, 341, 343
Of justification: 83-84, 308, 343

Saved, salvation: vi, vii, ix, 17, 23, 32-33, 35-36, 39, 45-48, 52, 58, 67-68, 82, 84-87, 90, 99-135, 137-142, 144-145, 148-149, 151-159, 161-166, 173-174, 180, 182, 185-195, 204, 207, 208, 210,

212, 214, 220-221, 229, 231, 233, 235-243, 249, 251-259, 265-267, 270, 273, 275, 277, 279, 284, 296-297, 303-320, 325-333, 335, 337, 339-346, 349-356

Savior: 194, 224
Jesus as: 48, 116, 119, 123, 125-126, 130, 136, 142, 156, 158, 181, 188-189, 219, 234, 245, 255-256, 308, 315, 318, 324, 329

Schreiner, Thomas R.: 128, 183

Secure, security: vi, xi, 102-104, 108, 193, 221-222, 233, 276, 306, 309, 312, 317, 327-328, 340-341, 351, 356

Self: 6, 19, 288-289
Worth: 287-288, 290-291
Crucifying: 288-289
Denial: 289
Self-centered: 289, 349

Self-determinism 37, 42, 52, 55-57, 131

Self-directed being: 22, 52, 56

Semi-pelagian: 22, 242

Shank, Robert: 321-322, 328

Shedd, William G. T.: 45, 89, 98, 100, 124, 136-137, 207, 214-216, 249

Sheep: 11-12, 162

Shipwreck of faith: 320, 326, 348-349, 355

Sin(s)

Original: 8, 33, 240, 242, 244
Racial: 239-240
Personal: 238-239, 245
Presumptuous: 296, 322-325, 357
Of ignorance: 296, 322-323, 325
Of Adam: 14, 21, 25-28, 31-32
Influence of: 78, 177

Sinful nature 85, 214, 242, 244

Sinners: iv, xi, 18-19, 23-24, 27-29, 85-86, 101, 148, 157, 159, 161, 193-195, 200, 203, 206, 209, 211, 224, 230, 234

Smith, David: 33

Soft determinism: 42, 44, 57, 66
See also compatibilism

Soteriology: x, xi, xii, 38-39, 43, 67, 69, 71, 304

Sovereignty Of God: 37, 45-47, 52, 71, 78-79, 87, 97, 169, 339
Divine: vii, 41, 71, 80, 305, 337, 339

Spectator role
And foreknowledge: 77

Spontaneity: 52, 54, 137
Liberty of: 53-55, 65, 69, 81

Sproul, R. C.: 260-261, 266, 334

Spurgeon, Charles H.: 64

Stanley, Charles: 306-308, 344

Stevens, William Wilson: 309

Strong, A. (Augustus) H.: 30, 33, 190, 262

Sublapsarianism: 36, 89-90, 189-190

Substitute, substitution: v, 192, 207, 209, 212, 222-223, 231-233

Substitutionary atonement: vii, 205, 212

Suffering: 4, 64, 78, 191, 215, 316, 326, 345, 348-349

Suffering of Christ: v, 31, 177, 206, 223, 231

Supralapsarianism: 36, 183, 191

Synergism, synergistic: 24, 121, 152, 260-261

T

Tampering with sin: 348

Taste: 191, 234, 315-317

Teleios: 298

Temporal succession: 57

Ten Commandments: 19, 209, 280

Thayer, J. H.: 286, 316

Theism
Classical: 61-62
Process: 61

Thelo: 6, 50, 136

Thiessen, Henry C.: 45, 89-91, 136, 189-190, 201

Time
God's relationship to: 70-71, 170, 176

Timeless
God as: 70

Toplady, Augustus: 64

Total depravity: 1, 17, 45-46, 52, 83, 87, 304

Total personality: 7, 28, 285-286

Tradition of the elders: 106

Traducian theory (of origin of soul): 14-15, 27-28

Transcendence: 61
Transformation, transformed: 227, 266, 284-285, 287-288

Trichotomy, trichotomous: 75

U

Unbelievers: 20, 68, 130, 138, 311, 313, 315

Unconditional election: 29, 35, 37, 44-47, 64, 68, 86-87, 265-266, 304-306, 328, 339
Of Jews: 102-104, 107, 110, 125, 139-140, 154-155, 188

Unholiness: 310

Union with Christ: vii, 31-32, 184, 187, 192-193, 212-218, 232-235, 239-240, 245, 278, 294, 343-344
See also "In Christ," "In Him"

Universal atonement: 197
footnote only
See Unlimited atonement

Universalism: 193, 227, 234

Unlimited atonement: 37, 190, 192, 234

Unlimited determinism: 38, 43, 60, 64-66, 69, 75, 80

Unpardonable sin: 322, 324, 326

V

Values, Four Basic: 291-292

Van Til, Cornelius: 23

Vessel, vessels: 129, 139, 282
Of honor: 128, 136, 183, 289-290
Of wrath: 137, 139
Earthen: 289-290
For destruction: 136

Vicarious: 207, 215, 217, 222

Vincent, M. R.: 126, 307

Vulnerable
God as: 62

W

Walvoord, John F.: 215, 249

Ware, Bruce A.: 90, 146, 166, 196, 356
footnotes only

Warfield, Benjamin B.: 64

Warning: 80, 276, 318, 320, 327-330, 332, 341-342, 352

Watson, Richard: 64, 76

Wesley, John: 64, 150

Westminster Standards: 41
Shorter Catechism: 41

Wiley, H. Orton: iv, 64, 221, 237

Will
Freedom of: 21-22, 47, 51, 53, 79, 314
Of God: x, 67
Divine: 72
Human: 22, 38

Wisdom: 4, 136, 177, 201, 292
Of God: x, 64, 78, 170, 177, 205, 246, 339

Woo, wooing, of Holy Spirit: 130-131

Word of God: 78, 85, 114, 123, 165, 177, 230, 257, 294-295, 315, 317, 339

Works: vi, vii, ix, x, 28, 45, 58, 86, 101, 105-107, 109, 111-112, 117, 121, 130-132, 141-142, 144-145, 153, 155, 158, 173-174, 204, 209, 218, 253-254, 267, 269, 303, 324, 345, 351

Worth
Of man: 11-12

Wrath
Divine: v, 100, 112-113, 133, 136-137, 139, 170, 192, 201, 203, 205-206, 209-210, 231, 233, 235, 265, 303, 308, 335

Wright, R. K. McGregor: 40

Y

Yarbrough, Robert W.: 152, 157, 159-160, 162

Scripture Index

Genesis

1:26 ....3, 10, 59
1:27 3
1:28 ....9, 10
1:29-30 10
2 11
2:17 ....9, 11, 80, 202
2:18 9
3:15 80
5:3 15
13:14-15 ....103, 105, 116, 117, 122, 123, 203
15:6 142
17:8 ....103, 105, 116, 117, 122, 123, 203
21:12 117
25:23 ....117, 120
50:19-20 135

Exodus

20:3-11 280
20:12-17 280
33:19 ....127, 141, 142
34:7 265

Leviticus

4:2 322
4:22 322
4:27 322
5:15 322

Numbers

15:24 322
15:25-26 322

15:27 352
15:27-31 ....296, 322, 323
15:30-31 ....322, 323, 324, 325
35:11 322
35:15 322

Deuteronomy

32:8-9 173

Joshua

20:3 322
20:5 322
20:9 322

1 Samuel

23:10-13 75

2 Samuel

12:23 236
18:29 277

2 Kings

13:19 75

Ezra

7:6 38

Psalm

8:4 1
8:5-8 11
8:6-8 10
19:13 322
81:14, 15 75

Proverbs

21:1 38

Ecclesiastes

10:5 322

S. of Solomon

15:17 137

Isaiah

29:16 136
42:1 185
42:9 75
45:9 136
48:18 75
53:6 ....16, 86, 206, 245
53:10 206

Jeremiah

2:2, 3 75
18:1-4 129
18:1-10 136
18:6 129
18:7-10 129
38:17-20 75

Ezekiel

3:6 75

Matthew

3:8 253
3:9 ....101, 105, 122
5:48 298
6:26 12
11:21 75
12:11-12 12
12:18 185
15:1-20 106
16:24 ....6, 50

16:28 316
17:5 321
18:10 236
21:29 .... 6, 50
22:14 187
22:37 5
22:39 288
23:37 .... 6, 50, 181
24:12 342
24:22 185
24:24 185
24:31 185
25:45 202
27:46 206

Mark

1:15 251
1:22 152
4:28 150
7:1-23 106
8:34 .... 6, 50
9:43-48 202
13:20 185
13:22 185
13:27 185

Luke

3:8 253
7:50 270
9:23 289
18:7 185
23:34 323
23:46 207
24:47 251

John

1:12 251
1:12-13 .... 151, 152,
154
1:19-12:50 157
1:33 295
3:1 156
3:3 .... 156, 295
3:3-7 .... 17, 86
3:5 .... 156, 295

3:5-6 295
3:14-15 156
3:15-16 188
3:16 .... 131, 158,
174, 190,
234, 251
3:18 .... 131, 133,
154, 158,
174, 251
3:36 .... 131, 133,
174, 251,
311
4:13-14, ... 188
4:14 .... 155, 188
5:21 162
5:24 .... 154, 158,
174, 346
5:33 157
5:36 .... 153, 155,
156
5:37-42 157
5:40 157
5:44 157
6:25-29 155
6:29 204
6:35 .... 155, 158
6:37 .... 158, 160,
161
6:39-40 158
6:44 .... 16, 22, 24,
51, 84, 86,
132, 159,
160, 161,
163, 257,
260, 293
6:51 155
6:65 .... 160, 161
6:70 .... 157, 159,
182
7:17 .... 6, 50, 162
7:37-39 155
7:40-43 162
8:24 158
8:33 152
8:33-40 .... 101, 103,
106, 122

8:47 162
8:51-52 158
10:7-11 155
10:10 349
10:26 162
10:27-30 .... 155, 158
10:28 .... 160, 163,
312
10:28-30 .... 308, 309,
310, 328,
351
10:29 .... 160, 161
12:32 .... 158, 159,
160, 162
13:18 .... 156, 182
14:6 .... 155, 156,
157, 158,
174
15:2 .... 236, 311,
312, 331,
332, 344,
351
15:5 290
15:6 .... 311, 312,
331, 332,
333, 344,
351
15:16 .... 156, 182
15:19 .... 156, 159,
182
18:10 159
19:30 206
20:30-31 153
21:6 159
21:11 159

Acts

2:10 164
2:22 .... 153, 180
2:23 .... 88, 175,
176, 177,
253
2:36 253
2:38 .... 251, 253
3:17 323

3:19.................251, 253,
          323
4:12.................174
4:28.................166, 170,
          180
5:31.................251, 253
11:18.................251
13:43-48 ....164, 165
13:48.................164, 165
16:19.................159
16:30-31 ....129, 132
16:31.................131, 174,
          251, 265
17:30.................148, 187,
          234, 251,
          253
20:21.................251, 253
21:30.................159
26:5.................175
26:20.................vi, 251,
          255

Romans

1:18-32 241
1:18-3:20 ....204, 208,
          218
1:19-31 113
1:32.................5, 113
2:1-16 269
2:1-3:8 ....113, 203
2:1-3:20 269
2:4.................137
2:6-13 ....204, 205,
          207
2:13.................269
2:14-15 4
2:15.................18
2:17.................103
3:3.................102, 213
3:8.................235
3:10.................204, 205,
          208, 269
3:20.................113, 205,
          208, 269
3:21.................217, 218
3:21-26 ....208, 209

3:22.................251
3:23.................16, 20, 86
3:25-26 209
3:26.................203
3:28.................212, 251
3:31.................219
4.................113
4:1-25 ....212, 251
4:1-8 121
4:3-5 ....269, 345
4:15.................113
5:1.................251
5:3.................58
5:8-10 237
5:12.................25, 26, 29
5:12-29 237
5:12-19 ....25, 26
5:15-18 26
5:17.................218
5:18-19 237
5:20.................113
5:21.................278
6:1-11 ....212, 214,
          215, 235
6:4.................215, 279,
          294
6:3-4 212
6:5.................279, 294
6:7.................278
6:8.................294
6:11.................212, 294
6:14.................113, 278
6:23.................16, 86,
          174, 202
7:5.................113
7:6.................113
7:7-25 113
8.................114
8:1.................212
8:7-8 ....16, 21, 22,
          51, 86,
          240, 294
8:12.................278
8:17.................215
8:28.................151, 214

8:29.................174, 175,
          180, 186,
          282, 284,
          285
8:29-30 ....45, 147,
          151, 152,
          170, 171
8:30.................147, 150,
          180
8:33.................185
8:35-39 312
9.................45, 97, 98,
          108, 113,
          136, 138,
          139, 141,
          144, 151,
          153, 156,
          166, 265
9:1-3 ....100, 115,
          119, 120,
          133
9:1-5 114
9:1-13 ....118, 119
9:1-29 142
9:3-5 ....114, 115,
          119, 120
9:6.................99, 100,
          103, 115,
          119, 120,
          122, 123,
          124, 125,
          127
9:6-13 ....99, 100,
          116, 118,
          119, 120,
          122, 123,
          125, 127,
          143
9:10-13 ....117, 120
9:12.................98, 120,
          124
9:14.................98, 99,
          100, 123,
          124, 125,
          126, 128
9:15.................127.128,
          129, 130

9:15-21 ....128, 183
9:16.................128, 131,
132, 137
9:17-21 128
9:18.................133, 135,
139
9:19-24 ....135, 137,
138, 139,
140, 141
9:25-29 ....139, 140
9:31-32 101
9:31-33 ....140, 141,
142
9:33.................188
10:1..................5, 134
10:3..................218
10:9..................5
10:11-13 ....142, 148,
188
10:13................234
11:2..................175, 181
11:7..................119, 134
11:7-11 135
11:11-14 134
11:22................150
11:28-32 134
11:29................313
12:2..................285, 286
14:5..................5
16:13................185

1 Corinthians
2:7....................170
4:1-2 59
4:7....................290
6:9-11 ....276, 295,
296, 353
9:17..................59
11:25................213
12:13................213, 311
13:10................298

2 Corinthians
3:14..................134
3:18..................149, 284,
285

4:7....................290
5:15-16 215
5:17..................281, 295,
296, 309,
350, 352
5:21..................206, 217
7:10..................254

Galatians
1:8-9 ....276, 346
2:16..................212, 251
2:19-20 214
2:20..................31, 212,
214, 216,
258
3:1-18 ....212, 251
3:6....................269
3:13..................206
3:15-18 313
3:19-4:10 ....171, 172
3:24..................171, 172
3:27..................212
4:5....................171
5:16-17 350
5:17..................297
5:19-21 ....276, 296,
353
5:21..................276
5:22-23 287
6:14..................23, 318

Ephesians
1.......................166
1:4....................138, 182,
183, 184,
189, 266
1:5....................170, 171,
172, 174
1:10..................82
1:11..................40, 82,
170, 173,
174
2:1....................23
2:1-3 ....16, 86
2:1-4 134

2:2-3 ....17, 86
2:6....................215
2:8-9 251
2:10..................295, 296
2:14..................212
3:2....................59
4:12..................299
4:13-14 298
4:18..................134
4:24..................4
5:3-7 ....276, 353
5:28-29 288

Philippians
1:6....................313
1:22..................185
2:12-13 58
2:13..................131
3:9....................217, 218
4:11..................312

Colossians
1:21-23 ....330, 342
3:1....................215
3:10..................3, 149
3:12..................185

2 Thessalonians
2:13..................185

1 Timothy
1:13..................323
1:18-19 348
2:1-4 194
2:4....................234
2:6....................191, 234
4:10..................234

2 Timothy
2:10..................185
2:11..................215
2:11-13 ....306, 307
2:12..................215
2:21..................290

2:25.................251, 253
3:17.................299

Titus
1:1.................185
1:7.................59
3:5.................295

Hebrews
2:1.................342
2:9.................191, 234, 316
2:11.................320
3:14.................317, 342
5:14.................298
6:1.................251
6:4-6.................315, 317, 322, 323, 325, 326, 327, 331, 342, 352
6:6.................251, 328
6:7-8.................331, 333
6:9.................328
6:11.................342
8:10.................5, 286
9:5.................209
9:13.................320
10:10.................320
10:14.................320
10:26-29.................320, 321, 322, 323, 325, 352, 354
10:27.................320
10:29.................318, 321
10:32.................316
11:25.................185
12:7-11.................348, 350
12:7-8.................352
12:14.................353
13:12.................320
13:22.................348

James
1:18.................295
2:6.................159
2:14-26.................276

1 Peter
1:2.................175, 181, 185, 186
1:3.................294
1:5.................vii
1:20.................175, 177, 178, 179
1:23.................295
2:3.................316
2:9.................185
2:24.................206
4:10.................59

2 Peter
1:3-4.................329, 330
1:10.................352
2:10.................325
2:20-21.................324, 325, 329, 330
3:4.................194
3:9.................137, 194, 234, 251
3:17.................175
3:18.................282

1 John
1:6.................276
2:2.................191, 234
2:3-4.................276, 296, 353
2:6.................342
2:9-11.................276, 353
2:15-16.................296
2:22-24.................332
3:2-3.................296
3:3-10.................276, 353
3:9.................297

3:10.................295, 296
3:14-15.................276, 353
4:1-3.................346
4:20.................276, 353
5:4.................295, 296, 353
5:11.................310, 311
5:13.................251
5:18.................353

2 John
7-11.................346
9.................332

Jude
3-19.................346

Revelation
17:14.................185
20:11-15.................202
21:8.................16, 86, 174, 202
22:17.................6, 50, 234

CPSIA information can be obtained
at www.ICGtesting.com
Printed in the USA
LVOW08s2124140417
530855LV00001B/7/P